B. P. Pratten

The Rivers of Great Britain, Descriptive, Historical, Pictorical

Rivers of the south and west coasts. Vol. 2

B. P. Pratten

The Rivers of Great Britain, Descriptive, Historical, Pictorical
Rivers of the south and west coasts. Vol. 2

ISBN/EAN: 9783337240738

Printed in Europe, USA, Canada, Australia, Japan

Cover: Foto ©Andreas Hilbeck / pixelio.de

More available books at **www.hansebooks.com**

W. H. J. Boot, R.B.A. del.

On the Wharfe. Bolton Abbey

RIVERS OF GREAT BRITAIN.

Rivers of the East Coast.

DESCRIPTIVE, HISTORICAL, PICTORIAL.

CASSELL & COMPANY, LIMITED:

LONDON, PARIS & MELBOURNE.

1892.

CONTENTS.

THE TYNE (Continued).

THE WEAR.—By JOHN GEDDIE.

THE TEES.—By AARON WATSON.

THE HUMBER AND ITS TRIBUTARIES.

By the REV. CANON BONNEY, D.Sc., F.R.S.

By EDWARD BRADBURY.

By CANON BONNEY.

By EDWARD BRADBURY.

By CANON BONNEY.

THE HUMBER AND ITS TRIBUTARIES *(Continued)*.

PAGE

By W. S. CAMERON.

By W. S. CAMERON.

By W. S. CAMERON.

THE RIVERS OF THE WASH.—*By CANON BONNEY.*

THE RIVERS OF EAST ANGLIA.—*By W. SENIOR.*

LIST OF ILLUSTRATIONS.

THE TEES:—

THE HUMBER AND ITS TRIBUTARIES:—

THE RIVERS OF THE WASH:—

THE RIVERS OF EAST ANGLIA:—

We are indebted for the use of Photographs on pages 1, 4, 5, 9, 12, 15, 17, 21, 24, 25, 29, 33, 35, 40, 43, 49, 57, 65, 71, 76, 77, 101, 105, and 109, to Messrs. J. Valentine and Sons, Dundee; on pages 11, 13, 16, 20, 35, 44, 46, 49, 92, 125, 243, 316, 329, and 334, to Messrs. G. W. Wilson and Co., Aberdeen; on pages 53, 73, 74, 93, 96, 106, 193, 205, 217, 250, 300, 316, 317, and 324, to Messrs. Poulton and Son, Lee; on pages 60 and 83, to Mr. T. Scott, Birmingham; on pages 79 and 88, to Mr. T. Foster, Coldstream; on page 85, to Mr. W. Green, Berwick-on-Tweed; on pages 88, 157, and 152, to Mr. H. Piper, Gateshead; on pages 116, 140, 141, 145, 146, 152, 153, and 204, to Mr. J. P. Gibson, Hexham; on pages 120 and 124, to Mr. J. Worsnop, Rothbury; on page 121, to Rev. G. Smith, Bedlington; on pages 145, 200, 208, 209, 211, 213, and 305, to Mr. E. Yeoman, Barnard Castle; on page 150, to Mr. C. C. Hodges, Hexham; on pages 154 and 155, to Messrs. G. M. Laws and Son, Newcastle-on-Tyne; on pages 181, 184, 189, 265, 269, 277, and 296, to Messrs. Frith and Co., Reigate; on page 212, to Mr. J. W. Cooper, Darlington; on page 224, to Mr. F. Pearson, Basford; on pages 238, 240, 252, 253, 263, 272, 273, 276, 284, and 290, to Mr. R. Keene, Derby; on pages 263 and 264, to Mr. J. W. Hilder, Matlock Bath; on page 258, to Messrs. Allen and Sons, Nottingham; on page 304, to Mr. M. Shuttleworth, Ilkley; on page 336, to Mr. G. A. Nicholls, Stamford; on pages 340 and 341, to Mr. A. Hendrey, Godmanchester; on page 345, to Messrs. Hills and Saunders, Cambridge; on page 352, to Mr. W. W. Gladwin, Maldon; on page 366, to Mr. Gill, Colchester; on pages 350, 357, 360, 361, 364, and 370, to Mr. Payne Jennings, Ashtead.

RIVERS OF GREAT BRITAIN.

BEN MACDHUI.

THE HIGHLAND DEE.

The Source: Larig and Garchary Burns—In the Heart of the Cairngorm Mountains—Ben Macdhui and Braeriach—"A Very Vulgar Place"—A Highland Legend—The Linn of Dee—Byron's Narrow Escape—The Floods of 1829—Lochnagar and Mary Duff—Influence of the Dee on Byron—Braemar and the Rising of '15—Corriemulzie and its Linn—Balmoral—The "Birks" of Abergeldie—Their Transplantation by Burns—What is Collimaukie?—Ballater; The Slaying of "Brave Brackley"—Craigendarroch—The Reel of Tullich and the Origin Thereof—The Legend of St. Nathalan—Mythological Parallels—The Muick—Morven: The Centre of Highland Song and Legend—Birse—Lumphanan Wood—The Battle of Corrichie—Queen Mary and Sir John Gordon—At Aberdeen.

AMONG the streams that meet together in the wild south-west of Aberdeenshire to form the Dee, it is not easy to decide which is chief, or where is the fountain, far up the dark mountain-side, where this parent rill has birth. Dismissing minor pretenders, we can at once state that the original is either the Larig or the Garchary Burn. The first is more in the main line of the river, whilst it has also more water; the second rises higher up, and has a longer course before it reaches the meeting-place. Popularly, the source of the stream is a place about the beginning of the Larig, called the Wells of Dee. Here Nature has built a reservoir perfect in every part. The water escapes from this fountain-head in considerable volume, so that it forms a quite satisfactory source, which we may well adopt. Here, then, our journey commences among

"The grizzly cliffs that guard
The infant rills of Highland Dee."

We are in the very heart of the Cairngorm Mountains, confronted on every side by all that is most savage and grand in nature—frowning precipices, mist-covered heights, sullen black lochs, an almost total absence of vegetation, an almost unbroken solitude. Here rise Ben Macdhui, Braeriach, and Cairntoul, whose streams, running down—often hurled down—their weather-beaten sides, rapidly increase the volume of our river. Braeriach fronts Ben Macdhui on the other side of the infant Dee. It presents to the view a huge line of precipices, dark and sombre, save when the hand of Winter, powdering them with snow, changes them to masses of glittering white. Even at a good distance away you hear the splash and dash of innumerable waterfalls, caused by the burns leaping the cliffs. If you venture to wander among those wilds you must know your ground well, for however bright the day may be one hour, the next you may be shrouded in mist, or drenched with rain, or battered by hail. The mist, indeed, is rarely absent. You see it clinging round the heights and moving restlessly up and down the hill-side like some uneasy and malignant spirit. As you walk you are startled at a huge figure striding along. It requires an effort to recognise a mist-picture of yourself—a sort of Scotch Spectre of the Brocken.

It was of these wild regions that an old Highlander once remarked to Hill Burton that it was "a fery fulgar place, and not fit for a young shentleman to go to at all." Let us not scorn the ingenuous native; Virgil has said, in the Eclogues (much more elegantly, 'tis true), very much the same thing about very much the same kind of scenery. All our way by Dee will not be among views like this. Indeed, at the mouth are scenes of rich fertility. It is on the fat meadows near Aberdeen that a portion of those innumerable flocks and droves are raised which have so great a reputation in the London market. These are the two extremes, but between them there is every variety of Highland scenery. He who has seen the banks of Dee has seen, as in an epitome or abridgment, all that the north of Scotland has to show. In the midst of variety one thing is constant, whatever landscape you may be passing through: you always have the great hill masses on the horizon. Thus the Dee is a typical Highland river. Even with the sternest parts soft touches are interwoven. Thus take the Lui, which, rising in Ben Macdhui, falls into the Dee at an early point of its course. The lower part of Glen Lui is remarkable for its gentle beauty. The grass is smooth as a lawn, the water of the burn which moves gently along is transparently clear, the regular slope is covered with weeping birches. The perfect solitude of this sweet valley has its own charm, though it be the charm of melancholy. Higher up, nearer Ben Macdhui, in Glen Lui Beg, the scenery is wilder, and the water dashes down more swiftly, as if it longed to be away from its wild source. We must go with it, and bid farewell to Ben Macdhui and the sources of Dee. And for farewell, here is a mountain legend.

At some time or other a band of robbers who infested this region had acquired a great store of gold. One of their number, named Mackenzie, proved that there is not honour among thieves. He robbed his companions and then hid the twice-cursed pelf in a remote and well-nigh inaccessible spot far up the slope of Ben Macdhui. The work of concealment took him the best part of a short summer night, for the sun rose precisely as he finished. He noticed that as its first beam fell over the ridge to the east, it marked a long burnished line of light over the ground where the treasure lay. This seemed to him to distinguish the spot beyond the possibility of error. Before his death he confided to his sons the secret of his hidden treasure. They were poor and greedy. The rest of their lives was devoted summer after summer to the hunt; but the grim mountain kept its secret well. Often the morning mist mocked their efforts, yet they succeeded no better when, on the anniversary of the burial, the sun rose in a sky of unclouded blue. One by one, prematurely aged, they passed away, till the last died a madman, revealing in his ravings the secret and the ruin of their lives. And still, somewhere on that mountain-side, the gold hoard lies concealed.

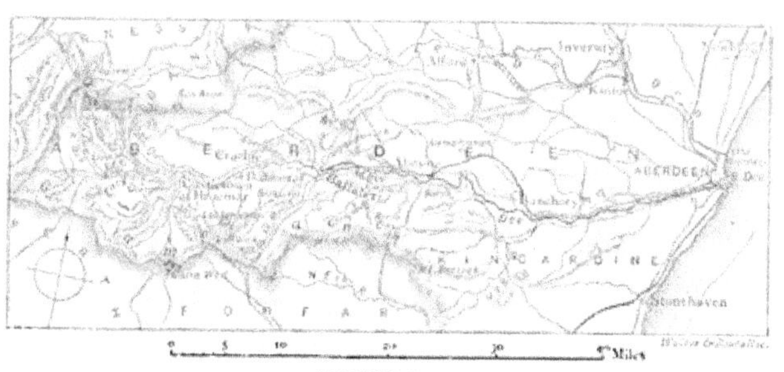

THE HIGHLAND DEE.

For some time after we leave the Wells of Dee, we are still in the midst of gloom. Dark black rocks rising on either side to a great height still shut us in, whilst the stillness is only broken by the roar of the wind, the rush of the water, or the (occasional) scream of the eagle; but when we get to the Linn of Dee, near Inverary, we may fairly consider ourselves back among our kind; nay, we are within the very uncharmed circle of the tourist, whereat we may rejoice or grieve as is our liking. This linn is caused by the river rushing through a narrow channel in the rocks over into a pool very deep, and (according to local tradition) unfathomable. Some hardy spirits have jumped across the channel, but if you try, and miss, you will never come out alive. Then your epitaph will be written in a guide-book paragraph, somewhat after the fashion of the lines in Baedeker telling the horrible end of that unfortunate officer who fell into the bear-pit at Berne. Lord Byron, when a boy, had a narrow escape here. "Some heather caught in his lame foot, and he fell. Already he was rolling downwards, when the attendant luckily caught hold of him, and was but just in time to save him from being killed."

LINN OF DEE.

LINN OF CORRIEMULZIE.

The great floods of 1829—those floods of which Sir Thomas Dick Lauder is the chronicler—wrought sad havoc here. A bridge spanned the stream at a height of thirty feet. The river, rising three feet higher, swept it away. We must turn to the annals of Strathspey to test the full havoc of the flood fiend, yet it wrought no mean ruin here. I pick out one or two cases. Near Inverey the rising water attacked six houses, destroying each in turn until all the inhabitants were huddled round the hearthstone of the last. Here the water burst in, forcing the poor people to take refuge on a knoll, where, without shelter, and in mortal terror for their lives, they crouched shivering through the night. There is a waterfall on the Quoich, near where it joins the larger river. This was spanned by a bridge so firmly bound to the rocks as to be (it was hoped) immovable. The flood struck it, and it was torn away, with tons of the adjacent rocks. It seemed, indeed, to those who lived through that terrible time, as if the very structure of the earth was breaking in pieces. The days were black with the ever-falling sheets of heavy rain; the nights were vivid with the ever-flashing lightning; whilst day and night alike the wind roared with demoniacal fury. The waters hidden in the bowels of hills and

LOCHNAGAR.

rocks burst forth, leaving great fissures and scars, which remain as a monument of the Titanic forces at work. Shocks of earthquake happened again and again. "I felt the earth hobblin' under me," said a peasant graphically. Many thought the end of all things was at hand. Yet it was in less sensational ravages that the flood wrought its most cruel havoc. The poor man's cottage left a hopeless ruin, the fertile field left a sandy waste—such were the most lamentable signs of its power. Human effort was powerless against it. What could be done with a flood which rose, as was noted at Ballater, not less than one foot in ten minutes? The ravages made have long ago been repaired. At Linn of Dee there is now a handsome white granite bridge, which was opened by the Queen as long ago as the year 1857.

It is odd that the poet of this essentially Highland river should be an English bard; for if we turn to see what our literature has to say of the Dee, we must turn to Byron. Yet Byron was, as he says, "half a Scot by birth, and bred a whole one." If his ancestors on the father's side "came over" (as he delighted to recall) with the Conqueror, he was not less proud to remember that his mother was of one of the best families of the "Gay Gordons," and that for over three centuries her people had possessed Gight. He went to Aberdeen in 1790, when but two years old; here he stayed till 1798, and during that time he visited again and again most of the finest spots on the Dee. Those mighty hills, those clear, flowing streams, were the earliest things he remembered, and he never failed to acknowledge how deep was the impression they made on him. "From this period I date my love of mountainous countries." Near the end of his life he sings, in "The Island"—

> "The infant rapture still survived the boy,
> And Lochnagar with Ida look'd o'er Troy."

His mention of Lochnagar—"dark Lochnagar"—reminds us how peculiarly his name is connected with that Deeside mountain of which he is the laureate. Here, too, sprang the strange child-love of the precocious boy for Mary Duff, with whose beauty the beauty of the country where he came to know her was indissolubly linked in his mind. The scenes in Greece, he says, carried him back to Morven (his own "Morven of snow"), and many a dark hill in that classic land made him "think of the rocks that o'ershadow Colbeen;" whilst the very mention of "Auld Lang Syne" brings to his mind the river Dee and

> "Scotland one and all,
> Scotch plaids, Scotch snoods, the blue hills and clear streams."

In Moore's biography there are needlessly ingenious arguments to prove that it was not the Dee scenery that made Byron a poet. Of course not. *Poeta nascitur non fit*, to quote the old Latin saying, which puts the matter much more pithily than Moore. But scenery and early impressions determine the course of a poet's genius as surely as the nature of the ground determines the course of the stream. How much Celtic magic there is in all Byron's verses—the love of the wild and terrible and impressive in scenery, as in life! Byron's poetry is before all romantic, and so is Deeside scenery. In his revolt against conventionalities, and even (it must be said) against the proprieties and decencies, we can clearly trace a true Celtic revolt against the dull, hard, prosaic facts of life. Can it be said that if Byron had passed his early years among the Lincolnshire fens or the muddy flats of Essex, "Don Juan" or "Childe Harold" would have been what they are—if, indeed, they had ever existed?

Moore under-estimated the influence of such scenes on Byron because he under-estimated the scenes themselves. "A small bleak valley, not at all worthy of being associated with the memory of a poet," says he. At this the local historian, good Mr. James Brown, who, having first driven a coach till he knew every inch of a large stretch of the country, then wrote an excellent Deeside guide, waxes very wroth. "It is really to be wished that Mr. Thomas Moore would not write upon subjects which he knows nothing about. Deeside a small bleak valley! Who ever heard tell of such nonsense!" Moore, however, did after his kind. He who sang the "sweet vale of Avoca" cared little for "dark Lochnagar." Indeed, there are some northern folk very much of Moore's opinion. Does not the old proverb tell us that

> "A mile of Don's worth two of Dee,
> Except for salmon, stone, and tree"?

But it is for those who love the stone and tree, the wild forests, the wilder hills, that Dee has its surpassing attraction. It adds a fine charm to the enthusiast's enjoyment of such scenery to know it is not everyone who can appreciate it.

But we turn now to interest of another kind, for at Castleton of Braemar we touch successive strata of historical events. There is Craig-Koynoch, where Kenneth II., too old for hunting himself, used to watch his dogs as they chased some noble stag, whilst his ears drank in the music of horn and hound. Here, too, in the old castle of Braemar, of which but a few remains are left, Malcolm Canmore, last of Scotland's Celtic kings, had a hunting seat in the midst of the mighty forest of which we still see the remains. There are still great herds of deer to be hunted, though the wolves and wild boars have long since vanished. Here, too, were the great possessions of the Mar family. It was to this place that John Erskine, thirty-ninth Earl of Mar, summoned the Highland clans under pretence of a great hunting party in Braemar forest, and began the rebellion of 1715. The standard was formally set up on the 6th of September, when the gilt ball which ornamented the top fell down, much to the consternation of the superstitious Celts.

A famous Jacobite song gives us the names of the leaders and the clans:—

> "I saw our chief come up the glen
> Wi' Drummond and Glengarry,
> Macgregor, Murray, Rollo, Keith,
> Panmure and gallant Harry;
> Macdonald's men, Clan Ronald's men,
> Mackenzie's men, Macgillivray's men,
> Strathallan's men, the Lowlan' men,
> O' Callander and Airly."

The hunting party, it should be noted, was not all a pretence. It took place on a magnificent scale, as Taylor the Water Poet, who was there (how or why it would take too long to explain), tells us. After he lost sight of the old castle, he was twelve days before he saw either house, or corn-field, or habitation for any creature but deer, wild horses, wolves, and such-like creatures. Taylor goes on to describe how a great body of beaters, setting out at early morning, drove the deer, "their heads making a show like a wood," to the place where the hunters shot them down. As we all know, the '15 was a disastrous failure—less terrible, it is true, but less glorious, than the '45. Mar turned out to be neither statesman nor soldier ("Oh for one hour of Dundee!" said the old officer at Sheriffmuir). He escaped with the Pretender to France, his vast estates were forfeited, and for a time there was no Earldom of Mar. His poor followers suffered more than their lord. All the houses in Braemar were burnt, save one at Corriemulzie. It was only the seclusion of that narrow glen, so beautiful with its birch-trees and its linn, that saved the lonely habitation. There are memories of the '45 about the district too. For instance, a little way down the river from Castleton is Craig Clunie, where Farquharson of Invercauld lay hid for ten months after Culloden, safe in the devotion of his clan, though his enemies were hunting for him far and near.

Ten miles or so below Castleton, we come upon another royal residence, which

BRAEMAR.

we all know as Balmoral, the Highland home of Queen Victoria. This place is now one of the most famous spots in Britain, and though its celebrity is of recent date, yet it has an old history of its own. As far back as 1451 it was royal property. In 1592 James V. gave it to the then Earl of Huntly. In 1652, on the downfall of the family, it came into the possession of the Earl of Moray. Enough of these dull details, which are best left in the congenial seclusion of the charter chest. In 1852 the Crown again—and let us hope finally—acquired Balmoral.

If anyone wonders why the Queen is so fond of her Highland home, it must be because the questioner has never seen it, since of all the dwelling-places of men it is surely the most desirable. It stands on a slight eminence near the Dee, which winds round it in a great bend. Swiftly the beautifully clear water rolls past. The low ground, richly fertile, is green in summer-time with various leafage. Behind the castle rises the graceful height of Craig-na-gow-an, clothed with the

VIEW FROM THE OLD BRIDGE, INVERCAULD, BRAEMAR.

slender birch-tree. The cairn on the top, to the memory of Albert the Good, reminds us of the great sorrow of Victoria's life. The castle lies at the foot of the hill, protected from the wild winter winds. In both near and remote distance we have the ever-beautiful background of the everlasting hills, immovable, and yet ever changing in place and appearance with each change of light and shade. Ben Macdhui in one direction is most prominent, dark Lochnagar in another. The scenery is "wild, and yet not desolate," as the Queen simply, yet truly, puts it. Its varied aspects give, from one point of view or another, examples of all Deeside views. The castle itself is built of very fine granite. It has a noble appearance, yet the architecture is of the simplest baronial Scotch style. It has all the traditional comfort of our island dwellings. It is, in a word, a genuine English home amidst the finest Highland scenery. What combination could be more attractive?

Two miles farther down is Abergeldie, of which the castle is occupied by the Prince of Wales when in these parts. Between the two is Crathie Kirk, where the royal household and their visitors worship in simple Presbyterian fashion in the autumn months. Abergeldie has an old reputation for its birks. There used to be a quaint old song in two verses which told their praise. In the first verse an ardent wooer entreats one of those innumerable "bonnie lassies" of Scotch popular poetry to hie thither under his escort. She is to have all sorts of fine things—

"Ye sall get a gown o' silk
And coat o' collimaukie."

What on earth is collimaukie? asks the reader. In truth I cannot tell, and I fear to look up the word in Jamieson lest it turn out to be something commonplace. The second verse is the young lady's reply. It is deliciously arch and simple:—

"Na, kind sir, I dare nae gang,
My minny will be angry.
Sair, sair wad she flyte,
Wad she flyte, wad she flyte,
Sair, sair, wad she flyte,
And sair wad she ban me!"

"Methinks the lady doth protest too much," and the probability is that she went after all. At any rate, the picture is perfect. You almost see the peasant girl mincing her words, biting her finger, with a blush on her young face. And what has become of this song, then? Why, Burns laid violent hands on the birks, and transferred them to Aberfeldy; which, thenceforth, was glorified with a most shady grove; in poetry, that is, for in fact there was not a single birk in the place for long afterwards, if, indeed, there is one even now; and, as far as my recollection goes, there is not. But we have still something to relate regarding those famous birks. It seems that the juice of the trees is carefully extracted, and the skilled natives, "by a curious process, ferment the same and make wine of it—which wine is very pleasant to taste, and thought by some to be little inferior to the wine of

Champagne and other outlandish countries." So far the local chronicler. We can only toss off a goblet (in imagination) of this extraordinary *vin du pays* to the prosperity of the birks ere the bend of the Dee hides them from our view.

Ballater is the next important place we come to. It is the terminus of the Deeside Extension Railway, and what is for us at present much more important, the centre of the most interesting part of Deeside. One mile south of it is an almost vanished ruin, the scene of a terrible tragedy, the memory of which—though it happened three centuries ago—is still preserved by a poem of a very different sort from the simple peasant idyll just quoted. One of the old tragic ballads which with such profound yet unconscious insight deal with the stormier human passions, tells the story of how Farquharson of Inverey slew, in shameful fashion, Gordon, Baron of Brackley. With what pithy expression the first two lines place you in the very heart of the subject!

> "Inverey came down Deeside whistlin and playin',
> He was at brave Brackley's yetts ere it was dawin'."

And then comes the proud, insolent challenge of the murderer—

> "Are ye sleepin', Baronne, or are ye waukin'?
> There's sharp swords at your yett will gar your blood spin."

Gordon is brave, but he will not go forth almost alone against so many to meet certain death till his fair, but false, young wife taunts him bitterly with his cowardice. Then he gets ready, though he knows how certain is his doom.

> "An' he stooped low, and said, as he kissed his proud dame,
> 'There's a Gordon rides out that will never ride hame.'"

There is a narrow glen near by which popular tradition still points out as the spot where they "pierced bonny Brackley wi' mony a woun'." The ballad closes in darkness and sadness, but one is glad to learn from contemporary history that the Earl of Huntly made a foray and avenged the death of his kinsman.

Hereby is the hill of Craigendarroch, which we cannot pause to climb, though from it we have a grand view a long way down the Dee Valley. Tullich I can only mention. Have you ever seen, by-the-bye, that extraordinary Highland tarantula called the reel of Tullich? It is perhaps the wildest, maddest dance ever invented. The legend of its origin is this:—One tempestuous Sabbath, about a century and a half ago, the congregation at the parish kirk there were without a minister. The manse was some way off, the roads were rough, and the parson got it into his head that nobody would be at church that day, so *he* need not go either. The people got tired of waiting; they began to stamp with their feet, then hidden bottles were produced, and then they danced and shouted till at last the whole thing degenerated into a wild orgie, during which the wind roared round the kirk and the sleet beat on the windows in vain. Then they invented and danced the reel of Tullich. Before the year was out all were dead, and by the dance alone are they now remembered. It is worth while quoting this strange story, for it is an example of the rare Presbyterian legend. A place on the river called the King's Pool reminds one of a Catholic myth. St. Nathdan, who once lived here, did penance for some sin by locking a heavy iron chain round his waist. He

BALMORAL.

then threw the key into this pool, saying he should know he was forgiven when he found it again. Long afterwards he went a pilgrimage to Rome, and on the Italian coast some fishermen, in return for his blessing, gave him a fish. Need I add that in the belly he found the key?

THE CASTLE.

The legends which hang like the mist round every rock and ruin have a weird fascination, but I must stop repeating them, or there will be room for nothing else. I cannot help noting, however, that there is a Deeside version of nearly every ancient myth. Thus one story tells how a Macdonald was suckled by a wolf quite after the fashion of Romulus. Another is of a giant injured by an individual calling himself Mysel, so that when the stupid monster was asked who hurt him, he could only say "Mysel" (myself). This is almost exactly the tale of the giant in the "Odyssey." But more curious than all is a reproduction of the famous apple legend, with Malcolm Canmore for Geisler and one called Hardy for William Tell. The resemblance is exact even down to the two additional arrows; but I can scarcely go so far as the old Deeside lady, who affirmed that

ABERGELDIE CASTLE.

since Malcolm Canmore flourished about the time of the Norman Conquest, and William Tell was contemporary with Robert Bruce, the Swiss legend was borrowed from the Scotch!

It is difficult to get away from a neighbourhood like Ballater, where there is so much worth seeing. The Muich here, running from the south, falls into the Dee. About five miles up is the Linn of Muich — linns and waterfalls are the peculiar glory of Deeside, I need scarcely say. A great mass of water finds here but one narrow outlet, over which it foams and struggles, and then falls fifty feet with a great splash into a deep pool. The heights of the precipice are clothed with old fir-trees, which also stick out of the crevasses of the rocks. The Muich rises away up at the foot of Loch-na-gar in Loch Muich, which means, they say, the Lake of Sorrow — so gloomy and sombre is that far-off recess in the hill. To the west of Loch-na-gar are the Loch and Glen of Callater — wild enough, too; and beyond is the Breakneck Waterfall, which is positively the last fall I shall mention. A stream makes a bold dart over a precipice. It seems like a thread of silver in the sunlight. Down it falls, with a thundering sound on the rock, scattering its spray around in a perpetual shower. A British admiral, some few years ago, slipped over a precipice near here. His hammer (he was specimen hunting) stuck in a crack, and there he held on for two awful days, and still more awful nights. The whole neighbourhood hunted for him, and at last, the black speck being seen on the cliff, he was rescued. Not a man of the rescuers would accept a farthing for what he had done. The Highlander has his faults, but there is always something of the gentleman about him.

Nearly due north of Ballater is Morven—the Morven of Byron, and (perhaps) of Ossian, though there are other places and districts in Scotland bearing the name. Morven is the centre of Highland song and legend. But if it is enchanted, it is also uncertain, ground, and must here be left untraced. We are still forty-three miles from Aberdeen; so we glide through Aboyne and Glentanner, leaving the beautiful castle of the one, and the equally, though differently, beautiful valley of the other, unvisited. Then in many a devious turn we wind round the northern boundary of the parish of Birse. "As auld as the hills o' Birse," says a local proverb, which shows that even in this land of hills the district is considered hilly. Here are some of their names: Torquhandallachy, Lamawhillis, Carmaferg, Lamahip, Duchery, Craigmahandle, Gamoch, Creagauducy. Grand words those, if you can give them their proper sound. Otherwise leave them "unhonoured and unsung," and unpronounced. The local chronicler is much perplexed by another somewhat inelegant Aberdeenshire witticism—"Gang to Birse and bottle skate." With absolute logical correctness he proves that in that inland and hilly parish there are no skate; and that, if there were, to bottle them would be contrary to the principles and practice of any recorded system of fish-curing. We shall not discuss with him this dark saying.

On the other side of the Dee is Lumphanan parish, in the "wood" of which Macbeth—according to Wyntoun, though not according to Shakespeare—met his death. His "cairn" is still to be seen on a bare hill in this district, though another tradition tells us that his dust mingles with the dust of "gracious Duncan" in the sacred soil of Iona. The Dee, now leaving its native county, flows for a few miles through the Mearns or Kincardineshire. It returns to Aberdeenshire in the parish of Drumoak, forming for the remaining fourteen miles of its course the boundary between the two counties.

It is here we come across the most interesting historical memory connected with Deeside, for it is a memory of Queen Mary. On the south side of the Hill of Fare there is a hollow, where the battle of Corrichie was fought in 1562. I do not wish to enter into the history of that troubled time. Suffice it to say that the Earl of Huntly, chief of the Gordons, and head of the Catholics, was intriguing to secure the power which Murray was determined he should not have. The Queen was with Murray, though her heart, they said, was with the Gordons. Anyhow, she dashed northward gaily enough on a horse that would have thrown an ordinary rider. Murray's diplomacy forced the Gordons into a position of open hostility, and his superior generalship easily secured him the victory at Corrichie. The old Earl of Huntly was taken, it seemed, unhurt, but he suddenly fell down dead—heartbroken at the ruin of himself and his house, said some; crushed by the weight of his armour, said others. They took the body to the Tolbooth in Aberdeen. Knox tells us that the Countess had consulted a witch before the fight, and was comforted by the assurance that her husband would lie *unwounded* that night in the Tolbooth. The remains, embalmed in some rude fashion, were carried to Edinburgh; for a strange ceremony yet remained ere the Gordon lands were divided among the victors. A Parliament in due time met in Holyrood, and the dead man was brought before his peers to answer for his treasons. A mere formality, perhaps, but an awfully gruesome one. His attainder, and that of his family, together with the forfeiture of his lands, was then pronounced. The battle was a great triumph for the Protestant lords; even the sneering, sceptical Maitland, says Knox, with one of those direct, forcible touches of his, "remembered that there was a God in heaven." There was one who looked on the matter with other eyes. "The Queen took no pleasure in the victory, and gloomed at the messenger who told of it." Indeed, there was a tragedy within this tragedy. Among the prisoners taken at Corrichie was Sir John Gordon,

BALLATER.

Huntly's second son, "a comely young gentleman," wild and daring, and, though then an outlaw, one who had ventured to hope for the Queen's hand. It was whispered that she was not unfavourable to him; some ventured to say "she loved him entirely." For such a man there was but one fate possible, and that was death. He was executed in the market-place of Aberdeen. Murray looked on at the death of his foe with that inscrutable

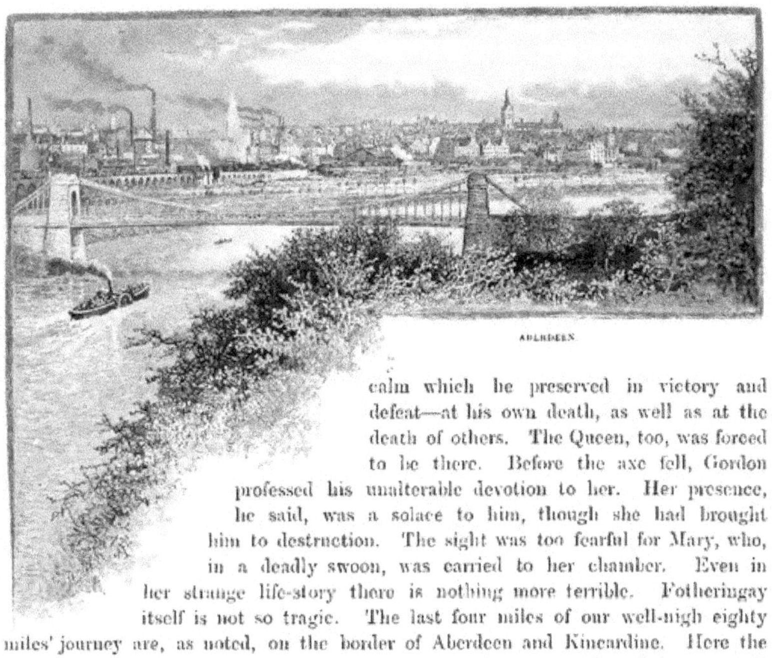

ABERDEEN.

calm which he preserved in victory and defeat—at his own death, as well as at the death of others. The Queen, too, was forced to be there. Before the axe fell, Gordon professed his unalterable devotion to her. Her presence, he said, was a solace to him, though she had brought him to destruction. The sight was too fearful for Mary, who, in a deadly swoon, was carried to her chamber. Even in her strange life-story there is nothing more terrible. Fotheringay itself is not so tragic. The last four miles of our well-nigh eighty miles' journey are, as noted, on the border of Aberdeen and Kincardine. Here the river enjoys a peaceful old age, after the wild turmoil of its youth. The water, still beautifully clear, moves placidly along amidst rich meadows; the near hills are low, with soft rounded summits. The dwellings of men give a cheerfulness to the scene. It is the very perfection of pastoral landscape. And then, at last, we come to Aberdeen and the sea. But on the wonders of that famous town I cannot here enter. Suffice it to say that our record of the Highland Dee is finished.

FRANCIS WATT.

BRIDGE OF TAY, KENMORE.

THE TAY.

The Tiber and the Tay—History and Legend—Perthshire and the Tay—The Moor of Rannoch—Blair—Pitlochrie—Killin—Kenmore—The Lyon—The "Rock of Weem"—The "Birks" of Aberfeldy—Dunkeld and Birnam—Invertuthil—The Loch of Clunie—The Isla—Strathmore—Dunsinane Hill—Scone and the Ruthvens—Perth—The Views from Moncrieffe and Kinnoull—Strathearn and the Carse of Gowrie—Dundee—The Tay Bridge, New and Old—View from the "Law"—"Men of Blood" and Men of Business.

"BEHOLD THE TIBER!" said the conquering Roman, when from one of the many 'vantage-grounds commanding the noble stream that sweeps past Perth, the Imperial eagles first saw as fair a scene as they had yet reached in their flight. The ardent lovers of the river—meaning all who know its banks well—have ever since felt, with Scott, half flattered by the traditional compliment, half scornful of the comparison of the puny and "dramlie" Roman stream with the broad, clear, and brimming Tay—the dusty Campus Martius with the green "Inches" of Perth—the featureless and desolate Campagna with the glorious stretch of hill and plain, water and woodland, overlooked from Kinnoull Hill or the "Wicks of Baiglie."

It is true that when this pioneer of countless hosts of Southern invaders and sightseers came hither, to admire and covet, the Tay flowed through a savage and shaggy land. There might have been a handful of the skin or wicker-work wigwams of the "dwellers in the forest" on the site of Perth, or at Forteviot or Abernethy, afterwards the capitals of the Picts, and a sprinkling of Caledonian coracles on the neighbouring waters. But if Perthshire and the Tay had a history before the coming of Agricola and the building of the lines of Roman roads and stations that converged upon their great camp, dedicated to Mars, near the meeting-place of this prince of Scottish streams with the tributary waters of the Almond and the Earn, it is utterly lost in the mists of antiquity.

History of the most stirring kind the Tay has known enough of since. Every glen and hillside is thronged with memories and legends of the days of romance, which, in Perthshire and on the banks of the Tay, came to an end only about a century ago, when some of the Jacobite lairds were still in exile for being "out" in the '45, and had not utterly given up hope of the "lost cause." Every old castle and little township has played its part in the strange, eventful drama of the national history; and by their record, not less than by its position, Perthshire can lay claim to be the heart, and the Tay to be the heart's blood, of the northern kingdom.

Perthshire is the Tay, almost as truly as Egypt is the Nile. It is the case that some of the head-waters of this many-fountained stream rise in other counties—that its furthest, if not its most important, source is in the desolate Moor of Rannoch—"a world before chaos," crudely compounded of bog and rock, where Loch Lydoch trails its black and sinuous length out of Argyllshire into Perth; that, further north, Loch Ericht, straight as a sword-blade, thrusts its sharper end miles deep into the mountains of Laggan, in Inverness-shire, hiding, as tradition tells us, the ruins of submerged fields and houses under its gleaming surface; and that the Isla draws from Forfarshire that portion of its waters which murmurs under the haunted old walls of Airlie and Glamis. True, also, a choice and lovely portion of Perthshire—many deem it the choicest and loveliest of all—drains through the Trossachs to the Forth; and that the Tay itself, after it has ceased to be a river, and has become an arm of the sea, overpasses the bounds of the "central county," and meets the ocean between the Braes of Angus and the hills of Fife—between the clustering spires and chimneys of busy Dundee and the crumbling towers that watch over the secluded dignity of St. Andrews.

All this notwithstanding, the periphery of Perthshire may roughly be said to embrace all the wealth of beauty reflected in the Tay, and all the wealth of memories that mingles with its flowing current. And richly endowed is this prince of highland and lowland streams, both with beauty and associations.

The centre of the basin of the Tay is somewhere in Glenalmond, between the sweet woodland shades of the "burn-brae" of Lynedoch, under which "Bessie Bell and Mary Gray" rest, with their lover at their feet, and the bare and stilly place where "sleeps Ossian in the Narrow Glen," and where murmurs along

> "But one meek streamlet, only one,
> The Song of Battles, and the breath
> Of stormy war and violent death;"

while above, on the summits of the hills, the grey stones and cairns still keep watch, and, interpreted by tradition, point out to us the place where Fingal once held sway in the very heart of Perthshire and of the Caledonian Forest.

Of the ancient woods that are supposed once to have clothed the country, remains may yet, perhaps, be seen in those glorious sylvan demesnes that surround Taymouth in Breadalbane and Blair in Athole; Dupplin, and Drummond Castle, in Strathearn, and Rossie Priory in the Carse of Gowrie; Scone Palace and Dunkeld, Moncrieffe and Kinnoull, overlooking the central and lower reaches of the Tay. Traces of them may also be found in the Woods of Methven, that once gave friendly shelter to Wallace, and in those ragged and giant pines that thinly dot the hillsides in Rannoch and Glenlyon, over which Bruce was once chased by the Lord of the Isles and the English invaders.

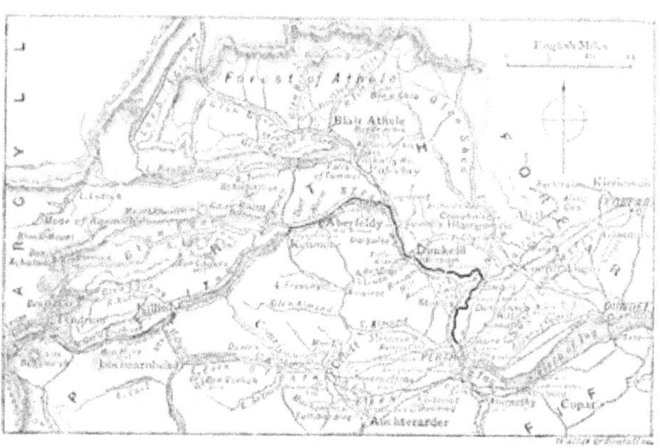

THE TAY.

But a new forest has grown up within a century, to shade once more the waters of the Tay. Whatever may have been the case in Macbeth's or Shakespeare's time, "great Birnam Wood" can no longer be seen from "high Dunsinane Hill" for the growth of trees—the "moving grove"—that has risen up between. The Bruar Water and its falls are now shaded from the sun and the northern blasts, as Burns longed to see them, by "lofty firs and fragrant birks," as well as by their craggy cliffs; and not content with thus fulfilling the poet's wish, the Lords of Athole, from the "Planting Duke" downward, have been nobly ambitious of clothing their once bare hills with forest to the summits. Beside the pillars of ruined Dunkeld Cathedral—almost as worthy of reverence as they—stand the two "Parent Larches," the first trees of their kind introduced into Scotland. Planted only a century and a half ago, millions of their seed and kin have now overrun Perthshire and the Highlands, proving themselves thoroughly at home in the soil and air of the Tay.

In the bleak Moor of Rannoch—the "furthest Thule" of Perthshire and of the more northern Tay sources—there are great blank spaces where the heather itself will scarce grow. There are only grey rock and black marsh—"bogs of Styx and waters of Cocytus," with scarce a sign of human habitation or even of animal life. But the logs of oak found embedded in the peat, and the hoary fir trunks that still keep a stubborn stand by Loch Lydoch and the banks of the Guar and the Ericht, show that even in this dreary region a great forest once waved. The "Black Wood of Rannoch" still clothes the southern side of the fine loch of the name; and here, indeed, the Scots fir is to be seen in all its pride and strength, rising above the beautiful growth of oak and birch coppice, and of heather of almost arboreal proportions. Escaping from Loch Rannoch, the Tummel roars down its rocky bed under the piny slopes and crags of Dunalastair, with a halt by the way in Loch Tummel, where, from the "Queen's View," looking back, a magnificent prospect is had of the lovely lake embosomed in woods and hills, dominated by the lofty shape of Schiehallion, with the lonely Black Mount and the more distant Grampians closing the background. Further down, opposite Faskally, the Garry joins it,

"BIRKS" OF ABERFELDY.

ABERFELDY, FROM THE WEST.

mingling the streams of Athole with the waters of Rannoch. Before the meeting, the Garry, leaving its parent lake high up near the borders of Inverness, has tumbled in white foam through leagues of the "Struan country," between banks thinly sprinkled

BRIDGE OF GARRY.

with birchwood and edging great tracts of moorland. Then the Erichdie, the Bruar, and the Tilt bring down their contributions from remote mountain corries visited only by the deer-stalker, through deep wild glens, gloriously wooded at their lower extremity. Where the Tilt runs into the Garry stands Blair, the Highland seat of the ducal family of Athole.

The date when "Blair in Athole" was first occupied as a stronghold of a powerful Highland chieftain is not told in the eventful annals of the Castle. Strategic considerations, from the points of view of war and of the chase, no doubt determined the selection of the site, inside the rugged jaws of the Pass of Killiecrankie, and on a shelf commanding the routes leading across the Grampians from the basin of the Tay to the valleys of the Spey and the Dee. The choice thus made in ruder days is thoroughly pleasing in these "piping times of peace," when the line of the Highland Railway threads its way through the narrow defile, and keeping the main valley of the Garry, skirts the miles of woodland, opening at intervals to afford peeps of the plain, massive white front of the Castle and the broad spaces of its surrounding parks. The way through Glentilt, traversed by the clans to join the Stuart standard at Blair or on the Braes of Mar, is free now only to the deer and the gillies.

Without going back to the Athole lines of the Comyns and the Stewarts, or to the joyous hunting scenes in which Queen Mary and other of the old line of Scottish Sovereigns bore a part, Blair has been a centre of historical and social interest ever since it became the chief seat of the Murrays. Montrose assembled the Royalist clans here, and set out upon the campaign which began with the defeat of the Covenanters at Tibbermore and the capture of Perth, and ended at Philiphaugh, where, in one day, the fruits of six brilliant victories were lost. Another darling of cavalier legend, Graham of Claverhouse, Viscount Dundee, lies buried in the old church near by. In the year of the Revolution he had relieved Blair Castle, where the clansmen of Athole had held out for the Jacobite cause against their titular chief, and having enticed General Mackay through the Pass, he rushed down upon him with all his force from the slopes of the Hill of Urrard, utterly routing and sweeping back the enemy through the narrow gorge of the Garry, and himself falling, shot through the heart, at the moment the Sassenachs turned to run.

Notable events happened here also in the "'15" and in the "'45;" and, to come to the recent memories which are cherished with pride in Blair-Athole, Queen Victoria has paid repeated visits to the locality, and was entranced by the magnificent prospects of wood and stream, rugged mountain and fertile strath, that are unfolded from the top of the Hill of Tulloch, and from other points of view in this beautiful district. It is a kind of "holy ground" to fervid Jacobites, one or two of whom are supposed still to linger in Perthshire, if extinct elsewhere. It is also a favourite resort of the increasing host of pilgrims in search of Highland sport and scenery, who invade Athole through the Pass of Killiecrankie, and gaze, with a delight in which there is no longer any tempering of fear of consequences, upon the lofty and impending banks, pine-clad to their summits, and the wilderness of rock and boulder below, through which the Garry glooms and flashes in alternate pool and fall.

Pitlochrie is a charming place to halt at before, or after, clearing this "gateway of the Highlands." The Tummel has now joined the Garry, and under the latter name the united streams have but a short way to go before they fall, at Ballinluig, into the stream which, from the place where it issues from Loch Tay, takes the name of the Tay. Were we to seek it still nearer to its sources, we should find ourselves in a district which, before the railway came to disturb its solitude, was as lone and wild as the lochans of the Black Mount or those corries of Ben Alder and Ben-y-Gloe whence the Tummel, the Ericht, and Tilt draw their springs. The line from Oban breaks into Perthshire and the basin of the Tay at Tyndrum, near the head of Strathfillan, not far from the scene of Bruce's defeat at the hands of the Lord of Lorn. Following, from near the base of Ben Lui, the infant Tay—here, however, bearing the names successively of the Fillan and the Dochart—the way leads past the sites of ruined castles and chapels, by cairns yet haunted by memories of the bloody feuds of former days, and wells to which legend still assigns wonderful healing virtues. On the left are bare mountain sides stretching away northward towards the hills that enclose the head of Glen Lochay and Glen Lyon; and to the right the range of alpine heights that culminate in Ben More and impend over Loch Dochart, its old castle, and its "floating island." St. Fillan lived and laboured in Strathfillan; Fingal is said to be buried in Glen Dochart; a hundred traditions cling to the rocks and waters here, and in Glen Ogle, and in the Glen of the Lochay, which, pouring over its pretty "linn," joins the Dochart just before the united stream falls into the head of Loch Tay.

Where the waters meet at Killin, a rich feast is spread for the eye of the lover of Highland scenery. Killin, with its wonderful mingling of wild mountain outlines, and the gentle, infinitely varied charms of the lake and running streams and wooded shores, is a painter's paradise.

Fifteen miles of the finest salmon-angling water in Scotland, overhung on the north by the vast bulk of Ben Lawers, and bountifully fringed by birch and other wood, separates Killin from Kenmore, at the lower end of the great Loch, whence issues, under its proper name, the Tay. The ruins on the little island near the outlet are those of the Priory erected by King Alexander I. beside the remains of his Queen, Sibylla, daughter of Henry I. of England—a quiet retreat for centuries of the company of nuns from whom the Fair at the neighbouring Kenmore takes the name of the "Holy Women's Market." Kenmore is as lovely in its own way as Killin; but here it is no longer wild Highland landscape, but Nature half-submissive to the embellishing hand of man. It is

"A piece of England ramparted around
With strength of Highland Ben and heather brae;"

and in the centre of the scene, set among ample lawns and magnificent walks and avenues, backed by the high, dark curtain of Drummond Hill, and looking towards the pine-clad heights opposite, stands Taymouth Castle, the princely seat of the Breadalbane family. Famous even among their sept for their politic ability and acquisitiveness, the Campbells, Lords of Glenorchy, who became Lords of Breadalbane, are said to have chosen this site, at the eastern limit of their vast possessions, with the hope of "birzing yont" into richer lands further down the Tay. To this day, the Breadalbane estates extend for a hundred miles westward of Taymouth, to the Atlantic Ocean.

Behind Drummond Hill is Glen Lyon, and a vista of its mountains—Schichallion lording it over the minor heights—opens up at the Vale of Appin, where the Lyon falls into the Tay. A long journey this tributary makes, among savage and solitary hills, and past haunts of Ossian's heroes and of the "Wolf of Badenoch," before it reaches the sylvan beauties assembled round Glenlyon House and Sir Donald Currie's Castle of Garth. But the most venerable of all the objects on the banks of the Lyon—not excluding the reputed birthplace of Pontius Pilate—is the "Old Yew of Fortingal," perhaps "the oldest authentic specimen of vegetation in Europe."

On nothing quite so venerable as this does the next outstanding eminence by the Tay—the "Rock of Weem"—look down. But Castle Menzies, for four centuries the home of the Menzies of that ilk, lies surrounded by fine woods at

BIRNAM, FROM BIRNAM HILL.

its base; further off is the site of the old Abbey of Dull; and beyond the Bridge of Tay—first place of assembly of the gallant "Black Watch," or 42nd Highlanders—are the Falls of Moness and the "Birks" of Aberfeldy. Mountain ash and pine have to some extent replaced the hazels and birches about which Burns so sweetly sings; but tourists come in larger flocks every season to Urlar Burn and to the pretty village near by. Grandtully Woods, and the old Castle of the Stewarts, which has been said to resemble more closely than any other baronial seat the picture drawn by Scott of Tully-veolan, attract many admiring eyes. Balleichan recalls memories of "Sir James the Rose;" and all down Strathtay, before and after the junction with the Tummel—at Logierait and Kinnaird, Dowally and Dalguise—the enchantments of a romantic past and of superb scenery combine to induce the traveller to linger over every mile of the valley.

DUNSINANE HILL.

Dunkeld and Birnam are ahead, however, and the temptations to delay must be foregone. There is no nook of Scotland more gloriously apparelled and richly endowed. Grand forests stretch for miles around, clothing the river-banks, filling the glens, and crowning to their crests Birnam Hill, Newtyle, Craig Vinean, Craig-y-Barns, and other heights that gather round the old cathedral town. Through the centre of the scene the Tay sweeps in smooth and spacious curves and long, bright-rippled reaches. All this loveliness is concentrated around the Palace and Cathedral of Dunkeld. Opposite is Birnam, and, a little above the line of arches of the fine bridge, the "mossy Braan," coming from Loch Freuchie and "lone Amulree," tumbles through the romantic dell of the Rumbling Bridge and the "Hermitage," and over its upper and lower Falls, before entering the Tay.

A single gnarled and wide-branched oak represents all that remains of the original Birnam Wood. The glory of the ancient Cathedral has also departed, or undergone a change. For some fifteen hundred years, it is reckoned, there has been a Christian house on this spot; and at as early a date Dunkeld ("Dun-Caledon") had a royal residence, probably on the site of the "dun" or fort on the "King's Seat." St. Columba is thought to have founded the church, and to have preached here to the natives of "Atholl, Caledon, and Angus;" and he is said to have found burial at Dunkeld. Adamnan and Crinan were among its Culdee abbots; and in the long line of its Roman Catholic bishops, whose diocese extended over the greater part of the basin of the Tay, Gawin Douglas, the poet and translator of the "Æneid," is not the only eminent name. Very stately without and beautiful within, the edifice of the Cathedral Church must have looked in its prime, before the Lords of the Congregation sent word to "purge the kyrk of all kynd of monuments of idolatrye," but to "tak guid heid that neither the windocks nor dooris be onywise hurt or broken"—a saving clause to which the zealous Reforming mob paid scant attention.

SCONE PALACE, PERTH.

The main portion of the Cathedral—the nave—has long been roofless, but the tower, in which the "Cameronian Regiment" of 1689 offered their brilliant and successful resistance to the victors of Killiecrankie, and stemmed the Highland tide rushing down on the Lowlands, still stands, and the choir has been restored and is used as the parish church. Within the walls, the "Wolf of Badenoch," Alexander Stewart, Earl of Buchan—that type of a savage and ruthless Highland chieftain—is buried; here also are the vaults of the Athole family, and a monument recording the deeds of the "Black Watch." Without, the beautiful lawns, gardens, and woods of Dunkeld Palace, one of the seats of the Duke of Athole, surround the Cathedral ruins, and come down to the river's edge. Fine villa residences are ranged along the hillside, and the town of Dunkeld offers every evidence of prosperity.

At Dunkeld, the Tay takes a long sweep eastward, until at the meeting with the Isla at Meikleour it forms a great elbow and resumes its southward flow. The Murthly estate, which belongs to the owner of Grandtully, occupies the south bank of the river along this portion of its course. From the earliest times royalty, like romance and poetry, has had the good taste to frequent these scenes. The wraiths of Neil Gow, the famous fiddler, and of the Highland caterans hanged in the "eerie hollow" of the Stare Dam, dispute with the ghost of Macbeth the honour of being the familiar spirits of Birnam Hill, once again magnificently clothed with wood. In Auchtergaven is the birthplace of Robert Nicol, the "Peasant Poet;" and here also stood the "Auld House of Nairne," which recalls the name of Caroline Oliphant, Baroness Nairne, the laureate of Jacobite song, and which, like her ancestral home in Strathearn—the "Auld House of Gask"—gave shelter to Prince Charlie. At the Royal Castle of Kinclaven, now a neglected ruin, many a Scottish Sovereign, from the time of Malcolm Ceanmohr and Queen Margaret, had solaced themselves after the chase or battle, before it was captured and recaptured, rebuilt and demolished, in the days of Wallace and Bruce.

The northern bank of the Tay is equally rich in scenic beauty and historical associations. Between the grounds of Delvine and Meikleour, and opposite the "Bloody Inches"—believed to preserve the memory of the spot where Redner Lodbrog, the Norse viking and skald, was beaten back to his ships—the important Roman station of Tulina, now Invertuthil, is supposed to have stood. Meikleour the Marchioness of Lansdowne has inherited from her ancestors the Mercers, descendants of a warlike Provost of Perth in the fourteenth century. The village is one of the quaintest and most charming of Scottish hamlets; and the great "beech hedge," ninety feet high, is among the many arboricultural marvels in the valley of the Tay. Hidden from sight among hills and woods, like many other lakes and famous sites of this district, is the Loch of Clunie, with its island castle, the hunting seat of kings and place of rest and retirement of bishops in the old days. The Lunan drains from it into the Isla; but to trace the Isla would be to write pages of description and history concerning Glenardle and Glenshee, Stormont and Strathmore, the slopes of the

Sidlaws and the passes through the Grampians into Braemar. We should have to give some idea of the beauties collected about Bridge of Cally, Craighall, and Blairgowrie on the Ericht; to visit the "Reekie Linn," the "Slugs of Auchrannie," and Lintrathen on the Isla; to seek the sites, mythical or otherwise, of Agricola's victory over Galgacus and of Macbeth's defeat by Macduff near Dunsinane Hill; and to speak of what makes Glamis and Airlie and Inverqueich, Alyth and Meigle and Coupar, and the rest of the country lying along the borders of Perth and Angus, memorable and attractive. It would even lead us as far as Forfar and its loch and castles, and the rival little burgh of Kirriemuir—the "Thrums" of recent delightful sketches of old world Scottish "wabster" and kirk life in Angus—and detain us to the end of the chapter.

We resume, instead, the line of the Tay below Meikleour and Kinclaven, and beyond the "Coble o' Cargill," replaced by the more prosaic bridge carrying the railway line from Perth to Aberdeen. This is the heart of Strathmore—the "great valley." Ballathy, Stobhall, Muckersy, and Stanley maintain the repute of the Tay for noble prospects of hill, wood, and stream. Stobhall was the seat of the Drummond family—still a power in Perthshire—before they removed to Drummond Castle on the Earn; and near by, at the Campsie Linn, beside an ancient cell of the monks of Coupar-Angus Abbey, is the waterfall over which—*teste* the author of the "Fair Maid of Perth"—Conacher, the refugee from the battle on the North Inch, flung himself to hide his shame. Macbeth's Castle, on Dunsinane Hill, and the field of Luncarty—where, nine centuries ago, the peasant ancestor of the Hays of Tweeddale, Errol, and Kinnoull is said to have turned the battle for the Scots against the Danes with his plough-yoke—might detain us. But now, close ahead, the explorer of Tayside views, fringing the right bank of the river for miles opposite the mouth of the Almond, and extending to the environs of the Royal City of Perth, the woods of Scone—

> "Towers and battlements he sees,
> Bosomed high on tufted trees."

This is Scone Palace, the magnificent mansion of the Earls of Mansfield, standing almost on the site of the ancient Abbey and royal residence of Scone. Modern Scone and all its surroundings are stately and spacious, but the relics of its early grandeur have disappeared from the landscape, and almost the only memorials of the days when it was the meeting-place of parliaments and councils, the crowning-place of kings, "the Windsor of Scotland," are the mound of the "Motehill," the sycamore tree planted by Queen Mary, and the cross which marks the place where stood the old "City of Scone." In its neighbourhood was fought the last battle that decided the supremacy of the Scots over the Picts and the amalgamation of the two nations in one. On the Motehill, Kenneth Macalpine proclaimed the "Macalpine Laws." Hither, according to tradition, the "Stone of Destiny" was brought, more than a thousand years ago, from the old capital of the Dalriadic Scots in the west—from Dunstaffnage or Beregonium—and the Sovereigns of Scotland continued to be crowned on it until it was carried off to England, as the trophy of conquest, by Edward I. It forms part of the Coronation Chair at Westminster; and patriotic Scots declare that the prophecy bound up in the fateful stone is still being fulfilled, and that where it is, the Sovereigns of a Scottish house rule the land. Though the Coronation Stone

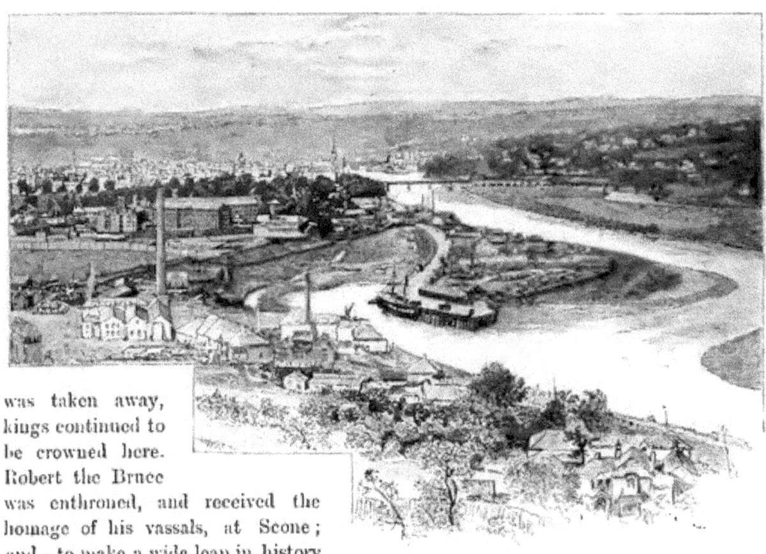

PERTH, FROM THE WEST.

was taken away, kings continued to be crowned here. Robert the Bruce was enthroned, and received the homage of his vassals, at Scone; and—to make a wide leap in history—Charles II. was crowned King of Scotland at the spot where his ancestors had been anointed and installed, before he set out on the unlucky expedition which ended at Worcester. Similar preparations were made for the coronation of the Old Pretender; but on the very eve of the event dissensions among his followers, and the approach of Argyll's army, caused him to take flight back to the Continent, leaving his adherents to their fate—an inglorious end to "an auld sang!"

Before Kenneth Macalpine's day, Scone was a place where councils of the Early Church met; and nearly eight centuries ago a monastery was founded there, and richly endowed by Alexander I., in gratitude for his escape from an attempt made by insurgent "men of Moray and the Mearns" to capture him at Invergowrie Castle, or "Hurley Hawkin," where two burns meet near the Church of Liff. The Abbots and the Abbey of Scone played a prominent part in the civil and ecclesiastical affairs of Scotland; and we find the patronage and lands of the High Church of St. Giles, in Edinburgh, bestowed upon it, on account of the expenses incurred by the monks at the funeral of Robert II. and coronation of Robert III., when the prelates and nobles encamped on the fields between the Abbey and the Tay trampled down the standing corn, besides eating and drinking their victuals, and also, as the deed of gift runs, "because, at similar times of unction and coronation, through the many and frequent great gatherings of the people, the monastery has

TAY STREET, PERTH.

sustained great damage in their buildings, and been burdened with heavy expenses." All cares and burdens came to an end in 1559, when the Reforming mob, having destroyed the Blackfriars' and other religious houses in the "City of St. Johnstoun," stormed out of Perth, and burned the Abbey of Scone. Its lands, after remaining a brief time in the hands of the unfortunate House of Gowrie, fell to the branch of the Murrays that became illustrious in law, statecraft, and literature, in the person of William, first Earl of Mansfield. The Abbey site is a clump of trees; and the "Royal City of Scone," expelled outside the park gates, has nothing to represent it but the prosaic village of New Scone.

The Ruthvens have no longer part or lot in this district, where they once lorded it over the stout citizens of Perth, and dared to put their Sovereigns in thrall. Their old home of Ruthven, or Huntingtower Castle, is opposite Scone, and not far from the junction of the Almond with the Tay, where, if we could believe tradition, stood the original Perth—Rath-Inveralmon—until it was visited by one of the many floods that have vexed its burghers, and was removed a mile or two downward to its present site, more close to the shelter of Moncrieffe and Kinnoull Hills and the tide-water of the Tay. All around are historical scenes—among them Methven and Tibbermore, made memorable by stirring passages in the careers of Wallace, Bruce, and Montrose. But at few spots has more history been made, or contrived, than at the Castle of the Ruthvens. Four or five generations of its lords made themselves illustrious or notorious in the annals of the "troublous times" that preceded the Union of the Crowns. Above all, they were zealous, not to say unscrupulous, partisans of the Reformation. It was the third lord who rose from a sick-bed, and, clad in armour, and "haggard and terrific" in visage, took a foremost share in the murder of David Rizzio. His son, the fourth Lord Ruthven, grandfather of the "great Marquis" of Montrose, had a hand in the same bloody business, and he it was who conducted Mary to Lochleven, and extorted from her the renouncement of her right to rule.

The year after this same fourth lord had been made first Earl of Gowrie was enacted the "Raid of Ruthven." The young King James was invited to visit Huntingtower Castle, on his way from Athole to Edinburgh, and was there detained by force by the Gowrie faction, whose professed object was to preserve him from evil counsel and wicked favourites. Here, when he wept, he was bluntly told, "Better bairns greet than bearded men." He never forgave the affront, and as soon as he got the power in his hands the ruin of the Ruthvens was decreed. Lingering at Dundee to plot, Gowrie was captured and beheaded, and this event, in the time of the second and last earl, led to the still more mysterious and tragic episode of the "Gowrie Conspiracy," which gave the Stuarts the desired opportunity to "root out the whole name and race." Every reader of Scottish history remembers the strange story—how, in the autumn of 1600, the King was summoned by the Master of Ruthven, at early morning, while buckhunting at Falkland, to ride to Perth to see a "pot of gold" discovered there; how, by his own tale, he found in the turret chamber to which he was led, not a treasure but an armed man, and a portrait on the wall, covered by a curtain, which, being drawn aside, revealed the features of the slain earl; how James shrieked for help, and his attendants, bursting in from the courtyard, found him struggling in the hands of Gowrie and his brother, both of whom were instantly despatched. But the scene of this was not Ruthven Castle, but old Gowrie House, the town residence of the doomed family, which stood on the site of the present County Buildings of Perth, close by the Tay; and the episode belongs to the annals of the "good city of Sanct Johnstoun."

Thanks to the civil and religious broils of former days, and to the spirit of modern improvement, nearly all the antiquities of Perth—the relics of days when it was the seat of the Court, the centre of trade and religious life, and the great "objective" of warlike operations and political intrigues have disappeared from the face of the earth. Of its Castle, which stood near the north end of what is now the Skinnergate, not a trace now remains; of its ancient walls, besieged and breached so often in the wars between Scots and English, scarcely a vestige. Four monasteries, and numerous other religious houses, once existed here; and according to information that reached Erasmus, their inmates led a specially delicate and lazy life. All disappeared—monks and monasteries together—at the Reformation, and the "rascall multitude," who had perhaps seen too much of their cowled and cloistered neighbours to cherish a deep respect for them, showed little scruple in spoiling "the monuments of idolatry," and in making free with the meat and drink with which buttery and cellar were found well stored, and bore in triumph through the streets the great dinner-pot of the Blackfriars, thus spreading abroad the last savour of the mediaeval religious life of Perth. Blackfriars Wynd and Street indicate the position of this Dominican convent, and King James VI.'s Hospital serves to mark the site of the only Carthusian foundation that existed in Scotland. In the former, James I. was done to death, and in the latter, richly endowed by him, the murdered poet-king was buried. The dark tale—the portents and warnings vouchsafed to the victim, the midnight clash of arms and flare of torches in the Monastery gardens, while James was gaily chatting with the Queen and her ladies before retiring to rest; the heroism of Catherine Douglas, who thrust her arm through the staple of the door as a bar against the traitors; the temporary escape of the king into the vault below the floor; his discovery, the savage struggle before he was despatched, and the terrible revenge that was wreaked by the widowed Joanna—is as familiar as the Gowrie tragedy itself.

The Church of St. John is still a venerable and venerated object in Perth; although it also has suffered from the hard usage of time and the Reformers, and its roof now covers, in place of the numerous shrines and chapels of Roman Catholic days, three Presbyterian places of worship. It was in St. John's that Knox preached his iconoclastic sermon; and many other conspicuous events in the civil and religious history of Scotland—and more particularly during the long struggle between Protestantism and Papacy, and between Episcopacy and the Covenant—were transacted within a stone-throw of its time-worn walls. Fourteen Scottish Parliaments, and a still larger number of Councils of Churchmen, are reckoned to have met in Perth previous to the Reformation. Here schism and martyrdom had begun a century and a half before Knox. Girdings and gibings at priestly ways crept even into the "Miracle Plays" annually performed on Corpus Christi Day; and the town and country around were "more infested with heresy than any other part of the nation." Cardinal Beaton watched from the Spey Tower while example was made of heretics by hanging and drowning them "for the encouragement of others:" to such good effect that in a few years the monasteries were in ashes, and the Lords of the Congregation, assembled at Perth, had proclaimed their resolution to spend goods and lives in the cause of the "true worship of God, the public welfare of the nation, and the common liberty," in token whereof the burghers set out on their southward march with ropes—"St. Johnston's ribands"—about their necks. Mary Queen of Scots and her son had small reason to remember with pleasure their visits to Perth; and after the Gowrie incident King James did all in his power to humiliate the town. It was here that the Assemblies of the Kirk and Parliaments, or Conventions of Estates, alternately proclaimed and disowned the authority of the bishops; the town was the centre of fighting in the long battle between Prelacy and Presbytery. Perth loyally entertained Charles I., and thirteen brethren of the Craft of Glovers—fateful number!—danced the sword-dance before him; and soon after, these selfsame swords were girded to oppose the King at Duns. Montrose captured and pillaged the town, after defeating the Covenanting troops outside at Tibbermore; the young Charles II. lodged in the Gowrie House, and after vainly attempting to run away from the ministers and their long prayers and exhortations, signed the Solemn League and Covenant, and professed, as King of Scots, penitence for the sins and follies of himself and his House. Then came Cromwell and his Ironsides, and built a citadel on the South Inch and a pier on the Tay with the stones of the ruined convents; and Claverhouse, Mar, and Prince Charlie have helped since then to "make history" at Perth and in its neighbourhood.

For nearly a century and a half the annals have been comparatively peaceful and prosaic; even inundation and plague do not trouble the townsmen as of yore. The Tay no longer makes trysts with its tributaries to meet "at the bonny cross of St. Johnstoun." Except in rare times of spate, it sweeps

ON THE FIRTH OF TAY.

THE NEW TAY VIADUCT, FROM THE SOUTH.

smoothly and sedately under the arches of the bridge, and past the green "Inches," with their spreading trees and spacious walks—the fields of pastime and of strife since long before the memorable battle of the North Inch, when the blade of Hal o' the Wynd, fighting "for his own hand," turned the scale in favour of the champions of Clan Chattan—to meet tide-water and commerce below the town. It is the benefactor and the crowning ornament of Perth, which has considerably grown and beautified itself of recent years, not the least of its sources of wealth being the amenities and romantic associations of the ancient city, and the glorious scenery of the Tay, of which it may be described as at once the gateway and the centre.

Within short walking distance of Perth are the Hills of Kinnoull and Moncrieffe. Tay, after leaving the town, turns sharply to the left between these two grand wooded heights—each of them rising over 700 feet above the river—and pursues its way, widening as it goes, between the rich low expanse of the Carse of Gowrie and the opposing shores of Fife. It were hard to decide which of these sentinel hills commands the more magnificent prospect. Each view might challenge comparison with any scene outside of the basin of the Tay for extent and for the mingling of all the elements of beauty in Highland and Lowland scenery. Yet, close as they stand to each other and to Perth, distinctly different panoramas, in foreground and in perspective, are unfolded from the summits of the two heights. They offer companion pictures, and not merely landscapes in duplicate, of the Tay from its sources in the distant blue ranges of the Grampians to the sea.

The top of Moncrieffe—or Moredun—beside the foundations of the old Pict fort or *dun*, is the right station whence to survey Strathearn—a valley that rivals that of the Tay itself in the place it holds in the national history and in the affections of the lovers of scenic beauty. Directly below the steep pine-covered crest of Moredun runs the winding Earn, separating the park and woods of Moncrieffe from the pleasant watering-place of Bridge of Earn. Near the confluence with the Tay is Abernethy, its "Round Tower" coeval, perhaps, with the introduction of Christianity to this part of the Tay, and its Castle Law on which, says tradition, Nechtan and other Pictish kings held their state during the two centuries and a half when this decayed little burgh was the capital of the land. Beyond, in the same direction, are the waters of the Firth; Mugdrum Island, long and low; Newburgh, and Norman Law, the Norsemen's look-out, rising on one side above old Ballenbriech Castle and the Fife shores, and on the other commanding the "Howe o' Fife" and the Loch of Lindores. Beside the venerable ruins of Lindores Abbey, close to Newburgh and the Firth, are buried the murdered "heir of Scotland," David, Duke of Rothesay, and James of Douglas—the "grey monk of Lindores"—the last of the ambitious race of the Black Douglases. In the same vicinity, in a glen or pass of the Ochils, stood another grim memorial of feudal or pre-feudal times, "Cross Macduff," now represented only by its pedestal, where the taker of life, if he could "count kin," within nine degrees, with the Thane of Fife, the head of Clan Macduff, could find refuge, and proffer the "blood-penny" in atonement.

Over against Moredun are the crests of the Lomonds and the green, smooth, wavy lines of the Ochils; and through Glenfarg to its foot comes the new main line of railway to the North by the Forth Bridge. Right opposite, behind Pitkeathly Wells, Kilgraston, the old kirk and "rocking stone" of Dron, and the ruins of Balmanno Castle, are the "Wicks of Baiglie," whence Scott asserted that the Romans and he could descry the site of Perth. But the eye is carried irresistibly westward along the skirts of the hills and the broad and teeming valley below, towards the Highland mountains that surround the sources of the Earn. Near at hand are Forteviot and its Holyhill—a Scoto-Pictish capital before Perth; Dunning and other villages and hamlets lying along the hill-foots, proud to this day of the memories of the martyrs for "Crown and Covenant," their sufferings at the hands of Montrose and Mar, and the former prosperity of their weaving crafts; and standing on rich flats by the waterside, or in picturesque glens running up into the Ochils, many a mansion and castle of the fighting and grasping Jacobite lairds of Strathearn, ill neighbours of yore to the Whiggish villagers. Over against the "Birks o' Invermay" lies Dupplin Castle (now the seat of Lord Kinnoull), with its loch, its grand woods, and the site of its battle-field, so disastrous to the Scots; and opposite Lord Rollo's park of Duncrub is Gask, still a home of the Oliphants, though the "Auld House" has disappeared. Further west, the Ruthven water comes down through Gleneagles and the lovely wooded "Den" of Kincardine, past the old castle and the single long street of Auchterarder, famous in ecclesiastical history. The Machany flows by Culdees and Strathallan Castles, and not far from Tullibardine, cradle of the noble House of Athole, and burying-place of the great race of Montrose. At Innerpeffray, where the old line of Roman roads and stations crossed the Earn, comes in the Pow, flowing by the ruins of Inchaffray Abbey and the woods of Balgowan and Abercairney; and further on, around Crieff, and thence upwards by Comrie and St. Fillan's, to Loch Earn, lies one of the most glorious districts, not alone of Earnside, but of Scotland. Drummond and Monzie Castles, Ochtertyre and Dunira, Lawers and Aberuchil, are among its grandly wooded demesnes; Glenturret, Glen Lednoch, and Glen Artney contribute each their charms of crag and waterfall, bosky dell and lone hillside, and there are innumerable remains of former days in the form of standing or ruined chapel and castle, and the sites of ancient feud and battle. Little of all this can, of course, be descried from the top of Moncrieffe Hill; but Ben Chonzie, and the Braes of Doune, and the Forest of Glen Artney, and behind them the shapely head of Ben Voirlich and other mountains that mirror themselves in Loch Earn or guard Glen Ogle and Lochearnhead, are full in view.

The abrupt front of Kinnoull Hill, on the other hand, commands more directly the lower course of the Tay and its estuary, widening out between the level expanse of the Carse of Gowrie, thickly sprinkled with farms and mansions, and the opposing shores of Fife, onward to where it is closed by the smoke of Dundee and the line of the Tay Bridge. From the pathway below the tower crowning the hill, one looks down—one almost fancies he might leap down—upon the woods and sward surrounding Kinfauns Castle, the residence of the family of Gray. Visible, too, from Kinnoull, or sheltering under the folds of the "Braes o' the Carse," which rise from the flat champaign to the heights of the Sidlaws, are innumerable sites and scenes, equally rich in beauty and in memories of days when Gowrie was busier making history than in raising grain. Among them are St. Madoes' Church and its sculptured Runic stones; Errol and Megginch, ancient heritages of the Hays; Kilspindie, where Wallace spent his schooldays, when he "in Gowrie dwelt, and had gude living there," and the seat, later, of Archibald of Douglas—"Auld Graysteel;" Fingask, the home of the stout old Jacobite family of Murray Threipland and of the "Lass o' Gowrie" of Scottish song; Kinnaird and Rossie Priory, the earlier and later possessions of the noble House of Kinnaird, champions in these parts, for generations, of the cause of Reform.

From Rossie Hill, or from the battlements of the fine old baronial tower of Castle Huntly, a nearer view can be had of the beautiful cultivated Carse and its surroundings of firth and hills; or from near the remains of the ancient Church of Invergowrie and the boundary line of the shires of Perth and Stirling you can look across the widest part of the great tidal stream—three miles of shining water or sandbank—to another famous old ivy-clad ruin, Balmerino Abbey, on the opposite and bolder shore of Fife. But as Kinnoull commands the grandest view of the upper part of the Firth of Tay, so Balgay Hill and Dundee Law are the stations to take up for a survey of its lower reaches and its meeting with the North Sea. Round the bases of these eminences the northern coast of the estuary curves outward, leaving a comparatively narrow platform on which, for a space of three miles or more, are grouped the forest of chimneys, spires,

DUNDEE, FROM BROUGHTY FERRY.

and masts of the city and harbour of Dundee. The passage between the sea front of esplanade and docks, and Newport and the line of handsome villas surmounting the rocky bank on the other side, is reduced to less than two miles; and still bending and narrowing, as the Fife shore, in turn, approaches, as if to meet Angus and seal the mouth of the Tay, the waters of the Firth measure only a mile across from Broughty Castle to Ferryport-on-Craig, where, skirted on either hand by broad stretches of sand and "links," they finally open, trumpet-shaped, to meet the German Ocean. Directly under the Law, from Magdalen Point to St. Fort, where begin the narrows and the busier part of Dundee, the line of arches of the

DUNDEE.

new Tay Bridge spans the Firth. The width from bank to bank is 3,440 yards—a little under two miles—including the curve which the long double file of piers makes in approaching the Dundee side. Slight as the structure looks, when first seen from the Law or the river, and compared with the wide expanse of water over which it is carried, it conveys, on more attentive view, an impression of security as well as gracefulness; it is not only a triumph of engineering skill, but a beautiful object in a striking and noble picture.

Far other are the impressions produced by the appearance, above the water level, and running for part of the way alongside its successor, of the foundations of the first Tay Bridge. This ill-fated undertaking had only been eighteen months open for traffic, when, on a wild night at the close of 1879, the whole of the central portion collapsed and fell into the raging Firth, carrying along with it a train, with its freight of seventy or eighty passengers, which was crossing at the time. Not a soul survived to tell the circumstances of the catastrophe—the most dramatic and one of the most disastrous in the annals of railway accidents in this country. But subsequent inquiry left no doubt that, in the original scheme of the structure, sufficient allowance had not been made for the tremendous pressure put upon it by the currents of air scouring through this funnel of the Firth; and that much of the work, both in the brick foundations and steel superstructure, had been "scamped" and left without proper inspection, so that the first occasion of maximum strain—a passing train, while a tempest was at its height—brought the inevitable result.

Dundonians love to survey their city and its surroundings from the "Law." The spectacle is one they may well be proud of. Marvellous has been the change here since Dundee consisted of only four straggling streets, meeting at the central "place" of the "Market Gait," and a congeries of narrow lanes running from these down to the harbour, consisting, as the local historian tells us, of rude jetties added to the natural haven opening between the headlands of the Chapel Craig and the Castle Rock. Even then, however—four centuries ago and more—it had an interesting history; even then the energy of its burgesses and its favourable position at the mouth of the Tay enabled it to carry on a brisk trade with the ports of Holland and the Baltic. Already its Castle, near the head of the Seagate, had suffered sieges; its Constables, the Scryngeours, were the standard-bearers of Scotland in the national war, and the town disputed with Perth which was the more ancient and honourable. Its situation at the foot and on the slope of the fine acclivity facing the sun and the Tay, got for it from its Lowland and Highland neighbours its name of "Bonny Dundee" and the "pleasant town." It has vastly increased its trade and importance since; but it has also increased its amenities; and even the casual eye overlooking it can see, by the handsome spires and towers rising beside the forest of masts and factory stalks that stretch along the shore, and by the open spaces—Albert Square, and the Baxter and Balgay Parks—that the town is mindful of art and air and beauty, as well as of business. The castles—the early building on the Castle Hill, and the later fortalice of the Constables at Dudhope—have disappeared to the foundations. But the fine old square tower of St. Mary's, in the Nethergate, is still a handsome and conspicuous landmark of Dundee, spite of all the competition of its modern buildings. Although it can hardly be part of the original structure erected by David, Earl of Huntingdon—the hero of the "Talisman"—in gratitude for his escape from manifold perils while serving under Richard Cœur-de-Lion in Palestine, it is a venerable and stately object, and the Dundonians have had this their chief antiquity carefully restored.

That Dundee has not more remnants left of its early consequence is due to the march of modern improvement, and to the hard knocks it suffered in times of civil war and invasion. After Pinkie, the English troops seized upon the Castle of Broughty Craig—which, like the Tower of St. Mary's, has been restored, and now guards the entrance to the Firth, with the pleasant backing of marine villa residences and stretches of links and sands much frequented by the good folks of the burgh—and Broughty besieged Dundee, and Dundee Broughty, for two or three years before the intruders were expelled. A hundred years later Montrose and his Irish and Highland kernes swooped suddenly down upon it from the upper valley of the Tay, and plundered and sacked the Covenanting place, the leader looking on from the "Corbie Hill," while the followers burned, slew, and wasted in the streets below. The townsmen magnanimously forgot this when, a few years later, the "Great Marquis" was brought into it, a captive in the hands of his enemies; and "though Dundee," says Wishart, "had suffered more by his army than any other within the kingdom, yet were they so far from insulting him, that the whole town testified very great sorrow for his woful condition." Next year—1651—Dundee had again to endure sack and capture, at the hands of General Monk, when the garrison was put to the sword, the town burned, and, as Carlyle says, "there was once more a grim scene of flames, blood, and rage and despair transacted upon this earth." Claverhouse is close by the town, and John Graham—that other "evil genius of the Covenant"—was Constable of Dudhope, and took his title from "Bonny Dundee."

The "bloody Mackenzie" was another of its sons or neighbours; Camperdown House, the home of the valiant Admiral Duncan, is behind Balgay and the busy suburb of Lochee. But, if it has reared many "men of blood," Dundee has been still more prolific in historians and poets, reformers and inventors, of whom Boece and Wedderburn, Halyburton and Carmichael, are representative names. Yet longer is the list of its merchant princes, and its munificent patrons of art and benefactors of the town, of whom the Baxter family are types. They have made of Dundee a great and busy centre of maritime commerce, and placed it first among the trading places of the kingdom in the importation and manufacture of jute; and they have not forgotten generous aid in endowing the town with public parks, museums, libraries, educational institutions, and other resources of civilisation, such as few seats of industry of its size can boast.

Dundee has spread over the green slopes and orchard grounds below the Law; but it has only increased the circumference of its fine environment of land and sea. Westward, the view extends over the fertile Carse, and range on range of the Grampians, amid which may be descried Ben Lomond and Schiehallion, and many a Highland peak besides. Behind the Law, the eye rises from the rich valley of the Dichty, flowing by Strathmartine and Claverhouse towards the sea at Monifieth Sands, to the Hill of Auchterhouse, Craig Owl, and other extensions of the Sidlaws, with glimpses of the heads of the loftier hills of Strathmore peeping over their shoulders; and, ridge behind ridge, these uplands subside as they stretch eastward, past many a storied and beautiful scene, towards Arbroath and the sea. Southward, beyond the Firth and the bridge, the rocky northern shores and hilly backbone of Fife are spread out like a map; and behind Newport and Tayport and the waste expanse of Tents Moor shimmer the waters of St. Andrew's Bay and the Eden Estuary, and rise the grey, weather-beaten towers of St. Rule's Cathedral and of Cardinal Beaton's Castle, beside the green links and white sand of St. Andrews.

John Geddie.

BROUGHTY FERRY CASTLE.

BEN AND LOCH LOMOND.

THE FORTH.

Comparative Poetry, Romance, and History—Loch Ard and Flora MacIvor—The "Clachan of Aberfoyle"—Lake of Menteith—The Trossachs and Loch Katrine—Ellen and Helen—Loch Achray—Ben Ledi—The View from Stirling Castle—Stirling Town—Bannockburn—The Ochils and the Devon Valley—Alloa—Clackmannan—Kincardine-on-Forth—Tulliallan Castle—Culross: Abbey and Burgh—The "Standard Stone"—Torryburn—Rosyth Castle—"St. Margaret's Hope"—Dunfermline: Tower, Palace, and Abbey—The New Forth Bridge—Inch Garvie and its Castle—Inverkeithing Bay—Donibristle House—Aberdour—Inchcolm, Cramond, Inchkeith, and May Islands—The Bass Rock—Kirkcaldy Bay—Edinburgh—Leith—Seton—Aberlady—Round to North Berwick—Tantallon Castle.

OTHER Scottish streams may dispute with the Forth the prize of beauty, and excel it in length of course and in wealth of commerce. There is none that can contend with it for the palm of historic interest. Nature herself has marked out its valley as the scene of the strife and of the reconciliation of races and creeds. Half the important events in Scottish annals have taken place on or near the banks of the river, and of the Firth—around Doune, and Stirling, and Edinburgh, and Dunfermline; under the shadow of the Campsie and the Ochil Hills; along the margins of the Teith and Allan, Devon and Esk; by the folds of the Forth, or by the shores of Fife and the Lothians. Its course forms no inapt emblem and epitome of the fortunes of Scotland and of the Scottish nation. Drawn from the strength of the hills, and cradled amid scenes of wild and solitary beauty, its deep, dark, winding waters flow through the "Debatable Land" of Roman and Caledonian, of Pict and

Scot, of Saxon and Gael. The fords and bridges which Highlander and Lowlander, Whig and Jacobite, have crossed so often on raid or for reprisal, have become bonds of union. The fertile carse-lands wave with the richer harvests for the blood shed in the battles of national independence, and in many a feud now ended and forgotten. The Forth, that "bridled the wild Highlandman," has become the symbol of peace and the highway of intercourse between South and North.

Poetry and Romance, as well as History, have made the Forth their favourite haunt. The genius of Scottish Romance, or of Scottish History, could nowhere find a prouder seat than Ben Lomond. At its feet are the waters of Loch Lomond, losing themselves to the north among the enclosing folds of the hills, and broadening out southwards to embrace their beautiful islands; while beyond, like a map, lie the mountains of the West, from Skye to Kintyre, touched here and there with gleams of loch and sea, and with blurs of smoke from factory stalk or steamer. From the other flank of the mountain issues the infant Forth. Ben Lomond presides over all its devious wanderings, from the source to the sea. It looks directly down upon "Rob Roy's country;" and close at hand, and within the basin of the Forth, are Loch Katrine and the Trossachs. The towers of Stirling, and even the "reek" of Edinburgh, may be descried on a clear day. Following the broad valley of the Forth, the eye can take in the sites to which cling most closely the heroic or pathetic memories of "the days of other years;" and over the whole glorious landscape Walter Scott has thrown the glamour of his genius.

Romance works with a charm more powerful than that of History itself in attracting visitors to the head-waters of the Forth and Teith, and in enhancing the marvellous natural beauties of their lake and mountain scenery. True, few except stout pedestrians and ardent anglers follow up the Duchray Water, past ivied Duchray Castle, to the corries that seam the base of Ben Lomond. But the path from Inversnaid, that skirts Loch Chon and the more famous and more beautiful northern head-stream of the Forth that issues from it, is not so unfrequented. Farther down, Loch Ard opens again, and yet again, a lovely mirror in which are reflected the changeful outlines and rich colours of its girdling hills and woods. Oak coppice, interspersed with the shining trunks of the birch and the dark green of the pines, climbs over every knoll, and clings to every crag, and even covers the little island on the lake, where Duke Robert of Albany hoped to find a refuge from his enemies. Above copse-wood and lake rise the brown slopes and grey precipices of Ben Vogrich and of Craigmore; while the conical head and broad flanks of Ben Lomond shoulder themselves into view, and close the top of the glen.

But the enchantment of Loch Ard would not be complete did not the form of Flora McIvor yet haunt the Linn of Ledeart, in the guise of the Highland Muse, as when first she startled and threw a spell over Edward Waverley; and did not her voice — wild and plaintive as the legends of the land and the genius of its race — mingle, as of yore, with the murmur of the stream. The pass by the lake-side still seems to have the commanding figure of Helen MacGregor presiding over it, and eyeing menacingly Saxon intrusion into this refuge of a proscribed clan. The "Clachan of Aberfoyle," now unexceptionable as a place of travellers' entertainment, can never be disassociated from the memorable experiences of a night's quarters at "Jeannie MacAlpine's." At the "Fords of Frew," we think, more than of anything else, of Rob Roy slipping the belt-buckle in midstream,

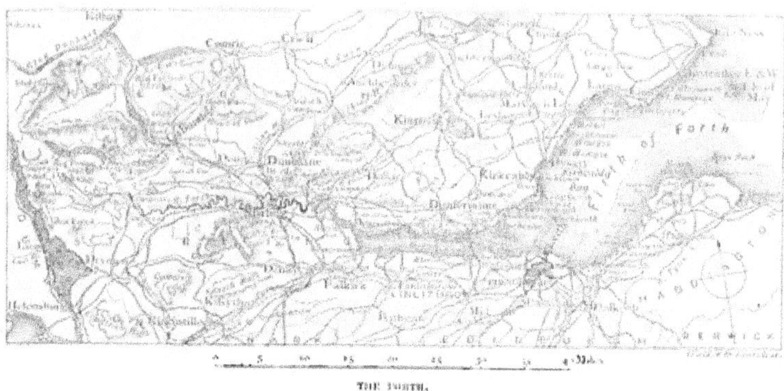

THE FORTH.

and of the moving and mysterious night interview on the neighbouring moor between Francis Osbaldistone and Di Vernon.

The "Clachan" is now all spick and span; but its surroundings are the same. The brawling waters tumble in white foam from Loch Ard, and, mixing with the Duchray, pour their deep sombre current—the Avondhu, or "Black River"—on past Gartmore to wind in labyrinthine folds through the level mosslands towards Stirling. And the natives of the Upper Forth, while they have forgotten the real history of their district, will show you, chained to the tree in front of the inn windows, the veritable "coulter" with which Bailie Nicol Jarvie did such credit to his Highland blood, and the selfsame oak-stump from which he hung suspended over the lake; nor have they wholly lost faith in the Fairy People—the *Daoine Shi*, or "Men of Peace"—with whom these hills and valleys have from time immemorial been favoured haunts.

From Aberfoyle, the direct road to Stirling, leaving the Forth, winds round the margin of the Lake of Menteith, overlooked by the outposts of the Grampians, and overlooking the rich beauty of a plain which rises on its southern side behind Bucklyvie and Kippen, to the lower heights and smoother outlines of the Campsie and Fintry Hills. Here, in the heart of Menteith, we are in the country of "the Graemes," and many legends of the great House of Montrose linger about this, as about other spots in the basin of the Forth. But the Lake of Menteith has still earlier and prouder memories. The Comyns and the Stewarts—the old lords of

Menteith—wielded almost regal power from their island-castle of Talla; and within bowshot is the larger isle of Inchmahone, where part of the ancient Priory still stands in the shadow of its planes and orchard trees. Mary Stuart spent part of

"ELLEN'S ISLE."

her childhood in the "Isle of Rest"—perhaps the quietest and sweetest period of her troubled life—when it was thought wise, after the battle of Pinkie, to remove the young Queen of Scots to a place of safety.

The Trossachs and Loch Katrine can be reached in a couple of hours, on foot, from Aberfoyle. More even than the Upper Forth and the banks of Lochs Ard and Menteith, these scenes at the head-waters of the Teith, immortalised in "The Lady of the Lake," are the abodes of the spirit of Highland romance and the shrines of tourist pilgrimage. Once this "fastness of the North" was the impregnable retreat of the proscribed clan of the MacGregors, whence they issued to harry the shores of Loch Lomond with fire and sword, and levy black-mail and empty byres in the Lennox. A century and a half ago it was still thought unsafe for peaceably disposed folk to approach the district, and in the memory of men still alive it had hardly acquired more than local fame for its beauty.

Walter Scott and his metrical and prose romances have changed all that. A stream of tourists flows steadily through the passes all the summer and autumn, and more fitfully at other seasons; and steamers, stage-coaches, and hotels have strangely altered the aspect of this "Scottish Lake Country." But the "everlasting hills" look down on it unchanged. The crest of Ben Lomond still dominates the western end of Loch Katrine, girt in by hill-sides, or opening into glens as stern and almost as solitary as when they echoed back the slogan of

THE TROSSACHS AND BEN VENUE.

Roderick Dhu. Round the lower extremity of the lake the mountains take closer rank and more varied forms; and the broken and impending precipices, the winding and opening waters, the wooded shores and islands, fringed with grey rock or "silver strand," seem, as when Fitz-James first set his foot here, an "enchanted land" over which Ben Venue and Ben An stand sentinels:—

> "High on the south huge Ben Venue
> Down on the lake in masses threw
> Crags, knolls, and mounds confusedly hurled,
> The fragments of an earlier world;
> A wildering forest feathered o'er
> His ruined sides and summit hoar;
> While on the north through middle air
> Ben An lifts up his forehead bare."

On the cloven side of Ben Venue is the "Coir-nan-Uriskin"—the Goblin's Cave or Hollow—deserted of its unearthly denizens since it has become an object of interest to the tourist. "Ellen's Isle," clad with wood to the water's edge, seems to shelter in the shadow of the northern shore. Cromwell's men, clambering up the pass, found that the women and children of the clan had sought refuge here; and one bold soldier swam out to the island to bring away a boat. Hardly had he touched ground when a woman—Helen Stuart—drew a dagger from below her apron and slew him. A minstrel's music has slightly changed the name and wholly changed the associations, and the spot is dedicated to another Ellen and to the gentler fancies, not the rude facts, of the days of old.

From the "Silver Strand" opposite Ellen's Isle you wind for a couple of miles through the "bristled territory" of the Trossachs before you reach Loch Achray, and "the copse-wood grey that waves and weeps" above the second of the chain of lakes. Ben An and Ben Venue hold the place of sentries to left and to right, and seem to have tumbled down into the narrow pass huge fragments from their splintered sides, to block the way against intruders into this old sanctuary of the Gael. In vain; their very efforts have but added to the wild impressiveness of the scene, and to the crowds that come to wonder and admire. It would be "to gild refinèd gold" to describe the beauties of the Trossachs—the scene where Nature seems to have tried to produce, within the narrowest compass, the most bewildering effects by mingling her materials of rock and foliage and falling waters. Their praises have been sung in words that linger in every memory.

Toilsome indeed must the path have been to trace when the wandering James V. came hither in pursuit of game. But a fine road now threads the depths of the ravine, and skirting Loch Achray, and passing the Trossachs Hotel and Church, brings us to Brig of Turk and the opening of "lone Glenfinlas," the haunt of Highland deer and of Highland legend. Every green nook and cranny, every glimpse of copse-wood and tumbling water, moss-grown hut and lichened rock, is a temptation to linger by the way. But Duncraggan must be passed; then Lanrick Mead, at the west end of Loch Vennachar, the meeting-place of the Clan Alpine, summoned by the "Fiery Cross;" and by-and-bye the sounding torrent of Carchonzie, where the Vennachar "breaks in silver" from its lake, and near it Coilantogle Ford, the scene of the deadly strife between James Fitz-James and Roderick Dhu. By this time the form of Ben Ledi—the "Hill of God," the high altar of the old Druidical worship—has lifted itself up mightily upon the left, and, furthest outpost in this direction of the higher Grampians, keeps watch over the "mouldering lines" of the Roman encampment on Bochastle, the Pass of Leny, and the modern village of Callander. It looks across to Ben Voirlich and the heathy solitudes of Uam-Var, where the "noble stag" was first started upon the eventful Chase, and abroad on a prospect which may compare, for richness, variety, and extent, with that from Ben Lomond.

Not less magnificent in its own way, and far more accessible, is the view from the bridge of Callander, where the most impressive features of the scene are Ben Ledi itself, the high crag that forms the background of the village, and the deeply wooded flanks of the pass, down which foam the waters of the Leny, coming from the "Braes of Balquhidder" and Loch Lubnaig, to hold romantic tryst here with the stream from Loch Vennachar, and between them to form the Teith. But we must downward with the Teith towards Stirling, only glancing at a few of the scenes on its banks—at the wooded glen of the Keltie, embosoming the far-famed Falls of Bracklinn; at Cambusmore, where Scott began his "Lady of the Lake;" and above all at the "bannered towers of Doune," its huge feudal walls rising above the Teith—walls saturated from dungeon to turret with memories of grim or pathetic events in the histories of the Stewarts of Menteith and Moray, and in the lives of Mary Stuart of Montrose, and of Charles Edward. Murdoch, Duke of Albany, is thought to have built Doune, and may have planted its "Dool Tree." When Murdoch was executed, along with his sons and adherents, on the "Heading Hill" at Stirling, it was on a spot where his eyes might fall upon the strong new castle upon which he had built his hopes of safety.

At Stirling Castle it will be convenient to take our next stand, and see "the mazy Forth unravelled." No baronial castle on the Rhine or Danube is more romantically and commandingly placed than these "towers of Snowdoun," or surveys a fairer scene. One can imagine the time—but yesterday in the geologist's record—when the broad valley of the river was filled with the sea, back to the roots of the Grampians, and when Stirling Rock, with its neighbour bluffs, the Abbey Craig and Craigforth, rose as islands or peninsulas over the waters, each with its slope towards the east and its front to the west. The sea has long receded, and Stirling now dominates the green and level floor of its fertile carse. Through the middle of the landscape meanders the Forth, in immense loops and folds—"a foiled circuitous wanderer"—

"Forgetting the bright speed he had
In his high mountain cradle,"

and using, as it would seem, every circumvolution and chance of tarrying or turning back, to avoid meeting with the Teith, the Allan, and the Bannock, at the base of Stirling Rock. From where the stream debouches from the hills into Flanders Moss, to where it meets the tide-water at Stirling Bridge, there is said to be a fall of only eighteen feet in some eighteen miles, measured "as the crow flies"—a distance increased fourfold by following the intricate gyres of the dark still waters. Below the Bridge, to which vessels are able to come up from the sea, the river still continues to double and turn as far as Alloa, in those "links o' Forth," each of which, according to the old rhyme, is "worth an Earldom in the North."

Flat and tame as are the immediate banks of the river, draining through ancient mosses, now turned for the most part into rich corn-bearing land, goodly sites are close at hand in the plain, on the slopes of the enclosing hills, or in the tributary valleys—among them Cardross, and Blair-Drummond, and Keir, all famous in the annals of Scottish law, agriculture, and literature; and Airth and Airthrey Castles, which carry the mind from the doughty deeds of Sir John the Graeme to those of Sir Ralph Abercromby. Of what lies within the valley of the Teith we have seen something. But the banks of Allan Water, behind the favourite Spa of Bridge of Allan and its embosoming woods and hills, are almost as well worth exploring; for they lead, to mention but a few of their attractions, to Dunblane and its beautiful old Cathedral, to Sheriffmuir, and to the Roman Camp at Ardoch.

The tide of Scottish history long flowed towards and around Stirling Castle. The time when it was not a place of strength and of strife is lost in the mists of antiquity. Early, too, it became the seat of kings; and the Castle, and the little burgh upon the slope behind, have witnessed many a stirring sight. Scottish Parliaments were held here, or in the Abbey of Cambuskenneth, whose ruined tower rises, on a "link of Forth," opposite what is now the railway station. Sovereigns were born and baptised, were wedded and buried, held joyous jousts, and committed foul deeds of blood and shame, on Stirling Rock or under its shadow.

The buildings on the highest platform of the Rock—still a fortified and garrisoned place—surround the "Upper Square." What is the Armoury was the Chapel, erected on the site of an older Chapel Royal, by the "Scottish Solomon," to celebrate, with pomp till then unheard of, the baptism of Prince Henry.

OLD BRIDGE OF FORTH, STIRLING.

Opposite is the Palace of James V., its front still embossed with the remains of rich carvings and uncouth sculpture. The Parliament House, built by James III. (now put to barrack purposes), and the building within which James II. stained his name and

STIRLING, FROM ABBEY CRAIG.

race with blood, by stabbing to the heart the Earl of Douglas, complete a group of buildings upon which have been indelibly impressed the character and the fate of the Sovereigns of the House of Stuart. The visitor to Stirling Castle can view Highlands and Lowlands from "Queen Mary's Look-out;" and then, for change of sympathy and impression, inspect the pulpit and communion-table of John Knox; or, if his faith be great, the dungeon where Roderick Dhu drew his latest breath. The windy hollow between the Castle and the "Gowling Hills," he is told, is Ballangeich, of which that hero of ballad adventure, James V., was "Gudeman." The most distant of these braes was the "Mote" or "Heading Hill," the old place of execution, where many a noble and guilty head has fallen—the Albany faction and the murderers of James I. among the number. Below the Castle, on the other side, are the King's Garden and King's Park, the scenes of the sports and diversions in the olden time, where James II. held tournaments, and James IV. delighted in his "Table Round."

Nor are the history and aspect of the town of Stirling unworthy of its noble station. It, also, is crammed with memories and antiquities—from the square tower of the West Church, grouping so well with the buildings on the Castle, and surmounting the hall where Knox preached and the infant James VI. was crowned, down to the burial-place of the murdered James III., under the tower of Cambuskenneth and close by the winding Forth.

But the historical fame and interest of Stirling rest perhaps more upon the bloody and decisive battles fought in its neighbourhood, than upon anything else. From the Castle ramparts one can look down upon Stirling Bridge, Bannockburn, and Sauchie; and Falkirk, Kilsyth, Sheriffmuir, and other stricken fields, reaching from the '45 back to Pictish and Roman times, are not far off. In memory of the Struggle for Independence, but especially of William Wallace, the presentment of a feudal tower, surmounted by a mural crown, rises to a height of over 200 feet on the summit of the Abbey Craig, the most commanding site, next to Stirling Rock itself, in the valley. The Bridges—the old and the new—lie midway between these two bold bluffs. But the former venerable edifice, though it could also tell its strange stories of civil broil, and, among others, of how an Archbishop was hung on its parapet three centuries ago, is by no means the structure where the "Protector of Scotland," watching the passage of the Forth (probably from the slopes of the Abbey Craig), taught so terrible a lesson to Cressingham and the English invaders. This, by all accounts, was a wooden structure placed half a mile above the moss-grown buttresses of the present Old Bridge of Stirling.

The fame of the battle fought at Stirling Bridge in 1297, and of the other fight, so disastrous to the Scottish cause, that took place a year later at Falkirk, has been quite obscured by the Bruce's great victory at Bannockburn. One never thinks of Stirling without remembering that near by is the field where was decided, for three centuries, and indeed for all time, the history and fortunes of Scotland. The banks of the Bannock are now peaceful enough, and the people of the village of that name, and of the neighbouring hamlet of St. Ninians, lying still nearer Stirling and the battle-ground, are occupied with nothing more warlike than the weaving of tartans. The slough in which the English chivalry sank, and were overpowered, is now drained and cultivated land. But a fragment of the "Boro Stone," where Bruce set up his standard, is still preserved; and the "Gillies' Hill," behind, commemorates the opportune appearance of the camp-followers of the Scottish army, when they hoisted their blankets on their tent-poles,

"And like a bannered host afar
Bore down on England's wearied war,"

putting a finish to the rout of Edward II.'s troops.

Leaving Stirling and Bannockburn and all their memories behind us, we can now embark upon the Forth, and follow its broadening stream towards the open sea. The fat carselands are still on either hand, rimmed in on one side by the furrowed flanks of Dumyatt and the Ochils, and bounded on the other by the Campsie Fells, crowned, far off, by Earl's Seat; while beyond, on a clear day such as we have bespoken for our readers, the Bens grouped around the sources of the Forth and Teith lift themselves into view, fronted effectively by the towers of Stirling and the Abbey Craig. As we face now east, now west, now north, now south, on our devious way, these objects shift place bewilderingly, and more and more the "foot-hills" of the Ochils come down to take their place and give a bolder character to the foreground scenery of the Forth.

Very beautiful, at all seasons and in all lights, is this historic range, with its wonderful variety of form and play of shadows. As tales of wild Highland foray and *stieve* Lowland endurance are mingled in its annals, so the pastoral and mountainous combine in this its southern aspect; and the result is harmony. From the summit of Ben Cleuch, the highest of the Ochils, and from other coigns of 'vantage, you can gaze down into peaceful, secluded glens, familiar only to the sheep and the curlew, or into busy valleys lined by thriving villages and factory stalks, from which arises the smoke of the bleaching, spinning, and other manufacturing industries that have long had a home in the heart of these hills. Or you can look abroad and take in at one sweeping glance the whole breadth of the

ALLOA PIER.

country from Glasgow to Dundee—from the Lammermoors and the North Sea to Ben Nevis and the hills of Arran.

But the greatest of the glens of the Ochils is that followed by the "clear-winding Devon," over many a rocky scaur and past many a busy mill-wheel, on

SALMON-FISHING NEAR STIRLING.

its way to join the Forth at Cambus. It would take a volume to do justice to the beauties, wild and soft, of the Devon Valley, and to the associations, warlike and peaceful, that have gathered around its noted places; to attempt to describe Crook o' Devon and Rumbling Bridge, the "Devil's Mill" and the "Cauldron Linn," and Dollar and Alva Glens; to collect the memories that cluster about Tillycoultry and Alva, and Menstry and Tullibody; to dwell upon the attractions of its excellent trouting streams; or to peer among the shadows that appropriately shroud the ruins of Castle Campbell—the "Castle of Gloom"—overlooking the "Burn of Sorrow," harried in revenge against Argyll for the burning of the "Bonnie House o' Airlie."

Unless one has a few days to spare that cannot well be better spent than in exploring Glen Devon and the nooks of the Ochils, he can only glance at the charming wooded valley and blue inviting heights as he follows the windings of the Forth, past the flat green "inches" of Tullibody and Alloa, under the North

CULROSS, FROM THE PIER.

British Railway Bridge crossing the river between these two islands, to the busy town of Alloa.

More than Alloa itself, with its fame for the brewing of ale, and signs of active shipping and manufacturing trade, the eye will be attracted by Alloa Tower and Park, now the seat of the Earl of Mar and Kellie; for here once ruled the old line of the Erskines, Earls of Mar; here Queen Mary paid repeated visits, sailing up the Forth to meet Darnley, under the conduct of Bothwell as High Admiral; and here her son, King James, spent part of his boyhood, under the eye of the Regent Mar and the strict disciplinary rod of George Buchanan.

CULROSS ABBEY.

Below Alloa the river straightens and widens, taking more and more the character of an estuary. One should not miss noting the scattered houses of the old town of Clackmannan, scrambling up the slope to its church and the ancient tower of the Bruces. Clackmannan is the place which Aytoun's recluse thought of selecting for rural retirement, because, "though he had often heard of it, he had never heard of anybody who had been there." It is more out of the world than ever, now that county business has flitted to Alloa. Its visage is not, however, so forlorn as that of Kincardine-on-Forth, the pier of which we now approach; for Kincardine has plainly seen better days, and has little expectation of seeing their return. It was once a busy shipbuilding and shipowning port; and close by was distilled the famous Kilbagie whisky, by which the tinker in the "Jolly Beggars" swore. Now there is no Kilbagie, and no shipping business to speak of; and Kincardine is a "dead-and-alive" place, and more dead than alive. There are many places like it all along the shores of the Forth—places favoured by special times and special circumstances of trade, which has since drifted or been drawn elsewhere.

The massive grey ruins of Tulliallan Castle are in the woods close behind Kincardine. This also was once a stronghold of the Bruces—in fact, it is "Bruce Country" all the way along this northern shore of the Forth, until we come to the last constriction of the estuary, over which the great railway bridge is being thrown at Queensferry. The spidery red limbs of this new giant bestriding the sea begin to come in sight after passing Kincardine Ferry and rounding Longannet Point. For now, especially when the broad mudbanks of the foreshore are covered at high water, the river takes a truly spacious expansion; the salt water begins to assert dominion over the fresh, and the line of the southern bank retires to the distance of three or four miles. It is no great loss; for Grangemouth and Bo'ness are little other than ports for the shipment of coal and pig-iron. The Carron Works show like pillars of fire by night and pillars of smoke by day, hiding Falkirk and Camelon and other spots of historic note. Further east the low shore-line is backed by a monotonous ridge that shuts us out from sight of the valley of which Linlithgow, with its loch and royal palace, is the centre; and even the woods of Kinneil, and the knowledge that along this crest, starting on the shore near the old Roman station of Carriden, run the remains of "Grime's Dyke"—the Wall of Antonine—fail to make the southern side a joy to the eye. There is metal more attractive near at hand, within the sweep of the Bay of Culross.

Culross—Koo'ross, as the name sounds familiarly to the ears of those who know it—cherishes a fond tradition that Turner the painter, who visited Sir Robert Preston at the Abbey in the beginning of the century, compared its bay with that of Naples, rather to the disadvantage of the latter. Local partiality is doubtless the father of the legend. Yet there are wonderful charms embraced by the curve of coast facing the south and the Firth, betwixt "Dunimarle and Duniquarle," with Preston Island and its ruined buildings in the string of the arc; the grey and white walls and red roofs of the little royal burgh, following the sinuosity of the shore, or struggling up the wooded slopes; the "corniced" roads and "hanging gardens" behind; crowning the near foreground, the Norman tower of the Abbey Church, the ruins of the ancient monastery, and the stately façade of the mansion of Culross Abbey (the design, it is said, of Inigo Jones); and behind, the forest, moorland, and cultivated tracts, rising towards the wavy green lines, fading into blue in the distance, of the Ochils and of the Cleish and Saline Hills. With the fresh light of morning or the soft colours of evening upon the waters and upon the hills, the scene may well be deemed lovely. Circumscribed as is the space, and few and insignificant as are the remaining actors, Culross and its vicinity have been the theatre of famous events, and have reared many men prominent in the civil and religious history of the country. Here St. Serf, the Apostle of Fife, is supposed to have been born, and to have died. Here St. Thenew, daughter of "King Lot of Lothian," landed from the rotten shallop in which she had been cast adrift at Aberlady, far down the coast, and gave birth to the more famous St. Kentigern, or Mungo, patron saint of Glasgow. From Culross downward, both shores of the Firth, and the islands in its midst, are strewn with the memorials and traditions of the early Culdee missionaries, whose humble cells later became the sites of the wealthier and more imposing religious houses of Catholic times. Besides St. Serf and St. Mungo, Fillan, Palladius, Adamnan, Adrian, Monans, and Columba himself, set their imprint upon these curving coasts and solitary islets; and Inverkeithing, Dysart, and Pittenweem; Abercorn, Inchcolm, Inchkeith, the May, and the Bass, are among the places sanctified by memories of the Early Church.

It was not till 1217 that the Monastery of Culross, of which only some fragments remain, was founded by Malcolm, Earl of Fife. At the Reformation the Abbey lands passed chiefly into the hands of the Colvilles of Culross, and this family, with the Erskines, the Cochranes, the Prestons, and the Bruces, have since successively had "the guidin' o't" in the burgh and the surrounding district. So far from the ecclesiastical eminence of Culross terminating with St. Serf, it has continued almost down to our own day; for the town, and the district back from it—at Carnock, and eastward along the hill-skirts to Hill of Beath and beyond—have witnessed the keenest struggles between Conformity and Schism—have been special scenes of the labours of Bishop Blackadder and Bishop Leighton the "Saintly;" of John Row, and of John Blackadder the Covenanter, who held his Conventicles under the wakeful and vengeful eye of Dalzell of Binns—him with the "vowed beard," whose hill-top for "glowering owre" Fife is on the opposite side of the Firth; and in later times, of Boston, of Ralph and Ebenezer Erskine, of Gillespie, and of other founders of the "Relief Church."

Culrossians might adopt the Bruce motto, "Fuimus," to describe their industrial as well as their religious past. More than once the burgh has been a spot favoured by trade, as well as by history. The celebrated Sir George Bruce, of Carnock, made its fortunes, as well as his own, by coal-mining and salt-making in the days of James I. of England. Remains, in the shape of a heap of stones, uncovered at low water, are seen of the "Moat"—an "unfellowed and unmatchable work; a darke, light, pleasant, profitable hell," as John Taylor, the "Water Poet" described it in the early years of the seventeenth century—constructed to work the minerals lying under the bed of the sea. But Culross's prosperity did not come to an end with them. Throughout Scotland its "girdles"—iron plates for baking the oaten bread of the "Land o' Cakes"—were also "unfellowed and unmatchable" for many a day. The first of note among the ancestors of the Earl of Rosebery was of the honest guild of the girdlesmiths of the burgh. A

DUNFERMLINE.

"Cu'ross girdle" will soon only be found in an archæological museum; their glory is departing, their use will soon be forgotten.

A lingering look may be cast in the direction of the "Standard Stone," at Bordie, where Duncan and Macbeth withstood the Danes; and of the Castlehill, or Dunimarle, near by, which lays claim to be the scene of the murder of Lady Macduff and her "pretty chickens" by the Usurper—a claim, however, disputed by the "Thane's Castle," near East Wemyss, by Rhives, and by other sites in the East of Fife. To this famous Whig shire we eventually come at Torryburn, for thus far, since leaving Stirling, we have been skirting on the left the shores of Clackmannan and of a sporadic fragment of Perthshire projected upon the Forth. In its scenic, social, and historic characteristics, however, the whole ground, from where the river begins to broaden, is "Fifish," and, from Dunmyatt to the "East Neuk," bears the traces, in place-names, legends, and ancient remains, of old Pictish possession, and of Norse, Saxon, and Highland incursions; of Culdee settlement and of Roman intrusion; and of all the later strife, in Kirk and State, in which Fife has "borne the gree." Neighbours have been ready to observe that the joint effects of geographical isolation and outside pressure are quite as deeply marked in the character, habits, and ways of the inhabitants; and that,

FORTH BRIDGE, FROM THE SOUTH-WEST.

besides occupying a separate "Kingdom," they are in many respects a "peculiar people."

Charlestown and Limekilns, after Culross, are but upstart villages, built by the Earls of Elgin as shipping-places for the coal, lime, and ironstone upon their Broomhall Estate. Before us, a prominent object by the shore, is the stark grey keep of Rosyth Castle. And now we are fairly in "St. Margaret's Hope," and under the shelter of the high ground projecting from the Fife shore, which narrows, by a full half, the width of the Firth, and forms, with Inch Garvie island as a stepping-stone in mid-channel, the natural abutment whence the Forth Bridge makes its flying leap to the southern bank. From the lee of this rocky ridge Queen Mary, having rested at Rosyth, set sail for the other shore, after her escape from Loch Leven Castle. On the beach here Sir Patrick Spens may have paced when the "braid letter" was put into his hands, sending him on the luckless voyage to bring back the "Maiden of Norway," while not far off

> "The King sat in Dunfermline tower,
> Drinking the blood-red wine."

But most famous of the events in the annals of the "Hope"—and one of the epoch-making accidents in the history of Scotland—was the landing, in 1069, of Edgar Atheling and his sisters in this safe harbourage, after grievous tossings by storms and ill-fortune. The then royal residence of Dunfermline is four miles distant, the road leading past Pitreavie, where, six centuries later, Cromwell, descending from the Ferry Hill, so terribly mauled the Scottish army. Tradition points out a stone where the weary Saxon Princess Margaret rested, on a way which became so familiar to her. For she found favour in the sight of King Malcolm Canmore, and made many journeys, by the haven and the ferry that bear her name, to Edinburgh, and to pilgrim shrines in the south. It might almost be said that civilisation, and the English speech, and the Roman hierarchy and influence, landed on the Scottish shores with Saint Margaret; and the whole district around the "Queen's Ferry" is redolent with memories of her to this day.

"Dunfermline Tower," or rather the foundations of what is considered the first royal seat there, are within the grounds of Pittencrieff, on the high bank overlooking the Lyne burn. Farther up, and more adjacent to the modern town, is the Palace, built in later times, and still showing a stately front, sixty feet in height, rising above the ancient trees and overlooking the beautiful Glen. Beyond these walls, and the crypt-like chambers which served as kitchen and other offices, little of the Palace remains. The mullioned windows are pointed out of the rooms in which Charles I. and his sister Elizabeth, the 'Winter Queen" of Bohemia, were born, and where Charles II. signed the "Solemn League and Covenant;" but within, as without, they only look into "empty air."

The Palace communicated by underground passages with the Abbey, founded and dedicated to the Holy Trinity by Malcolm Canmore and Margaret in 1072, and enlarged and beautified by the munificence and piety of their successors. Beyond fragments of the walls, nearly all that remains of the monastic buildings is the Frater Hall, with the delicate Gothic tracery of its west window. But close behind is the Abbey Church, surrounded by its graves, its rookery, and the old houses of the town; and it still ranks as one of the proudest and best-preserved specimens of Anglo-Norman church architecture in Scotland. Rich and quaint are the carvings on its doorways, and dim and mysterious is the light that falls through its illuminated windows as you tread your way between the massive old pillars, and literally over the dust of kings and princes, to the spacious and lightsome New Abbey Church. This portion of the Abbey structure was rebuilt seventy years ago, and in the course of the operations the workmen came upon the tomb and remains of Robert the Bruce—recognisable, among other evidences, by the gigantic stature and by the breast-bone, from which a piece had been sawn to reach the heart that Douglas sought to carry to the Holy Land. The tomb of Malcolm and Margaret is at the east end, and without the present limits of the church; and within, besides "The Bruce," there are buried a score of Scottish Sovereigns and princes, including David I., the builder of monasteries and the "Sair Saunt for the Crown," and Alexander III., whose fatal mischance near Kinghorn was the beginning of the national troubles.

One may range far before finding a group of buildings so intrinsically beautiful, so historically interesting, and so fitly set amid their surroundings. For Dunfermline has many things else, old and new, to attract the visitor—from the "Oratory Cave" of Queen Margaret, to its handsome municipal buildings and Free Library and Baths, the gifts of Mr. Andrew Carnegie. It is a "live place," and not one existing merely on the memories of its past; for it has extensive and growing industries in coal and linen. But it will always be more the "City of Kings" than the seat of trade.

From the old Bartizan Tower of the Abbey Church, one can survey a dozen shires, and—contrast as strange as the light and shadow in the churches below—a glimpse is caught, beyond North Queensferry Point, of the limbs of the New Forth Bridge. This gigantic work represents the second undertaking adopted by the North British Railway and the supporting companies for shortening the journey to the North by throwing a bridge over the narrows at Queensferry. The first plan of a suspension bridge was abandoned, after the catastrophe that befell the structure on the Tay; and the design (by Sir John Fowler and Mr. Baker) now happily completed is that of a cantilever bridge, founded on three sets of piers—at the edge of the deep-water channels on the north and south sides, and on Inch Garvie island in the middle—united, over the fairways of navigation, by central girders. The whole space spanned is over a mile and a half, but fully a third of this distance is occupied by the viaduct approaches to what may be termed the bridge proper, supported at a height of 165 feet above mean sea-level upon a series of stone piers. At this elevation the line is carried across the Firth, which reaches from 30 to 35 fathoms in depth in the channels between Inch Garvie and the north and south shores. Except the supporting bases of stone, the whole central structure is of steel, wrought and fitted in the works on the southern side; and it is estimated that not less than 50,000 tons of metal have been used in the work.

From the three main piers, columned "towers of steel" rise to a height of 630 feet above high-water mark, that on Inch Garvie being wider than the two others. They are formed of tubes of $\frac{3}{4}$-inch steel, 12 feet in diameter at the base, inclining inwards and towards each other, and united by cross members, in the shape of the letter "X," for purposes of strength; and from these the intricate bracket-work of upper and lower members, with their connecting struts and ties, stretch out over the Firth, and approach each other near enough to be united by the two 350-feet lattice girders over the fairways. The two great

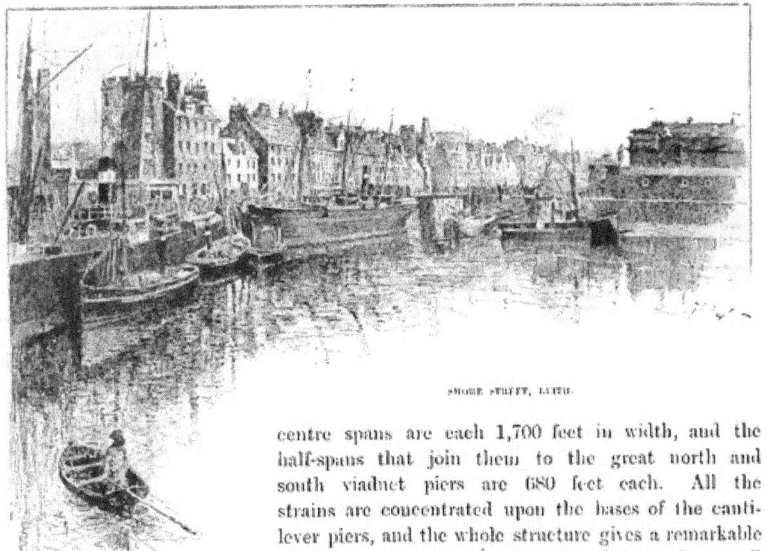

SHORE STREET, LEITH.

centre spans are each 1,700 feet in width, and the half-spans that join them to the great north and south viaduct piers are 680 feet each. All the strains are concentrated upon the bases of the cantilever piers, and the whole structure gives a remarkable impression of combined lightness and strength, as well as of colossal size. From 3,000 to 4,500 men were employed for several years upon the Bridge, of which it may almost be said that half of the work is under water and out of sight. Its cost has to be reckoned in millions; and, connected with it, new lines have been or are being constructed, by which passengers and goods will henceforth be carried by the shortest available route from south to north, in despite of the obstacles interposed by the Forth, the Ochils, and the Tay.

Of all the objects dwarfed and changed by the Bridge, Inch Garvie and its Castle have perhaps suffered most. Built long ago to protect the upper waters against the pirates that infested the Outer Firth, it has often since played a part in schemes of national defence. "Roy of Aldivalloch" held Inch Garvie with twenty musketeers against Monk's troops, at the time of Cromwell's invasion; and it was afterwards manned to repel Paul Jones. Now, looking down upon it from the summit of the great pier, it seems as if a good-sized stone would crush, like a toy, the queer admixture of old and new buildings huddled upon it. From this great height, both expanses of the Firth, with their bounding shores, lie spread below like a map.

The southern shore, now become once more rich in interest and beauty, has complacently drawn nearer hand. Looking westward, and withdrawing the eyes from the fine amphitheatre of hills that enclose the upper course of the Forth, Blackness Castle—one of the four royal fortalices specially mentioned in the Treaty of Union, and the scene of many stirring events in the national annals: Edinburgh, Stirling, and Dumbarton being the others—is full in sight, upon its peninsula. Nearer are the woods of Abercorn, whose history goes back to Roman times, and earlier; closer still, the magnificent colonnaded front, the sea-terraces, the deer-

EDINBURGH, FROM THE FIFE SHORE.

parks, and the stately lime avenues of Hopetoun House, the seat of the Earl of Hopetoun; and almost below, and on the hither side of Port Edgar Harbour, the ancient town of South Queensferry. The last few years have made "a mighty difference" in many ways to the little burgh, but have not materially altered the somewhat grimy features of its main street, which runs eastward, at the base of the hill, towards the Bridge, the "Hawes Brae," and the "Hawes Inn," where, it will be remembered, Jonathan Oldbuck and his young friend Lovel descended from the Edinburgh Diligence, and cemented acquaintance over a magnum of port, and where, also, adventures first began to overtake the hero of "Kidnapped."

Turning eastward, this southern shore is prolonged in the wooded knolls of the Dalmeny estate, and round the projecting point, and on the very sea-marge, is the old, but now renovated, Castle of Barnbougle, once the seat of the Mowbrays.

Behind it is Dalmeny House, with beautiful sward and woodland extending as far as Cramond, where Lord Rosebery keeps a boat to ferry the public across the Almond water into Midlothian.

These latter objects, as has been said, are out of sight from the Bridge, but on the northern side one sees well into the deep inlet of Inverkeithing Bay, where the old royal burgh, dating from before William the Lion's time, lies stranded in mud. It is still proud of having witnessed the last assembly of the Culdees, and the first movement of Scottish "Voluntaryism," and boasts also of containing the "palace" of Queen Annabella Drummond, and the birthplace of Admiral Greig, of the Russian service. For miles the domain of Donibristle follows the advancing and retiring points of the Fife shore, which, now that the outer Firth opens up, recedes away northward as well as eastward. Within the half-circle of Dalgety Bay are the ruins of old Dalgety Church, and what remains of Donibristle House. The estate belongs to the Earl of Moray, the owner of Doune and of many broad lands in the north. The mansion was accidentally burned thirty years ago; but destined for longer remembrance is its burning, not accidental, three centuries since, when took place the tragedy of "the Bonnie Earl o' Moray." The "Bonnie Earl"—son-in-law of the famous Regent Moray—was in 1591 slain, as he was escaping from the blazing building, by Gordon of Buckie and other retainers of Lord Huntly, with the connivance, as was suspected, of James VI. The ballad-writers have their explanation, for

"The Bonnie Earl o' Moray,
He was the Queen's love."

An Earl and Regent Moray of an earlier stem—Randolph, the companion of the Bruce and of the Black Douglas—had his home at Aberdour, the next indentation in this singularly beautiful coast. The line had soon to give place to the Douglases, Earls of Morton, who have ruled here for some five centuries, though their old castle, overlooking the lovely bay, with its projecting bluffs and shining sands, now a favourite resort for bathers and summer visitors, has been long untenanted. The wily and unscrupulous Regent Morton came hither to amuse himself with gardening, in the intervals when, from choice or compulsion, he was not in the thick of political intrigue. Edinburgh was always in view from Aberdour, and nature and simple country pursuits could not hold him long. Through the high beech groves and hanging woods, one of the most charming of walks leads for three miles to Burntisland. But the charm is no longer what it was, for the railway line running athwart the slope has played havoc with the trees.

Outside Aberdour, and partly shielding the bay, is Inchcolm Island. It would need a volume to do justice to the islands of the Forth. Some we have already glanced at. "St. Colme's Inch," where, as Shakespeare tells us, the routed Norsemen were fain to crave permission of the Thane of Cawdor to bury their dead, is the most famous of them all—except perhaps the Bass. The square tower and mouldering walls of its Abbey, rising close to the narrow isthmus where the isle is almost cut in two by the sea, are still prominent objects in the view. The Monastery was founded in 1123, by King Alexander I., in gratitude for his miraculous rescue from shipwreck, and entertainment here by a hermit who followed the rule of St. Columba. It once owned rich possessions in half a dozen shires, granted in part by a Lord Alan Mortimer of Aberdour, whose body the monks flung overboard in a storm while crossing to the island, thus giving a name to the inner channel of "Mortimer's Deep." Invaders, pirates, and rebels, as well as the hand of time, have since sorely visited the island, but still portions of the old buildings stand, and are even habitable.

Cramond Island, almost opposite Inchcolm, hugs the other shore, and there is a road across the sands to its little farmhouse at low tide; while in the mid-channel there are many rocky islets, some of them the chosen resorts of cormorants and other sea birds. Further down, half-way between Leith Pier and Kirkcaldy Bay, Inchkeith stretches its length for nearly a mile across the Firth. Inchkeith, also, has harboured anchorites and stood sieges; and there are many curious legends connected with its coves and caves. But its most prominent feature is now the white lighthouse perched upon its highest crest; and barely visible to the eye are the powerful batteries that sweep, on the one side, Leith Roads, and on the other side the North Channel, between the island and Pettycur Point, where also great guns are mounted for the defence of the Forth. Then a long way farther out, at the very entrance to the Firth, and visible only in clear weather and easterly wind, runs the long rock wall of the May Island. In other days the May was a great resort of pilgrims, who held it a merit to reach a place so difficult of access, and barren women especially found a blessing in drinking from the well that had refreshed St. Fillan and St. Adrian. There was a religious house here connected with the Priory of Pittenweem on the adjacent Fife coast, but the monks found it by-and-bye most convenient to reside on shore. Though the light of faith has gone out, another light—a guide to the commerce entering the Firth—has been kept burning upon the May for two centuries and a half. Now its only residents are the lighthouse-men and their families, and its only regular visitors are myriads of sea-fowl.

The Carr Rock and Fidra Island lights mark, with the May, the entrance to the Firth; and scattered along the East Lothian coast, from Fidra eastwards, are numerous little islands, "salt and bare." But none of them have the fame or the aspect of the "Bass." This huge mass of rock, heaved up by some convulsion of nature, like North Berwick Law and other great bluffs on shore, presents seawards its precipitous cliff, rising sheer to a height of 400 feet, while towards the land it shows a green slope descending steeply to the landing-place and the remains of its old prison castle. The crevices of the rocks are filled with the nests of the solan-goose and other sea-fowl, and the air around is alive with their cries and the sweep of their wings. But otherwise it is impossible to imagine a spot with the aspect of grim isolation more thoroughly impressed upon it. St. Baldred is said to have lived and died on the Bass Rock; but it came most conspicuously forward in history when it was made the prison of the Covenanters, charged with no other offence than that of following their consciences against the will of the King; and afterwards, when its Jacobite garrison held out for years after every other place in the kingdom had submitted to William of Orange.

But on the way from Inchcolm to the Bass, what a marvellous series of noble land and sea pieces, of famous or hallowed sites, we have passed! It were hard to say whether scenic beauty and historical associations cluster more closely upon the shores of the Firth, or upon the surrounding amphitheatre of hills. In the profile of the hills of Fife, the broad-shouldered Lomonds, with their double or triple heads, overtop all—the East Lomond looking down upon the ruins of the old royal hunting seat of Falkland, the scene of Rothesay's cruel pangs, and the western heights upon Loch Leven and the Island Castle, whence Mary made her romantic escape. More in the foreground are Dunearn, crowded by the remains of a Pictish fort, and the steep, rugged front of the Binn of Burntisland, overhanging the town of that name. Rossend Castle—a favourite residence of the Queen of Scots, where took place the incident that cost the enamoured French poet Chastelard his life—fronts the sea at the west end of Burntisland harbour; and to the east, behind a beautiful sweep of sand and "links," rises the cliff at which an evil fate overtook Alexander III. and Scotland.

PORTOBELLO.

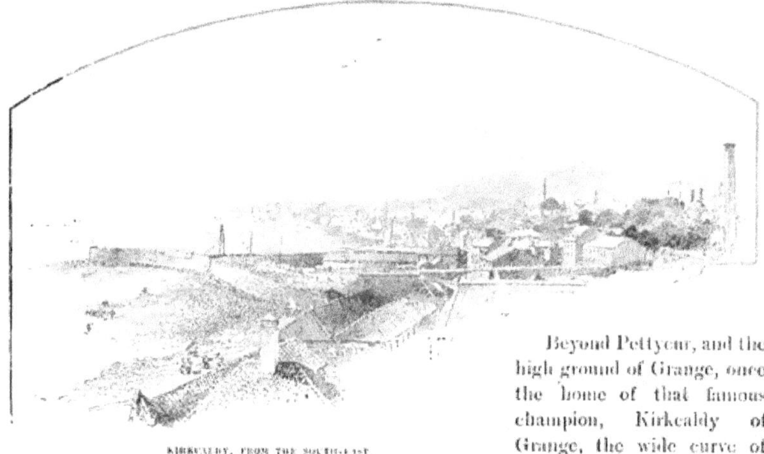

KIRKCALDY, FROM THE SOUTH-EAST.

Beyond Pettycur, and the high ground of Grange, once the home of that famous champion, Kirkcaldy of Grange, the wide curve of Kirkcaldy Bay opens up. The old burgh of Kinghorn is at one extremity, and the still more ancient town of Dysart at the other; and the middle foreground is largely occupied by the houses and shipping of the "Lang Toun." The very names of Kirkcaldy ("Kirk of the Culdees") and of Dysart ("Desertum") point to the antiquity and the sanctity of the origin of places that to this day are strongly "Churchy." The grotesque folk-tale relates that the devil was "buried in Kirkcaldy," and that his complaint that "his taes were cauld" led the good-natured inhabitants to build house to house, until now the town, with the villages connected, stretches some four miles in a straight line. The story may have had its origin in some of the apostolic doings of St. Serf, who had for a time his "desert" in one of the caves in the red cliffs at Dysart; or else in some magic feat of the wizard Michael Scott—the friend of Dante and Boccaccio—whose weird tower of Balwearie is an uncanny neighbour of the "Lang Toun." The ruins, close by the shore, of Seafield Tower and of Ravenscraig Castle—the latter the home of the line of "high St. Clair," and of the "lovely Rosabelle"—are now strangely backed by floor-cloth factories.

Kirkcaldy has, however, other and even better things to be proud of; for here Adam Smith was born; here Edward Irving taught and preached, with Thomas Carlyle, the dominie of a competing school, as his friend and companion on excursions to Inchkeith, and to quaint nooks of the Fife coast. The author of "Sartor Resartus" had kindly recollections of the folks of the "Kingdom"—"good old Scotch in all their works and ways;" and with strong unerring touches brings before us their "ancient little burghs and sea villages, with their poor little havens, salt-pans, and weather-beaten bits of Cyclopean breakwaters, and rude innocent machineries."

Portentous for length is the mere list of these surf-washed Fife towns—beloved of wandering artists and haunted by memories and traditions of the olden time—that are sprinkled along the coast eastward. Mention cannot be avoided of Wemyss, Easter and Wester, with their caves and coal-pits rendering upon the sea, and their castles, old and new; of tumble-down Methil and the "ancient and fish-like flavour" of Buckhaven; of Leven and Lundin, their Druidical stones and stretches of breezy links, the delight of golfers; of Largo, where the Law looks down upon "Largo Bay" and its brown-sailed fishing boats, upon the cottage of "Auld Robin Gray," and upon the birthplace of the famous Scottish admiral, Sir Andrew Wood, and of Alexander Selkirk, the "original" Robinson Crusoe; of Elie, most delightful of East Coast watering-places; of St. Monance and its picturesque old church and harbour and ruined tower; of Pittenweem and the remains of its priory, on the site of St. Fillan's cell; of Anstruther, Easter and Wester, the scene of "Anster Fair," and the home of Maggie Lauder; of Cellardyke, Kilrenny, and, quietest and remotest of them all, "the weel-aired ancient toun o' Crail," where Knox preached and Archbishop Sharp was "placed," situated close by Fife Ness, with its wind-twisted bents, its caves, and traces of Danish camps and forgotten fights.

The smell and the sound of the sea are about all these Fife burghs and fishing villages, and not less saturated with romance and history are the old-fashioned mansion-houses of the lairds of the East Neuk, that seek shelter in every fold of the land. For Fife was the true soil of the "cock" or "bonnet" laird, whose proverbial heritage was "a wee pickle land, a good pickle debt, and a doo-cot." Little better than a ruined dove-cote—or "a corbie's nest," as the Merry Monarch called Dreel Castle, the old tower of the Anstruthers—shows many a crumbled seat of the long-pedigreed Fife gentry. But they were the nurseries of famous men—witness the Leslies, Alexander and David, and a host besides—who found not only their native shire but their native country too narrow a field for their talents and their ambition. In this, as in other respects, the shores of Fife offer an epitome of Scottish history, and the quintessence of Scottish character.

Turn now towards the Southern shore. The spell even of the coasts of Fife cannot long detain us, when Edinburgh, seated on her hills, and queening it over the waters, with the couchant lion of Arthur's Seat beside her, is in view. As Stirling presides over the "Links of Forth," and the upper courses of the river, Edinburgh Rock with its Castle appears the Guardian Genius of the Firth. Round the base of this "Bass Rock upon land," the masses of buildings seem to swirl and surge like a tide-race of human life, and to climb, in broken wave upon wave, crested by the spires and roofs of the Old Town, and overhung by the murky spray of its proverbial "reek," all up the steep slope to the battlements of the Castle. Stirling itself is scarcely its peer for dignity of situation or for renown. From the highest platform of the Rock, where hooped and battered Mons Meg guards the old chapel of Canmore and Margaret, to the profoundest depths of the shadows cast by the tall and beetling houses of the Grassmarket, the West Port, and the Cowgate, it is haunted by traditions; and its history, like its aspect, is most sombre and most striking.

Looking from the windows of the rooms which Mary occupied, and whence the infant James was let down in a basket to the bottom of the rock, one glances across the "plainstanes" of the Grassmarket, the scene of Jock Porteous's slaughter, to the Old Greyfriars Churchyard and its graves of martyrs and of persecutors, to the dome and towers of the old and new University buildings, and to the piled and crowded buildings, thinning out and becoming newer as they descend the warm slopes of Morningside and Newington towards the bluffs of Craiglockhart, the whinny slopes of the Braids, and Craigmillar Castle, behind which are the finely pencilled lines of the Pentlands, the Moorfoots, and the Lammermoors. Or the eye can follow the impending walls of the many-storeyed houses of the Lawnmarket and the High Street, as far as the "Crown" of St. Giles and the Parliament House—each of them part and parcel of the national life—and so on by the Canongate and its memorable old "lands" and closes, towards the spot where the Palace and the ruined Abbey of Holyrood, shouldered by breweries and canopied by the smoke of gasworks, shelter under the Salisbury Crags. Or looking away from the grim Old Town, one may travel far before seeing anything to compare with the stately front of Prince's Street, facing its gardens and the sun, and turned away from the cold blasts of the north; the Calton Hill and its monuments; the serried lines of the New Town streets and squares, broken by frequent spires and towers, and sweeping away in one direction towards the wooded sides of Corstorphine, and in the other joining Leith and its shipping; while beyond, if the day be fine, the glorious view is bounded by the Firth and its islands and the hills of Fife, melting in a distance where land, sea, and sky are indistinguishable.

Too often, viewing it from the "clouded Forth," the grey city, its castle, and its subject hills are swallowed up in the "gloom that saddens heaven and earth" during the dismal Edinburgh winter and spring, and the uncertain summer and autumn. Sometimes they show huge and imposing, like ghosts in the mist, or rise like islands over the strata of smoke and haze in which Leith lies buried. But there are gloriously fine days at all seasons of the year, even in this much-abused climate, and then the long pier, the shipping in the roadstead, the tangle of masts and rigging in the spacious docks, and the warehouses, churches, and close-built houses of the port of Leith make a brave show in the low foreground of a lovely picture. To the west, the wide arms of the Granton breakwaters enclose a harbour, built at the cost of the Duke of Buccleuch. Nearer to Leith is the white pier-head of Newhaven, with stalwart fishermen, and comely fishwives in white "mutches" and short petticoats, grouped about its quays. Leith itself is an old as well as a brisk seat of trade and shipping. The large business it continues to conduct with the ports of the Baltic and the North Sea it has carried on for many centuries, and in these days it has extended its commercial relations to nearly all parts of the world. Many of the most famous episodes in the national annals began and ended in Leith. But royal embassies no longer land or embark there; it is happily exempt from hostile invasions and bloody civil and religious feuds.

Eastward from Leith, sewage meadows and brick- and tile-works suddenly give

THE BASS ROCK, FROM NORTH BERWICK.

place to the mile-long front of the Portobello Esplanade, with its pier and bathing coaches and strip of sand, dear to Edinburgh holiday-makers, and with the outline of Arthur's Seat as a noble background to the masses of handsome villas and lodging-houses. Beyond comes a string of little seaside watering-places, fishing and shipping ports—Fisherrow, Musselburgh, Morrisonhaven, Prestonpans, Cockenzie—which, with the country behind them, vie in picturesqueness of aspect with the Fife towns opposite. A high ridge, the last heave of the Lammermoors, marks the limits of this belt of coast country—the old approach of hostile armies from the South—which might dispute with the district around Stirling the title of the "Battlefield of Scotland." Carberry Hill, where Mary fell into the hands of the Lords of the Covenant, overlooks the woods of Dalkeith Palace and the Esk, not far above where, between Fisherrow harbour and Musselburgh, that classic stream enters the sea. A continuation of Carberry are the Fawside braes, and right underneath the ruined castle on the sky-line, and between it and Inveresk Church, was fought the battle of Pinkie, so disastrous for the Scots, when the little burn trickling through Pinkie Woods "ran red with blood." It was on this ground, too, that Cromwell was out-manœuvred by Leslie, and compelled to fall back, "to make the better spring" upon Dunbar; and by the venerable bridge

TANTALLON CASTLE, LOOKING EAST.

across the Esk, the Young Pretender led his troops from Edinburgh, on hearing that the Royalist forces were advancing by the coast upon the capital. The site of the battle of Prestonpans is in the fields beyond the tumbledown old town of that name, which boasts—and looks as if it boasted truly—of being the first place in Scotland where coal was worked and salt manufactured from sea-water. In the more thriving looking village of Cockenzie, they point out the house in which "Johnnie Cope" was soundly sleeping when the Highlanders, making a circuit of the high ground behind Tranent, and crossing the marsh at Seton, "sprang upon him out of the mist" of a September morning.

Seton, with its woods and wild-flowers, its lovely sweep of sands, the remains of its ancient church, and the Castle standing on the site of the Palace of the

Earls of Winton, is redolent of memories of the "high jinks" of Queen Mary and of other members of the unfortunate House of Stuart, in whose mischances the loyal Setons faithfully shared. The parks of Gosford, their trees strangely bent and twisted by the east wind, line the coast for miles, and the great white front of Lord Wemyss's mansion is a shining landmark. Then comes Aberlady Bay, an expanse of sand and mud at low water, but at high tide a broad arm of the Firth, running up close under the walls of the venerable Parish Church and pretty village of Aberlady, and skirting the favourite golfing links of Luffness and Gullane.

From here all the way round to North Berwick, the sea-margin, with its long stretches of grassy turf, interspersed with bent hillocks, whins, sand "bunkers," and other hazards dear to the devotees of cleek and driving-club, may be said to be sacred to the Royal Game of Golf. Four or five spacious golfing courses interpose between; and ardent pursuers of the flying gutta ball have been known to play across the whole distance of seven or eight miles. Numbers of them take up their quarters at Aberlady or at Gullane, placed idyllically upon the edge of the common and the ploughed land, with views extending across the green links and the sea to Fife, and landward over the rich fields of East Lothian to the Lammermoors, with the nearer Garleton Hills, Traprain, and North Berwick Law; a few also at the beautiful old village of Dirleton, beside the ivied ruins of its Castle.

North Berwick, however, is the golfer's Mecca on this side of the Firth; and bathers, artists, and other seekers after the pleasures of the sea-shore succumb to its attractions in increasing numbers every season. The sands and the links, the sea lapping upon the beach, or chafing round Craigleith and the other rocky islets and points, exercise a potent spell. But North Berwick's great lion, and a conspicuous landmark over sea and country for a score of miles around, is the natural pyramid of the "Law." It rises immediately behind the town, in lines as steep and symmetrical as if built by art, and from its summit, nearly 1,000 feet high, an almost unrivalled view is obtained over the Forth and the Lothians. Though one would hardly guess it, looking at the clean streets and handsome hotels and villas that line the shore, North Berwick is a burgh and port of great antiquity.

That it never throve to any remarkable extent in its earlier history may possibly be in part due to its dangerous proximity to Tantallon Castle, the hold of the Douglases, Earls of Angus. Every visitor to North Berwick, after he has surmounted the Law and wandered his fill by the beach, makes an excursion to Tantallon Castle. The coast eastward is bold and precipitous, and fretted by the waters of the North Sea, for we are now at the very lip of the Firth of Forth; and the Bass Rock, lying opposite the beautiful curve of Canty Bay, looks like a mass of the shore-cliffs washed bodily out to sea. Just where the coast is wildest and least accessible one sees—

"Tantallon's dizzy steep
Hang o'er the margin of the deep."

The eyrie of the Douglas is now a mere shell; but the extent and immense thickness of the walls still proclaim its strength in the days when it was a proverb to "ding doon Tantallon and make a bridge to the Bass." On three sides it was protected by the sea, and

> "Above the booming ocean leant
> The far-projecting battlement."

On the land side were those gate-works and walls which Marmion cleared, after bidding bold defiance to the "Douglas in his hall," and behind which the turbulent Earls of Angus, for their part, so often bade defiance to their Sovereigns. James V. once brought up against it "Thrawn-mu'd Meg and her Marrow," and other great pieces of mediæval ordnance from Dunbar, where three lords were placed in pawn for their safe return. But he failed to "ding doon Tantallon"; that feat was reserved for the Covenanters.

Now the spirit of Walter Scott seems to haunt the ruins, in company with the ghosts of "Bell-the-Cat," and the other dead Douglases who built or strengthened these storm-battered walls. The Magician of the North has waved his wand over the Forth from Ben Lomond to Tantallon and the Bass!

JOHN GEDDIE.

NORTH BERWICK, FROM THE HARBOUR.

BERWICK-ON-TWEED.

THE TWEED.

CHAPTER I.

FROM BERWICK TO KELSO.

Leading Characteristics—The View from Berwick—Lindisfarne—The History and Present State of Berwick—Norham Castle and Marmion—Lady-kirk—Tillmouth—Twisell Castle and Bridge—Ford Castle and Flodden—Coldstream—Wark Castle—Hadden Rig.

"A BONNY WATER" was the phrase used of the Tweed by a peasant-woman whom Dorothy Wordsworth met when she came to spy out the Border river. Homely as the expression is, it would not be easy to find another quite so meet. To grandeur, to magnificence, the stream can make no claim, either in itself or in its surroundings. Of screaming eagles, of awful cliffs, of leaping linns, of foaming waves, it knows nothing. No more horrid sound is heard in its neighbourhood than the cry of the pale sea-maw; its banks are rarely precipitous, never frightful; it has not a single waterfall to its name; and, save where its surface is gently ruffled by glistening pebbles, it flows smooth as (*pace* the poet) the course of true love usually is. Yet of charms more gracious how profuse it is! In its careless windings, its silvery clearness, its sweet haughs and holms, its affluence of leaf and blade, its frequent breadth of valley, it is dowered with all the amenities of a large and generous landscape, distributed into combinations of incessant variety. Nor does it owe much less to art and association than to Nature. It glides or ripples by some of the most impressive ruins, ecclesiastical and secular, in all Scotland. At point after point it shines, for the inner eye, with "the light that never was on sea or land." If over other Scottish streams as well the magician's wand has waved, the

HIGH STREET, BERWICK, WITH THE TOWN HALL.

Tweed is twice blessed, since it can speak not only of "Norham's castled steep" and "St. David's ruined pile," but of Ashestiel, and Smailholm, and Abbotsford. And then its course takes it through the very heart of the Debateable Land—birth-place of myth and legend, of fairy tale and folk-song—battle-field where hostile races and envious factions and rival clans have met in mortal strife. For centuries it was the wont of its waters to reflect the fire-bale's ruddy glare, of its banks to resound with the strident Border-slogan; and until long after the coalition of the Crowns its fords continued to be crossed by reiving marchmen in jack and helmet, driving before them their "prey," or scurrying before the avenging "hot trod," led on by blaring bugle-horn and mouthing bloodhound.

A bonny water it truly is, but not a brisk. Except in time of spate, it pursues its way, not wearily, it may be, but certainly lazily, and even wantonly, often wimpling into curves and loops which half suggest that, forgetful of its destiny, it is about basely to wind back to whence it came, and calling to mind Mr. Swinburne's

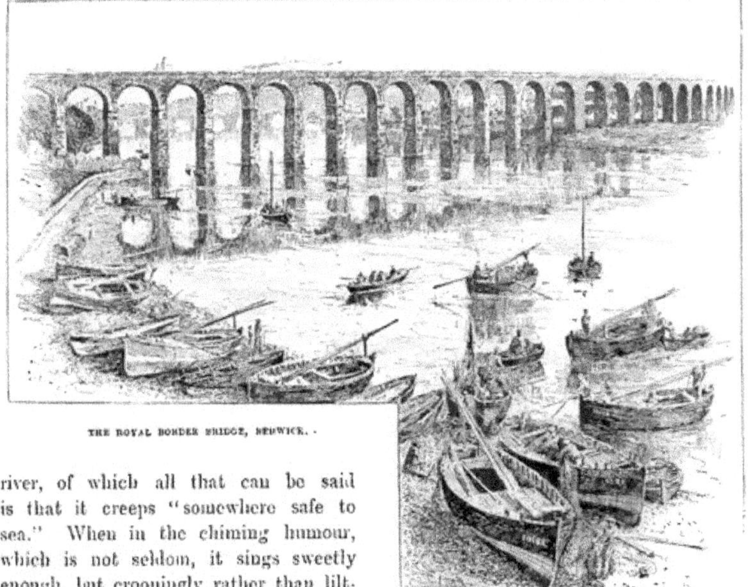

THE ROYAL BORDER BRIDGE, BERWICK.

river, of which all that can be said is that it creeps "somewhere safe to sea." When in the chiming humour, which is not seldom, it sings sweetly enough, but crooningly rather than liltingly—less to you than to itself, or in accompaniment to the birds that pour out their lavish strains along its banks. Not that there is any particular reason why it should take life more seriously. To things commercial it does not condescend. It is tidal only to Norham, and none but mere cockle-shells can get even so far. And if it has a drainage basin second only to that of the Tay among Scottish streams, it has never been alleged that in this respect there is any failure of duty. Let it be said, too, that while it rarely hastes, on the other hand it seldom rests. The "mazes" to which it is addicted are not usually "sluggish;" to the spiky rush or the cool shiny discs of the water-lily it shows no special favour; while dark pools "where alders moist and willows weep" are only to be found by those who seek. Exciting the influences of the stream are not; but they are at any rate cheerful.

One whose only knowledge of the Tweed is gained from what can be seen of it at Berwick, and when the tide is out, would not be likely to think of it more highly than he ought to think. For even at its "latter end" it seems to have no great sense of the dignity of life; it rolls neither broad nor deep, and does little more than trickle into the larger life to which it has all along so indolently tended. Nor is it here altogether happy in the surroundings which it owes to art and man's device. Berwick itself, rising from the water's edge to the top of Halidon Hill, and partly girdled by its fine wall, used as a promenade in these piping

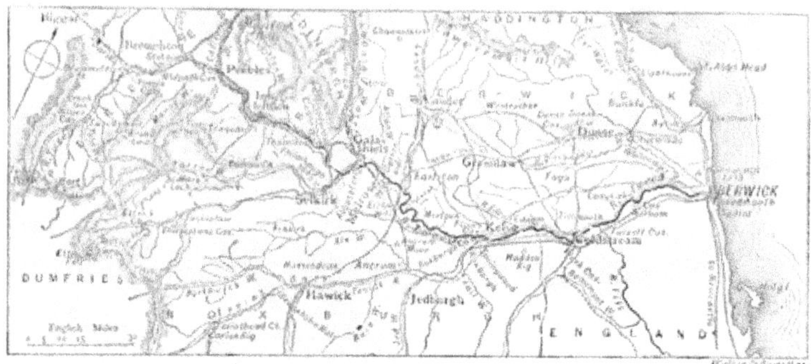

THE COURSE OF THE TWEED.

times of peace, looks quaint, and comely as well, seen from the opposite or southern bank. But when one has crossed the stream by the old bridge—Berwick Bridge, which has stood here since the time of James I.—and looks across at Tweedmouth, exactly opposite, and at Spittal, which has thought fit to spring up a little farther east and just at the river's mouth, the impression is less pleasing. Neither of these places is pretty in itself, while for their size they make an amazing amount of black smoke. Then there is Robert Stephenson's great railway viaduct, the Royal Border Bridge, which it is the fashion to praise up to the skies, as it well-nigh reaches them. As a successful bit of engineering, it is no doubt all very well; but an addition to the beauties of the scene it is not, whatever guide-books and gazetteers may say. In other directions, however, and farther afield, the outlook is more satisfactory. Away to the south the grey and rugged Cheviots make a glorious horizon-line; while out at sea are the Farne Islands, with their memories of St. Cuthbert, most austere of Western ascetics, and of Grace Darling, whose heroism puts so strange a gloss upon the holy man's abhorrence of womankind. The remnants of the ancient Abbey of Lindisfarne are among the very few examples of Saxon architecture which the destructiveness of the Danes has left to us; and that even these ruins remain, is due to no negligence of theirs. When they descended upon the island in the seventh century, not for the first time, they made a brave attempt to leave a desert behind them; but the massive strength which the builders of the church had intended to oppose to "tempestuous seas" was able in

VIEW FROM THE RAMPARTS, BERWICK.

some degree to withstand their "impious rage." The abbey no longer shelters St. Cuthbert's remains, which must be sought in the Cathedral that looks down upon the Wear. But the old Saxon arches and columns have a stronger interest than this could have invested them with; for was it not here, in Sexhelm's Vault of Penitence, dimly lighted by the pale cresset's ray, that the hapless Constance de Beverley, after solemn inquisition, was doomed to her terrible death, the while her betrayer was listening to the song which so melodiously contrasts the traitor's fate with the destiny of the true lover?

Berwick-on-Tweed is certainly not happy in having no history. Its beginnings are not clearly ascertainable; but it was for long a Saxon settlement, until the Danes, attracted by the rich merse-lands through which the Tweed flows, helped themselves to it. Then came the turn of the Scots, who held it off and on from about the time of Alfred the Great until John Balliol renounced the authority of his liege lord, to whom he had sworn fealty at Norham. When an English army approached, the citizens were by no means alarmed, although it was led by Edward himself. "Kynge Edward," they cried from behind their wooden stockade, "waune thou havest Berwick, pike thee; waune thou havest geten, dike thee." But they were better at flouting than at fighting; and they soon had bitter reason for lamenting that they had not kept their mocks to themselves. The place was stormed with the most trivial loss, and nearly eight thousand of the citizens were massacred. Some brave Flemings who held the Red Hall were burnt to cinders in it; and the carnage only ceased when the sad and solemn priests bore the Host into Edward's presence and implored his mercy. Then the impetuous monarch, who in his old age was able to say that no man had ever asked mercy of him and been refused, burst into tears, and ordered the butchery to stop. But the lion's paw had fallen, and Berwick was crushed. When Edward sat down before it, it was not only the great Merchant City of the North, but ranked second to London among English towns; he left it little more than a ruin, and it has never since been anything but "a petty seaport." Through its gates the king went forth to play the *rôle* of the conquering hero in Scotland; and when his over-lordship had been effectually vindicated, the Scottish barons and gentry met here to sulkily do him reverence.

Two-and-twenty years later there came another turn of the wheel. When Robert Bruce wrested his native land from the feeble hands of the second Edward, Berwick shared in the emancipation. Its capture was held to be an achievement of the first order, and after it, as Leland tells us, "the Scottes became so proud . . . that they nothing esteemed the Englishmen." But presently a weaker Bruce reigned in the North and a stronger Edward in the South. In due course the town was again beleaguered by an English force. A Scottish army under the Regent, Archibald Douglas, came to its relief; but the English held a strong position on Halidon Hill, and, met by their terrible showers of clothyard shafts, the Scots turned and fled, leaving Berwick to its fate. Thus it once

NORHAM CASTLE.

more became English, and never again did it change masters, though it was allowed to retain many of its privileges. In these later days, however, it has had to part with one after another of its peculiarities, and now it is substantially a part of the county of Northumberland.

That a place which has received so many rude buffets should have few very ancient remains is not to be wondered at. The present walls, which stand almost intact, and in excellent preservation, though the town in its recent prosperity has straggled outside their line, have a very respectable antiquity, dating as they do from the closing years of the sixteenth century; but of the older fortifications, which embraced a much more considerable space, scarcely a vestige is left, except an octagonal tower; while of the castle, which frowned over the stream where the north bank is steepest, little beyond the foundations has survived. A part of the site has been appropriated to the uses of a railway station, which by a well-meant but unhappy thought has been made to take a castellated form. The fortifications were dismantled some forty or fifty years ago, but there is still much to recall the ancient importance of the town as a place of arms. Nor have the citizens lost the military spirit which was bred into their forbears. They are proud to tell the stranger within their gates that there is almost as large a garrison here as at Edinburgh; and even the tavern-signs bear witness to a traditional love of arms.

The parish church dates only from the Puritan period. It is said to be

JUNCTION OF THE TILL AND THE TWEED.

"quaint" when it is only ugly; and to be a plain specimen of the Gothic when it is not Gothic at all, except in the opprobrious sense in which the term was first applied to mediæval architecture by the superior persons of the Restoration. There being no tower—the Puritans had no taste for "steeple-houses"—the parishioners are summoned to service by the bells of the Town Hall, in the High Street, where also the curfew is still rung at eight of the clock every evening. Although the Anglican is here the Established Church, the prevalent form is the Presbyterian, which has many places of worship, while various other communions are also well represented. But there seems to be some want of resource in finding distinguishing names for the various churches and chapels, for there is a Church Street Church, and hard by a Chapel Street Church, while several places of worship are nameless. Among these latter is one which bears on its front the legend "Audi, Vide, Tace"—intended, presumably, for a concise exposition of the whole duty of the pew in relation to the pulpit.

Not a great way from the first of the bends in which the stream indulges, and within sight of the towers of Longridge, the Whiteadder from the Lammermoors, reinforced by the Blackadder, renders up its tribute. Two miles above this point the river is crossed by the Union Suspension Bridge, which, built by Sir S. Brown in 1820, is said to have been the first structure of the kind erected in these islands, while as bridges go along the Tweed it is also quite an antiquity; for, until the beginning of the century, there was only one between Peebles and Berwick, a space of more than sixty miles. Now they are many, yet there has been little sacrifice of beauty to utility, for, as a rule, when not picturesque,

TILLMOUTH HOUSE, FROM THE BANKS OF THE TILL.

they are at least neat and modest. Hereabouts the valley is fairly broad, the banks rising on either hand into a long succession of rolling meadows green with herbage, or of furrowed fields red with tilth, in the prime of summer smothered with tender shoots of corn all aglow with the bright yellow blooms of the runch — to the wayfarer a flower, to the husbandman a weed. So curve to curve succeeds until Norham Castle comes in sight, standing on a lofty cliff of red freestone which rises almost sheer from the water on the southern bank, and disdainfully rearing itself high above the trees that have presumed to grow up around it.

When this ancient little village first had a stronghold no one seems to know. As early as 1121 a fortress was built here by Bishop Flambard, of Durham; but it was not the first to occupy the site. After the death of "this plunderer of the rich, this exterminator of the poor," the castle was so roughly handled by David I. that in 1164 we find another Bishop of Durham, Hugh Pudsey, virtually rebuilding it, and adding a massive keep. But warrior-priests were not much to the mind of the king who suggested the assassination of Thomas à Becket, and so, some ten years after he had rebuilt it, the bishop was prevailed upon to pass it on to William de Neville; and from this time onwards it appears to have been treated as a royal fortress. Thus it came about that more than once it was the scene of conference between William the Lion and the English King whose only association with the noble beast was through his brother. And here also came Edward I., to decide between the thirteen claimants to the crown of Alexander III., and to do a little business on his own account as well. A memoir of the Dacres on its condition early in the sixteenth century speaks of the keep as impregnable; but it was nothing of the kind. Like all these Border strengths, it was always being taken and retaken; and only a few years before this memoir was written, James IV., then on his way to Flodden, had brought up Mons Meg against it, and with the "auld murderess's" help had possessed himself of it. Pudsey's massive keep still remains, though in a greatly shattered state, and shorn of its mighty proportions; there are also bits of other parts of the castle, the whole enclosed within a wall of ample circuit.

In the days when it held a royal garrison, Norham had various castellans, some of them men of distinction in their day; but the most famous of them since the "tale of Flodden Field" was told, has been "Sir Hugh the Heron bold." This "Baron of Twisell and of Ford" passed among men as William Heron; but Hugh was more poetical, and so his baptismal name was changed. Nor, at the time selected for the Lord of Fontenaye's visit, was he here to be twitted with his witching lady's gallantries. Two years before this his bastard brother had taken part in the

FORD CASTLE.

FLODDEN FIELD.

slaughter of the Scottish Warden of the Middle Marches, Sir Robert Ker of Cessford; and as Sir William himself had been in some sort accessory to the crime, Henry had thought it well to deliver him and one of the actual murderers up to justice, so that at this time he was lying in durance at Fastcastle. This, of course, is the fault of the facts, not of the poetry. Nor need it be disappointing to find Sir Walter himself saying that the Marmion of the romance is "entirely a fictitious personage." When, indeed, it is remembered that one of the Marmions did verily come here, though long years before—in the reign which witnessed the triumph at Bannockburn, instead of the overthrow at Flodden—the poet might very well have been astonished at his own moderation. The errand of the real Marmion was a good deal more romantic than that of his imaginary descendant. At a great feast in Lincolnshire he had been endued with a gold-crested helmet by a lady who had nothing better to do than to drive a brave man into mortal peril. Her charge to him was to "go into the daungerest place in England, and ther to let the healme be seene and known as famous." So he sped him here to Norham, and within four days of his coming, Philip of Mowbray, the guardian of Berwick—now in the hands of the elated Scots—appeared before the walls "with the very flour of the men of the Scottish marches." The castellan at this time was a Grey of Chillingham, who drew out his men before the barriers, and then bade the knight-errant, "al glittering in gold, and wearing the healme," to ride like a valiant man among his foes, adding, "and I forsake God if I rescue not thy body, dead or alyve, or I myself wyl dye for it." Thereupon the knight mounted and rode into the midst of the enemy, "the which layed sore stripes on him, and pulled hym at the last out of his sadel to the ground." But now Grey and his men "lette prick yn among the Scottes" and put them to rout; and he of the "healme," though "sore beten," was horsed again and took part in the chase. As it must have been this visit which made the poet bring his Marmion to Norham, so no doubt it was the deed itself, coupled with an event which actually happened at Tantallon, which suggested the knight's precipitate retreat when he had bearded the Douglas in his halls.

Just above the castle is the village of Norham, with its pretty little church—all but the eastern end, where there is a poor Decorated window, in the Norman style, and still interesting, in spite of the drastic restoration it has endured. It stands in a churchyard which well repays the careful tendance it receives, for it is of exceptionally choice situation, separated by a row of limes from the cosiest of rectories, and by little more than another fringe of foliage from the Tweed, whose waves babble of rest and peace as they ripple by the cells where lie the simple village folk who ended their toilsome lives in their beds, and the warriors who came to a ruder end before or behind the castle walls. Here the northern bank is lofty and pleasantly wooded, as, a little below, is the southern bank. In its approach to the castle the stream bends round to the south, and its waters move less leisurely, as though, fresh from contact with a scene consecrated to peace on the earth and good-will among men, they cannot abide these grim stark ruins, with their memories of weeping captives and

TWIZELL BRIDGE.

cruel deeds. If the keep yet looks down with something of insolence upon its lowly neighbour on the strath far beneath, it is, for all that, a parable against itself, testifying that it is not to "men of might" but to "men of mean" that the inheritance has been decreed. For while its strength and splendour have for

JUNCTION OF THE TILL AND THE GLEN.

ever fled, the humble sanctuary has renewed its youth; and, though the forms of faith suffer change, it has a good hope that in the far summers which we shall not see it will still be fulfilling its gracious and hallowed offices.

Within sight of Norham, on the opposite bank, amidst a delightful bit of woodland scenery, is the tiny village of Ladykirk, named, by a reversal of the usual order, from its church, dedicated to the Virgin, and built about the year 1500 by James IV. as a votive gift for his preservation from drowning while crossing a ford at this spot. Thus says tradition, which has so much to answer for. But the story is not improbable. There certainly was a ford here, which was more than usually dangerous when freshets were running; and James, though not a serious-minded or scrupulous man—being, indeed, one of those who prefer to indulge and repent rather than abstain—was not without an easy kind of piety. From Ladykirk onwards to Tillmouth, walking along the banks, there is a rapid succession of varied delights. On one side or the other, when not on both, the stream is edged with lovely copses; and the path, breast-high with tufted grass and tangled briar, runs past many a thicket beloved of the yellow linnet and the spotted thrush, and athwart many a glen where in simpler days fairies held their dainty revels and laid their sprightly plots.

The Till not only augments the waters, but adds to the beauties, of the Tweed. "The sullen Till," Scott calls it in his poetry; but here he is tuning his harp to a minor key to sing the disaster at Flodden; and he can mean no more by the uncomplimentary expression than

THE GLEN AT COUPLAND.

when in his prose he speaks of it as deep and slow. A very leisurely water it certainly is, and the country through which it flows—past Ewart Newtown, where it is joined by the Glen, which rises on the slopes of the Cheviots as Bowmont Water, and passes through scenery of which that at Coupland may be taken as typical—is not on the whole interesting. But the epithet is less than just if applied to its mouth and the reaches immediately below, for here it flows through a deep, winding, and gloriously wooded glen. On the peninsula where the streams meet and blend, stands a fragment of what was once "a chapel fair," dedicated to St. Cuthbert; for when the roving saint had tired of Melrose and induced his custodians to launch him upon the Tweed in a stone coffin, this "ponderous bark for river-tides" glided "light as gossamer" until it landed here. The coffin used to be shown in two pieces beside the ruin (it was broken by the saint's guardian spirits, to save it from being degraded to an ignoble use); and Sir Walter, who would appear to have seen it, says that it was finely shaped, and of such proportions that with very little assistance it might have floated. To "Tillmouth cell" it was that Clare was conveyed by the pious monk when some "base marauder's lance" had at once rid her of her persecutor and avenged the betrayal of Constance; and here she spent the night in prayer. And to Tillmouth also it was that Friar John was attached, that "blithesome brother at the can" who in evil hour "crossed the Tweed to teach Dame Alison her creed," and being interrupted in the exposition by her churl of a husband, and being on principle an enemy to strife, incontinently fled "sans frock and hood." A boon companion the worthy John must have been, but not a safe guide for Marmion or another, since—

"When our John hath quaffed his ale,
As little as the wind that blows
And warms itself against his nose,
Kens he, or cares, which way he goes."

The mere fragment which is all that is left of Twisell Castle stands high above the Till, near its mouth, overlooking Tillmouth House, embosomed in trees a little farther up the Till, and Twisell's "Gothic arch," the picturesque single-span bridge which the foolhardiness of James allowed the van of the English army to cross on the morning of Flodden. Begun in 1770 by Sir Francis Blake, the castle was in the builder's hands off and on for the space of forty years; but it was never completed, and never occupied, although Sir Walter, whose conscience failed him in the matter of castle-building, was pleased to praise it as "a splendid pile of Gothic architecture." William Heron, the castellan of Norham, was, as we have seen, "Baron of Twisell," but his chief seat was Ford Castle, farther up the Till, on the eastern bank; and it was here, and not at Holyrood, that, according to the original legend, which did not quite suit the poet's purpose, the Scottish king fell victim to Lady Heron's charms. The story goes that, having taken Norham and Wark, he had stormed Ford, and was only deterred from demolishing it by its fair castellan's blandishments; and the Scottish chroniclers represent Lady Heron as preening her feathers expressly that the susceptible monarch might lose his chance of striking an effective blow. The whole story is now known to be devoid of truth. The unromantic fact is that Lady Heron deceived neither her husband nor his captor. When the battle of Flodden was fought she was far enough away from Ford Castle, imploring Surrey to make terms with the King of Scotland for the safety of her husband. That James took the castle by storm is no doubt true, but when he departed for Flodden he set it on fire, which was about the worst he could do under the circumstances.

Although the castle which Lady Heron's husband extended and strengthened was sorely knocked about by the Scots in 1549, portions of it remain to this day. From the windows a clump of firs which crowns the Hill of Flodden, known as the "King's Chair," on the west bank of the Till, is clearly visible, as it is from the Tweed, from which it is only about three miles distant, to the south; and the present proprietress of the castle, the Marchioness of Waterford, has had a ride cut through the woods straight up the famous height. The chamber occupied by the king may still be seen, and through its large window he must on the fateful morning have looked across the Till upon the gleaming tents of his forces. The position was one of considerable strength; but James recklessly threw away this and every other advantage. Against the remonstrances and appeals of his wisest counsellors he refused to permit Borthwick to open fire upon the English van as it was crossing Twisell Bridge, and so allowed the enemy to cut off his base. And now that the time was come for holding his hand, he resolved to strike; so, firing his tents, he amid profound silence marched down, and the fight began. When night came to enforce a truce, Surrey was in doubt whether the battle was at an end. But the Scots had lost their king, and with him his natural son the boy-Archbishop of St. Andrews, and the flower, and much more than the flower, of their nobility and gentry, and even of the clergy, and there was nothing for them but to draw off under cover of the darkness and carry to their homes the news of the most disastrous blow their nation had ever suffered. Many long refused to believe that their beloved king had fallen, and stories got abroad of his having gone on pilgrimage to win forgiveness for his sin against his father on the inglorious field of Sauchie, but they vainly waited for his reappearance, and there is no reason to doubt that the "King's Stone" pretty accurately marks the spot where he fighting fell. When Sir Walter exclaims—

"Oh for one hour of Wallace wight,
Or well-skilled Bruce to rule the fight,
And cry 'St. Andrew and our right!'
Another sight had seen that morn,
From Fate's dark book a leaf been torn,
And Flodden had been Bannockbourne"—

we hear the patriot as well as the poet. Yet it is the truth that the Scots at Flodden fought no less valiantly than their ancestors had done at Bannockburn. But their king, though a gallant soldier, as in many respects he was a wise statesman, and, like most of his house, an accomplished man, was as bad a general as ever led brave men to destruction; while Surrey could not only head a charge, but play a cunning and wary game. It was not the first time the men had met. Ten years before, the English noble had handed to the Scottish king his bride, Margaret Tudor—then, a girl of fourteen, her mind teeming with dreams of imminent happiness; now, a sad and lonely woman, awaiting tidings of the strife betwixt her husband and her brother which all her tears and caresses had been impotent to avert.

At Coldstream, a couple of miles or so farther up the Tweed, pleasantly girdled with trees, we are still in the thick of military memories. Not far from where Smeaton's bridge gives a choice view both up and down stream is the first ford of any importance above Berwick. Here Edward I. crossed in 1296; here also Leslie and his Covenanters crossed in 1640 on their way south. At Coldstream, too, rather more than twenty years afterwards, the general who could make a king and hold his tongue disbanded his regiment as soldiers of the Commonwealth and re-embodied it as the Coldstream Guards before setting forth to undo the work in which the Covenanters had borne so large a share. It was by this ford, again, that Marmion, in his haste not to miss the fighting, made his perilous passage across the stream, having spent the night at Lennel's Convent, of which "one frail arch" is all that is left.

COLDSTREAM BRIDGE, FROM UP-STREAM.

A little above the spot "where to the Tweed Leat's eddies creep," on the southern bank, is a fragment of Wark Castle. According to Leland, it was "causid to be made" by Henry II. It twice repulsed attack at the hands of David I.; and when on the second occasion he had reduced it by blockade, he thought it well "to ding it doon." But it was rebuilt by Henry, and gave the Scots much further trouble before its final demolition—probably just after the union of the Crowns, when so many Border strongholds were dismantled. When, about the middle of the fourteenth century, David Bruce laid siege to it, the governor himself, Sir William Montague, mounted on a "wight" steed, penetrated the investing lines one dark and stormy night, and carried word to the king, Edward III., of what was happening at Wark, and so the siege was raised. The castle had been Edward's wedding-gift to the Earl of Salisbury, and the countess was here when he relieved it. She was naturally grateful, and her liege complacent; and the gossips say that in this wise began the romance of which one incident was the establishment of the Order of the Garter. The king was certainly in a perilous situation, for had he not just rescued the lady from one?

As the stream is traced upwards, the banks not seldom break into cliffs, the valley gains in breadth and richness, and away to the north the skyline is broken by the round top of Dunse Law. Nearly midway between Coldstream and Kelso the Tweed ceases to be the Border river, and enters the shire of Roxburgh, and a little higher up it takes toll of the "troutful Eden," which on its way

RUINS OF WARK CASTLE.

down from the slopes of Boon Hill has watered the village of Ednam (Edenham), where "the sweet poet of the year" was born. A couple of miles or so away to the south is Hadden Rig, scene of the fight between the English and Scottish Marchwardens in 1542. Sir Robert Bowes, Governor of Norham, had, with three thousand horse, ravaged a large part of Teviotdale, and was marching on Jedburgh, when he encountered George Gordon, Earl of Huntly, and, with several of his colleagues and many of his men, was taken prisoner. Fighting on the English side was the exiled Earl of Angus, who only by a desperate exercise of strength and activity escaped capture and the traitor's doom which would inevitably have followed.

THE TWEED.

CHAPTER II.

FROM KELSO TO TWEEDSWELL.

Kelso and its Abbey—Roxburgh Castle—Floors Castle—The Teviot—Ancrum—Carlenrig—The Ale—The Jed and Jedburgh—Mertoun—Smailholm Tower and Sandyknowe—Eildon and Sir Michael Scott—Dryburgh—The Leader and Thomas the Rhymer—Melrose—Skirmish Hill—Abbotsford—The Ettrick and the Yarrow—Ashestiel—Innerleithen—Horsburgh Castle—Peebles—Neidpath—Manor—Drummelzier—The Crook Inn—Tweedswell.

WHEN Burns came to Kelso in the spring of 1787, and stood upon the bridge which preceded Rennie's fine piece of work, he is said to have reverently uncovered his head and breathed a prayer to the Almighty. A less religious nature than his might well have been moved to the devotional mood, for there can be few scenes so charged with inspiring and exalting influences. If Leyden did not quite hit the mark in saying of the Tweed here that she "her silent way majestic holds," it is only because she chants as she goes: august her course certainly is, for she rolls broad and brisk, and flows into queenly curves. On the one hand is Sir George Douglas's place, Springwood Park, the entrance dignified by some glorious bronze beeches; on the other are the stately ruins of the Abbey; and beyond, the town, neat and clean, gleaming white in the sunshine. Up stream, full in front, stands the palatial Floors Castle, not far from where the Teviot pours its hurrying tide into the Tweed; below bridge the spacious current ripples between thickly wooded banks. The town itself has many interests, modern as well as ancient. For some months towards the end of last century a boy, slightly lame, and much given to poring over old romances, attended the old grammar-school adjacent to the abbey, and still carried on there, though in a new building; and here began that acquaintance with the Ballantynes which was to have such ruinous issues. With another true minstrel also, though one who sings in a lower key, the town has associations. The Free Church, one of the white spired edifices visible from the bridge, was built for Horatius Bonar, who during a long ministry here wrote some sacred songs which men will not soon let die. Against the Free Church nothing need be urged except its newness; but the parish church—octagonal, with a huge slated roof, divided into as many sections—is a building of simply audacious uncouthness, a sight to make "sair eyes." It has been said to be the ugliest parish church in Scotland, and the statement might be amplified and still remain true. During the eighteenth century the parishioners were pleased to commend themselves to the divine mercy in the dismantled abbey, a low vault having been thrown over the transept; while right overhead, under a roof of thatch, certain of their fellows were all the while enduring the rigours of human justice. This felicitous arrangement survived until about 1771, when one Sunday the falling of a lump of plaster from the roof sent the congregation scampering out with the words of an oracular prophecy attributed to Thomas the Rhymer ringing in their ears. Then they set up this detestable building, fashioned in the style of an auction mart, within a stone's-throw of the venerable walls in which they were too superstitious longer to assemble themselves together!

The remains of the Abbey are not considerable, consisting of a part of the central tower, about half of the west front, bits of the transept walls, and some fragments of the choir. The style is an interesting mixture of Romanesque and Early Pointed; thus there are round-headed doorways with zigzag mouldings, and series of those intersecting arches which mark the transition from the one style to the other; while the two surviving arches that support the central tower are Early Pointed. Less graceful than the remains of Melrose Abbey, which are much later, they have a massive dignity distinctly superior to those of Dryburgh, which come nearer to them in style. In Burton's opinion, there was no other building in all Scotland which bore so close a resemblance to a Norman castle. It was of course its position in the Debateable Land which prompted its builders to invest it with such strength and solidity. And the days came when it needed all its power of resistance, and more besides, since it often had to bear the brunt of battering-ram, of cannon-shot, and of the still more deadly faggot. Its visitations culminated in 1545, the year when the Earl of Hertford, better known as the Protector Somerset, made his terrible descent upon the northern kingdom. On this occasion it was bravely held by about a hundred defenders, including a dozen of its monks; but it was breached and stormed, and "as many Scots slain as were within." Thus it came about that there was only a remnant of the brotherhood left for the Reformers to expel fifteen years later; and the iconoclasts on principle must have found the wrecking of the building an easy enough task. When the vast possessions of the monastery came to be dealt with, the prudence, if not the generosity, of James VI. reminded him that he had favourites. In the previous reign the abbacy had been conferred upon James Stuart, one of the king's natural sons, while others of his bastards battened upon the revenues of divers other abbeys. On its practical side, it is clear, the Reformation came none too soon.

The Abbey of Kelso, like those at Melrose and Jedburgh, and several more in other parts of Scotland, owes its foundation to David I., the pious son of a pious mother—"St." David, as he is often called. Standing at his tomb at Dunfermline, the first of the Jameses, whose taste ran to poetry rather than to piety, and to pursuits yet more frivolous, is said to have uttered the much-quoted remark that his predecessor was "ane sair sanct for the Crown," thinking the while of the revenues which had been alienated to religious uses. The reflection is generally taken seriously, but the wisest of the Stuarts must have meant it at least as much in jest as in earnest. David was, in truth, anything but an ignorant, impulsive fanatic. His training at the refined court of Henry I. had rubbed off "the rust of Scottish barbarity," as an outspoken English annalist puts it; and coming to his kingship an educated and accomplished man, he set about reducing his rude realm to order and civilisation; and in fulfilment of this mission castles were built, burghs erected, and religious establishments founded. Those were the palmy days of monasticism, when religious houses had not come to be filled with ecclesiastics of the type of Friar John of Tillmouth, and the Abbot of Kennaquhair in the "Monastery;" and if it can be said of St. David that "he succeeded in reducing a wild part of Scotland to order," it is chiefly because he gave so powerful a stimulus to the agencies of the Church.

KELSO, WITH RENNIE'S BRIDGE.

Between Kelso Abbey and Roxburgh Castle, represented by a small fragment on a ridge just where the Teviot and the Tweed mingle their waters, a close connection is to be traced, for the fortress was once a royal residence, inhabited by St. David himself; and when his one son Henry died within its walls, the body was borne into the church, and there with solemn pomp interred. And when three centuries later James II., at a spot said to be marked by the large holly near the margin of the Tweed, was killed by the bursting of "The Lion" while attempting to wrest the castle from the hands of the English, his son was carried by the nobles into the abbey to be crowned. The catastrophe turned out well neither for the castle nor for its English defenders; for when it occurred, the queen, Mary of Gueldres, held up her boy of seven in view of the troops, and the assault was resumed with such fury that Lord Falconburg had to capitulate. The castle had often been taken by the English, and now, in the exasperation of the Scots at the loss of their king, it was torn stone from stone. Even then it was not to avoid further associations of the same hateful kind, for after the battle of Pinkie in 1547, when the Scots had to smart for their triumph at Ancrum two years before, the

Protector Somerset formed a camp among the ruins, and compelled the neighbouring country to come in and pay tribute and "take assurance." It was in carrying out his mission of exacting submission from the recalcitrant that honest Stawarth Bolton visited the mourning Elspeth Brydone at Glendearg, and thought to console her for the loss of her husband by offering himself as his successor. The ancient town which grew up in the shadow of the castle has been literally anni-

DRYBURGH ABBEY, FROM THE EAST.

hilated; the present village of Roxburgh is a little further eastwards. Floors Castle, the princely seat of the Duke of Roxburghe, stands on the north bank of the stream, fronted by a spacious lawn. It was built by Vanbrugh, but was transformed to something approximating the Tudor type by Playfair, the Edinburgh architect. Judged by Vanbrugh's achievements elsewhere, the change was most likely an improvement; but the effect has been to give the fabric a composite look which does not appreciate its other attractions—its superb situation, its magnificent proportions, its undeniable air of distinction.

Something must, in passing, be said of the Teviot, so full of history, of legend, of folk-song, and of romance, and endowed with such various and abundant beauty. Its most romantic association is with Branxholm Hall, cradle of the House of Buccleuch—the "Branksome Hall" where the "nine-and-twenty knights of fame" hung their shields; now a comely family residence, with the ancient tower for nucleus, standing on a steep bank north of the stream, about three miles from Hawick, the town where Sir Alexander Ramsay was captured by the Knight of Liddesdale, to be cruelly starved to death in the dungeon of Hermitage Castle. Denholm, birthplace of Leyden, with Rubershaw, and many another spot, must be passed over. But at Ancrum Moor we must give ourselves pause for a little, for here in 1545 the Scots "took amends" on the most ruthless and destructive raiders who ever crossed the Tweed. In 1544 Sir Ralph Evers, Governor of Berwick, with Sir Brian Latoun, had made an incursion in the course of which, according to Evers' own inventory, the "towns, towers, barnekynes, parysche churches, bastill houses" which they "burned and destroyed" amounted to 192; while of cattle they had "lifted" 10,386, of "shepe" 12,492, and of nags and geldings 1,296—and these are only some of the details. For these achievements a grateful monarch made Evers a lord of Parliament, and he was celebrated in song as one who, having "burned the Merse and Teviotdale," still was ready "to prick the Scot." The praise was well deserved, for the next year he and Sir Brian made another raid, and beat their record. Returning towards Jedburgh, laden with booty, they were followed by Angus and by Norman Leslie, and while they were halting on Ancrum Moor, Sir Walter Scott of Buccleuch came up with a body of retainers. He had a long account to settle. The outworks of his Castle of Branxholm had been burned; all his lands in West Teviotdale and on Kale Water had been harried; and the Moss Tower, near the junction of Kale with Teviot, had been made "to smoke sore." By his counsel Angus took up a position on the piece of low ground called Peniel Heugh, and having drawn the invaders into ambush, an easy victory was won. Evers and Latoun both fell, and a thousand prisoners were made. The scene of the battle is also known as Lilliard's Edge, from the "fair maiden Lillyard," who took part in the fight, and "when her legs were cutted off" by the English louns, "fought upon her stumps." The column on the hill, visible for miles along the valley of the Tweed, as well as in Teviotdale, has nothing to do with this lady's heroism, nor with the Scottish victory, but, as the peasantry are surprised to be told, commemorates the Battle of Waterloo.

RUINS OF ROXBURGH CASTLE.

Another place on the Teviot, Carlenrig, not far from the source, near the Dumfries border, is celebrated as the scene of Johnnie Armstrang's execution in the course of James V.'s hanging and hunting expedition. His keep was at Hole House, in Eskdale; but at the head of thirty-six bravely attired horsemen he came to Teviotdale and presented himself to the king, expecting to be received with favour. When James ordered him and his merry men to instant execution, he is represented as making a variety of large offers for pardon—as that he would bring in by a certain day, either quick or dead, any English subject, were he duke, earl, or baron, whom the king might name. But, his terms being all rejected, he said proudly, "It is folly to seek grace at a graceless face." So—

"John murdered was at Carlinrigg,
And all his gallant companie;
But Scotland's heart was ne'er sae wae
To see sae mony brave men die."

Among the Teviot's vassal-streams are the Ale, whose "foaming tide" William of Deloraine swam in his night ride to Melrose; and the brawling Jed, which gives its name to the royal burgh on its banks—famous for "Jethart staves," a species of battle-axe, and for "Jethart justice," the equivalent of "Lydford law" in the West of England. One of those who came into the hangman's hands at Jedburgh was Rattling Roaring Willie, the jovial harper at whose feet the "last minstrel" sat, with such excellent results. He could not brook that the tongue of the scoffer—

"Should tax his minstrelsy with wrong,
Or call his song untrue:
For this, when they the goblet plied,
And such rude taunt had chafed his pride,
The bard of Reull he slew.
On Teviot's side in fight they stood,
And tuneful hands were stained with blood,"

and so forth. But the minstrel's memory had etherealised the facts. The squalid prose of the story is that a drunken brawl arose at Newmill, on the Teviot, between Willie and a rival from Rule Water, known as Sweet Milk; that they fought it out there and then; and that Sweet Milk was slain on the spot.

Above Kelso—to return, with apologies, to the Tweed—the valley opens out, and the trees grow thicker, while the larch and the fir begin to come more into evidence. At Mertoun House, Lord Polwarth's seat, environed with groves, one of those Introductions to the cantos of "Marmion" which so hamper the movement of the poem, while they contain some of the poet's finest lines, is dated. Sir Walter was passing Christmas here, and even then, when the boughs were all leafless, "Mertoun's halls" were fair. In another of the Introductions much that is interesting in a biographical sense is said about the large gabled tower which, as it stands four-square to all the winds that blow, is one of the most prominent objects in the landscape for miles along the valley. It is the Smailholm

MELROSE ABBEY, FROM THE SOUTH-EAST.

Tower of the mystical "Eve of St. John," and is built among a cluster of crags a few miles north of the stream, in the parish which contains Sandyknowe, a farm-house leased by Sir Walter's paternal grandfather from Scott of Harden. Thus it happened that from his third to his eighth year young Walter was often sojourning in the parish of Smailholm; and long afterwards, as the shattered tower and crags amid which the "lonely infant" had strayed and mused until the fire burned, rose up before him in vision, he confessed the poetic impulse which came to him in this "barren scene and wild." The tower, anciently the property of the Pringles of Whytbank, now of Lord Polwarth, is a typical Border peel—not a castle, but simply a large square keep of enormous strength, the walls being nine feet thick; the chambers built over one another in three storeys, with communication by a narrow circular stair; the roof a platform; the whole enclosed by an outer wall. Much nearer the river, on the other side, is another Border strength, Littledean Tower, the keep of the Kers of Nenthorn; and close at hand stands the old shaft of the village cross, where in more stirring days than these, at the "jowing" of the bell, the men of the barony, armed with sword and lance, and sometimes with a "Jethart stave" (the Scots never took kindly to the twanging of the yew), would assemble in their hundreds to guard their own byres, or, mounted on their vigorous little ponies, to prick across the Border to empty their neighbours', and belike to ruin them "stoop and roop."

The huge three-coned hill which can be seen from below Kelso, and remains in sight for many miles, although it is constantly shifting from left to right, from front to rear, so mazy is the way of the stream, is, of course, the famous Eildon. Tradition says that it was split into three by the magician Scott, not Sir Walter of that ilk, but "the wondrous Michael," more formally, Sir Michael Scott of Balwearie. Indeed, most of the more striking phenomena in these parts are ascribed to "Auld Michael" when they are not credited to "Auld Nickie" or Sir William Wallace. The theory is that he was under the constant necessity of finding employment for a spirit with an enormous appetite for work. On one occasion he bade him "bridle the Tweed with a curb of stone;" and the dam-head at Kelso, constructed in a single night, was the result. The division of Eildon into three was another night's task; and it was not till he had set the industrious demon making ropes out of sea-sand that he himself could find any rest. If these incidents have a legendary look about them, it is certain that Sir Michael himself was no myth. He was profoundly versed in all the learning of the Dark Age; and it is probable that he was one of the ambassadors who sailed "to Noroway o'er the faem" to bring about the return of Alexander's fair daughter. If he was less of a magician than his distant descendant, it was through no fault of his own. He was a diligent student of all the abstruse sciences, and wrote freely about them; and he was credited with uncanny attributes by the learned as well as by the vulgar of his day. While Sir Walter was in Italy he was complaining that the great Florentine had thought none but Italians worthy of being sent to hell. He was reminded that he of all men had no right to grumble, since his ancestor figures among the magicians and soothsayers of the "Inferno."

MELROSE ABBEY: THE EAST WINDOW.

However Eildon got its present shape, it forms a singularly picturesque object in the landscape. And the scene that lies rolled out before anyone who chooses to climb either of the summits is one of the fairest that mortal eye ever rested upon. To the south the view is bounded only by "Cheviot's mountains lone;" to the north, by the Lammermoors; eastwards, the Tweed valley, lustrous in its vesture of green of many shades, spreads itself out for miles beyond Dryburgh and St. Boswell's, although the stream itself, from its way of hiding itself between deep and woody banks, is constantly vanishing from sight; westwards, beyond Abbotsford, to give variety to the view, the valley is less luxuriant, and the hills are larger, and instead of being divided into trim fields and meadows, or covered to their tops with bonny birks and hazels, present an unbroken surface of pasture-land, relieved only by patches of broom. To the south-west the outlying Ettricks keep ward over the valley where the shepherd-poet roamed and dreamed; full in view to the north-west, at the foot of the lovely Gala Water, is busy, brand-new Galashiels, blotting the blue with its smoke, and in other ways as well "sinning its gifts;" while nestling at the foot of the hill is Melrose, now a town rejoicing in "suburbs" and a hydropathic institution.

The glory of Dryburgh Abbey is its situation and immediate surroundings, in which it is certainly superior to Melrose, and even to Kelso. To get to it you leave the public highway, cross the water, and presently pace along a shady avenue, to find it at last bosomed in trees, seated on a grassy flat that slopes gently down to the river, whose music may be heard as its waves ripple by, almost insulating the site—for nowhere, perhaps, does the Tweed curl into so many loops as between Mertoun and Abbotsford. And Nature, not content with furnishing an incomparable situation and almost incomparable surroundings, has done her best with ivy and other creeping plants to hide the scars left by the hands of violent men. What now meets the eye is the western gable of the nave, a gable of the south transept, with a five-light window, and a bit of the choir and north transept—sufficient to show that the abbey was much smaller than either of its neighbours. The transept and choir are First, the nave—rebuilt in the first half of the fourteenth century—Second, Pointed, while the conventual buildings, south of the abbey, show the transition from Romanesque to Pointed. At Melrose there is not a vestige of the monastic buildings left; here they are in better preservation than the Abbey itself. The most perfect of them is the chapter-house, over against which are some immemorial yews. The founder was Hugh de Morville, Lord of Lauderdale and Constable of Scotland; the stone—an obdurate brownish sandstone—was hewn from the quarry on the Dryburgh estate which yielded its substance also for Melrose. Ravished and burnt by Edward II., the monastery was at once rebuilt, partly at the charges of Robert the Bruce. Then it was burnt by Richard II.; but it was not actually ruined until the devastating wars which broke out in the reigns of James IV. and V., when it was twice ravaged by Evers and Latoun, and once by the Earl of Hertford, who left it much as we now see it, save for the healing work of Nature and of Time. One feature of the ruins to which a peculiar interest attaches is the gloomy vault in which the "nun of Dryburgh" for years immured herself, never quitting it until dark, returning to it at midnight, and persisting in this strange mode of life until at last the night came which had no morrow, when they buried her in the adjoining graveyard. She never explained herself, but the common belief was that she had vowed never to look upon the sun during the absence of her lover, who came not back, having fallen in the affair of '45.

How it came to pass that the dust of "Waverley" lies in St. Mary's aisle we know from Allan Cunningham. When Sir Walter was stricken down in 1819, and was believed to be at the point of death, the Earl of Buchan, the eleventh of his line, made a somewhat fussy though well-intended appeal to Lady Scott to prevail upon her husband to be buried here beside his forbears the Haliburtons of Newmains, to whom the abbey once belonged; and Sir Walter, without seeming greatly impressed, promised that the earl should have the refusal of his bones, since he seemed so solicitous. Things, however, did not shape themselves quite as the nobleman had anticipated. Sir Walter recovered, and the earl had for three years been sleeping with his ancestors in St. Moden's Chapel before that sad September day when the writer whose nimble pen had traced its last word was borne here, and sorrowfully laid beside his wife, whom six years earlier he had followed to the same hallowed resting-place. In the chapel now lie his eldest son, Colonel Sir Walter Scott, and Lockhart, his "son-in-law, biographer, and friend." The aisle, it should be added, contains the dust of other families of note, including the Haigs of Bemerside, who have flourished there ever since the days of Malcolm IV., and who form the subject of one of the barbarous couplets said to have been written by Thomas the Rhymer before—all too tardily—he was appropriated by the fairies.

The Earl of Buchan spoken of above had a weakness for setting up monuments, and in indulging it he showed more public spirit than good taste. Close by his suspension bridge he built "an Ionic temple" of red sandstone, with a statue of Apollo under the dome, and a bust of Thomson perched on the top. As time went on, the statue was so much damaged (it may be hoped that something higher than a spirit of destructiveness was the motive of the image-breaking) that it had to be removed, though the bust still holds its place. A furlong or two up the stream, on a thickly timbered eminence, facing the Border, he put up a colossal statue of Wallace, hewn out of the same incongruous material, but painted white, though the paint has long since vanished. Wallace suffered many things during his life, but it was not a Sassenach who did this.

Between Dryburgh and Melrose the Tweed is swollen by Leader's "silver tide" from the Lammermoors. On the banks of this water St. Cuthbert tented his flocks in the days of his youth; while at Earlston—formerly Ercildoune—two miles above the confluence, lived Thomas the Rhymer, whose surname appears to have been Lermont or Learmount, and who is believed to have lived in a castle of which a tower is still shown. There is no doubt that Thomas had a real existence; but whether he posed as a prophet, and had commerce with the fairies, and was finally spirited away by a hart and hind that were seen calmly parading the village, is more questionable. The poet, however, is clear enough about it all. With much detail he tells how, when the message came to the Rhymer to follow the deer, he "soon his cloaths did on," and—

> "First he waxe pale and then waxe red,
> Never a word he spake but three:
> 'My sand is run; my thread is spun:
> This sign regardeth me.'"

Then, having bidden farewell to the Leader, he crossed the flood and was seen no more of men.

ABBOTSFORD.

With the situation of St. Mary's Abbey Dorothy Wordsworth was fain to avow herself disappointed. When she came to Melrose she found it "almost surrounded by insignificant houses," which is even truer now than it was then; and she adds that even when viewed from a distance the position did not seem happy, for the church was not close to the river, "so that you do not look upon them as companions to each other." This has been rebuked as "somewhat captious;" but one presumes to think it nothing of the kind. In itself, however, the Abbey is fair beyond description; it would be as difficult to adversely criticise as it is to adequately praise it. To justly appreciate its proportions, graceful and imposing even in its ruin, and with the central tower bereft of its rood-spire, it should be seen from one of the summits of Eildon; yet its details, when minutely scrutinised on the spot, are still more admirable. Burns, before his time in his appreciation of Gothic architecture as in some other things, speaks of it as "a glorious ruin;" to Sir Walter's mind it was "the finest specimen of Gothic architecture and Gothic sculpture which Scotland can boast." It is, in sooth, one of the crowning achievements of the Gothic, with most of its merits and almost none of its faults. Exuberantly ornamented, it never oversteps the thin line which separates richness from redundancy. Even the great east window, built after Richard II.'s devastations in 1385, when the Gothic had passed its prime, has a grace and harmony which justify all the admiration usually accorded to its size; while it is preserved from the stiffness which is the besetting sin of the Perpendicular by the foliaged tracery that knits the long mullions together. The window in the south transept, also in five lights, is, however, to be preferred before it, although considerably smaller; it is in the Second Pointed, or Decorated style, to which the greater part of the ruin belongs, and the lines into which its mullions flow are of indescribable loveliness. The carving on capital and corbel, on boss and buttress, has an elaborate yet dainty beauty such as is seldom met with on either side of the Tweed, and must of a truth be the work of hands that were made cunning by love of art and patient by a sense of pious duty.

The first Abbey of Melrose, built of oak and thatched with reeds, occupied a nearly insulated site two miles down the river, where the village of Old Melrose now stands. It was a "Chaldee" foundation, as Mrs. Dods would say—was founded by Aidan of Lindisfarne, was the home of the St. Boisil after whom St. Boswell's is named, as well as of St. Cuthbert, was destroyed by Kenneth, after an existence of three hundred years, and, though rebuilt, sank into decay and ruin. Then, five hundred years after St. Aidan, came St. David, who, when the new monastery had been built, brought, Cistercian monks from Rievaulx to fill it. Its experiences at the hands of the second Edward and the second Richard, of Evers and Latoun, and of Hertford, were identical with those of Drybargh, and the dismal story need not be repeated. After the Reformation a part of the nave was used as the parish church, a barbarous wall of brick being put up at the west end, rising into an equally sightly vault to keep out the weather. Although these additions are a grievous eyesore, it was rightly decided, when early in the present century a church was built, to let them be, lest their removal should leave the ruins less secure. In 1832 these were repaired, and the circumstance that the Duke of Buccleuch allowed Sir Walter Scott to superintend the work is guarantee that it was done with a tender and reverent hand. The bell which counted the slow hours for the drowsy monks still tells the time, with quite as much accuracy as could be expected or desired.

To the cloisters access is had by a low door at the north-east end of the nave—the entrance through which William of Deloraine was led to the wizard's grave. One of the tombs bears an incongruous printed label, "Michael Scott;" but the identification rests on evidence which would not even satisfy an antiquary—on nothing else, in truth, than the story of the "last minstrel," who was not scrupulous as to matters of fact. Nor is there anything but tradition to show that the magician was buried in the Abbey at all. In this instance, moreover, tradition is divided against itself, for one story has it that he was interred in the monastery founded by St. Waltheof at Holme Coltrame, in Cumberland. In one particular, however, the stories agree: they both aver that the magic books were buried with the wizard, or preserved in the monastery where he died; and here we have the hint of which Sir Walter has made such splendid use in the "Lay." There has been much controversy, by the way, over the question whether the ruins were ever explored by Scott by moonlight. Old John Bower, who for many years was the keeper of the abbey, maintained that he could never have done so, since he had never borrowed the key from him at night; and a verse has been quoted from Sir Walter himself against those who find it hard to believe that the sweetest lines in the "Lay" were not written from "personal experience":—

> "Then go and muse with deepest awe
> On what the writer never saw,
> Who would not wander 'neath the moon
> To see what he could see at noon."

The lines are not characteristic, and probably are not genuine. But whether Scott was "too practical a man to go poking about the ruins by moonlight," as Tom Moore contended, or was not, is surely a trivial and even irrelevant question. If Scott never saw the Abbey except when it was being flouted by "the gay beams of lightsome day," it does not follow that the passage is mere moonshine. Peradventure it is poetry.

Other doubtful interments here, besides that of the magician, are those of Alexander II. and his queen Joanna. But probably the Abbey does contain the heart of the great Bruce, believed to have been deposited here, in fulfilment of the king's written wish, after Douglas's unsuccessful attempt to bear it to the Holy Land. Nor is it open to doubt that some of the Douglases themselves came here to rest after their stormful lives. The doughty earl who was slain at Otterburn was not "buried at the braken bush," as says the ballad, but beneath the high altar of this Abbey. Hither also was borne Sir William Douglas, the so-called Flower of Chivalry, when Ramsay's murder had been inadequately avenged on Williamhope, betwixt Tweed and Yarrow, by Sir William's godson and chieftain, William Earl of Douglas. It was the wanton defacing of these tombs that nerved the arm of Angus at Ancrum Moor; and when one remembers the scathe wrought upon and within these walls by Lord Evers, it seems to be of the very essence of irony that this should be his place of sepulture. Yet it was not in scorn that he was interred amid the evidences of his destructiveness, but as a mark of honour to a brave albeit pitiless foe.

In the churchyard, under the fifth window of the nave, is the tomb of a modern worthy, Sir David Brewster, who lived at Allerly, near Gattonside, and died in 1868. Elsewhere is the grave of faithful Tom Purdie, marked by a monument raised by Scott himself, from whose pen proceeded the inscription. "In grateful remembrance," runs this model epitaph, "of his faithful and attached service of twenty-two years, and in sorrow for the loss of a humble but sincere friend." Poor Tom! he could not have gone about with a prepossessing aspect if he sat for Cristal Nixon in "Redgauntlet." Yet when he was brought before Sir Walter on a charge of poaching, and with mingled pathos and humour set forth his hardships and temptations—a wife and children dependent upon him, work scarce, and grouse abundant—the Sheriff's heart was touched; so Tom, instead of being haled off to prison, was taken on as shepherd, and afterwards made bailiff. Sir Walter was not infallible. He was grossly imposed upon by the Flemish guide at Waterloo. But perhaps no one ever lived who better understood the Lowland peasant; and in this instance he had no reason to question his insight. Purdie identified himself with all Scott's concerns, talked of "our trees" as the plantation at Abbotsford proceeded, and of "our buiks" as the novels came out, and never ceased to amuse his generous master with his quaint humour, or to gratify him by his efficient service.

A little above the centre of the town the stream is crossed by a suspension foot-bridge, which connects Melrose with Gattonside, granted to the Abbey by its founder, and still celebrated for its orchards. The footpath which follows the windings of the river, with wooded slopes on either hand, leads past Skirmish Hill, at Darnick, the scene of the "Battle of Melrose," one of many consequences of the disaster at Flodden, which left the realm with a king in long clothes. The gallant attempt made at the king's own suggestion, and in his presence, by Sir Walter Scott of Buccleuch, to cut the leading-strings in which the Douglases insisted upon keeping the high-spirited monarch, was frustrated by the inopportune return of the lairds of Cessford and Fairnyhurst, and Buccleuch and his men had to flee for their lives.

In the neighbourhood of the picturesque bridge which carries the Galashiels road across the river, and gives the passing traveller a glimpse both up and down stream which must make him hunger for more, is the site of the curious old drawbridge, if so it may be called, which belonged to the Pringles of Galashiels, afterwards of Whytbank, and consisted of three octangular towers or pillars, from the centre one of which the ward would, for a consideration, lay out planks, and so extemporise an elevated footway. It was this service which Peter refused to do for the sacristan of Kennaquhair when the holy man was bearing to the monastery the Lady of Avenel's heretical book. "Riding the water" on a moonlit night, he thought, would do the monk no harm; and so, though a "heavy water" was running, Father Philip had to ford the stream, with results so discomforting and mysterious. It was not only with Peter and his laird that the monks of St. Mary's had disputes. Even when the monastery was founded they were not quite unsusceptible to sports dear to the profane, for in the charter which gave them rights of forestry it was thought necessary to except hunting and the taking of falcons. As they waxed sleek they did not grow less selfish, or less tenacious of their rights; and so there was much contention between them and their neighbours, whose opinion about them sometimes found vent in catches of poetry. The men of God do not appear to have retaliated in verse. But there was the pulpit, and there were penances.

Betwixt this point and Abbotsford the Alwyn and Gala Waters flow in—the one babbling down a glen which is in parts prettily wooded, and is recognised as the Glendearg where the Lady of Avenel spent the sad years of her widowhood; the other reeking with the chemical abominations of Galashiels. As the ascent is continued, the valley grows somewhat less rich in beauty, nor is it improved by the flaring red houses which look down upon Abbotsford from the slopes on the opposite bank. When Sir Walter acquired the estate—or, rather, the first bit of it—it must have been much less attractive than now. It was then a farm, a hundred acres in extent, and there was hardly a tree upon it. He was his own architect; and it was one of his boasts that there was not one of the trees which had not been planted under his direction. The house for which he is thus to be held responsible is scarcely imposing, nor can it be said to have the merit of consistency. You can see at a glance that it grew, rather than was made. On the whole, it is pleasing to the eye rather than to the architectural sense; and if, as has been said, its gables and sections and windows and turrets and towers are a little bewildering in their multitude and variety, one still ventures to think that it is better as it is, plentiful as may be its lack of plan, than it would be if it conformed more strictly to the conventional castellated type.

The interests of Abbotsford are many and great. It is indeed "a romance in stone and lime," every outline, as Lockhart says, with little exaggeration, "copied from some old baronial edifice in Scotland, every roof and window blazoned with clan bearings, or the lion rampant gules, or the heads of the ancient Stuart kings." And Sir Walter was from his earliest years a diligent gleaner of curiosities; so that, apart from many precious mementoes of himself, the rooms which the Hon. Mrs. Constable Maxwell Scott, his great-grand-daughter, throws open to the public, form a museum of the rarest interest. But, after all, it is chiefly the desire to make acquaintance with the scenes amid which the sanest and shrewdest of our great writers since Shakespeare spent the most eventful years of his blameless life that draws to Abbotsford its crowds of pilgrims. It was here that he wrote most of his works; here that he met the great disaster of his life in a spirit which showed in combination the loftiest chivalry and the nicest commercial integrity; here that he piously submitted himself to the stroke of death. The story of his return to Abbotsford to die is full of pathos. "As we rounded the hill at Ladhope, and the outline of the Eildons burst on him," says his biographer, "he became greatly excited; and when . . . his eye caught at length his own towers . . . he sprang up with a cry of delight." Then they bore him into the dining-room, and his dogs "began to fawn upon him and lick his hands, and he alternately sobbed and smiled over them until sleep oppressed him." The next day he felt better, he said, and might disappoint the doctors after all. But his strength continued to leave him, and he was often delirious and unconscious. One day, about two months after his return, he sent for his son-in-law, who found him with eye "clear and calm," though in the last extreme of feebleness. "Lockhart," he said, "I may have but a minute to speak to you. My dear, be a good man—be virtuous, be religious—be a good man.

GALASHIELS.

Nothing else will give you any comfort when you come to lie here." These were almost his last words. Four days afterwards he breathed his last, in the presence of all his children. "It was a beautiful day—so warm that every window was open, and so perfectly still that the sound of all others most delicious to his ear, the gentle ripple of the Tweed over its pebbles, was distinctly audible as we knelt around the bed, and his eldest son kissed and closed his eyes." Surely this man died "in the odour of sanctity" as truly as Waltheof of Melrose or any tonsured saint of them all.

The Ettrick, which joins the Tweed not a great way above Abbotsford, no longer flows through a "feir foreste;" where once there was "grete plentie" of hart and hind, of doe and roe, mighty flocks of sheep now graze. Of Ettrick House, where the pastoral poet was born; of Thirlestane Castle, the strength of "Ready, aye ready" John Scott; of Tushielaw, where another of the Scotts, Adam of that ilk, was hanged by the king who had no mercy for Johnnie Armstrang; of Carter haugh, where the "fair Janet" met "young Tamlane," and by strength of love won him from the thraldom of the Fairy Queen; of Selkirk, whose burly "souters" (*sutors*) gave so good an account of themselves at Flodden Field—of all this there is no space to speak. Nor can there be anything but barest mention of the Yarrow, whose bonnie holms and dowie dens were dear to Wordsworth and other modern poets, as they were to the old folk-singers of the Border. St. Mary's lone and silent lake, with its swans that "float double;" Henderland, where Cockburne's widow mourned her knight "sae dear;" Dryhope, where the "Flower of Yarrow" was wooed and won by Walter Scott of Harden; Newark's stately tower, where the last minstrel's trembling fingers tuned his harp and swept its strings—these and other scenes must all be left unnoticed. But the Yarrow is perhaps the most benign of Border streams, and it has inspired the sweetest and saddest of Border songs, not excepting even the "Flowers of the Forest," or "Annan Water." And of them all, none is more sad or sweet than that which tells the story of the Baron of Oakwood, who was slain on its "dowie banks," and there found by his "ladye gaye."

> "She kissed his cheek, she kaimed his hair,
> She searched his wounds all thorough;
> She kissed them till her lips grew red
> On the dowie howms of Yarrow."

It is near Philiphaugh that Yarrow and Ettrick wed—Philiphaugh, famed for its memories of Outlaw Murray, and still more for the crushing defeat which Montrose here suffered at the hands of David Leslie. The most princely of apostates was taken completely by surprise, and the men who until now had carried all before them were fleeing for their lives before he could strike a blow. Leslie is said to have butchered many of his prisoners in cold blood, some being shot in the court-yard of Newark Castle, while others were precipitated from a high bridge over the Tweed. It would be pleasant to believe that the story is not true, or is at all events exaggerated. The latter part of it is certainly inaccurate, if not wholly false, for in those days there was no bridge over the Tweed in this region. Sir Walter, however, was at the trouble to point out that there is a bridge over the Ettrick only four miles from Philiphaugh, and another over the Yarrow, either of which might have been the scene of the massacre.

Above Clovenfords, celebrated for its vines, the Tweed has burrowed for itself deeper banks, while the valley broadens; and if the braes amid which it insinuates itself are less cultivated, and not so thickly wooded, the water itself moves more swiftly and sings more cheerily, and shines more lucidly than ever, displaying the tawniest of beds. Presently the emulous Cadon Water flows in, and then comes Ashestiel, an earlier residence of Sir Walter, where most of the cantos of the "Lay" and of "Marmion" were written. West of Thornilees stands a fragment of one of many ruined peels which line the stream on both sides, forming an unbroken line of communication, for they were sufficiently close together for the fire-bale's warnings to be passed on from one to another. Beyond this the valley contracts, as the stream winds round a great hill fertile of little but screes, but before long it again opens out; and then comes the solitary bit of prosaic scenery of which the Tweed is guilty. The braes on either side, though not lofty, are nothing but uncomely sheep-walks; the banks themselves are utterly commonplace. The interval, however, is a brief one, and almost before the stranger has recovered from his surprise at finding the bonny water so demeaning itself, he is once more raised to the admiring mood. For he is now at Innerleithen, nicely placed on the lower slopes of an enormous brae, where Leithen Water comes down from the Moorfoot Hills to keep tryst with Tweed. Here are mineral springs, with properties not dissimilar from those of the Harrogate Wells; and to drink the waters of these "filthy puddles," in a more or less serious spirit, many in summer come this way. The good people of the town will not need to be told that for the opprobrious expression here quoted no one but Mrs. Dods is responsible. For when one of the least pleasing, though not the least powerful, of the "Waverley" books saw the light, Innerleithen made haste to identify itself with the *locus in quo;* the St. Ronan's Club was started; and the St. Ronan's games are still kept up. The incident was not a bad thing for Innerleithen, and Sir Walter, being a good-natured man, did not protest; but the wayfarer must not be disappointed if he fail to see much correspondence between the scenery of the book and that of the place. Yet let him not scorn the pious faith. Would not he himself be glad to believe, if there were any shadow of reason, that the lines had fallen to him in the veritable place where Captain MacTurk swaggered, and took his Maker's name in vain, and angrily resented imputations upon his piety; where Mr. Winterblossom appropriated the tit-bits of the table and made phrases; where the omniscient Mr. Peregrine Touchwood circumvented Mr. Valentine Bulmer; where, above all, the immortal Meg spurned "riders" from her door, and rated her "huzzies," and railed at the "stinking well" and all who frequented it?

Over against Innerleithen lies the parish of Traquair, with its burn and its "bush." A little to the south of the stream is Traquair House, a seventeenth-century residence tacked on to a much older tower. If the books could be believed, it would be the original of the Baron of Bradwardine's house. "Waverley" himself, however, was of a different opinion. The ruins of Horsburgh Castle, the seat of the family of this name, now for more than a hundred years abandoned to owl and bat, are about a couple of miles or so below Peebles. The town itself has a lovely situation at the point where Eddlestone Water babbles into the Tweed, and at the foot of a glorious brae, broad and lofty, and covered with fir and larch, with rolling hills all around, making a mighty amphitheatre. No wonder that it should have risen to the dignity of a holiday resort with a "season;" or that in other days the Hays of Yester should have been glad to come in from Neidpath Castle to winter in their town-house, the quaint old building in the High Street now known as the "Chambers Institute." In very early days Peebles was a dwelling-place of kings; and by the time of that James who was addicted to "the profane and unprofitable art of poem-making," it was renowned for its games, which were sung either by the monarch himself or by some brother minstrel of not much later date.

PEEBLES, FROM A LITTLE BELOW NEIDPATH.

But about the middle of the sixteenth century the Earl of Hertford came here, and then the town had to make a fresh start. The castle has disappeared from the head of the High Street without leaving a wrack behind. Of the Cross Kirk, built in the thirteenth century by Alexander III., little beyond the shell of the tower and a gable remains, and even the pitiful ivy has not been able to make it a sightly relic. There used to be here also the still older church of St. Andrew; and William Chambers has received much praise for having "restored" it—an exceptionally brutal use of a much-suffering term. The only other building of any note is the "Cross-Keys Inn," many-gabled and picturesque and comfortable. It has seen better days, for it was once upon a time the town-house of the Williamsons of Cardrona; but the crowning glory which it claims is that of being the "public" of Dame Dods, yclept the "Cleikum," which had for sign a large picture of St. Ronan catching hold of the devil's game leg with his episcopal crook. If you ask for evidence, you are pointed to the legend above the doorway, "The original Cleikum Inn, 1653"!

The stream has now been traced up for a distance of well-nigh seventy miles, yet Peebles is not much more than five hundred feet above the sea-level; herefrom the ascent is more obvious, though still quite gradual, for in the thirty miles or so yet to be traversed the rise is not more than a thousand feet. As they ripple by the town the waters sing a pretty song; but a stone's-throw or two above the comely old bridge which spans them close to where the castle frowned

NEIDPATH CASTLE.

upon all who sought to cross it with hostile intent, it glides smooth and silent, as though it had fallen asleep. Now the valley narrows into a glen, winding and profound; and at Neidpath, in full view of the town, the river dwindles into the merest burn, which it would be no great feat to leap across. But what a burn, and what a glen! Nothing yet seen, or still to be seen, is quite so superb as what now meets the view. For here the braes on either side are steep, and of immense height, and smothered to their tops with firs and larches; and the stream winds more than ever, at one moment widening into still deep pools, at the next shrinking into a dancing rapid; and all around, wherever the eye turns, it rests upon large swelling hills, robed with verdure, and girdled with timber, and crowned with grey cairns. Surely the glen was not much more lovely in the days before the last Duke of Queensberry, to spite the next heir of entail, or to put money into his mistress's purse, barbarously cut down the noble avenue by which the castle was approached, and provoked Wordsworth to gibbet him in an indignant sonnet. Burns, by the way, was aroused to an even finer show of wrath by the similar havoc which "Old Q." had wrought at Drumlanrig, in Nithsdale.

Neidpath Castle, however, has pleasanter associations with the bards. From the southern branch of the Frasers it passed to the Hays of Yester; and to the ninth lord of Yester, first Marquis of Tweeddale, is credited the earliest surviving lyric inspired by the Tweed. Here are two of the verses:—

> "When Maggie and me were acquaint
> I carried my noddle fu' high;
> Nae lint-white in a' the grey plain,
> Nae gowdspink sae bonny as she.
>
> "I whistled, I piped, and I sang,
> I woo'd, but I came nae great speed;
> Therefore I maun wander abroad,
> And lay my banes far frae the Tweed."

The man who wrote this pretty piece held his castle for Charles II., but it was unable to stand the brunt of Cromwell's cannon, and was not merely captured, but ruined. It was long untenanted, but has now by repair and addition been made habitable, though not more picturesque.

Where the Manor Water joins the Tweed they show the grave of the "Black Dwarf," and the cottage which he built with his own hands—with some help from compassionate neighbours—on land which he appropriated without asking any one's leave. The portrait is not very highly coloured: Elshender of Mucklestane Moor had scarcely a sourer or more splenetic humour than David Ritchie, though he may have been a trifle more comprehensive in his misanthropy. Yet David had great sensitiveness to natural influences, and, though he had a reputation in the parish for heresy, would speak of a future state with intense feeling, "and even with tears." Poor "bow'd Davie!" There was little in common betwixt him and his kind, and it seemed to him that his tale of mercies was not a long one; yet there have been many who would be willing enough to part with some of their advantages in exchange for his firm grasp of "the mighty hopes that make us men."

As the bridge at Stobo is approached the stream broadens out again, and strolling along the pleasant, shady road cut in the hill there is much to delight the eye, and something as well to please the ear—on the right splendid plantations, climbing up the brae; on the left the water, gleaming through the fluttering leaves, and beyond it a grassy level—where the patient kine make music with their bells—rising into fine slopes of sward, while above these are broad belts of timber. Close beside the stream, above Drummelzier, is the ruined castle of this name, and hard by, but high up the brae, where it must have been almost inaccessible, are some fragments of Thanes or Tinnis Castle, used as a citadel or redoubt by the garrison. Of an early laird of Drummelzier historians relate that when after long absence he came home from the East, where he had crusading been, he was surprised to find his faithful spouse nursing a strapping boy. The lady, however, was able to explain: while she was walking along the banks one day, the spirit of the Tweed had issued forth; and how could a weak woman prevail against a spirit? So the boy was called Tweedie, and founded the great family of that name, whose legend was, "Thole* and think." This, however, one supposes, is to be taken as a considerate exhortation to their victims rather than as a motto for their own guidance. So interpreted, it is not less frank than the device of the Cranstouns, "Ye shall want ere I want," or that of the Scotts of Harden, "Reparabit cornua Phœbe." Moonlighting is no invention of the nineteenth century.

But Drummelzier's most famous association is with Merlin the seer, Merlin Wylt, the Wild, as he is called, to distinguish him from Merlin Ambrosius, who is believed to have uttered his oracles and succumbed to Vivien's enchantments in the preceding century. The story goes that after the battle of Arderydd, in or about the year 573, he fled to the wilds of Tweeddale, and here passed the remainder of his life with a reputation for insanity; that he prophesied that he should die from earth, water, and wood, and accordingly, being pursued by a band of unappreciative rustics, he leapt into the Tweed here and was impaled upon a stake; and that they buried him where the Pansayl brook flows into the river, the spot being marked by the scraggy thorn which is visible from the churchyard. For anyone not blessed with a mighty intuition it is not easy to be sure of anything about Merlin except that he was, and was not. Mr. Veitch, however, paints an impressive picture of Merlin as no wild man of the woods, but as "a heart-broken and despairing representative of the old Druidic nature-worship, at once poet and priest of the fading faith, yet torn and distracted by secret doubt as to its truth." In the same volume—that on the history and poetry of the Border—the eloquent professor remarks that we are "apt to interject into ancient actors and thinkers modern ideas, at which probably they would have stood amazed."

Beyond Merlindale, "hearsed about" with black firs, the stream expands until it becomes broader than it is at many points within a dozen miles of its mouth. The Edinburgh road bears it company nearly from Broughton to its source; but instead of crossing to the western bank some way above Drummelzier, it is pleasanter, if you have no "machine"—that is, are not driving—to keep along the eastern bank for some two or three miles farther, when a delightful saunter across a magnificent haugh, besprinkled with the yellow tormentilla and many another timid wild flower, brings you to Stanhope Bridge, and so again to the highway. A few years ago, when the Tweed had one of its spasms of turbulence, this bridge was swung bodily round to the bank, while several others higher up were swept clean away. As the Crook Inn is approached the stream has again become attenuated; the valley, too, has straitened, the hills are less abrupt and barren than those seen in the distance a few miles below, and occasionally a small plantation is espied, where the mavis and the merle may be heard flooding the air with their amorous minstrelsy. The Crook, beloved of anglers, who have tender memories of its luscious mutton, as well as of the good sport which can almost always be had in this part of the stream, is still the comfortable place it used to be before it classed itself as a hotel and acquired fashionable habits.

* Suffer in patience.

For the remaining ten or twelve miles the course is one of utter solitude and of growing wildness—not even a shepherd's hut in sight, and no tree, except here and there a stunted hawthorn or a lonely rowan; the braes less verdant, and more given to yielding screes; no sound to be heard but the irritating squeal of the stone-chipper, the low, long-drawn whistle of the "whaup," or the pleading cry of the peewit. Of animated nature no other sign meets the eye save little groups of sheep clinging to the braes—the fierce-looking black-faced variety it may be, or the half-breeds with their still more ferocious-looking streaked visages, or the meeker "cheeviots." So the slow ascent continues until at last Tweedshaws, the solitary farmhouse, is reached, and then, leaving the road a little way up Flocker Hill, you stand at last at Tweedswell, the putative source of the stream. Looking around, you see on every hand huge hills rising in the distance, and making between them a vast circle—Black Dod, and Clyde Law, near which the great western stream rises, and Moll's Cleuch Dod, and Lochraig, and many another, while just behind Flocker Hill, Hart Fell rears its giant form. When Merlin Wylt roamed the wilds of Tweeddale a mighty forest waved over them; now the evidence of their former glory of rowan and birch and hazel must be looked for in the peaty soil which stains the head-streams as they furrow their way down the braes. Later in the year these hills, at present so swart and void, will be brightened with scatterings of purple; and then, under a sunnier sky, their plight will seem less blank and savage. But now they show an aspect stark and grim; for the time of the broom is not yet, and to-day the sun is sulking behind the murk, and their gusty tops are all asmoke.

W. W. HUTCHINGS.

HART FELL.

AMONG THE FELLS.

THE COQUET.

The Fisherman's River—"Awa' to the Border"—Peat-Hags—Eel-Fishing—Alwinton and Harbottle—The Village of Rothbury—Brinkburn Priory—Weldon Bridge and Felton—Warkworth Hermitage and Castle—The Town of Amble—Coquet Isle.

THERE'S a gentleman that will tell ye that just when I had ga'en up to Lourie Lowther's, and had bidden the drinking of twa cheerers, and gotten just in again upon the moss, and was whigging cannily awa' hame, twa land-loupers jumpit out of a peat-hag on me or I was thinking, and got me down, and knevelled me sair eneuch, or I could gar my whip walk about their lugs; and troth, Gudewife, if this honest gentleman hadna come up, I would have gotten mair licks than I like, and lost mair siller than I could weel spare; so ye maun be thankful to him for it under God."

So, with all the generations of Pepper and Mustard frisking about him, did honest Dandie Dinmont explain to his wife how he came by a battered face and a wounded head.

The "peat-hag" is a characteristic not only of the Scottish Border-land, but of wide tracks on the English side, and a very remarkable feature it makes in a wild landscape, being a sort of black precipice made in the green hills by some sudden sinking of the apparently bottomless peat. It is all ancient peat-land together where the river Coquet rises—"Coquet, still the stream of streams," as one of the poets of "The Fisher's Garland" has observed; "the king of the stream and the brae," as has been remarked by another poetical brother of the angle. Other northern rivers the fisherman mentions with respect, and perhaps with joyful remembrance of pleasant and successful days; but of the Coquet he never speaks except

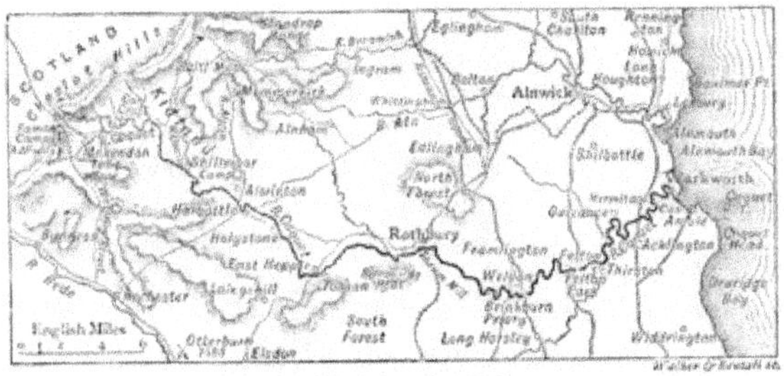

THE COURSE OF THE COQUET.

with glowing enthusiasm. No tuneful fisher who was friendly with the muse ever failed to give the Coquet a preferential mention in his verse. Now it is—

"Nae mair we'll fish the coaly Tyne,
Nae mair the oozy Team,
Nae mair we'll try the sedgy Pont,
Or Derwent's woody stream;
But we'll awa' to Coquet side,
For Coquet bangs them a'."

And now it is—

"There's mony a saumon lies in Tweed,
And many a trout in Till,
But Coquet—Coquet aye for me,
If I may have my will."

A much beloved stream, indeed, is the Coquet, rising in an acre or two of marshy land, losing itself for a while among the peat, then winding into the sunlight round the feet of the green hills, and—after many a mile of joyous wandering—plunging into deep embowered woods and mossy thickets, where, to all but its familiars, it is unsuspected and unseen.

All around Coquet Head lies the Debatable Land. Mounting the dark hill of Thirlmoor one may look far away over Roxburghshire, whence, in former rough times, there was many a raid into the rich Northumbrian lands. The district known as Kidland lies along Coquetside, from the Cheviots eastward, and here in the stormy moss-trooping days no soul could be induced to live, even if he were tempted by the offer of free lands. The hills are now covered with sheep; there is a shelter for the shepherds on the top of Thirlmoor; yet to this day Kidland is a country bare of habitations, shrouded for great part of the year in mists; dank, rainy, treeless;

swept by fierce winds, treacherous by reason of its numerous bogs. The wild duck may be shot at Coquet Head, but for the most part it lives and breeds here in great safety, too remote from men, too fortunate in its wild surroundings, to be much or frequently incommoded by the English enthusiasm for sport. It is possible, perhaps, to be in as deep a solitude on Dartmoor, but scarcely possible to be so far from the musical church bell and the cheerful cottage smoke.

But even in this wild region there are remains of our old civilisation, and numerous relics of "the grandeur that was Rome." What are known as the Ad Fines Camps are situated close to Coquet Head; the Watling Street crosses the young stream not far from its source on Thirlmoor; the Outer and the Middle Golden Pot, Roman milestones of an unusual design, are within easy reach of where the river encloses the ancient camps in one of its forks. These stations were of considerable extent when they were made, and were serviceable in after ages as the meeting-place of the Wardens of the Middle Marches of England and Scotland when they assembled to punish offences against the Border laws. Wild stories of lawless times are told by the shepherds on the hills. There was a "Thieves' Road" over Kidland, along which, doubtless, many a herd of stolen sheep or kine has been driven. Many fights there were in these parts, and much pursuing of raiders from the other side of the Border. The Northumbrians, it must be admitted, were no better than their neighbours, and not the least less inclined to thieving. Even a judge was stolen on one occasion, as he was going the rounds of the King's Justiciaries, and was kept in prison until his captors could exact from him their own terms.

The country below Coquet Head is veined by little streams, which pour into the river at brief intervals, so that what was but lately a thread of water hidden among the moss soon becomes a laughing, sparkling river, though even so low down as Blindburn, four or five miles from the source, it may, in very dry seasons, be bridged by a lady's foot.

The first house is at Makingdon, rather more than a mile from Ad Fines Camps, and fifteen hundred feet above the level of the sea. There are occasional houses at intervals of a mile or two along the far-winding course of the river to Alwinton. Of one of these a Mrs. Malaprop of the hills remarked that "it was in a very digested state," meaning thereby that it stood grievously in need of repair. A descendant of the true Dandie Dinmont lived at Blindburn farm-house until a few years ago, and kept up the famous breed of terriers, giving to each pair the immortal names of Pepper and Mustard. The traveller into these regions is dependent upon the kindly hospitality of the sparse inhabitants, for there is no house of entertainment within many miles, and a weary distance must the shepherd trudge over the moors before he can forgather with his kind.

The Coquet flows through wild and exceedingly rocky scenery between Blindburn and the next house, which is Carl Croft, and anglers, even with long waders, find no inconsiderable difficulty in fishing the stream. Those of the more discerning sort make their way up one of the tributaries, the Carl Croft or the Philip

Burn, or, by preference, the Usway—the largest and wildest and most beautiful of the feeders of the Coquet—which joins the river at Shillmoor, distant from the small village of Alwinton only about five miles or so. Near the point of junction the Coquet falls, in leap after leap, among rugged and dangerous rocks. Good eel-spearing may be had here in due season. It is usual to make up a party of ten or a dozen, chiefly composed of the shepherds of the district, and to set out on moonless nights, each man with a torch and four-

HARBOTTLE.

ALWINTON BRIDGE.

pronged fork, or "cleek." Those who have tasted its joys say there is no sport in these islands equal to that of spearing eels in the Coquet, with Border shepherds for company. Sometimes, indeed, eels are not the only prey. The river swarms with bull trout, and how is it possible to resist the temptation of cleeking a fine plump fish if it comes within reach of one's spear? Such sport is dangerous, however, being against the laws, and numerous have been the conflicts, in times not long past, between the hillmen and the watchers, their hereditary foes. On some occasions the poachers have played sly tricks on those who have intended their capture. They have sent out rumours of their intention to have "a gey night;" then they have sat in some lonely place drinking whisky and telling stories the night through, issuing thence in the morning, when the watchers had convinced themselves of a hoax, to sweep the Coquet and all the neighbouring streams.

The chief resorts alike of shepherds and of anglers are the villages of Alwinton and Harbottle, distant about two miles from each other, and near to where the Coquet winds out of the hills and flows between rich meadow-lands, that slope away to the distant Cheviots on the one hand, and to the nearer Simonside Hills on the other. Alwinton has the large allowance of two inns to about eleven houses. It is one of the most ancient of the Border villages, and had a church in 1293, to which fled one Thomas de Holm, escaped from the prison of the neighbouring town, but taken by Simon Smart and Benedict Grey, who "beheaded him at Simonsett, and hung his head up on the gallows at Harbottle," as a

THE COQUET AT FARNHAM.

warning to all like evil-doers. Alwinton has its peel-tower, at about half a mile from the present village; but at Harbottle there are far more striking memorials of a stirring past. There is Harbottle Castle, for example, a ruined mass of masonry on the summit of a steep hill between the village and the river. It must anciently have been almost the strongest place on the Borders, when what is now a small village was doubtless a fairly considerable town. "Here Botl," the place of the army—such is the name which it is said to have borne before the Conquest, when it contained a stronghold held by Milred, the son of Ackman. "Robert with the Beard," the lord of Prudhoe, founder of the family of De Umfraville, came into possession of all the surrounding lands in 1076, on condition of defending the countryside against wolves and the enemies of the king. The castle, of which there are portions still remaining, was built in the reign of Henry II., and was the prison and place of execution of all offenders taken in the liberty of Redesdale. Sitting by the castle of Harbottle in these days, and listening to the joyous music of the Coquet stream, the imagination vainly endeavours to piece together the meagre fragments of the past into some consistent whole; for the quiet aspect of things, the sweet rural peace, and this

"Place of slumber and of dreams
Remote among the hills,"

make it seem incredible that a great Scottish army can ever have sat down before it, and that the place can have been strong enough to resist a determined siege.

When Harbottle has been left behind, the river no longer strains through narrow passes or hurries by great ramparts of riven cliff. It broadens out, indeed, into a quiet, smiling stream, with a brown shingly bed, and with occasional large masses of reeds, in which an otter may hide. There are now frequent small villages along its course, the most interesting of these being Holystone, where there is a well in which, as Alexander Smith has related—

"The king and all his nobles and his priests,
Were by Paulinus in Christ's name baptised,
And solemnly unto his service sealed.
And then Paulinus lifted up his hands,
And blessed them and the people."

No less than three thousand Northumbrians are said to have received the sacrament of baptism at this place, a statement which will seem the less incredible if we consider that Northumbria was then the most powerful and populous of the Saxon kingdoms. The famous well lies by the junction of two Roman ways, in a little grove of fir-trees, where the water still bubbles up actively through the sand and gravel. There is above it a stone cross with this inscription: "In this place Paulinus the Bishop baptised 3,000 Northumbrians, Easter, DCXXVII."

Under the brow of Simonside, which is a huge shoulder of mountain thrusting itself up suddenly from the ascending land, there are a few cottages, and one great house, and a mill where are manufactured the Cheviot tweeds. This is the village of Tosson. Hence one looks away across the Coquet to the long range of the Cheviot hills, which seem surprisingly near, and yet are separated from Coquetside by many a mile of rich and pleasant pasture land. The ancient village of Rothbury is close at hand, with its one long street dipping down from the moorside to the Coquet banks, with its picturesque "Thrum Mill," its ancient church tower, and its great expanse of furze-bestrewn moors, amid the nearest of which Cragside, the residence of Lord Armstrong, is set. "An Act of Parliament is out of breath before it reaches Rothbury," say the people of the place. It is a saying which has survived from the pre-railroad days, when this portion of the wild Border land seemed as much cut off from the rest of England as if it had been islanded by the sea. Nor, indeed, is the sea so far away. On clear days one may behold it from the top of Simonside, a thin grey streak, scarcely distinguishable from the greyness of the sky.

A turbulent little town was Rothbury in its earlier days. It was here that Bernard Gilpin took down from the church door a glove which had been hung up as a challenge to all and sundry, and then preached a powerful sermon on the wickedness of private war. In the same church many years ago an old man who was listening to a condemnation of robbery rose up and said, "Then the de'il I give my sall to, but we are all thieves." Happily that broad statement no longer applies. The people of Rothbury and the region beyond are honest, stalwart, hard-working, prosperous folk, given to no pursuit more lawless than the occasional poaching of bull trout.

And of bull trout, which easily passes for salmon with the unwary, it is well that a word should be said. The *salmo eriox* has long established its title to the Coquet as its own exclusive stream. "On the Coquet it goes by the name of salmon," says a writer on angling, "there being no true salmon in that river. Bull trout very rarely takes fly or bait of any kind, except when it is in the kelt state, when it is ravenous. It reaches fifteen and twenty pounds in weight." A noble fish, it will be remarked; but why should it have laid exclusive claim to the Coquet, with that river lying, as it does, between such salmon-haunted streams as the Tyne and the Tweed? This is a puzzle which the scientific mind finds itself incapable of solving to this day. A generation since it was maintained that the bull trout devoured the young of salmon, and it was decided, therefore, that the *salmo eriox* should itself be destroyed. By the connivance of the local landowner every specimen of the bull trout was killed as it entered the river from the sea. Breeding ponds for salmon were then established at Rothbury, and 17,000 young fish were turned into the Coquet in a single year. Many of these were branded for future identification, but, so far as was known, not a single fish of the whole 17,000 ever came back to the stream in which it was bred. Some were caught in the Tyne, and some in the Tweed, and some in more distant rivers, but never did the bite of a true salmon reward the patient angler by Coquetside. Worse than all, too, the common trout deteriorated, for they had fed on the spawn of the *salmo eriox*. These things becoming apparent, as much anxiety was shown to get the bull trout back to the river as there had been eagerness for its destruction. The bull trout is now, in fact, strictly preserved under the salmon laws. There is a Coquet Fish Conservancy Board; and the catching of bull trout in Coquet, alike by nets and by more artificial expedients, is now a considerable industry, much of the so-called salmon exported to France and Spain being no more than the *salmo eriox* of the English Border. There are those who will not even yet believe that the Coquet cannot be made a salmon river. Now and then some angler confidently announces that he has caught a true salmon in this delightful and prolific stream. Such tales are listened to with interest, but are not believed. Even experienced fishermen are capable of confounding the bull trout with its nobler brother of the streams.

ON THE COQUET, BRINKBURN.

At the foot of the long street of Rothbury, and just on the lower outskirt of the village, is the Thrum Mill, the name of which is explained by the fact that the river here strains through a narrow chasm, or thrum, in a piled-up bed of freestone rock. The mill is an object of the conventionally picturesque description, with a moss-grown waterwheel, and with a tumbling torrent for foreground. A bridge here crosses the Coquet, and to the left, halfway up the steep side of a heathery hill, rises the mixed Gothic and Elizabethan mansion of Lord Armstrong.

The site has clearly been chosen for the wildness of its surroundings, for whatever changes may be wrought by cultivation, and however the growth of plantations may soften the harsh brown and softer purple of the heather, untamed Nature will still assert itself here, like Hereward's wife at Ely, as "captive but unconquered." At Cragside there is one of the noblest of English picture galleries, the contents of which have been brought together by an exceedingly catholic taste, and by a

AT FELTON.

liberality of expenditure only possible to "wealthy men who care not how they give." Here are Linnell's "Thunderstorm in Autumn," Millais' "Chill October," David Cox's "Ulverstone Sands," Leslie's "Cowslip Gatherers," Wilkie's "Rabbit on the Wall," Rossetti's "Margaret and her Jewels," and some of the finest works of Turner, Landseer, Phillip, Müller, and, coming down to living artists, Sir Frederick Leighton.

From Rothbury the Coquet takes a long sweep through the fields and then plunges into the woods of Brinkburn. There are here, one reads, great and dangerous holes in the river bed; but so there are at many places on the Coquet, and not at Brinkburn more remarkably or permanently than elsewhere. Such holes are made by the swirling water of the floods, and may change their situation with every spate. Their more particular association with Brinkburn may arise from the fact that the bells of the priory are believed to have been cast into a hole in the river, from which whosoever recovers them, says the tradition, will come into possession of treasures galore. Brinkburn was one of the earliest religious settlements on the disturbed and lawless English side of the Border. Exceedingly courageous must have been those monks who decided to accept the rough chances of life at Brinkburn Priory. They had the protection of the deep woods, indeed. Even now one may pass by Brinkburn without suspecting what rich memorials of a past age and a venerable faith are hid within its leafy coverts. It is not merely embosomed, but buried, in trees. So, too, it must have been when the monks were here, for the story goes that a party of marauding Scots had already passed the priory, and was well on its way toward places under less saintly protection, when the monks too soon set the bells a-ringing for joy at its departure, with the evil result of revealing their hiding-place, so that the Scots, returning, fell upon the black canons of Brinkburn while they were assembled to offer up prayers of gratitude for their deliverance from danger.

This priory of Brinkburn was founded in the reign of Henry I. by a certain Sir William de Bertram, Baron of Mitford, by Morpeth, who endowed it liberally from his extensive lands. Its monks were of the order of St. Augustine. Of their history little is known, but it must have been troublous enough, and there is reason to think that they were more than once under the necessity of flight. Having resolved to build a church, the Lord of Mitford determined that it should be such a one as would do honour to his name. The present extensive remains still speak eloquently of the original beauty of the edifice. Of the church, partially restored in 1858 by the present owners of the estate, the Cadogan family, it has been remarked that, "the richest Norman work is here inextricably blended with the purest Early English, and the fabric must be regarded as one of the most fascinating specimens of the transition from one to the other that there is in the country." Out of the ruins of the monastery, and above the cellars in which the monks may have hidden themselves in times of trouble, the present manor house of Brinkburn has been built. It stands not far from the banks of the Coquet, which are here somewhat narrow and steep, with rocky projections, and with no route for the angler except in the bed of the stream, or amid an almost impenetrable confusion of shrubs and brambles and trees. At one point the piers of a Roman bridge may be discerned when the water is low; there is a quaint old watermill by the side of the stream; at a spot but a short distance away, it is averred by a pleasant tradition, the Northumbrian fairies were buried, and there they sleep, like King Arthur under the castle of Sewingshields, until faith shall return to the earth.

The most widely known of all the villages below Rothbury is Weldon Bridge, at which one arrives when the Coquet has left Brinkburn Woods. It is the main resort of those anglers who love quiet fishing, and are not adventurous enough to make their way into the hills. Much has it been besung by the poets of the craft. "At Weldon Bridge," says one

> ". . . there's wale o' wine,
> If ye hae coin in pocket;
> If ye can throw a heckle fine,
> There's wale o' trout in Coquet."

It is but a little place, this Weldon Bridge, with a large inn, before whose doors the river flows in gentle music. For the last two or three miles the stream has been characterised by the most capricious bendings, and henceforth, but with rather larger sweeps, it preserves the same wilful habit until it reaches the sea. There are pleasant walks along its banks down to Felton, sometimes diverging into low-lying woods, sometimes climbing the hill-sides among farms, and occasionally leading to some ancient ford. At Felton itself the hills close in more narrowly, and the pleasant little village stands on a declivity amongst trees, whilst the river streams through a rocky pass. There is a dam at Felton which furnished material for rather a feeble joke to the late Frank Buckland. He found the fish falling back exhausted from vain attempts to leap the weir, and he posted up a "notice to salmon and bull trout," telling them to go down the river and take the first turn to the right, when they would find good travelling water up stream, and assuring them of the good will of the Duke of Northumberland, who meant to make a ladder for them by-and-bye. The fact that an inspector of fisheries, like Buckland, should have believed that salmon went up the Coquet with the bull trout is a curious illustration of the indeterminate ideas which have until lately prevailed on the subject of the varieties of fish by which this river is frequented.

Felton is one of those villages at which it is pleasant to spend a night. Its bridge is almost as beautifully situated as that of Bettws-y-Coed. One stands upon it in the evening, and leans one's arms on the parapet, and looks towards the hills which environ it, and the comfortable village inn, and the quiet cottages, and feels how glorious a land is this England in which we live. There is nothing else to do or to enjoy, unless the river is low, as Frank Buckland saw it, and the fish are crowding up the stream; and then the sight is one that is for the existing moment very exciting and is afterwards difficult to forget.

Felton is an ancient place. The old religion lingers there. The Protestant Reformation scarcely penetrated to north Northumberland, and many of the chief families of the district are still attached to the more ancient forms of faith. Attached to Felton Park is the Roman Catholic chapel of St. Mary. There are remains of a more antique edifice of the same faith about two miles away, the Church of St. Wilfred of Gysnes, given to the canons of Alnwick in the twelfth century. Felton is on the old Northern Coach Road, and is not now far away from the rail. Whosoever desires to make acquaintance with the whole of the

Coquet should alight at the neighbouring station of Acklington. He may then go downward to Warkworth, to Amble, and the sea; or he may go upward to Brinkburn, to Rothbury, and the moors.

From Felton until Warkworth is in sight there is little over which one need linger. The country is level more or less, and the river seems to flow in a deep trench, with a fringe of trees on either side of it. At one place it comes through a deep break in the solid rock, which seems as if it must originally have been quarried. One speculates in vain as to the mighty force of the water by which such passages must have been hewn. These clefts for rivers are not uncommon,

MORWICK MILL, ACKLINGTON.

but they are incomprehensible. The water, one is compelled to feel, was but a minor element in their formation. A mile and a half from Warkworth there is another weir, a great straight wall of cement, with a passage for fish on either side. Yet though the fish may go up to left or right, as they may choose, there is what persons addicted to sport might call "an even chance" in connection with their coming down. If they take the ladder to the right they will get off to sea, but if they come down to the left they will fall into a trap, and will, in all probability, be eaten on French dinner tables as salmon. For, at Warkworth, or within a short distance of it, is the great fishery of Mr. Pape, who has not only the weir to assist his operations, but has the right—acquired by paying a rent to the Duke of Northumberland—to stop up one of the fish passes at the extremities of the

WARKWORTH CASTLE.

THE VILLAGE OF WARKWORTH.

weir, which privilege he exercises so ingeniously that every fish that chooses the left side of the river for its downward passage gets into his trap, from which it may be lifted out at will.

Can Edmund Spenser ever have been at Warkworth? If not, how does he come by this description?—

"A little lowly hermitage it was,
  Down in a dale, hard by a forest's side;
Far from resort of people that did pass
  In travel to and fro; a little wide
  There was an holy chapel edified,
Wherein the hermit duly wont to say
  His holy things each morn and eventide;
Thereby a crystal stream did gently play,
Which from a sacred fountain welled forth alway."

Except as regards the little stream and the sacred fountain this is accurately descriptive of the hermitage at Warkworth. The Coquet is here a tolerably broad river indeed, so that to reach the lowly hermit's cell one must make employment of the boatman's art. A little church hewn out of rock, and with a certain architectural skill—that is the famous hermitage of Warkworth. A wood grows high above it; there is a pleasant walk by the riverside below; and above the cave there are some steps by which the hermit is supposed to have ascended to his garden ground. The Hermitage is, as Bishop Percy says—

> "Deep hewn within a craggy cliff,
> And overhung with wood."

Never did hermit choose a lovelier spot for his orisons; but this hermit of Warkworth was a man of industry and taste. He used the hammer and the chisel well. He made for himself a chapel, a confessional, and a dormitory, and none of these did he leave without ornament. There is a groined roof, and there is a rood above the doorway, and there is the recumbent figure of a lady with upraised hands. Whosoever chooses to weave legends about the hermitage of Warkworth is at liberty to do so, for nothing is certainly known of the hermit. The received tradition is to be found in Percy's "Reliques," where a member of the family of Bertram by mistake slays his sweetheart and his brother, and expiates his double crime by isolating himself from his kind. The Coquet is very beautiful here, with a mile walk through woods and meadow lands. After the Hermitage a sweet bend of the river brings Warkworth Castle in sight. It stands high up on the summit of grassy slopes, which have a few shrubs scattered about them. Here it was that, according to Shakespeare's narrative of events, Henry Hotspur read the letter of "a pagan rascal—an infidel," who would not join him in his designs against the Crown. The next scene is in the Boar's Head Tavern, Eastcheap, with Poins and Prince Hal. Shakespeare was so far adherent to fact that Hotspur actually lived at Warkworth Castle. Edward III. had conferred it on the second Lord Percy, and until the middle of the fifteenth century the Percies preferred Warkworth to Alnwick. The Castle is one of the most beautiful and perfect ruins in England. It is not only finely situated, but is unique in design, suggesting less of strength than of taste in constructing a palace which must also be a stronghold. A living novelist, the best of our story tellers, has made Warkworth the starting-point of one of his Christmas tales, and has most admirably conveyed to the reader the feeling of the place. Whom should I mean but Mr. Walter Besant? The church where his hero did penance, and where his heroine bravely stood beside her lover, is at the foot of the village street, which slopes upward to the height on which the Castle stands. Just beyond the church is the great stone archway through which the town must be entered, standing at the inner side of the bridge over the Coquet stream. Altogether, the village does not amount to much. It has a few good inns, and a few old-fashioned cottages. But it is as sweet a place as is to be found in all the countryside, and is therefore much in favour with persons in search of a brief, quiet holiday.

In Warkworth, small as it is, one feels everywhere the influence of the past. History seems to keep guard over it as an important part of its story. In 737 it was conferred by King Ceowulph on the monastery of Lindisfarne. The town was burnt in 1171 by the army of William the Lion, who was something of a poltroon. King John visited the place in the thirteenth century, and did much mischief farther up the river. General Forster and his Jacobites were here in 1715. That very Mr. Patten who is a principal figure in Mr. Besant's "Dorothy Forster" writes:—"It may be observed that this was the first place where the Pretender was so avowedly pray'd for and proclaimed as King of these realmes."

From the turrets of Warkworth Castle one looks over a wide expanse of land and sea. The coast line is visible for great distances, beyond Alnmouth and Dunstanborough on the one hand, and almost to Tynemouth on the other. The great towers of Alnwick are in sight, and mile on mile of the most fertile land in Northumberland, and mile on mile of rabbit-haunted sandhills by the sea. Just beyond the Castle the land slopes downward, past a cottage or two, and a little wood, and a great clump of whin-bushes, to the Coquetside, and then the river flows through flat marsh-land until the small seaport town of Amble is reached. I have never seen those Essex salt marshes in which Mr. Baring-Gould lays the scene of his powerful "Mehalah," but whenever I read the book I am reminded of the country from Warkworth to the sea. Amble has grown up on a steep above the river; but there are flat spaces all round about it, and the river seems to stagnate where barges and schooners lie grounded in the mud, and beyond the harbour there are great level fields between "the bents" and the sea. Not a cheery place, by any means. Amble is one of the smaller outlets of the Northumberland coal trade. In very early days the Romans had some sort of encampment here, and in the Middle Ages Amble had its Benedictine monastery. It is now an exceedingly prosaic little town, with a harbour quite out of proportion to its size, and with an evident intention of "getting on."

"The bents" are the grass-covered sandhills which time and the winds have piled up between the ancient landmarks and the present limits of the tide. They rise to very considerable heights, and stretch, in great undulations, along many a mile of shore. The Coquet flows down between them to a wide waste of sand when the sea is out, and one may trace its waters, should they be discoloured by flood, on either side of the Coquet Island, which the river must have worn from the mainland very long ago. The island is a low, level strip, containing some sixteen acres of ground. It has a peculiar history of its own. There was a monastery upon it in the seventh century, and here the Abbess of Whitby is said to have met St. Cuthbert, who, for this occasion, had overcome his generally invincible dislike to women. St. Cuthbert's own island is in sight from the Coquet, and if the Farnes were not in the way one's range of vision might extend to Lindisfarne. In later times than those in which Cuthbert taught religion to a rude people the hermit of Warkworth had a rival hermit in the recluse of Coquet Isle; a far more dismal place to reside in, for all around it rage the terrible winter storms of the North Sea. Persons interested in the art of "smashing" may be interested to hear that Coquet Island was resorted to by the makers of false coins—"hard hedds" they were called in those days—so early as 1567. The place was taken by the Scots

HUNTING ON COQUETSIDE.

(From the Picture by Colonel Lutyens, by Permission of Major Browne, Doxford Hall, Northumberland.)

during the Civil Wars, and there its history ends, except so far as it is continued by shipwreck and disaster at sea. On Coquet Island a lighthouse now stands, tall and white, so that its walls may be seen far away over the sea in the daytime, and its lamps for many a rood at night. Gulls and terns and puffins and guillemots play around it and make their nests amid its sandy turf; and there comes "the dunter," as the fishermen call it, the porpoise as it is called in more ordinary speech, to devour the bull trout as it is making towards the comparative safety of the Coquet waters. All this may be changed a few years hence, for Amble is developing its trade, and hereafter masts of assembled shipping, and a black prospect of "coal-shoots," may be the characteristic features of Coquet mouth.

AARON WATSON.

KEILDER MOORS (WITH PEEL FELL TO THE RIGHT).

THE TYNE.

CHAPTER I.

THE NORTH TYNE.

Peel Fell—Deadwater Bog—Keilder Castle and the Keilder Moors—The Border Peel—Border Feuds and Friendships—The Charltons—Bellingham—The Reed—Tyne Salmon—The Village of Wark—Chipchase Castle—Haughton Castle and the Swinburnes—Chollerford and the Roman Wall—The Meeting of the Waters.

THE clouds which are dragging themselves along the summit of Peel Fell were but lately dappling a bleak English landscape with their shadows, and are now being carried by the indifferent winds beyond that border-line over which, at peril of their lives, mail-clad men in earlier and ruder times were wont "to go to Scotland to get a prey." The last house in England, a lonely but pleasant homestead, with its wide sheep-walks and its patch of cultivated land, stands under the shelter of a ridge where the brown waste rises into high moorlands; and beyond it, the fell looms very darkly, save where a beam of sunlight traverses its purple slope, with such bright decisiveness as if it were Ithuriel's spear. Up above Alston, in Cumberland, where the South Tyne comes wandering from the mountain slopes, you may find cottages and farmsteads which were built almost as far back as it is safe to carry a noble pedigree; but here, where the North Tyne oozes out of the fells, we are in a country which was constantly raided from both sides of the Border; and so, for many a mile round about, there is nothing ancient but the castle and the peel tower, the Roman road over the moss, and the Roman wall chaining together the windy ridges of the moors. How could there be, indeed, when the Borderer of former times was accustomed to see his house "all in a low," and was happy and fortunate if he could but drive his cattle in safety to the nearest peel? If a farmhouse dates back a hundred years or so it seems to belong to a venerable past, and if there is in these parts any more noble residence which does not proclaim to the wanderer that it was built for the purposes of defence, it will belong to a day later than that on which James I. crossed the Border to assume the English crown.

Peel Fell is the westernmost spur of the Cheviot range. Beheld from afar it seems to be a hill of gentle and inviting slope; but is, in fact, more craggy and broken than any of its kindred hills, which, of all the uplands of our country, are, except for the presence of the shepherds and their sheep, the most solitary. On the summit one stands 1,975 feet above the level of the sea. In these days a railway crosses the Border near to Peel Fell. It has kept to the winding course of the river from Newcastle upwards, and now it plunges into that Debateable Land which was for so long a period the excuse of Border feud and foray, and which was not definitely assigned either to the Scots or the English until 1552. Along the very path which this railway keeps there went, on many a memorable day,

"Marching o'er the knowes,
Five hundred Fenwicks in a flock;"

for their old enemies the Grahams kept the Border beyond the fells, and there was not among the Montagues and Capulets such wild and deep enmity as existed between the Tynedale and the Liddesdale men. It must have been ill-marching enough, for the route lay over Deadwater Bog, where, in case of misfortune and retreat, the Fenwicks would have an advantage over their pursuers in their superior knowledge of the sounder spots of ground. In this Deadwater Bog, it is maintained, the North Tyne takes its rise, though here, as in so many cases in which great rivers originate otherwise than in well-defined springs, there is division of opinion and of faith. The Deadwater is a curving silvery thread in a black setting of peat-moss. It belongs wholly to the English side of the Border, and after its leisurely circuit of an almost level plain it ripples into a wider channel and fuller light through a mask of waving reeds. But between the stations of Saughtree in Scotland and Keilder in England there is a wet ditch within a railway enclosure, and here, say some of the people of the district, and here the Ordnance Survey also asseverates, we must look for the actual origin of the North Tyne. I would gladly debate the question with the Ordnance Survey, if only to prove that the Tyne is an English river up to the remotest spot to which it can be traced; but it is "ill fechtin'" with those who are appointed to settle questions of boundaries, and whose decisions are held to be final however much they may be disputed; and as the little Deadwater and the small stream which insists on counting honours along with it eventually join together and form the indisputable North Tyne, it will be the discreeter course to let the Ordnance Surveyors have their will.

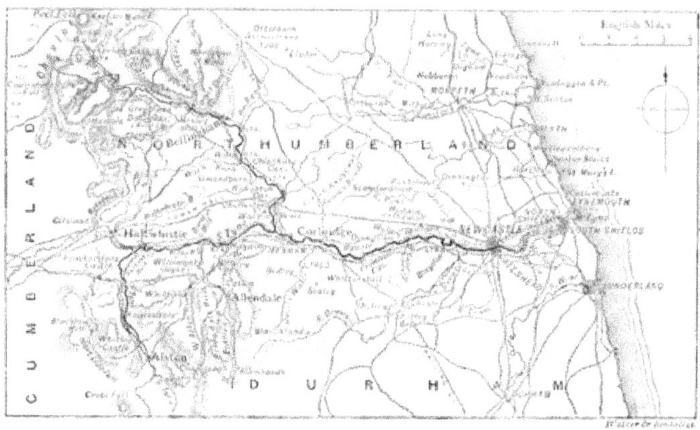

THE COURSE OF THE TYNE.

The Tyne has scarcely become a distinguishable stream when it commences to take toll of its tributaries. First of all it is broadened and deepened by the junction of the Keilder Burn, whereupon it assumes such dimensions that a wooden bridge is thrown over from bank to bank. Keilder is here a name common to some of the chief features of the landscape—Keilder Castle, Keilder Burn, Keilder Moors. The castle is not one of the old Border strongholds, as might be assumed from its situation, but was built in the latter part of the last century by Hugh, last Earl and first Duke of Northumberland. It is approached by a road over the moors, and through a forest of young fir-trees. Its square tower is half hidden in a wood of more ancient date, and it has for background a fair expanse of purple hills. Between the castle and the fells there is a "forest primeval," as old, it may be, as that which Longfellow describes in the opening of "Evangeline," and far more strictly preserved; for not even the scant natives of the district are permitted to enter here, lest perchance they might disturb the game.

On Keilder Moors, to the North of Tynehead, three miles hence, there is as good sport as anywhere in South Britain. All varieties of moor-fowl wend thither. The heron may be seen rising, like an arrow shot from a bow, from Keilder Burn;

sea-birds wander thus far inland from Holy Island and the Farne Isles, and even make their nests and breed their young at this distance from their kind. The frequent hooting of the owl may be heard here in the night-time, and the distressed cry of the plover resounds all day over these heathery solitudes, where, but for such shrill voices, the silence and the utter loneliness might be felt as a burden, and the bare, desolate country, stretching to the bare, desolate hills, might seem too horribly remote from the kindly haunts of men. But wild as this country now is, and far scattered as are its inhabitants, there must, "in the dark backward and abysm of time," have been a numerous people here, for there are traces of ancient camps on most of the hills, and within two miles' compass there must have been at least six settlements of the aboriginal inhabitants of these islands, perhaps of those very Picts whose disorderly valour caused the building of the Roman wall.

KEILDER CASTLE.

The woods of Keilder are still in sight when the yet inconsiderable "water of Tyne" is swollen by the broader and more impetuous Lewis Burn, which, after a turbulent career through picturesque glens amid the fells, ploughs its way deep among the pebbly soil of the haughs, and then makes a fatal junction with the more distinguished stream.

"There's wealth o' kye i' bonny Braidlees,
There's wealth o' youses i' Tine,

says the old ballad. It was the habit of the Borderer to regard other folks' possessions as his own, as they might be for the taking, and of these "youses" and kye the hardy wooer remarks to her to whom his speech is here addressed, "these shall all be thine." Here, looking down from the moorlands on the confluence of the Tyne and the Lewis Burn, one sees how this portion of the north country must always have been a rich pastoral land, very alluring indeed

GREYSTEAD BRIDGE.

to the reivers who lived beyond Peel Fell. The "haughs" are the flat pastures among the hills and by the side of streams. There is a fair, broad prospect of these where the two "waters" come together. Their monotony is here and there broken by dark bands of sheltering trees. Over the sheep and cattle grazing on these lowlands the ancient peel towers kept guard. There were both peels and castles, indeed. The Border peel was a solitary square tower, with stone walls of enormous thickness. Into the lowest of its compartments cattle were driven when there was an alarm of visitors "from over the Border." To the upper storeys those who fled for shelter and safety ascended by means of a ladder, which they drew up behind them, then defending themselves as best they might until their neighbours could be summoned to the conflict by the fire which on these warlike occasions was always hung from a gable of the roof. It was not only to steal cattle and sheep that the marauders came. There were often deep blood-feuds to avenge. The Robsons, who are declared to have been "honest men, save doing a little shifting for their living," made a raid on the Grahams of Liddesdale, and brought home sheep which were found to be afflicted with the scab. Their own flocks died in consequence, and the Robsons became very angry therefor, so that they made a second raid into Liddesdale, and brought back seven Grahams as their prisoners, all of whom they incontinently hanged, with the intimation, quite superfluous under such circumstances, that "the neist time gentlemen cam to tak their schepe they were no

DALLY CASTLE.

to be scabbit." Such acts bred constant retaliation, and in Northumberland to this day there is no very kindly feeling to persons "from the other side of the Border."

The remains of castles and peel towers crowd together somewhat when we have passed the pleasant little village of Falstone, which seems from time immemorial to have been occupied mainly by the Robson clan. At Falstone, where there are two rival but not unfriendly churches nestling among the trees, was discovered, a while ago, a Runic cross raised to the memory of some old Saxon Hrothbert, from whom, the name being the ancient form of Robert, it is probable enough that the doughty Robsons sprang. There was a peel in the village itself, but this has been long since incorporated with the laird's house. Another stood a short distance away, on the opposite side of the Tyne, below Greystead—where we reach the first important bridge over the North Tyne; and within a short distance of a point where three valleys unite their streams there stood two castles related to each other by a deadly feud, and two peels made famous by a wild friendship. Dally Castle—there are now but a few low, earth-covered walls remaining—occupies the summit of a hill distant about a mile and a half from the south bank of the Tyne. Tarset Castle—recognisable only as a green mound—stood on the north bank, close to where the river is joined by the Tarset Burn. The popular legends have connected these old Border strongholds by a subterranean passage, which is believed to have been haunted through many generations. Here a vivid superstition has heard carriages rolling underground, and has seen long processions emerge from an opening which no country wit had the skill to find. In Tarset Castle lived that Red Comyn who was slain by Robert Bruce, and of whom one of the Bruce's friends "made siccar" by thrusting a dagger to his heart when he had been left for dead. Sir Ralph Fenwick occupied Tarset Castle in 1526, but was driven out by the Charltons, though this must then have been one of the strongest places on the Borders. At some other and undetermined period—so the popular legends say—Tarset and Dally Castles were occupied by families which were at feud with each other, but it so fell out that the Lord of Tarset was smitten by the charms of his enemy's sister, whom he met by stealth in some retired spot on the moorlands. There, one day, he was set upon by the Lord of Dally and killed, and a cross was thereafter set up to his memory—perhaps by the lady for whom he had died—the site of which is pointed out to this day.

Far different from the relations which existed between the lords of Tarset and Dally were those of Barty of the Comb and Corbit Jack, who inhabited neighbouring peels further up the Tarset Burn. Barty awoke one morning to find that all his sheep had been driven over the Border. Straight he repaired to his faithful Corbit Jack, and the two friends set off together over the fells; whence Barty of the Comb returned with a sword wound in his thigh, the dead body of his "fere" on his shoulder, and a flock of the Leathem sheep marching before him. The record of such occurrences is preserved only in the stories of those who rejoice in male prowess, and who relate how Barty "garred a foe's heid spang alang the heather like an moan;" but that they had a very pathetic side also the touching ballad of "The Border Widow" might help us to understand.

The old feuds were kept up long after all reason for them had ceased to be, and when no more raiders came from the Liddell to the Tyne the men of the neighbouring valleys fought with each other, from lack of more useful employment. It was the wont, for example, of a descendant of this same Barty of the Comb to appear suddenly at Bellingham Fair, with a numerous following of Tarset and Tarret Burn men at his back, and, raising a Border slogan, to behave as if Bellingham had been Donnybrook. This was at the beginning of the present century only, when, according to Sir Walter Scott, the people of North Tynedale were all "quite wild," a statement which is not borne out by other authorities, though this "muckle Jock" of Tarset Burn can by no means have had such manners as stamp the caste of Vere de Vere.

The home of those Charltons who drove Sir Ralph Fenwick out of Tarset Castle, and even out of Tynedale, "to his great reproache," observes an old writer, was at Hesleyside, which is nearly two miles from Bellingham northwards. Here a tower was erected in the fourteenth century. There were other powerful Charltons in the immediate neighbourhood—at the Bowere, a mile further up the Tyne, for example, where there lived Hector Charlton, "one of the greatest thieves in those parts," if old stories tell true. It was Hector who bought off two men that were to be hung, and then let them loose to prey on the King's lieges, taking for himself, as became a man boastful of his shrewdness, a due share of their spoil. Also it was the lady of Hesleyside who, in place of a sound meal, would sometimes serve up a spur on an otherwise empty dish, by way of hint that the larder had need to be replenished; and Hesleyside, proud of its past, still keeps this spur as an heirloom. But out of strength, as says Samson's riddle, there cometh sweetness. The later generations of Charltons have been a cultured race, and it was a rare collection of choice books which was dispersed at the Hesleyside sale a few years ago. Of the ancient tower nothing now remains, the present mansion of the family, situated amid woods which are conspicuous for many miles around, having been built at a comparatively recent period.

At Bellingham, where several fairs are still annually held, and which has been, so long as local history goes back, the central market town of this remote district, we find amid the billowy moorlands a sweet pastoral country, set about with well-timbered lands. The village took its name from the De Bellinghams (now extinct), a family which tried to drive out the Charltons of Hesleyside, and came to no good thereby. Under Henry VIII. Sir Alan de Bellingham was the Warden of the Marches. The village is somewhat commonplace, but has a very interesting church and beautiful surroundings. A mile away Hareshaw Lynn comes tumbling down, between seamed cliffs and verdurous precipices.

"'Tween wooded cliffs, fern-fringed at falls,
All broken into spray and foam."

For two miles there is a succession of beautiful cascades, which sing their wilful tune under a dappled archway of clinging shrubs and bending trees. Bellingham Castle has disappeared, like the family by which it was erected, but the old church, with its strong stone roof, bears witness of how in the days of the Border feuds even the House of God had need to be built so that it might be defended against wary and ruthless foes. The structure is in the early Norman style. The stone roof was probably added after the church had been twice fired by the Scots. The nave seems to have been used for much the same purpose as the peel towers, the narrow windows having obviously been intended as much for defensive purposes as for the admission of light. At Bellingham, as indeed throughout all this wild Border country, one may gather a plentiful store of song and legend—tales of how a man whom Bowrie Charlton had slain was buried at the Charlton pew door, so that his murderer dared not to go to church again whilst he lived; of how St. Cuthbert appeared in the church to a young lady who sought a miracle, and how the said miracle was but half completed because of the fright of the young lady's mother; of how other miracles were wrought at St. Cuthbert's Well; and of many another strange event of superstitious times. "The past doth win a glory from its being far," but Bellingham is a very humdrum village now, with no more exciting occurrences than its fairs.

BELLINGHAM CHURCH.

Shortly after the North Tyne has dreamed leisurely along through Bellingham village, its quiet ways are suddenly disturbed by the inrush of a water which is almost as wide as its own, and greatly more turbulent. The Rede has come down from the wild and bare region which the Watling Street traversed on its way to Jedburgh and beyond. Its springs are in the slopes of the Cheviot range north of Carter Fell. Forcing its way over a rock-strewn bed, it flows under the dark shade of Ellis Crag, and by the battle-field of Otterburn, and, with many a capricious bend or lordly curve, past the ancient Roman station of Habitancum, where, until a splenetic farmer destroyed all but its lower

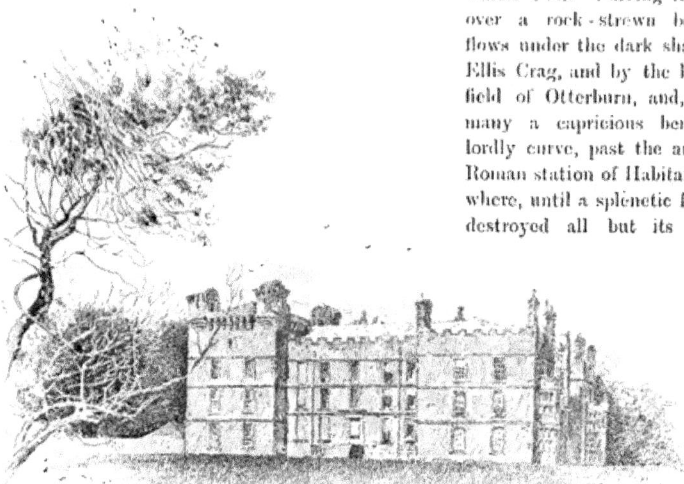

portions, the heroic figure of "Rob of Risingham," one of the most ancient of English sculptures, might be seen. The Rede is a stream which drains an enormous acreage of moor. A day's rain will swell it into a broad and boisterous torrent, with wide skirts extending far over the haughs. Famous for salmon-breeding is the Rede, and it is only by constant watching that the men of Redesdale are prevented from taking, out of all due season, what they regard as their own. When there is no "fresh" in the river the fish may be seen lying crowded together in the shallow pools, so that it

CHIPCHASE CASTLE.

is possible to wade in and take them without intervention of net, or gaff, or rod. But it is an exasperating circumstance that, plentiful as the salmon are, the season for rod-fishing in Redesdale is short, in spite of the law which permits it to be pursued for most months of the year; for as the fish come up here for the spawning season only, there are not more than some two months during which they may become the angler's legitimate prey. Doubtless such scenes as that which is depicted by Sir Walter Scott in "Guy Mannering" have been witnessed in Redesdale on many a former day. Salmon-spearing from "trows" was common down to at least the middle of the present century, the "trow" being a sort of double punt, pointed at the bows and joined together by a plank at the stern, and the spear, or "leister," being a barbed iron fork attached to a long pole. The Tyne has a Salmon Conservancy Board in these more severe times, and if trow or leister were to be seen on the river they would be seized as spoil of war.

The narrow streak of gleaming water which made a silvery line across Deadwater Bog has now taken toll of wide lands—

> "The struggling rill insensibly has grown
> Into a brook of loud and stately march,
> Crossed ever and anon by plank and arch."

Far more than this it has done, indeed, for no longer would any plank be capable of spanning its waters. The North Tyne, which, with all its winding, keeps a much straighter course than the Rede, is now beyond all doubt a river, and such a river as, being liable to sudden and mighty floods, called "freshes" or "spates" in these parts, is of a width altogether out of proportion to the ordinary depth of its waters. Very pleasant and cool and shady are the banks of the North Tyne on hot summer days, and of such varying beauty, withal, that the angler whose thoughts are not too intently fixed on his creel, and on those stories of extraordinary luck with which he purposes hereafter to entertain his friends, may lose all sense of his occupation in that "peace and patience and calm content" which, says Izaak Walton, seized upon Sir Henry Wotton, "as he sat quietly on a summer's evening, on a bank, a-fishing." He is a fortunate angler who can take "a contemplative man's recreation" on such a river as the North Tyne, where he may camp out for a month together, well assured of sport; but where he need not feel lonely unless he wills, for a moderate walk will generally suffice to bring him to a village and an inn.

Among the oldest of these villages is Wark, some five miles below Reedsmouth. In course of centuries of change it has fallen from its high estate, for it was once the capital of North Tynedale, and a session of the Scottish Courts was held on its Moot Hill when Alexander III. was King of Scotland, great part of Northumberland being also under his rule. Wark is a very unpretending village now, with a modern church, and a school founded by a philanthropic pedlar, and nothing about it half so interesting as its history. A mile away stands Chipchase

Castle, which looks bright and new as it is seen from the railway, and yet is one of the most ancient and famous strongholds on the Borders. Not all of it is equally ancient, however, for in the time of James I. the present noble manor-house was added to the "keep" of earlier days by a descendant of that Sir George Heron who was slain in "The Raid of the Reidswire," and who is called in the ballad which celebrates that event, "Sir George Hearoune, of Schipsyde House." Ballad-writers were clearly not particular in the matter of proper names, for Sir George's patronymic was known well enough to the Scots, seeing that after his death they made presents of falcons to their prisoners, grimly observing that the said prisoners were nobly treated, since they got "live hawks for dead herons."

There was a village of Chipchase in Saxon times, and there are remains of a fort much older than the keep which has been incorporated with the existing mansion. Peter de Insula, a retainer of the Umfravilles of Prudhoe, which is further down the Tyne, lived here in the thirteenth century. The Herons, who followed him, were of the same family as the stout baron who is celebrated by Sir Walter Scott:—

> "That noble lord
> Sir Hugh the Heron bold,
> Baron of Twisell and of Ford,
> And captain of the hold."

The race has died out, as is the case with so many of the famous families of Northumberland; but coal sustains what a warlike lordship built, and Chipchase Castle is to this day as proud and stately a place as in the time of the noblest Heron of them all. There are grim stories told of what took place there in former rude times. Sir Reginald Fitz-Urse, says tradition, was starved to death in the dungeon of the keep, and another unfortunate knight, pursued by the swords of intending murderers, lost himself in the chambers of the castle walls, and never issued alive therefrom. The peel tower of Chipchase is almost as large as a Norman keep, and is more ornamented than was common in most structures of the kind. The more recent castle is held to be one of the noblest examples of Jacobean architecture that have come down to us.

Mr. Algernon Charles Swinburne, the poet, has recently reminded the world, through the medium of some Border ballads which but indifferently represent the dialect of Northumberland, that he is himself a Borderer. Long ago he wrote glowingly of "the league-long billows of rolling, and breathing, and brightening heather," and of "the wind, and all the sound, and all the fragrance and freedom and glory of the high north moorland." It is probably from Sir William de Swyneburn of Haughton Castle that he is descended. Haughton stands on the opposite bank of the river to Chipchase, and a brief space lower down. Here Archie Armstrong, the chief of a famous moss-trooping clan, was starved to death long ago—by accident, and not design, let it in justice be said. Sir William de Swyneburn was treasurer to Margaret of Scotland, and is credited with having had a great and insatiable greed for his neighbours' lands. He was succeeded in his tenure of the castle by the Widdringtons, one of whom is celebrated in the ballad of "Chevy Chase." It was he, indeed, for whom the poet's

"——heart was woe,
As one in doleful dumps;
For when his legs were smitten in two
He fought upon his stumps."

HAUGHTON CASTLE.

But there was a Sir Thomas Swinburne at Haughton in the reign of Henry VIII. He was Warden of the Marches, and it was through his neglect of a prisoner that Archie Armstrong came to his death. Haughton Castle has a fine look of antique strength, but is nevertheless, in the main, a modern building. The original castle was burned down at some unrecorded time, and its ruins were restored and made habitable in the early part of the present century. Close by, it is sad to say, a former owner had a paper-mill, where forged assignats were manufactured for the purpose of being passed off as the genuine French article during the Duke of York's expedition to Flanders in 1793. To Sir William de Swynburn the people around Haughton are still indebted for the convenience of a ferry, for one which he established so far back as the reign of Henry II. plies in the old fashion—by an overhead rope and pulley—to this day.

Past Haughton Castle the river strains and rushes between narrowing banks. Lower down, at Chollerford, it has changed its course somewhat in the lapse of

AT WARDEN.

centuries, and the waters of North Tyne now flow over what was the abutment of an ancient bridge. At this spot let the chance visitor take the poet's advice:—

> "Here plant thy foot, where many a foot hath trod
> Whose scarce known home was o'er the southern wave,
> And sit thee down, on no ignoble sod,
> Green from the ashes of the great and brave;
> Here stretched the chain which nations could enslave,
> The least injurious token of their thrall,
> Which, if it helped to humble, helped to save;
> This shapeless mound thou know'st not what to call
> Was a world's wonder once—this was the Roman wall."

Here, indeed, the great bulwark against northern barbarism approached the Tyne on either of its banks. The river is now crossed by a bridge which was built in 1775, but there still exist substantial remains of that by which the Roman legions crossed over to the great stations of Procolitia and Cilurnum. Procolitia was one of a trio of important stations near to this portion of the North Tyne, and is some three or four miles away. Not many years ago no less than 16,000 coins, besides some rings, and twenty Roman altars, were discovered on this site. The coins ranged from the days of the Triumvirate to those of Gratian. The altars were all dedicated to Coventina. Who Coventina may have been, the antiquaries inquire in vain. Of her neither Greek, nor Roman, nor Celtic mythology has kept record. What is clear is that she must have been worshipped by the first cohort of Batavians, which kept guard here when these altars were made. At Cilurnum, now known as the Chesters, nearer by three miles to the bank of the Tyne and the ancient Roman bridge, altars were raised to more various deities. A cohort of Asturians was in garrison here. With the exception of Newcastle, probably, and Birdoswald certainly, this was the most important station on the Roman wall, and is at this time far the most wonderfully preserved. One may stand in the grounds of Mr. John Clayton, at the Chesters, and, with slight exercise of the fancy, reconstruct a Roman city in Britain, so materially is the imagination assisted by what recent excavations have disclosed. Agricola is believed to have built Cilurnum in 81 A.D. It existed as a camp before the wall was built, and covered a space of six acres of ground. Coal was found on one of the hearths when the place was first unearthed, a curious proof of the long period during which that mineral has been in use in the district through which this river flows. Among the statuary discovered was a well-preserved figure which is believed to represent the river-god of North Tyne :—

> "The local deity, with oozy hair
> And mineral crown, beside his jagged urn
> Recumbent."

At Chollerford the even course of the river is broken by a long curving weir, over which the "wan water" comes down magnificently in seasons of flood. "The water ran mountains hie" at Chollerford Brae, says an old ballad; but that is clearly an exaggeration. Nevertheless, Chollerford is not the place at which one would choose to cross the river at flood-time, and without a bridge, as happened with "Jock o' the Side," when he was hotly followed by pursuers from Newcastle town. It is odd how ancient and mediæval and ballad history centres around this quiet spot. Half a mile away is Heaven's Field, where Oswald of Northumbria gathered his army around him, set up the standard of the Cross by the Roman wall, adjured his troops to pray to the living God, and overthrew in one of the most important battles of our early history the far larger forces of heathenesse. Here we are approaching the point where the North and the South Tyne, making a fork of swift, clear-shining water, unite their streams to form the great river of which Milton, and Akenside, and many another poet, have admiringly sung. By the ancient village of Warden, the two streams, as an old writer says, "salute one another;" and where they meet there is a stretch of water as wide almost as a lake, reflecting on still days the high-towering woods and the misty hills which divide North and South Tynedale.

ALSTON MOOR.

THE TYNE.

CHAPTER II.

THE SOUTH TYNE.

On the "Fiend's Fell"—Tyne Springs—Garrigill—Alston and the Moors—Knaresdale Hall—The Ridleys—Haltwhistle—Allendale—Haydon Bridge and John Martin—The Arthurian Legends.

WE are in Cumberland, amid the wilds. How did St. Augustine contrive to penetrate to such a region as this? The land is desolate, bleak, solitary. A desert of heathery hills; here and there a reed-fringed stream; in front the wild and stern face of Cross Fell! A seldom-trodden height, this Cumberland mountain, seeming to stand sentinel over all the country round. On its lower slopes, the three great commercial rivers of the North have their rise. We have come here in search of the source of the South Tyne, but a short morning's wandering would lead us also to the sources of the Wear and the Tees. Cross Fell is 2,892 feet above the level of the sea, and to half that elevation we have ascended to reach these moors in which it seems to be set. The "Wizard Fell," some poet has called it. The "Fiend's Fell" it was called of old. To reach it from Alston one must trudge wearily afoot, or hire such vehicle as may be obtainable where travellers seldom come. The road winds about over windy uplands, ever rising nearer to the drifting clouds. A lead-miner's bothie stands beside it here and there, and one is constantly passing places where the miners have "prospected" for ore. All the roadside, indeed, has been explored and broken. The South Tyne is making music all the way, for it flows downward to one's right, and is constantly tumbling over rocks and forming cascades over little precipices. It becomes a hasty, tumultuous river almost immediately after its birth, increasing in volume with a celerity quite wonderful to see, and seemingly impetuous to lose the cold companionship of these bleak and barren hills, which, despite their sternness, are all aglow with colour, and pulsating with rapid waves of light.

To the right, brown ridges of high moorland; to the left, slopes more broken, strewn over, as it would seem, with masses of light-purple rock; beyond all, the dark ridge of Cross Fell closing-in the lonely valley. A streak of brighter and fresher green than any that is visible on the hillsides indicates where a hidden thread of water percolates the moss. Then there is a glint of silver here and there. Finally, the eye lights upon a sedgy pool, in the centre of which there is perceptible that throbbing movement which tells of the presence of a spring. This, then, is the source of the South Tyne. Before its waters have travelled far from here they will be crossed by a rude, ancient bridge, and swollen by many a little tributary from the hills.

From the summit of Cross Fell at certain seasons the mysterious and terrible "helm wind" blows. When no breeze disturbs the air, and when, over all the country round, there is a clear and bright sky, a line of strangely tortured and curving clouds will form itself along the ridge of the mountain. Then the shepherds will hie to where shelter may be found, for they know that a wind will soon be blowing before which no human creature can stand upright, and that may uproot trees, and unroof houses, and carry dismay into the valleys far below. It was the fiends holding revel, said the early inhabitants of these regions; wherefore St. Augustine erected a cross on the highest part of the fell, collecting his monks around him, and holding a religious service there, whereby if the fiends were made less harmful they were by no means dispossessed. The nearest inhabited place is Garrigill, which is a prominent object in the valley as one ascends the moor from Alston. A Cumberland village is a series of white gleaming spots against the hillside—a collection of whitewashed walls and grey-blue roofs of stone. This of Garrigill is like so many others, except as to the height at which it has been built, and its bright contrast with the gloom of its surroundings. There is a pleasant shadow of trees about its housetops. There is a village inn, and a village green, and a village well. The young river flows past quickly, merrily, with the music of numerous little falls. The people of these hill regions are miners for the most part. Lead was worked in these mountain sides at times so far back as the Roman occupation of Britain, and some of the miners, if they had kept a record of such things, might show a pedigree longer than that of those whose ancestors were engaged in Senlac fight. Their chief quarters are at Alston and at Allenheads, but their bothies are scattered about these moors. The town of Alston is four miles below Garrigill. It is a pretty, white-looking town, high up on the slope of the moors. Of its two principal streets one is parallel with the river Nent, and the other with the South Tyne, the two streams here joining to make a fairly considerable river. At Alston we are again on the track of St. Augustine's footsteps. He may even have

FEATHERSTONE CASTLE.

FEATHERSTONE BRIDGE.

founded a place of worship here, and it is in keeping with the tradition of his having Christianised Cumberland that the church should bear his name.

White Alston, with the wild brown moors beyond it, stands between the broad, open desolateness of the mountain region and a lovely district in which the South Tyne laughs under the threading branches of ancient woods, or broadens out by sunny haughs, as if to rest itself between strife and strife.

Just below Alston we once more set foot on Northumbrian soil. The Ayleburn and the Gildersdale waters flow from opposite directions along the county boundaries, the one from high moorlands, by the old manor-house of Randalholme, the other from the peaty morass where once flourished the great forest of Gildersdale. Henceforth the country assumes a more gentle aspect. The lead-mines have been left far behind; the river lies broad in the sunlight, or darkens under the shadow of trees; there are gentler undulations in the hills, and

> "Long fields of barley and of rye
> That clothe the wold and meet the sky."

The remains of Whitley Castle, which is the modern and inappropriate name of a Roman station, are to be seen shortly after the Gildersdale Burn has joined the Tyne, and here, also, one comes upon an ancient Roman road, the Maiden Way, along which it may have been that "a woman might walk scatheless in Eadwine's day." Hereabouts the river is pleasantly fringed, and cool, and full of shadows and deep reflections. At brief intervals it is joined by some new tributary, pouring noisily out of a little valley of its own. Of these one of the most interesting is the Knar, which comes down in a boisterous and scurrying manner from a region of wilderness and lofty fell, where the red deer lingered latest in these parts, and where the remains of ancient forests may be discovered in the soft and treacherous moss.

Very rich in interest and beauty are some of the glens through which these mountain rivulets flow, with sudden precipices, and narrow defiles, and rock-strewn gorges, and the charm of moss and fern and overhanging tree. Knaresdale Hall, which is no more than a farmhouse in these days, is some distance lower down the South Tyne than the spot at which the Knar Burn brings its contribution to the constantly broadening stream. It dates back to rough seventeenth century times, and was as strongly built as became the home of the doughty lairds of Knaresdale. But the noblest of South Tyne castles is that of Featherstone, or Featherstonehaugh. It stands in a fine park opposite to where the river is joined by Hartley Burn. When Lord Marmion was feasting full and high at the castle of Norham, on Tweedside—

"A northern harper rude
Chanted a rhyme of deadly feud;
How the fierce Thirlwalls, and Ridleys all,
Stout Willimondswick,
And Hardriding Dick,
And Hughie of Hawdon, and Will o' the Wall
Have set on Sir Albany Featherstonhaugh,
And taken his life at the Deadman's Shaw."

For "the rest of this old ballad" the notes to "Marmion" refer us to "The Minstrelsy of the Scottish Border." But the ballad has not an old line in it. It is simply one of those sham antiques which it amused Surtees, of Mainsforth, to pass off upon one who trusted to his good faith and his familiarity with Border legend and story. The incident which it records is probably as imaginary as the old woman from whose recitation the words are declared to have been taken down.

Featherstone Castle is not built upon elevated ground, as is the case with most of the strong places of the Borders. It stands in a quiet vale amid wooded heights. The Featherstones claimed to have lived there for many centuries, the first of the family, according to tradition, being a Saxon chief of the eighth century. No pedigree can be safely and certainly traced back so far; yet, undoubtedly, the Featherstones were a very ancient race, and maintained their footing here through all the long troubles of the Borders. The nucleus around which the castle has grown was a square peel, of more elaborate ornamentation than was common. It has been declared, indeed, to be "the loveliest tower in the county." At this day it forms but one feature of a splendid group of castellated buildings, with many of the walls overgrown with ivy, and with a Gothic chapel as one of its main features. Near by is the lovely little glen of Pynkinsclengh, concerning which Mother Shipton predicted strange things, as yet unrealised. In Pynkinscleugh it was that Ridley of Hardriding endeavoured to carry off the daughter of the Lord of Featherstonehaugh on her wedding-day, and caused her death thereby, for she ran between the combatants' swords; and this she did so hastily and impetuously that she was slain.

The "Willimondswick" mentioned in the ballad of Surtees was one of the very numerous Ridleys of this district. Willimontswick disputes with Unthank Hall the honour of being the birthplace of Bishop Ridley the martyr. He was, in all probability, the only peaceful man of his family, for these Ridleys were through many generations a hard fighting, hard-riding, and turbulent race. From the record of scarcely any deed of violence on the Borders is the name of a Ridley absent. The ballads tell how—

"But an' John Ridley thrust his spear
Right through Sim o' the Cathill's wame;"

and how—

"Alec Ridley he let flee
A clothyard shaft ahint the wa';
And struck Wat Armstrong in the ee."

To such men as these the good Bishop Ridley, about to yield his body to the flames, wrote that, "as God hath set you in our stock and kindred, not for any respect to your person, but of His abundant grace and goodness, to be, as it were, the bell-wether to order and conduct the rest, so, I pray you, continue and increase in the maintenance of truth, honesty, and all true godliness." Bell-wethers they were, indeed, these Ridleys, and to some rough purpose, too.

Unthank Hall, to the tenants of which the martyr also wrote letters of farewell, is a recently rebuilt mansion, the near neighbour of Willimontswick, and on the opposite side of the Tyne to the quiet little country town of Haltwhistle. We are here again within a brief distance of the Roman wall. Haltwhistle may have been garrisoned by some of the assailants of that stupendous rampart. There are ancient earthworks on the site of what is known as the Castle Hill, one side of which is defended by an artificial breastwork of precipitous appearance. The former "Castle of Hautwysill" is now no more than a tall barn-like building, with a loop-holed turret resting on corbels. The chancel of the church is a survival from the old rough-riding days, and dates back to the thirteenth century; but there was too much fighting in the little town for much that was ancient in it to have survived into the present century. Haltwhistle has now a growing population of 1,600, and is as sweetly situated as heart could desire.

This little town is made attractive not only by its neighbourhood to the Tyne, but through the wild and fantastic beauty of Haltwhistle Burn, which flows down from the desolate, dreary, and cruel-looking Northumberland lakes, where the winds

HALTWHISTLE.

HAYDON BRIDGE.

that ruffle the surface of these forlorn waters

"Wither drearily on barren moors."

Yet there are fine sights enough above the ravine through which Haltwhistle Burn has ravaged and torn its way—wide views of fir-clad slopes, and wide-stretching farm-lands, and rolling moors, and dark precipices, and the ever-pleasant valley of the Tyne. Such another sight there is, with even a more extensive prospect, from the heights above the little hamlet of Bardon Mill. Southward lie Willimontswick, and the ancient chapel of Beltingham, and Ridley Hall, and the confluence of the Allen and the Tyne, and the grey, bright-looking village of Haydon Bridge; northward may be seen the important Roman stations of Vindolana and Borcoviens, and the far-reaching, dipping, and bending line of the Roman wall. Backwards, over the ground which we have traversed from Cross Fell, Saddleback and Skiddaw are in sight, and half the peaks, fells, and ridges of the great Cumbrian group.

A little below Bardon Mill the River Allen joins the South Tyne. What the

Rede is to the northern, the Allen is to the southern branch of the river—the largest and longest of its affluents. It is formed by the joining of two streams which rise on the extreme southern borders of Northumberland, and which flow some three or four miles apart until they are within about five miles of their confluence with the Tyne. The Allen is one of the loveliest and most retired of streams, flowing between picturesque rocks, and sheltered and darkened by hanging woods. There are here:

> "Steep and lofty cliffs,
> That on a wild secluded scene impress
> Thoughts of more deep seclusion."

Of all northern rivers this is the one which is most praised for the wild and yet tranquil variety of its scenery, for the charms which the quiet angler finds in the turns and windings of its rocky pass, and for the beauty and diversity of the foliage which clothes its steeply ascending vale.

At Haydon Bridge, when the water is low, there lies a great expanse of shingle, polished into whiteness by the floods. White are the houses also, with roofs of bluish stone; and there is an aspect of great quaintness about the little village, which seems to have been founded in Saxon times, and to have borrowed much of its older building material from the Roman wall. Of its former state there are still some small remainders in the chancel of an old chapel, and a cottage here and there on the height. It was at Haydon Bridge that John Martin, the painter of "The Last Judgment," and "The Plains of Heaven," and "Belshazzar's Feast," was born, and here, up to his twelfth birthday, he evoked the wonder of the simple folk with his rough drawings, a number of which, with the family eccentricity, he once exhibited upon his father's housetop.

From here it would be easy to make an excursion into King Arthur's country. Not, indeed, to

> "The island-valley of Avilion,
> Where falls not hail, nor rain, nor any snow,
> Nor ever wind blows loudly."

Avilion is Glastonbury, it is said; but all about this ruder country there is store of Arthurian legend, mostly of that coarser sort to which belongs the story of the "bag pudding" which "the Queen next morning fried." The King and Queen Guinevere, the King's hounds, and the lords and ladies of his court, lie all together in an enchanted sleep in a great hall beneath the Castle of Sewingshields, near to the Roman wall; or so the legends say.

And now we are once more approaching Warden Mill. To the North and South Tyne we must henceforth bid adieu. From this point they will flow together in the same bed. One has come down from the Scottish borders, a holiday stream, for forty-three miles; the other, not without doing its share of work by the way, has hurried over thirty-nine miles from the Cumberland fells. Thirty-six miles more, over half of which extent the Tyne is a great labouring, work-a-day river, and we shall meet the breezes and the billows of the northern sea.

HEXHAM ABBEY.

THE TYNE.

CHAPTER III.

FROM HEXHAM TO NEWCASTLE.

Hexham and the Abbey Church—Dilston Hall—The Derwentwater Rising—Corbridge—Bywell Woods—Prudhoe and Ovingham—Stephenson's Birthplace—Ryton and Newburn—The Approach to Newcastle.

UNTIL it becomes a tidal river, which does not happen till the huge pillar of smoke that announces Newcastle comes in sight, the Tyne in ordinary seasons is a broad and shallow stream, with occasional deep and quiet pools dreaming in shadowy places. Below Warden its banks are open on either side to the far-away hills, and it has but a bare, starved look among these level and almost naked shores. Yet it is a rich, fertile, and famous country, through which now flows this "water of Tyne." Hexham, renowned for its market-gardens, is close at hand. Its roofs peer out of a wide circle of trees, and above them all, massive and conspicuous, stands sentinel the broad square tower of the Abbey Church.

"The heart of all England" is a designation which was long ago claimed for their town by the Hexham folk. Just as Boston is held to be the hub of the universe, so Hexham was declared to be the centre of our right little, tight little island. Hence radiated such Gospel light and such imperfect learning as illumined these wild northern parts in Saxon times. Mr. Green has said of St. Wilfred, whom he calls Wilfrith of York, that his life was made up of flights to Rome and returns to England, which is but a churlish description of a great career; for St. Wilfred, the most magnificent and wealthy ecclesiastic of his period, not only restored York and built the church at Ripon, but erected here at Hexham an abbey and a cathedral of which Richard, the Prior, who assisted to restore it from its ruins, wrote:—"It surpassed in the excellence of its architecture all the buildings of England; and, in truth, there was nothing like it at that time to be found on this side of the Alps." The time to which Prior Richard refers was the latter portion of the seventh century. Wilfred, who was trained at Lindisfarne, visited France and Italy in his youth, and came back full of great architectural ideas. There were then, it is probable, no stone churches in England. At any rate, the first five churches of stone were York, Lincoln, Ripon, Withern, and Hexham; of which Wilfred certainly built three. Never had bishop a vaster diocese. Wilfred, Archbishop of York and Bishop of Hexham, had supreme ecclesiastical control over a district which—during his lifetime, and when he was in misfortune—was divided by Theodore of Tarsus into the four bishoprics of York, Hexham, Withern, and Lindisfarne. Of Wilfred's cathedral of Hexham nothing remains but the underground oratory, built about 674. The church was fired by incursive Danes in 875. Three centuries later the canons of Hexham piously went to work to rebuild and restore; but then the unruly Scots made a raid into England, taking Hexham on their way, and not only destroyed the restored buildings, but slaughtered the townsfolk, and burned to death two hundred children whom they found at school.

Hexham was once, says Prior Richard, "very large and stately." However, it diminished in importance under the influence of successive battles, tumults, incursions, and changes. Hexham ceased to be the seat of a bishopric at an early period of its history; and though the monks donned armour and girded swords to their sides when Henry VIII.'s commissioners came, declaring that, "we be twenty free men in this house, and will die all or that you shall enter here," their bravery nothing availed them, and the dissolution of the monastery still further depressed Hexham in the list of English towns. There is a story that the last Superior was hanged at the priory gates, and several of his monks along with him. The beautiful Abbey Church was restored, greatly to its detriment, in 1858. But even the restorers could not spoil it utterly, and it still gives an air of grandeur and stateliness to the quiet town which it adorns.

It is all an old battle-field, the land around Hexham. "Wallace wight," who is frequently heard of on Tyneside, generally to his disadvantage, and part of whose body was hung up on the bridge at Newcastle when he was executed, came here and slaughtered the people in 1297. One of the decisive battles of the Wars of the Roses was fought close by Hexham in 1464, on which occasion, as one of the most romantic stories in our history narrates, Queen Margaret and her son found shelter and hiding in a robbers' cave. "Hexham," writes Defoe, "is famous, or rather infamous, for having the first blood drawn at it in the war against their Prince by the Scots in King Charles's time." A good deal of the blood of the families of these parts was shed for the Stuart cause, then and long afterwards. Three miles below Hexham, and near to the scene of the Yorkist and Lancastrian battle, Devil's Water flows into the Tyne, past the grey old tower which is all that remains to attest the former splendour of the Earls of Derwentwater. This Devil's Water—which was Dyvelle's Water in bygone days, so called from an ancient family of these parts—tears its way swiftly between high and verdurous walls of rock—

> "It's eddying foam-balls prettily distrest
> By ever-changing shape and want of rest."

The hill-sides of Dilston are clothed in magnificent woods. The scene is such as those which the old-fashioned writers were wont to describe as "beautifully sylvan." There are wild wood-paths and beds of fern, the green tangle of underwood, and the varied shade and brightness of interlacing boughs. And hence, with hesitation and a doubtful mind, the last Earl of Derwentwater set out on that rash and unlucky expedition which caused him the loss of his head.

The ancient village of Corbridge—the quietest of country villages now, with

PRUDHOE CASTLE.

extensive market-gardens occupying ground on which the Roman legions may have camped—lies but a short distance away, and it was on Corbridge Common

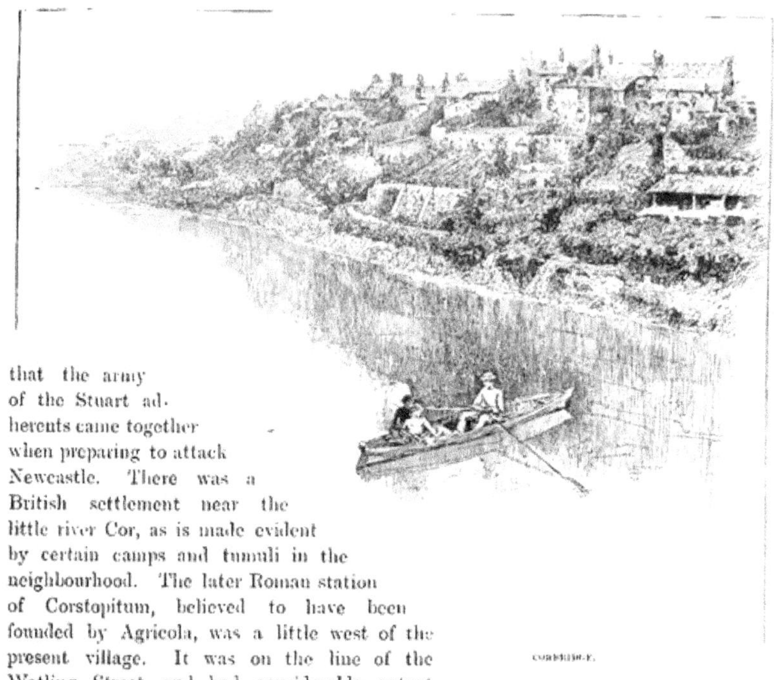

CORBRIDGE.

that the army of the Stuart adherents came together when preparing to attack Newcastle. There was a British settlement near the little river Cor, as is made evident by certain camps and tumuli in the neighbourhood. The later Roman station of Corstopitum, believed to have been founded by Agricola, was a little west of the present village. It was on the line of the Watling Street, and had considerable extent and importance. Many of the fragments of it have been worked into existing buildings, for the stations of the Roman wall, and the wall itself, were during many generations so many quarries for those who succeeded the first conquerors of our island. For a few years before and after Wilfred's time there may have been a period of quiet, during which a monastery, and, it is believed, even a king's palace, was established; but thenceforward, for long afterwards, Corbridge is mentioned in history only when it is overtaken by some great trouble. When King John arrived here in 1201 he conceived the idea that the place must have been destroyed by an earthquake, so complete and so extensive was the ruin that had been wrought. Yet three times again the town was burnt by the Scots. Even this, however, did not prevent the return of the people, and the founding of a new town of Corbridge, which sent a member to our earliest Parliaments, and only abandoned the privilege when the Corbridge folk became too poor or too indifferent to defray his "proper cost." The bridge which gives the village its name is the only bridge over the river which was not washed away or broken in the great flood of 1771.

BYWELL CASTLE.

From Corbridge to Bywell the winding course of the Tyne has as various a beauty as heart could desire. There are wide, open reaches, and still, deep, shadowy spaces between overhanging woods, and passages of lively water scourging a rocky bed. Bywell itself is an idyllic place. There are stories of how it was once a bustling town, much liable to attack from moss-troopers and all manner of Border thieves. Old records have it that so late as "the stately days of Great Elizabeth" it was "inhabited with handicraftsmen, whose trade is in all ironwork for the horsemen and borderers of that county, as in making bits, stirrups, buckles, and such others, wherein they are very expert and cunning, and are subject to the incursions of the thieves of Tynedale, and compelled, winter and summer, to bring all their cattle and sheep into the street in the night-season, and watch both ends of the street, and when the enemy approacheth to raise hue and cry, whereupon all the town prepareth for rescue of their goods, which is very populous, by reason of their trade, and stout and hardy by continual practice against the enemy." A quaintly confused statement this, but sufficiently explicit as to the uncertain conditions under which the artificers of Bywell lived. The place now sleeps quietly under its woods, lulled by the waters of the Tyne as they fall over Bywell Weir, and seems to dream of its past. "The antique age of bow and spear" has left for memorial a ruinous square tower, all mantled over with ivy, and hidden, with the exception of its battlements, in the surrounding trees. This ruin is a portion of a projected castle of the Nevilles, Earls of Westmorland; but the building was never completed, or, indeed, carried far, for the last Earl of Westmorland of the Neville family took part in that "rising of the North" of which Wordsworth's "White Doe of Rylstone" tells the sorrowful tale.

Any traveller by Tyneside whom night should overtake would be amazed to see fires gleaming out of the hillside about two miles below Bywell. They are unaccounted for by the presence of any town. The river, indeed, is about to plunge through clustering woods, and there is an aspect of solemn quiet all around. Here, nevertheless, in a small and unpretentious way, the industrial career of the river Tyne begins. The fires between the river and the hill are those of coke ovens, and they burn where, in his sturdy boyhood, Thomas Bewick, the great wood-engraver, used to play. Cherryburn House, his birthplace, is close by, and on the

NEWBURN.

other side of the river—that is to say, on its north bank—stands the ancient village of Ovingham, where a tablet against the wall of the church tower announces his grave. The brother of Dora Greenwell was incumbent of the parish for a while, by which means it came about that the poetess spent much of her youth at Ovingham. On the south side of the river, directly facing Ovingham, on a hill which is like a huge mound, stand some fragments of Prudhoe Castle. A ruin it has been for three centuries at least, and it is a very picturesque and interesting ruin still.

After a shady passage between high-banked woods, the river emerges to the broad light of day once more in front of the village of Wylam, which is one of the oldest, one of the most dismal and miserable, and one of the most famous, of the colliery villages of Northumberland. Here is George Stephenson's birthplace, a little two-storeyed cottage, standing solitary by the side of a railway. The Roman wall ran along the high ridge of ground beyond Wylam. Some interesting portions of it still remain at Denton Burn, which is over above Newburn, from two to three miles further down the Tyne. At Denton Hall lived Mrs. Montague, first of blue-stockings. Here Johnson was a visitor, and Reynolds and Garrick were occasional guests. There is a "Johnson's chamber" and a "Johnson's walk" to this day.

The village of Newburn lies about half-way up the heights, on the north side of the Tyne. Here was the last spot at which the river could be forded, for though Newburn is seventeen miles from the sea, as the river flows, it is reached twice a day by the tide. Across this ford the Scots troops under Lesley poured in 1640, to overcome the king's troops on Ryton Willows. The spot is still marked on the maps as a battlefield, and the event is spoken of as "the battle of Newburn."

A little below this place the Tyne is joined by a muddy little brook, known as Hedwin Streams. Here, as it is contended, the jurisdiction of Newcastle begins. From time immemorial—legally defined, I believe, as a period which came to an end with King Richard's return from Palestine—the mayor and citizens of Newcastle have claimed a property in the bed of the river Tyne from Spar Hawk, within the Tyne Piers, to Hedwin Streams here at Newburn, and the claim is still asserted once in five years; when, on what is known as "barge day," the Newcastle Corporation proceeds up and down the river in a series of gaily decorated steamboats, on board which high revel is held. And near Newburn, indeed, Newcastle may be said really to begin. It is five miles to where the city is blackening the atmosphere and dimming the sky with its smoke, but here are clearly discernible the fringes of its dusky robe. To our right, as we pass downward, lies the village of Blaydon. Prosaic Scotswood is on the left, and beyond it are the vast, mile-long works of Armstrong, Leslie, and Co. Where these works are was once one of the pleasantest of valleys. Now the furnaces vomit forth their flames, and the air is filled with smoke and the mighty clang of labour.

OVINGHAM.

THE HIGH-LEVEL BRIDGE AND GATESHEAD.

THE TYNE.

CHAPTER IV.

FROM NEWCASTLE TO THE SEA.

The Growth of Tyneside—"The Coaly Tyne"—Newcastle Bridges—Local Industries—Poetical Eulogies—Tyneside Landscapes—Sandgate and the Keelmen—Wallsend—Jarrow and the Venerable Bede—The Docks—Shields Harbour—North and South Shields—The Tyne Commission—Tynemouth Priory—The Open Sea.

FROM Newcastle to the sea, twelve miles by water, the Tyne is a vast tidal dock. It stands second among the rivers of the kingdom for the extent of its commerce. The Thames takes precedence in the number of vessels which enter and leave, and the Mersey stands before it in respect of the total tonnage of the ships by which it is frequented; but the Tyne ranks second to the Thames in the number of vessels which enter the port, and second to the Mersey in the bulk of its trade. But more remarkable even than the commerce of the river are its great industries. From Gateshead to the sea on the one hand, and from Newcastle to the sea on the other, there is a constant succession of shipyards, chemical factories, engineering establishments, glass-works, docks, and coal-shoots. Newcastle, it has been remarked, owes its rise to war, its maintenance to piety, and its increase to trade. A very neat and true saying. But trade has done more for the Tyne than for Newcastle. It has, since the beginning of the century, increased the population of the chief Northumbrian town from 30,000 to 160,000; but it has increased the population of Tyneside to half a million or more.

Milton did the river a huge injustice when he called this the "coaly Tyne." His intention was innocent enough, no doubt, since he meant only to acknowledge its celebrity in connection with coal. But it is the fate of these indecisively descriptive phrases to be misunderstood. The Tyne is a brighter and clearer stream than the Mersey, is immeasurably purer than the Thames, is only occasionally muddied like the Humber, and is at no time discoloured by coal. When there are floods in the upper reaches, so much brown soil is carried down by the impetuous water that the current of the river can be traced far out to sea; but at ordinary seasons the local colour of the Tyne approaches that of the sea itself, and is, in fact, a deep, clear olive-green. What is insufficiently understood, however, is that the local colour of a stream is that which is most seldom disclosed. Water takes its hue from the sky above it, and from the light which plays about its face. Hence Spenser's beautiful and much assailed phrase, "the silver-streaming Thames." Hence, also, the Tyneside poet's eulogy of his native stream:—

"Of all the rivers, north or south,
There's none like coaly Tyne."

The Romans threw three bridges across the river. There was one which crossed with the wall at Chollerford; and there was one which crossed with the Watling Street at Corbridge; and there was a third, earlier and far more important than the other two, which linked together what were afterwards to be named the counties of Durham and Northumberland. The bridge at Newcastle, built by Hadrian on his first visit to these northern parts of Roman Britain, was deemed of so much importance that at Rome a medal was struck to commemorate its erection. Also it gave its name to the Roman station which stood on the heights above. Newcastle first became known to history as Pons Ælii, in honour alike of Hadrian's bridge and of Hadrian's family. And ever since that day the town has been famous for its bridges. There was one which resembled London Bridge in having shops almost from end to end. It endured, says an eloquent local historian, "from the times of the Plantagenets, and through the Wars of the Roses, past Bosworth and Flodden Fields and the Armada, down to the encounter of the King and Parliament, to the Commonwealth, the Restoration, and the Revolution; and beyond the rebellions of 1715 and 1745 it kept its accustomed place across the stream, surviving the daily pressure of the tide, the rage of inundations, the bumping of barges and keels, the shocks of civil war, the negligent inattentions of peace." But at length large portions of it were swept away by the great flood of 1771, one of its houses being carried whole as far as Jarrow Slake, some miles farther down the Tyne.

On the bridge of Hadrian two lofty hills looked down. The Tyne has here at some remote period scourged its way through a deep ravine, and Newcastle, and its opposite neighbour, Gateshead, are built partly around the feet of commanding eminences, and still more extensively on the summits of these hills. Old Newcastle was a town of stairs. Communication between its upper and its lower portions was, with the exception of one narrow and steep street leading from the bridge, maintained by means of long flights of stone steps, which still exist, and are up to this day extensively used. All the succeeding bridges were built on the site of that of Hadrian. "The Low Bridge" was the name given to the last of these from the time when the High Level was built. It is the Swing Bridge which now crosses the Tyne at the point selected so many centuries ago, this swing bridge being a gigantic iron structure, with a great central span that is moved by hydraulic power, and leaves two openings of such extent that the *Victoria*, the largest vessel in Her Majesty's Navy, has been able to pass through without grazing either of the piers. But notable as is the Swing Bridge as a work of engineering, it is inferior even in this respect to the High Level Bridge, and very far inferior in grace and beauty. The High Level does for the higher portions of Newcastle and Gateshead what all the bridges from Hadrian's time have done for the lower portions. It is a foot and carriage way between the neighbouring towns; but it is also more than this, for at a height of twenty-seven feet above the roadway, under which a full-rigged ship can sail, there is a railway viaduct along which passes the main line to Scotland. One of the most wonderful of the world's bridges, the High Level is also one of the most handsome and well proportioned, so that it has probably been painted more frequently than any bridges but those of Cumberland and Wales. It is an appropriate thing that in the Swing Bridge and the High Level Bridge, which are likely enough to last for centuries to come, Newcastle should have memorials of its two greatest engineers, the High Level having been built by Robert Stephenson, and the Swing Bridge by Lord Armstrong.

Gateshead has been disparagingly described as "a dirty lane leading to Newcastle;" but this was in the days that are no more. It is now a great congeries of lanes, streets, roads, and alleys, dirty and otherwise. But for a large town thus intervening, we might see how rapidly the land slopes upward from the riverside to the two-miles-distant crown of Sheriff Hill, which is on the road southward to Durham, to York, and through the fair English shires to London. It was on the summit of Sheriff's Hill that the Sheriffs of Newcastle—a place which boasted of such officers because it was a county as well as a town—received the King's Judges when coming on Circuit. Thus far they advanced to meet them into the county of Durham. There was a splendid procession through Gateshead, over the Low Bridge, up the steep "Side," into Newcastle, and to the Assize Courts. Gorgeous trumpeters made proclamation; the gilded and hammerclothed carriages of the Mayor and Sheriffs were guarded by halberdiers; a tall official walked in front, with a great fur cap of maintenance and a most amazing sword. When the judges, sated with hospitality, and with the gaol-delivery completed, set off on horseback towards Carlisle, they were presented with money to buy each of them a dagger, to guard themselves against robbers and evil men.

COAL TRIMMERS.

A COAL STAITHE.

Gateshead was the site of a Saxon monastery that was certainly in existence in 653. It does not seem to have done much in the way of civilising the people, for when Walcher of Lorraine was made Bishop of Durham by the Conqueror, the Gateshead folk murdered him on the threshold of their church. This was not the present church of St. Mary, which is the most prominent object in Gateshead when the spectator stands on Newcastle Quay, but it probably occupied the same site. Gateshead was a domain of the Bishops Palatine of Durham, except for a short period during which it was annexed to Newcastle, and they built a palace there, no portion of which building now remains.

Between the two great Tyneside towns the river is narrower than at almost any point of its course from Hexham to the sea. Formerly it washed on either side over a shelving beach, and was but a shallow, inconsequential stream. There is a drawing of Carmichael's, made about the end of the first quarter of the century, in which some boats are unloading in the centre of the Tyne. Carts are drawn up beside them, and the horses in the shafts are not standing in water to the depth of their knees. The shores have been partly built upon and partly

NEWCASTLE-ON-TYNE.

dredged away since those days, and there is now a depth of twenty-five feet at low water at Newcastle Quay. The High Level Bridge strides across the river to a point which must have been just outside the walls that Rufus built around his castle. The great well-preserved Norman keep is only a few yards away. On the same eminence, and a little nearer to the river, stands the Moot Hall, or Assize Courts, which—all the rest of Newcastle being a county in itself—is still a part of the county of Northumberland. Here it must have been that the station of Pons Ælii was built, in a position admirable alike for watch and for defence. Much the greater portion of old Newcastle clustered around this elevated spot for many centuries. At a distance of not much more than a hundred yards is the ancient church of St. Nicholas, with its famous lanterned steeple, of which a local poet has sung that

"If on St. Nicholas ye once cast an e'e,
Ye'll crack on't as lang as ye're leevin'."

The Quayside at Newcastle has a long line of handsome stone buildings, intersected here and there by narrow "chares" that lead into the old district of Pandon, where the Saxon Kings of Northumberland are said to have had a palace in the olden time. The quay on the Newcastle side of the river is broad and spacious, but there is no quay space to speak of at Gateshead, where dreary and half-ruinous buildings cluster to the edge of the quay wall. Many of the ancient branches of local trade have died, or are dying, out. From the Tyne much wool was formerly shipped for the Netherlands; to Tyneside came the glass-blowers who were driven out of Lorraine by the persecutions, and here they settled once for all, soon exporting more glass from the Tyne than was made in the whole of France. The first window-glass was manufactured at Newcastle, and used in the windows of the church at Jarrow. There is a Tyneside glass industry still, but it no longer maintains its former eminence amongst local trades. Coal export, iron shipbuilding, chemical manufacture, engineering—these are the employments by which all others have been dwarfed on the banks of the Tyne.

In the whole of England, so far as my experience goes, there is only one town that is grimier, murkier, or more appalling in appearance than the towns on the lower Tyne as they are seen from the railways which run along either bank of the river. Bilston in Staffordshire is of more fearful aspect than either Hebburn, or Walker, or Felling, or Jarrow. On Tyneside, too, one may look away to the bright open country, to where there are low sunlighted hills on the horizon; but at Bilston an eye which searches over a landscape of blackened and withered grass only beholds more forges. In these northern latitudes, again, the skies are very cloudy and wonderful; and in the Black Country one never becomes aware that Nature can work miracles with her clouds and skies. From the river itself the blackness, the squalor, the apparent dilapidation, of these Tyneside towns are not so conspicuous. The Tyne is like a bending shaft of sunlight, making darkness not only visible but sublime. There is a quaint variety and picturesqueness about the wharves and "staithes" and factories which line its banks. The chemical works are like belated castles, about which hives of Cyclopean industry have grown up, for they thrust tall wooden towers into the air, round which there goes a platform that seems to be intended for sentries on the watch. From Newcastle Quay downwards, ships of all sizes and varieties are anchored at either side of the stream. Some are loading, some are discharging their cargoes, some are waiting to load. There are others which glitter in all the glory of new paint, having but lately been released from the stocks on which they were built. Shipyards, where new vessels are being constructed, may be found here and there between the chemical factories and the engineering works; and just now there is in every berth of every yard a new vessel in some stage of its construction. Out of these heterogeneous materials the sun sometimes builds up magnificent effects on the Tyne. Doubtless, on dull days, as Mr. William Senior has mournfully observed, "the smoke hangs like a funeral pall over the grimy docks and dingy river-banks, and the pervading gloom penetrates one's inner being;" but there are seasons when this grimy stream becomes a painter's river, indescribably striking and grand.

Below Newcastle Quay, at Sandgate and its neighbourhood, was the sailors' and the keelmen's quarter. Tyne sailors were the best that our country produced; and so it happened that the visits of the press-gang were frequent at the Sandgate shore. Many a fight there was before the captured men were carried off. All the folks of the neighbourhood, save such as had gone into hiding, would assemble for battle. The dialect of the place and the manner of these fights may both be surmised from these lines of the local muse:—

"Like harrin', man, they cam' i' showls,
Wi' buzzum shanks an' aud bed-powls—
Styens flew like shot throo Sandgeyt.

Then tongs went up, bed-powls got smashed,
An' heeds wes cracked, an' windors crashed.
Then brave keel laddies took thor turn,
Wi' smiths an' potters frae the Burn;
They cut the Whiteboys doon like corn,
An' lyed them law i' Sandgeyt."

QUAY AT NEWCASTLE.

The Roman Segendunum, which covered about three acres and a half of land, stood near to the river where it comes once more into a straight course after having taken a great bend southward shortly after leaving Newcastle. The wall thus enclosed a great bight of land between Pons Ælii and its eastern extremity, probably made useful in the landing of troops. From Segendunum it would be possible to signal to the important Roman stations at the mouth of the Tyne. But of Roman rule there is now nothing to remind us except after long search. The fame of Wallsend has been carried over the world by its coal, though, curiously enough, no coal is ever brought to bank at this place now.

Rather more than half-way from Newcastle to the sea, and over the river from Wallsend, the flames of the Jarrow furnaces leap into the air. At two widely separated periods of our history, Jarrow—the Saxon Gyrwy—has reached a distinction and importance altogether out of proportion to its size and the advantages of its situation. Here, as Mr. Green has beautifully observed, "the quiet grandeur of a life consecrated to knowledge, the tranquil pleasure that lies in learning and teaching and writing, dawned for Englishmen in the story of Bede." And of late years Jarrow has become the seat of an immense industry, whose results are to be met with in all parts of the world and on every sea. The first screw collier, the *John Bowes,* was built at Jarrow. It revolutionised the coal trade, and has made an almost inconceivable change in the commerce of the Tyne. Esteemed a large vessel in its day, it may occasionally be seen in Shields Harbour—for it still carries coals to London—dwarfed into insignificance by the passing to and fro of its gigantic successors. It is probable that the smallest steamer now built in the Jarrow shipyards is larger than the *John Bowes.* The place which gave the little steamer birth has grown into a considerable town, with a mayor and corporation, and some expectation of a member of Parliament by-and-bye. In all England, so far as I know, there is no sight which gives so powerful and weird an idea of a great industry as do the Jarrow furnaces when the flames are leaping from their lofty mouths on a murky night. The fire plays and burns and glows on voluminous clouds of smoke and steam; the Tyne is illumined by blazing pillars and rippling sheets of flame; everything shorewards is gigantic and undefined and awful, "'twixt upper, nether, and surrounding fires."

How different was the quiet Gyrwy on which Bede first opened his eyes! Beyond the furnaces and the shipyards the river broadens out suddenly over a space which is like a great bay. At low water this is nothing more than a huge acreage of mud, with quicksands beneath. To the right. Jarrow Church and Monastery stand on a lonely eminence; to the left, the little river Don flows sluggishly into the Tyne. After the landing of Hengist, says Gibbon, "an ample space of wood and morass was resigned to the vague dominion of Nature, and the modern bishopric of Durham, the whole territory from the Tyne to the Tees, had returned to its primitive state of a savage and solitary forest." All round Jarrow there was morass only—so much we should know from its ancient name, which means "marsh" or

SHIELDS HARBOUR: THE HIGH LIGHTS.

"fen," if there did not now remain something of the ancient appearance of things. The one piece of irredeemable land is this Jarrow "Slake." The river Don must have scoured out a wider estuary in Bede's day and before, for twice at least it was used as a haven—once by the Romans, who anchored their vessels at its mouth, and once by King Egfrid, who found shelter in it for the whole of his fleet. Of Bede's monastery—he was born at Monkton, close by—only a few broken walls remain, but they are attached to a large and interesting church, which has a good example of a restored Saxon tower. Ruin swept over the monastery again and again in its early days. In less than a century after Bede's death, the Danes were spreading themselves over England; the Cross went down before the hammer of Thor; and one mournful illustration of the reasserted supremacy of heathenism was to be found in the ruined monastery of St. Paul at Jarrow. When the monks of Lindisfarne, bearing with them the body of their saint, turned round to look upon Jarrow on their way to Chester-le-Street, they saw quick tongues of flame shooting upwards, and the wild, active figures of marauding Danes visible in the midnight glare. That same year a great battle was fought near the monastery, and the Vikings were overcome; whereat the monks crept back to their former quarters, rebuilt dormitories there, and enjoyed eighty years of peace; but in 867 a fleet of Baltic pirates sailed up the Tyne, and so plundered and burnt Jarrow Monastery that "it remained desolate and a desert for two centuries, nothing being left but the naked walls."

In the whole course of the river there is no finer sweep of water than that which stretches from Jarrow Slake into the harbour of Shields. On the north side we have passed the Northumberland Docks, which have a water-space of fifty-five acres, and are entirely devoted to the lading of coals. On the south side are the Tyne Docks of the North-Eastern Railway Company, which have a water space of fifty acres, and are employed equally for coals and general merchandise. The one is the main outlet of the great Northumberland coalfield, the other of the still more productive coalfield of North Durham. With the Albert Edward Dock, constructed more recently than either of these, and fit for ships of heavier draught, this is the whole dock accommodation of the Tyne; for, as I have had occasion previously to remark, the river itself, from the sea to two miles above Newcastle, is a huge tidal dock, which is available in all weathers, and in all states of the tide, for the largest vessels that float. What this phrase means may be seen to the full in Shields Harbour, where, on either side of the broad stream, vessels lie chained to the buoys in tier beyond tier, leaving a wide passage in mid-river along which great steamers are for ever passing to and fro.

The story of how the Tyne has been developed from a shallow and perilous stream into one of the noblest rivers of the kingdom makes a curious history, much too long to relate in this place. All the more extensive changes have been effected since the middle of the present century. The Tyne had a foreign as well as a domestic coal trade so early, at least, as the year 1325; but so little had at any time been done for its accommodation that there are many now living who remember how a small vessel might be stranded on sandbanks some five or six times in the course of its passage from Newcastle to Shields. Indeed, the reckless emptying of ballast into the bed of the river, and the utter neglect of means for keeping a navigable passage—things which seem altogether incredible in these days—at length brought matters to such a pass that the small passenger steamers often stuck fast at some portion of their journey, wherefore there was always a fiddler on board, to keep the passengers entertained till the rising of the next tide. It was whilst the Newcastle Corporation still successfully asserted its jurisdiction that such things were, and were growing worse; but as strong young communities grew up along the banks of the Tyne, the oppression and neglect of Newcastle became intolerable, and in 1850 the Tyne Commission was formed, with results that cannot have been foreseen by its founders; for the river has been widened and deepened over an extent of fifteen miles or more. Docks have been made, the Tyne has been straightened where "points" projected dangerously, enormous stone breakwaters have been built out into the sea, and where, in 1851, there were thirty vessels ashore in one confused heap, the British Navy might now safely ride at anchor, even in the teeth of a north-east gale. The transformation of the Tyne from its former dangerous condition into such a harbour of refuge as does not exist elsewhere on our coasts is one of the noblest pieces of

THE RIVER AT TYNEMOUTH CASTLE.

engineering that our century has seen, and there is no other great engineering work the fame of which has been so little noised abroad.

About Shields Harbour the seagulls pursue each other in play. They come all the way from the Farne Islands, and when the sun has gone down, and the western sky is still full of crimson and orange light, they may be seen circling ever higher, and gathering in bands, and finally setting off in a straight line northwards, calling to each other meanwhile with their shrill, baby-like cries. There is a space of a quarter of a mile or so between the twin but rival towns of North and South Shields. They divide, somewhat unevenly, a population of something over a hundred thousand persons between them. South Shields is of more rapid and most recent growth, but both the towns originated in the erection of a few fishermen's sheds, or shielings, which existed so long ago at least as the reign of Edward I. There were then, and for very long afterwards, two mouths to the Tyne, one of which ran parallel with the present main street of South Shields, and made an island of the Roman station which was founded here.

The whole aspect of the land round about has been changed by the deposit of ballast from ships. At many points of the Tyne there are artificial hills and embankments. Some of these are made by the refuse of chemical works; a more numerous and more lofty class are composed entirely of sand and shingle which was brought over-sea as ships' ballast. One of the earlier employments of George Stephenson was the minding of an engine that was employed in building up these huge ballast-heaps, which give a very singular appearance to some of the towns on the banks of the Tyne. South Shields was a spot greatly favoured for the discharging of this refuse, and it therefore happens that what was low and, for the most part, level ground, is now absurdly uneven, some of the streets being built upon the ballast, whilst others are far overtopped by mountains of sand and shingle that it would cost large sums of money to remove.

JARROW CHURCH: THE SAXON TOWER.

At North Shields there are terrifying flights of innumerable stairs. The lower quarters, both of North and South Shields—those, that is to say, which are nearest to the river—are incomparable as examples of old maritime towns. Something there is at Greenwich of the same character, and something more at Wapping; but nowhere is there such a salt-sea savour about the whole aspect of things.

The sailors, it should be observed, seem to have exercised their own discretion in the naming of streets. There is "Wapping," and "Holborn," and "Thames Street," and what not. These places are narrow thoroughfares running parallel with the river, and are accessible therefrom by means of wooden stairs and cramped passages between high blocks of buildings. The houses facing the Tyne, more particularly on the north side, seem less to have been built than to have been cobbled together. They are made indifferently of brick and wood and stone; they have platforms standing on wooden piles; they are kept out of the river by stout timbers that the tide washes, and that are green with salt-water moss or white with clustering limpets. There is all manner of variety among them, and nothing could be more quaint, ramshackle, or interesting as a reminiscence of an older world. It is the sailors' quarter now, as formerly, this odd assemblage of narrow streets and strange houses. Now, as in freer days,

> "Up to the wooden bridge and back,
> To the Low Light shore down in a crack,
> Rambling, swaggering, away goes Jack,
> When there's liberty for the sailors."

"The Low Lights" is that portion of North Shields which is nearest to the sea. A square white lighthouse stands on a wooden fish-quay, which projects far into the river; another similar lighthouse—"The High Lights"—occupies the top of a neighbouring hill. A ship making the river must have both of these lights in line, as if they were occupying different heights of the same tower. Light-

TYNEMOUTH, FROM THE SEA.

houses swarm about the mouth of the Tyne. There is a flash-light at the end of "The Groin," a reef which runs into the river from the South Shields side, thus assisting to make a beautiful sheltering bay between this point and the South Pier. There is a gleaming red light on the promontory at Tynemouth, and a vivid electric light flashes over the sea from Souter Point, two or three miles south of the Tyne. At the Quay by the Low Lights, in the herring season, there is a perfect forest of bare poles, and a great acreage of decks, on which brown fishermen are at work hoisting their catch, or mending their nets, or scouring their boats, as the case may be. The lettering of these craft indicates that they come from Kirkcaldy, from the Berwickshire coast, from Yarmouth, from Lowestoft, and from the Isle of Man. There are from two to three hundred of them in the season, and the river has no finer sight than the departure of these herring boats to sea when the wind is fresh enough to fill their sails. Should the evening be calm, they are towed outward in groups of five or six by a steam tug; and a pleasant voyage it is to the herring grounds; whence, when the sun has not long risen, the boats may be seen racing back again to get the best of the market at the Low Lights Quay. There are steam trawlers also at this busy mart in the early morning. It is all fish that comes to their nets, and some of it very queer fish too. A singularly odd mixture of scaly creatures may be seen lying about in heaps on the Quay—ling, skate, plaice, soles, cuttlefish, cat and dog fish, and cod, the biggest of which find their way to the London market; turbot, suggestive of aldermanic banquets; and a host of small fry too numerous to mention. The burly fishermen stride about in their oilskin coats, plentifully besprinkled with silvery scales, and glittering in the morning sunlight. The fishwives keep up a constant clatter of talk, in voices made shrill by their daily cry of "Fe-esh, caller fe-esh!" The auctioneers are very clamorous over their business, and for three hours all is hurry and shouting, and competition and confused haggling as to prices and sales.

On the north side of the Tyne the rocky promontory of Tynemouth shoots out into the sea. It is the termination of a high chain of banks extending from North Shields to the coast. On these stands the brigade house of the first of the volunteer life brigades; by which one is reminded that if South Shields invented the lifeboat, North Shields has a kindred claim to distinction in the origination of those brave bands of volunteers that watch our coasts in seasons of storm. Between the brigade house and Tynemouth Light, overlooking the entrance to the harbour, stands a colossal statue of Lord Collingwood, a Tyne seaman, mounted on a massive stone pedestal, and guarded by four of the guns of Collingwood's ship, the *Royal Sovereign*. A little further seaward, "their very ruins ruined," surrounded by British, by Roman, and by English graves, are the beautiful remains of Tynemouth Priory, which was built so sturdily, despite a certain apparently fragile character of style, that these ancient walls seem likely to bid defiance to storms for almost as many centuries to come as have already passed them by. A small chapel, built of wood, and dedicated to St. Mary, was the primitive and humble beginning from which sprung the great and powerful monastery of Tynemouth. One of the Kings of Northumberland (Edwin) erected this early in the seventh century, at the instigation of his daughter, who took the veil here. Tynemouth soon gained a reputation for sanctity, and grew so much in public favour that the chapel had to be rebuilt of stone ere long. Many were its vicissitudes during the subsequent warlike years. The priory at the mouth of the Tyne suffered even more frequently from fire and foray than the monastery at Jarrow. But the monks, as attached and devoted in the one case as in the other, returned after each fresh assault; until, in the reign of Henry III., they reared a monastic pile fit to be compared with Whitby for beauty and fame. After the dissolution, unfortunately, it became the prey of whosoever chose to make use of it for building materials; and it was not till the present century that the folk at the mouth of the Tyne began to understand that they are responsible for its preservation. In its rich and prosperous days the walls enclosed the whole of the promontory on which the Priory ruins stand; but now there remain only a small lady-chapel, a few scattered walls, a portion of a groined roof, a fine Norman gateway, and a magnificent remnant of the church. In the grounds where the monks formerly took their exercise red-coated soldiers may now be seen at drill. Pyramids of cannon-balls are piled amid the ruins; there is a large powder-magazine beside what may have been the entrance to the church. It is now fortified and garrisoned, in fact, this promontory where the godly men of old looked away over the wild North Sea. The Tynemouth cliffs have thus, it may be presumed, been brought back to their earliest uses, for the Romans had a station here, and before the Romans came the Britons must have had a camp on the spot, since recent excavations have revealed the existence of British graves.

Shooting outward from the Tynemouth shore, the mighty rampart of the North Pier makes division between the river and the sea. Such another pier comes outward from South Shields; and between them these two great works of engineering make a comparatively narrow channel for ships where there was formerly a wide and most dangerous estuary. Terrible indeed are the storms which sometimes rage over them and assail them with the battery of their waves. In a north-east gale the white water leaps above the summit of the Tynemouth cliffs. Outside the piers and beyond the bar the waves seem to be miles long, and when they narrow themselves to enter the river they rise to a height so appalling that the topmasts of a sailing-ship running for shelter may, with every dip the vessel makes, be lost to the view of those on shore. "The next instant," says Mr. Clark Russell, of a ship which he had been watching from Tynemouth when a storm was raging, "she had disappeared, and before another minute had passed I was straining my eyes against the whirling snow and looking into a blackness as empty as fog, amid which the pouring of the hurricane against the cliffs, and the pounding of the ponderous surges a long distance down, sounded with fearful distinctness. For three-quarters of an hour I lingered, peering to right and left of the beach at my feet, as far as the smother of flying flakes would let me look. But I saw no more of the brig." Such incidents were mournfully common before the piers were carried out to their present length. The Tyne was notorious for the number of its wrecks. No more than nine or ten years ago, indeed, I saw fourteen ships ashore in or near the mouth of the river, the spoils of a single night of storm. But this was the last occasion of so much calamity. For some years past now the Tyne has, most happily, almost been free from all disaster but collision.

As we round the Tynemouth cliffs the fishing village of Cullercoats comes into sight, rather over a mile away, with the dim, far-projecting Newbiggin Point a few miles beyond. On bright days a flash of light may reveal the white lighthouse at

Coquet Island, by Warkworth town. Round the rocky promontory close at hand there is a little bay, a projecting point of rock, and then a long stretch of yellow sand, broken almost at its centre by a brown, weedy reef of rocks, among which the pools linger when the tide goes down. This is "Tynemouth Sands." Here the

TYNEMOUTH, FROM CULLERCOATS.

pleasure-seekers come in crowds the summer through, rejoicing in the fine weather, and yet desiring a storm, a sight which, once beheld, would leave its memory within them their whole lives through.

"Oh, hear us when we cry to Thee
For those in peril on the sea,"

runs the touching sailors' hymn, and to those who live about the mouth of a river like the Tyne it has a deep meaning and thrilling pathos, such as those who have never heard it sung when the tempest was blowing outside cannot fathom or understand. For storms only those who live inland have any longing, for though these have heard of the wildness, they do not know the terror of the sea.

AARON WATSON.

IN WEARDALE.

THE WEAR.

William of Malmesbury on the Wear—Its Associations—Upper Weardale and its Inhabitants—Stanhope—Hunting the Scots—Wolsingham—Bollihope Fell and the "Lang Man's Grave"—Hamsterley—Witton-le-Wear—Bishop Auckland—Binchester—Brancepeth Castle—The View from Merrington Church Tower—Wardenlaw—Durham—St. Cuthbert—His Movements during Life and Afterwards—The Growth of his Patrimony—Bishop Carileph and his Successors—The Battle of Neville's Cross—The Bishopric in Later Times—The Cathedral, Without and Within—The Conventual Buildings—The Castle—Bear Park—Ushaw—Finchale—Chester-le-Street—Lumley and Lambton Castles—Biddick—Hylton—Sunderland and the Wearmouths—The North Sea.

"BRITAIN," says William of Malmesbury, "contains in its remotest parts a place on the borders of Scotland where Bede was born and educated. The whole country was formerly studded with monasteries, and with beautiful cities, founded therein by the Romans; but now, owing to the devastations of the Danes and Normans, it has nothing to allure the senses. Through it runs the Wear, a river of no mean width and tolerable rapidity. It flows into the sea, and receives ships, which are driven thither by the wind, into its tranquil bosom." With the mending of a few phrases, almost the whole of this description by the twelfth-century chronicler could be transferred to the Wear, and to the Durham and Sunderland, of our own day. The Scots have earned the right to be classed with the Danes and Normans as the pillagers of the fanes and castles of this centre of the ecclesiastical and political power of ancient Northumbria. Their modern successors, as destroyers of objects that "allure the senses," are the mine-owner and the mill-owner, the railway and the blast-furnace, the chemical works and the dockyard. The march of modern industry has taken the place of the foray of the Borderers in the valley of the Wear, as on the neighbour streams of the Tyne and Tees; and, like the fires of Tophet, the smoke of its burning goes up day and night. Yet there are compensations. The Wear does not quarrel with the good fortune that has clouded its once pure air, muddied its whilom clear stream, and disturbed its "tranquil bosom" with keels that no longer depend upon the wind for their coming and going. The wealth that has come to it with peace and the development of its mineral resources and shipping trade is not despised, although it be soiled with honest coal-dust.

Besides, those who are acquainted with the Wear know that it has higher boasts than its importance as a channel of navigation and outlet of trade. Even in its busiest parts—from Sunderland and Monkwearmouth to Chester-le-Street and Lambton—venerable associations with feudal and monkish times struggle for notice with the evidences of modern prosperity and enterprise. At Durham decisive victory is won by the memories of the past over the grimy allurements of the present. From the Cathedral City we carry away impressions of the picturesque grouping of its old houses and bridges, of the ruins of its strong Norman keep built by the Conqueror to repress the turbulent townsmen, and of the magnificent fane which covers the bones of St. Cuthbert and of the Venerable Bede, rather than feelings of respect for its manufacturing industry, or even for its distinction as the seat of a Northern University. We remember the former glories of the County Palatine, the semi-regal power and pomp of its Prince-Bishops, the odour of miracle that drew throngs of pilgrims to its saintly shrine, and the treasures that had an equally potent attraction for grasping kings and barons and for marauding Borderers, in preference to statistical and other testimony of the growth of its trade and population. All up the valley of the Wear, to Bishop Auckland and Witton, and to Wolsingham and Stanhope, commerce has pushed its way, and the very sources of the stream have been probed by the lead-mining prospector. But beauty is there also, and in possession—the beauty of stately woods, embowering princely piles, like Brancepeth Castle, the very stones of which are part of the national history; of clear reaches of the river, sweeping under fragments of religious houses, such as Finchale Priory, gently draped by time with moss, lichen, and ivy; of old bridges and mills and quaint bright villages and wide stretches of fertile land. Beyond all these comes a wilder and barer district, where the hills draw closer to the river, and cultivation and population become more rare, and where at length, over the massive and rounded outlines of the fells, as we rise towards the great "dorsal ridge" of England, we catch glimpses of the Cumberland Mountains and of the Cheviots.

To trace the Wear upwards or downwards is like ascending or descending the stream of English history; from the busy present we move back into the feudal age, and at length into the quietude of primitive Nature. Primitive Nature holds her ground staunchly on Kilhope Law and the "Deadstones," and over other great bare tracks of rolling upland, near the meeting-point of the shires of Cumberland, Northumberland, and Durham, whence the Welhope, the Burnhope, the Rookhope, and a host of lesser moorland streamlets, bring down their waters to feed the infant Wear. In spite of the mining prospector and the railway projector, many of these fells and dales are more lonely to-day than they were three, or even ten centuries ago. Of the great tangle of lines that cover like a cobweb the lower valleys of the Tyne and Wear, only one or two outer filaments find their way into the neighbourhood of Upper Weardale, and all of them fail by many miles to reach the solitudes of Killhope Moor.

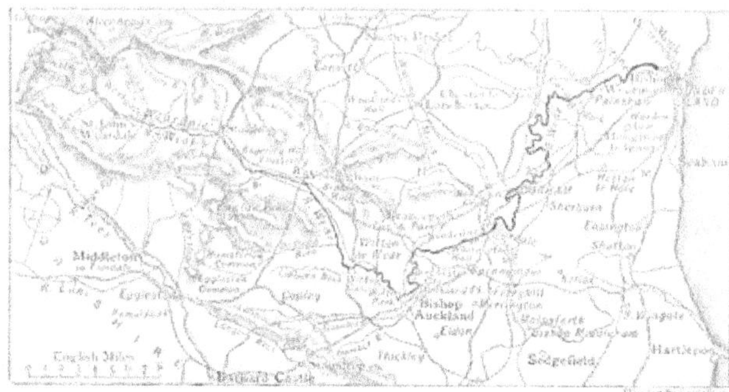

THE COURSE OF THE WEAR.

The smoke of one of the great "workshops of England" may hang darkly upon the eastern horizon, but it is still too distant to pollute the pure air of the hills. Roads, indeed, cross these wildernesses of "ling" and peat-moss—west and east from Alston and Nenthead into Weardale; north and south, from the valleys of the Allen and Derwent to the Tees—through tracts that, in the early part of the century, were traversed only by bridle and footpaths; but these serve in a measure to concentrate any passing traffic, and to leave the open moors more lonely than before. The travelling chapman with his pack, the drover, and the gipsy, promise to become as extinct, as wanderers of the fells, as is the moss-trooper from the Debateable Land, or the pilgrim on the way to St. Cuthbert's shrine. Their occupants are the wild creatures of the hills and the flocks of black-faced sheep; with a sprinkling of shepherds, who preserve in their dialect and customs many relics of what Durham and the Wear were before the Coal Age. There are mining communities scattered up the valleys and along the hill-slopes; and at Burtreeford, a little above the bridge at Wearhead—the old rendezvous for the wrestling and other sports of Weardale Forest—is what is reported to be the richest vein of lead-ore in England. The lead-miners, like the other dalesmen, are in some ways a race apart, rough and unsophisticated, like the features of the district they occupy, but hearty, sincere, and full of sturdy independence of thought, and free from many of the vices which mark their class elsewhere. It is true now, as it was at the time of the "Raid of Rookhope," when the Tynedale reivers were seen pricking over the moss by Dryrig and Rookhope-head to harry the lands of the Bishopric, that

"The Weardale men they have good hearts,
And they are stiff as any tree."

The Middlehope and the Rookhope flow into the Wear from the north, below St. John's Chapel in Weardale, through some of the wildest country in the Forest; and still farther down, upon the same band, Stanhope burn meets the parent stream at Stanhope. This ground was the favourite hunting-field of the old Bishops of Durham, and in Stanhope Park they had

STANHOPE BRIDGE.

ROGERLEY.

their lodge, where, at stated seasons, they came with a great crowd of retainers to chase the buck and roe. These gatherings are not yet wholly forgotten in the legends of the district. It was the duty of the Auckland vassals of the See to erect the necessary buildings for the housing of the Bishop and his joyous company, including a temporary chapel, where, it may be supposed, the rites of the Church had, on a good hunting day, rather perfunctory performance. The turners of Wolsingham provided the three thousand trenchers for the feeding in the open air; and the Stanhope villeins had the task of carrying the provisions and conveying the surplus venison and game to the palaces at Bishop Auckland and Durham. Often there was more serious sport afoot in Weardale Forest—for instance, when Edward III. hunted the nimble host of Scots whom Lord Moray and the Douglas brought across the Border in 1327 to pillage the Palatinate. The invaders were mounted on hardy

WOLSINGHAM.

HARPERLEY.

little horses, and with their bags of oatmeal at their backs, were themselves as well prepared as their steeds to rough it and pick up their living on the moors. After having been frightened from the neighbourhood of Durham by Edward's approach, they led him a fine wild-goose chase over the hilly country between the Tyne and the Wear. At last the English van, under Rokesby, descried the Scots encamped upon a strong height south of the Wear. To the challenge to come down and fight upon the level, the enemy prudently replied that they were on English ground, and "if this displeased the King, he might come and amend it;" they would tarry for him. There were skirmishing and great noise and bonfires kept up all night; but next morning the King, surveying the ground from Stanhope Park, found that the Scots had shifted to another hill. On the twenty-fourth day of the chase, the English passed the river and climbed the mountain, but found only three hundred cauldrons and a thousand spits, with meat all ready for cooking; also ten thousand pairs of old boots and shoes of untanned hide. The invaders had cleverly outwitted their pursuers, and were already leagues off on their homeward way over Yadsmoss and the western extremity of the county, carrying with them hurdles they had made for crossing the marshy ground where the English could not follow.

Stanhope is a populous little township on the north side of the Wear, well sheltered by the hills on both banks. Its church and market records go back for five hundred years; and its rectory revenues, mainly drawn from tithes on lead-ore, are among the richest in England. There are rocks and grottoes and beautiful walks along the river margin, as well as around Stanhope Castle, which may stand near the spot where once rose the old forest seat of the bishops. Below Rogerley and Frosterley the valley begins to open; the bare heathy hills withdraw to a more respectful distance; and between them and the river there interpose fine stretches of rich woodland and cultivated fields. For the scarped faces of limestone and marble quarries and the crushing-mill of the lead-mine, one begins to see rising here and there the pit-head machinery of the colliery and the smoke of the iron furnace; from a moorland stream the Wear changes to a lowland river. Wolsingham, which now divides its attention between agriculture and mining, was once on a time the place of hermitage of St. Godric of Finchale, and the villagers held their lands for the service of carrying the Bishop's hawks and going his errands while attending the Weardale Chase. South of Wolsingham is the long dark ridge of Bollihope Fell, and the spot, marked by a pillar, known as "the Lang Man's Grave." Here, says tradition, two huge figures were seen one clear summer evening engaged in mortal strife, until at length one of them fell; and on the place next day was found the dead body of a tall stranger, who was buried where he lay. Below Wolsingham the Wear flows by the grounds of Bradley Hall, an old lordship of the Eures of Witton and afterwards of the family of Bowes; and beyond Harperley the Bedburn Beck comes in, after draining the wild moorland tracts of Eggleston and Hamsterley Commons, and winding through some pretty wooded grounds and pastures. The scattered houses of Hamsterley are on the brow of a hill at the junction of the lead-measures with the great northern coalfield, and for generations its "hoppings," or rural festivals and sports, have been famous in this part of Durham. Some of the most charming "bits" on the Wear are around Witton-le-Wear. The stream bends and twines under the shade of the high wooded banks upon which the village is placed, and the sides of its tributary brooks are not less richly and picturesquely clothed. The centre of all this beauty is Witton Castle, at the meeting of the Linburn with the Wear. It was long the seat of the valiant race of the Eures, who held it on military service from the Prince-Bishops. It is now a possession of the Chaytors, who have preserved part of the old castellated keep, and restored the rest of the building in something like the original style.

The course of the Wear has now brought us close to Bishop Auckland, and to Bishop Auckland Palace and Park, all that remains to the Bishops of Durham out of the score of manors and castles which they once held. After Durham Castle, however, Bishop Auckland Castle was always their favourite and most princely seat. It is wedged into a nook between the Wear and the Gaunless, and from the high ridge sloping down to the latter stream it commands magnificent prospects of the country around. The town may be said to have grown up under the shadow of the Bishop's residence, but has in latter days discovered other and more dependable means of support, in manufactures and in the mineral wealth of the district. It is no longer, as in Leland's day, "a town of no estimation," either in trade or population. Formerly it had an ill name for insalubrity; but though the steep narrow streets running down to the Wear remain, it has done something to amend its reputation in this respect. Its chief architectural boasts, outside the Castle bounds, are perhaps the great parochial Church of St. Andrews, founded and erected into a collegiate charge by Bishop Bek nearly six centuries ago, and the fine double arch of Newton Bridge, erected by Bishop Skirlaw in 1388, spanning the Wear at one of the most romantic spots in the course of the river. But with the Park and Palace to be seen, the visitor does not linger long outside the Gothic doorway—itself a poor evidence of episcopal taste—that divides the Bishop's demesne from the Market Place. From the Park and its far-reaching lawns and woodland, the great group of buildings which have been added to and altered by a long line of Bishops of Durham is separated by a battlemented stone screen and arches. Bishop Bek began in earnest the work of beautifying and strengthening the Castle, which had to serve the prelates as a fortified place as well as an episcopal residence. His successors have at intervals zealously, if not always wisely, followed in his footsteps as a builder and renovator. The Bishops dispensed princely hospitality at Auckland; and in Rushall's time it was thought only "fair utterance" for the household to consume a fat Durham ox per week, and to drink eight tuns of wine in a couple of months; and it was this same Bishop who built "from the ground the whole of the chamber in which dinner is served."

The place suffered badly, however, in the hands of Pilkington, the first Protestant Bishop, who "built nothing, but plucked down in all places;" and still more deplorable were its fortunes in the storm of the Civil War, when, after having entertained Charles I. as king, the Palace received him as a prisoner, and was afterwards committed to the tender mercies of Sir Arthur Hazelrigg, who pulled down part of the castle and chapel to erect a mansion for himself. Bishop Cosin, on the Restoration, repaired this "ravinous sacrilege" to the best of his ability; and the chapel, as we find it, is largely his work, and fitly covers his tomb. Hazelrigg's hands also fell heavily on the fine Park, where he left "never a tree or pollard standing." But this also has been repaired, though one will look in vain now in the leafy coverts by the banks of the Gaunless for the herds of wild cattle that once frequented them. Perhaps the Park is put to better use as the favourite and delightful resort of the townsfolk and visitors of Bishop Auckland.

Not far below Newton Bridge and Auckland Park is Binchester, marking the place where the Wear was crossed by the great Roman road of Watling Street, in its straight course across the county from Piercebridge on the Tees to Lanchester on the Browney, and Ebchester on the Derwent. Roman remains, in the form of sculptured stones, of votive altars, and of baths, have been discovered at Binchester, which may be the Binovium of Ptolemy; and here a cross-road from the south joined the old military way, coming past the sites of what are now Raby Castle, Staindrop, Streatham, Barnard Castle, and other scenes in Langleydale and Teesdale and on the banks of the Greta, since immortalised by history and legend. An older seat of the great family of the Nevilles than Raby Hall itself—Brancepeth Castle, beyond Willington—is near at hand. It got into their possession when the grandson of the Neville who "came over with the Conqueror" married the heiress of the Saxon family of Bulmer. From the Bulmers the Nevilles are supposed to have derived their badge of the "Dun Bull;" and one of their race may have been the hero of the legend that accounts for the local nomenclature by telling how "Sir Hodge of Ferryhill" watched the track of

WITTON-LE-WEAR.

the savage boar—the "Brawn's path"—from Brandon Hill, and dug a pitfall for him at the spot still marked by a stone at Cleve's Cross, near Merrington. Brancepeth was the rendezvous of the "grave gentry of estate and name" in the North, who came to aid the Northern Earls, Westmorland and Northumberland, in the unhappy rising in Queen Elizabeth's time that cost so many of them their heads as well as their lands. It now belongs to Viscount Boyne. In spite of its low situation and the too intrusive neighbourhood of the great Brancepeth Collieries,

BISHOP AUCKLAND PALACE AND PARK.

it is a noble and massive feudal pile, and in its general effect has been pronounced "superior to any other battlemented edifice in the North of England." In the Baron's Hall are memorials of the battle of Neville's Cross; but for the most interesting memorials of the noble family that ruled the Borders from Brancepeth or from Raby, and by turns formed alliances with, and plotted against, the king, one must go to the old church of St. Brandon, and look at the effigies in carved oak or stone of the Nevilles.

On the other or south side of the Wear are Whitworth Hall, the historic seat of the Shaftos, and Spennymoor, made memorable by a terrible colliery disaster; and by Sunderland Bridge, near the inflow of the Browney, you cross to the vicinity of deep and haunted Croxdale. Behind all these rises the high ridge upon which are perched Ferryhill and the lofty tower of the old Church of Merrington. This is a commanding historic site for surveying the County Palatine;

and on a clear day the view ranges all up the valley of the Wear to the mountains of Westmorland and Cumberland, and south-east and east to the mouth of the Tees and to the Cleveland Hills in Yorkshire. Near by are many scenes of note in the annals of Durham. It was in Merrington Church that the usurping Comyn made his last stand in his "lewd enterprise" of seizing the Bishopric in 1141; and it was the gathering-place of the English forces that assembled to repel the Scots before Neville's Cross. Eldon, which gave its name to the eminent Lord Chancellor; Thickley, where were reared those stout Cromwellians, General Robert and Colonel John Lilburn; Mainsforth, the home of Surtees, the historian of Durham and friend of Walter Scott; and Bishop Middleham, the residence of the Bishops for two or three centuries after the Conquest, are all within easy reach. To the north and north-east, Brancepeth and Ushaw College, and the town and towers of Durham, are in sight, and between the Wear and the sea rise Penshaw, Wardenlaw, and other heights, and the smoke of collieries innumerable.

Wardenlaw receives most countenance from tradition for the claim that it is the spot where St. Cuthbert made selection of the last resting-place for his bones, weary of long wanderings by land and sea. But, on the ground of situation, the honour might be disputed by a score of other sites commanding a view of the rich valley, the winding river, and the "guarded cliff," crowned by the "Cathedral huge and vast," that is at once a monument and a symbol of the grand old Saint of the North. To visit Durham, or even to see its three great square towers rising in stern and severe majesty over the Wear and the masses of houses and foliage clustered beneath, is to feel that the Age of Miracle is not yet past. Or, if the ancient phases of faith and life be indeed dead or dying, there has nowhere in England been left a more solid and impressive memorial of their former strength than the Cathedral of Durham. The Apostle among the Angles, dead these twelve centuries, seems to haunt his ancient fane, and to cast the influence of his austere spirit over the narrow streets and lanes of the venerable town. The spell by which these stately arches and massive towers rose, and which, in other centuries, drew towards Durham great crowds of pilgrims, and wealth and secular and ecclesiastical power unequalled in the North, is not yet wholly broken. To this day the town stands somewhat aside, with an air of proud seclusion, from the rush and din of the great highways of commerce that pass so near. It gives, indeed, a part of its mind and time to the manufacture of mustard and carpets and the raising of coal, but it does not give its whole heart, like its neighbour cities, to trade. It is a centre of academic culture and learning, and has its thoughts not unfrequently cast back into a darker but splendid past. St. Cuthbert's body may follow the way of all flesh, but his will and his character are still living and acting powers in Durham.

Whether chance or heavenly inspiration directed the choice of site, the selection of Durham as the stronghold of the religious feeling and of the temporal power of the North was a happy one. For centuries it was the core, not only of the Vale of Wear and of the County Palatine, but of ancient Northumbria. To the credit of the Scots, to whose account Durham and the Wear had afterwards to set down so terrible an array of losses and grudges, it has to be said that this region of the North was originally missionised and converted to Christianity from the further side of the Tweed. When the greater part of Saxon England was in heathen darkness, a spark of light was struck at Holy Island and Lindisfarne, and a little later at Jarrow and Monkwearmouth, and never after was it extinguished. It was carried thither by apostles of the Early Scottish Church, and when Oswald, King and Saint, granted Holy Island, close by his royal residence of Bamborough, to St. Aidan as a site for a monastic house and a centre of missionary effort, the germ was planted of the future See of Durham. Cuthbert also came from the other side of the Border—a Border, however, which did not exist in those days as a barrier of ecclesiastical and political power. He was a native of the pleasant vale of Lauderdale, and came as a member of the brotherhood of Melrose to reinforce the band of holy men whose home was at Lindisfarne, and whose special field of labour was the region between Tees and Tweed. The zeal and the austerities of his companions were not enough to satisfy the ardent soul of Cuthbert; neither was Holy Island a retreat secluded enough for the practice of those penances and prayers by which he sought to mortify the flesh and to propitiate Heaven in favour of his work. His fame for piety was such that he was promoted to be Bishop of Hexham, and afterwards to be head of the Monastery of Lindisfarne; but, laying down these charges, he retired to the surf-beaten refuge of the Farne Islands, and there spent the solitary close of his days. Even in his lifetime, St. Cuthbert's fasts and prayers had, according to the belief of that time, been efficacious in working miracles; and it may be judged whether his brethren were likely to allow the tales of wondrous cures wrought at the touch or word of the holy man to suffer in repetition, or to permit so valuable a power to die with him. On his death-bed, it is said, he exhorted his companions to hold fast by the faith, and, rather than submit to the violation of a jot or tittle of the doctrine and ritual committed to them, to take up his body and flee with it to some spot where the Church might be free, and finally triumphant.

WILLINGTON.

The body of the saint thus became not merely a precious property, in which resided thaumaturgical virtues, but a symbol and pledge of monastic and churchly privileges; and it travelled farther and met with more adventures after death than in life. The pagan Norsemen became soon after the curse and the terror of the

BRANCEPETH CASTLE.

Northumberland coasts. Their first descent was made exactly eleven centuries ago—in 789—and four years later they returned and ravaged Lindisfarne, as well as Jarrow and other churches; but the monks, on coming back to their ruined home, found the incorruptible body of their saint intact in its shrine. Still later, in King Alfred's time, the Danes hove down upon the shores of England, and the brethren had again to flee for their lives from the marauders. This time, however, because they were not sufficiently persuaded that another miracle would be vouchsafed for the preservation of the precious remains, or for some other good reason, they did not leave the saint to the mercies of the invaders. Church legend has repeated with many marvellous particulars the story—

> "How when the rude Danes burned their pile,
> The monks fled forth from Holy Isle—
> O'er northern mountain, marsh, and moor,
> From sea to sea, from shore to shore,
> Seven years Saint Cuthbert's corpse they bore";

how, also, among other strange experiences, the corpse in its stone coffin floated "light as gossamer" down Tweed from Melrose to Tillmouth; and how, after an excursion to Ireland and to Craike Abbey, it was brought back once more to familiar ground by Wear and Tyne, but never again to Lindisfarne.

It was perhaps because the saint or his guardians thought that the risks of disturbance were too great on Holy Island that the relics sought refuge at Chester-le-Street, and there rested for more than a century. And now began the period of power of the bishopric, united to that of Hexham. Alfred the Great had, on regaining the control of his realm, largely endowed the episcopal seat rendered illustrious by the sanctity of Cuthbert and the learning of Bede. The lands between Tyne and Tees became "the patrimony of St. Cuthbert," and to these were added large possessions or authority in adjoining districts. The king decreed that "whatever additions the bishopric might acquire by benefaction or otherwise should be held free of temporal service of any kind to the Crown"—Cuthbert's dying wish put into the form of a royal grant. The bishop thus became, within his own domain, a vice-king, exercising civil as well as spiritual jurisdiction. Lands and vassals were added by a natural process of selecting the service least onerous in this world and offering the greatest rewards in the next; and the nucleus was formed of the County Palatine, which retained, down to the present century, some of the properties of an *imperium in imperio*. In the time of Ethelred the Unready, the spoilers returned, and the monks and the canonised remains were again driven forth, this time as far as Ripon. There came a time when it seemed safe to move back to Chester-le-Street, but the saint does not appear to have relished reinstatement after eviction. The returning company of monks halted on high ground overlooking the fair Vale of Wear and the likely site of Durham, then an insignificant village, and known as "Dunholm." At the top of the hill the precious burden became miraculously heavy, and the bearers had to set it down. Three days of prayer and fasting were required before inspired direction was obtained

DISTANT VIEW OF DURHAM.

through a monk, or a dun cow—tradition is contradictory on the point—and the *cortège* finally halted in a grove of trees on the platform of the high peninsula formed by the bend of the river. Here first rose a "tabernacle of boughs," and then a humble cell—the "White Church"—on the spot, as is supposed, now occupied by the church of St. Mary-le-Bow, in the North Bailey. In a few years' time the bishop, Aldune, set to work to erect, upon the site of the present cathedral, a "roof divine" to worthily cover the bones of holy Cuthbert; and as the monkish rhyme (translated) runs:—

"Arch follows arch; o'er turrets turrets rise,
Until the hallowed cross salutes the skies,
And the blest city, free henceforth from foes,
Beneath that sacred shadow finds repose."

All this happened nine hundred years ago. In counting upon rest, St. Cuthbert and his brethren had reckoned without the Scots and the Normans. Aldune's low and crypt-like structure did not last a century. It was rebuilt in statelier form by Bishop William de Carilepho, and Turgot the Prior; Malcolm of Scotland, then on his way to meet Rufus at Gloucester, also laying a foundation stone. Normans and Scots thus set their hands to the work of repairing the ruin they had made. It was the way of Durham and St. Cuthbert's shrine to thrive more by the assaults of enemies than by the benefits of friends. In the meantime, the fame and importance of the place had vastly increased. King Canute had made a pilgrimage to the shrine of the patron saint, having travelled the distance from Trimdon to Durham, by way of Garmondsway, with naked feet and clad in pilgrim's weeds. He added liberal gifts and fresh franchises to the see, and encouraged the monks to bring the remains of the Venerable Bede, the father of English Church and secular history, from Jarrow Monastery to be laid beside those of Cuthbert. Another great conqueror and sinner—William of Normandy—after he had wreaked terrible vengeance on the town that had become the centre of Saxon feeling in the north, and that had slaughtered his Norman garrison and his Norman Bishop, showed great respect for the shrine and patrimony of the saint: he even wished to look with his own eyes upon the incorruptible body, but a timely illness that seized him after saying mass in the cathedral baulked his purpose. Flambard, Pudsey, and the other successors of Carilepho, were not so much churchmen as great feudal lords, exercising almost regal sway on the Borders and a powerful influence at court. The privileges and revenues of the Prince-Bishops of Durham were a prize that the Sovereign himself might covet. They raised armies, coined money, levied taxes, appointed sheriffs and other judicial officers, and, in spite of their vows, exercised the right of presiding in court when sentences of life or death were adjudged upon criminals. In other respects their sacred office sat lightly upon them, and they caroused and hunted and intrigued and plotted on a grander scale than any baron of their time. Besides being Bishops of St. Cuthbert's See, they were titular Earls of Sadberge, and they found it easy to shuffle off the sacred for the secular character, or the secular for the sacred, as suited them. At the same time they never forgot the tradition of their patron saint, or failed to seize an opportunity of magnifying the office and increasing the dignity and power that centred in the "Haliwerk," or Castle, and the Cathedral. Thus Flambard divided his energies between building strong castles and completing the great church, and endowing public hospitals and his own bastard children. Hugh de Pudsey's wealth—such of it as the rapacious hands of the Anjou kings left—was spent on similar objects; to him Durham town owes its first charter, and the Cathedral its famous "Galilee Porch," or Lady's Chapel, an ingenious compromise, as we are told, between the inveterate ascetic prejudice of St. Cuthbert against the presence of women, and the necessity of allowing the sex access to the chapel dedicated to the Virgin. In Bishop Anthony Bek's days the See may be said to have reached the zenith of its splendour. He was little less than a Sovereign within his extensive domains; was right-hand man of Edward I. in planning and in seeking to carry out the subjugation of Scotland; led the van with his Northumbrian levies at Falkirk, and carried away the Stone of Destiny from Scone to Westminster; and, dying, left all he had to St. Cuthbert and the Church.

Signal revenge did the Scots work for these wrongs in the time of later bishops; England was never engaged in foreign war or domestic broil but they seized the opportunity of crossing the Border, and the See and the city of Durham caught the brunt of their attack. That was a crushing check, however, which they suffered in 1346, in the days of the learned Bishop Hatfield, when David of Scotland, taking advantage of Edward III.'s absence on his French wars, crossed the Border and with a great host of hungry horsemen was harrying the country up to the gates of Durham. England was not altogether defenceless; for the king had left behind him able guardians of the North Country, in the persons of his Queen Philippa and the Prince-Bishop. The "Haliwerk folk" assembled for the protection of their beloved fane, and the Nevilles and other great lords called together their retainers to fight under the standard of St. Cuthbert. The two armies met at the Red Hill, a broken and hilly piece of ground a short distance west of the city; and after having hung long doubtful, the fortune of war went utterly against the Scots, who left their king in the hands of the victors. A group of monks took up their position at the "Maiden's Bower," and signalled to another company upon the central tower of the Cathedral how it went with the battle; and when at length the invaders were put to rout, a solemn "Te Deum" was chanted, and this commemorative custom was continued almost to our own day. Lord Ralph Neville, who led the protecting troops, caused the monument to be raised which has given its name—"Neville's Cross" —to the battle; his body, with that of other members of the great family that once ruled at Brancepeth and Raby, is buried in the nave; and over his grave was placed, with his own standard, the banner wrested from the King of the

Scots. Though Queen Philippa was so good a friend to Durham, yet the churlish patron saint could not brook her presence near his shrine, and when she took up her quarters in the Prior's house she had to flee hastily in the night in her bed-gear. Not more hospitable was the welcome given to Margaret of Anjou, when fortune went finally against the House of Lancaster and she fled for refuge to Durham. The town and the Prince-Bishops had ventured and suffered much for the Lancastrian cause in the Wars of the Roses; but they dared not risk the vengeance of the victorious side, and hurried the despairing Queen across the

DURHAM CATHEDRAL AND CASTLE.

Border into Scotland. More troubles awaited Durham at the time of the Reformation. For six years Cardinal Wolsey held the diocese, but confined his duties to drawing its rich revenues. His successor, Tunstall, was a man of rare moderation for his time. Though a Reformer, like his friend Erasmus, he was inclined to remain attached to the "old religion," and he suffered at the hands of both parties as they successively came uppermost. In his days the monasteries—including that of Durham and the older foundations of Monkwearmouth and Jarrow, which had long been annexed to it as "cells"—were suppressed; and the curious reactionary movement known as the "Pilgrimage of Grace" may be said to have had its beginning at Durham. It was renewed, with like disastrous consequences, in the time of the first Protestant Bishop, Pilkington, in the famous enterprise of the

"Rising of the North," when Queen Elizabeth's partisans, the Bowes of Streatham, rose to notice over the ruin of the Nevilles and Percys, Earls of Westmorland and Northumberland. The Bishopric was temporarily suppressed during the Commonwealth; and the Cathedral interior suffered from being the place of con-

CHESTER-LE-STREET.

DISTANT VIEW OF LAMBTON CASTLE.

finement of the Scottish prisoners from Dunbar. But amends came at the Restoration, and whatever can be said against the personal or political character of Bishops Cosin and Crewe, they were princely builders, entertainers, and benefactors of the Cathedral and city. Other eminent men have since occupied the episcopal throne and palace — chief among them for learning and good works being Butler, the author of the "Analogy"; but since the year 1836 almost the whole of the old temporal distinctions and franchises have been stripped from the "Fighting Bishopric," and Her Majesty is the Countess Palatine of Durham, and keeps "the peace of St. Cuthbert" as well as that of the Sovereign.

Durham and its cathedral have an aspect worthy of their history. No such grandly imposing combination of massive Norman strength and solemn religious beauty is presented by any other architectural pile in England. Seen from

Framwellgate Bridge or any other of the many favourite points of view, it looks, what it has been in the past,

"Half house of God, half castle 'gainst the Scot."

About its outward shape there is that air of "rocky solidity and indeterminate endurance" which so impressed Dr. Johnson in its interior. Half the majestic effect of Durham Cathedral is derived, however, from its situation, settled firmly and boldly upon the highest platform of the rocky promontory washed by the river, its huge central tower rising sheer above all its surroundings—the focus of the picture; its two lesser towers squarely fronting the west; the pinnacles of the eastern transept, or "Nine Altars," balancing them on the other side; and, grouped around, the Castle and its lowering Norman keep, and the high masses of other buildings that surmount the beautiful green "Banks" and walks descending steeply to the Wear. Nearer at hand, after climbing and threading the narrow streets to the "Castle Green," the exterior view of the great Cathedral is still profoundly impressive if somewhat monotonous. On the north door hangs the knocker and ring, to which the offender against the laws could cling and claim sanctuary, or "the peace of St. Cuthbert." Within, the long arched roof and lines of alternate round and cruciform pillars are almost overwhelming, not so much on account of their height as of their ponderous strength and massive dignity. Many styles are represented, as many hands have been employed, in the interior; but the pervading spirit is the masterful and dominating genius of the Norman. The original work of Carilepho and Flambard is represented by the nave and choir. Bishop Pudsey's hand is manifest in the Transition-Norman of the "Galilee" at the west end, under the light and delicate arches of which repose the bones of the Venerable Bede. The "Nine Altars," extending eastward beyond the choir, is still later work, and was not completed until about the year 1230. In the graceful elegance of its slender shafts of stone shooting up to the extreme height of the roof, and broken only by the rich carvings of the capitals, and in the light that floods it through the beautiful "rose window" and other inlets, it forms a contrast to the somewhat sombre and heavy grandeur of the main portion of the Cathedral, and is one of our finest examples of the Early English style of church architecture. Here, however, was the "most holy place" in the Durham fane; for here is the platform of "the Shrine of St. Cuthbert," and under it the remains of the hermit of Lindisfarne rest after their long wanderings; and beside them lie other relics—"treasures more precious than gold or topaz"—among them the head of St. Oswald, "the lion of the Angles," and bones of St. Aidan. It was long believed that the place of the patron saint's sepulture was a mystery, revealed alone to three brothers of the Benedictine Order, who, under oath, passed on their knowledge, upon their death-bed, to other members of the monastery.

"Deep in Durham's Gothic shade
His relics are in secret laid,
But none may know the place."

But excavations made in 1827 have left little doubt that the spot pointed out in this Eastern Transept is that which contains the veritable remains of the "Blessed Cuthbert." Above it hung his banner and "Corporax Cloth," carried before the English host to victory at Falkirk, Neville's Cross, Flodden, and other fields; and the miraculous "Black Rood of Scotland," another of the spoils of war of the Bishopric, was among the treasures of Durham Cathedral until it was lost at the Reformation.

The chapter-house, the cloisters, and the dormitory represent most of what remains of the Monastery of Durham. Its priors took rank as abbots, and vied with the bishops of the See in piety and spiritual influence if not in temporal power. In the library and treasury are preserved many valuable manuscript relics of the monastic days, and in the great kitchen of the Deanery one may form an idea of the scale on which the old Benedictines lived and feasted. Other interesting ecclesiastical and secular buildings are collected upon the rocky platform above the Wear; but next to the Cathedral, the Castle takes first rank. It has long ceased to be the seat of episcopal state, as it has ceased to fulfil any warlike purpose in the land. It has been rebuilt, restored and added to many times since the Conqueror founded it to hold in check the Scots and to overawe the burghers; and it now helps to accommodate the Durham University—an institution which Oliver Cromwell first sought to establish, but which was only brought finally into existence upon the redistribution of the revenues of the See in 1837. Norman strength and solidity, so majestically exhibited in the interior and exterior of the Cathedral, become grim and sinister in the lines of the Castle, and in what remains of the fortifications that enclosed the ancient "Ballium." Bishop Hatfield rebuilt the Great Keep and the Hall named after him, in which Bishop Anthony Bek, that "most famous clerk of the realm," feasted Edward Longshanks on his way to conquer Scotland—the Hall which, before or since, has royally entertained a score of different Sovereigns as guests of the Prince-Prelates of Durham. But these restorations were made on the earlier foundations, and Keep and Hall and Norman Chapel retain many of the old features, and something of the old spirit.

Feudalism and romance quickly disappear from the scene when Durham is left behind, and the Wear, now becoming navigable for small craft, is followed farther on its course to the sea. There is an air of mournful solitude about the fragmentary ruins of Beaurepaire, or Bear Park, the retreat of the Priors of Durham, and of seclusion at the Roman Catholic College at Ushaw, founded for the use of the French refugees from the Revolution, and even at Sherburn Hospital, Bishop Pudsey's great foundation for lepers, now converted to other charitable purposes. But the squalor of colliery rows intrudes upon the picturesque, and the clash of machinery puts to flight the old spirit of monastic calm. This eastern side of the county of Durham is a vast busy workshop—a Northern "Black Country;" and earth and air and water, and even the minds and thoughts of the inhabitants, seem to have an impregnation of coal-dust and engine-smoke. Finchale, three or four miles below

MONKWEARMOUTH CHURCH.

Durham, is still, however, a lonely and retired spot; and a charming road through Kepyer Wood leads to the interesting ruins of the Priory erected by Bishop Pudsey's son, near the place where the good Saint Godric dwelt in hermitage. There are still some remains of the beautiful Decorative work to be seen through the screen of ivy; and the effect is deepened by the situation, on a promontory round which the river makes a bold sweep, and by the fine woods of Cocken that enclose and form a background to the buildings.

Chester-le-Street and Lumley and Lambton Castles are the next places of note by the Wear. Something already we know about Chester, and how narrowly it escaped being the civil and ecclesiastical capital of the County Palatine, and the custodian of the bones of St. Cuthbert. Its business is now mainly with coal and ironstone; but it grumbles a little still over the golden chance it missed, and the baser minerals it has to put up with :—

> "Durham lads hae gowd and silver,
> Chester lads hae nowt but brass."

It is supposed to have been a Roman station; but at all events its importance was considerable in Saxon times. The Church of St. Mary and St. Cuthbert is six hundred years old; and the most remarkable of its features is perhaps the "Aisle of Tombs," a row of fourteen recumbent effigies supposed to represent the ancestors of the Lumley family, who have lived or had possessions hard by since before the

LOOKING UP THE RIVER, SUNDERLAND.

Norman Conquest, and whose pedigree is so long that James I., compelled to listen to its recital, conjectured that "Adam's name was Lumley." Camden has it, however, that a Lord Lumley of Queen Elizabeth's time, who brought this collection of monuments together, "either picked them out of demolished monasteries or made them anew." The family are now represented by the Earl of Scarborough, whose seat, Lumley Castle, overlooks the Wear and the deep wooded valley through which, coming from Houghton-le-Spring and Hetton-le-Hole, runs the Lumley Beck. It is a goodly and in parts an ancient pile, but since the collieries have crowded around it, Lumley sees little of its owners, and has to be content with the range of old family portraits in the Grand Hall, a companion set to the stone effigies in the church.

Lambton Castle is not only surrounded but undermined by pit workings to such an extent that the ground and the fine semi-Norman, semi-Tudor building upon it—the home for many centuries of the Lambtons, now Earls of Durham—threatened to collapse, and are partly supported by the solid brickwork with which the old mines were filled. Lambton belonged of old to the D'Arcys; but, according to the legend, it was after it came into the hands of the present family that the famous fight between the heir of the estate and the "Worm" took place. The county, as would appear from its traditions, once swarmed with loathly "worms" or dragons; and this one took up its station by coiling itself around the "Worm Hill," and also frequented the "Worm Well." The heir of Lambton encountered it in armour "set about with razor blades," and the monster cut itself to pieces, the penalty of victory, however, being that no chief of Lambton was to die in his bed for nine generations. The most eminent name in the Lambton pedigree is that of John, first Earl of Durham, the champion of Reform, and the Greek temple that crowns the summit of Penshaw Hill, on the opposite or south side of the Wear, is erected to his memory.

At Biddick the great Victoria Railway Bridge crosses the Wear by a series of large spans at a height of 156 feet above the stream. The "Biddickers," now good, bad, and indifferent, like other "keelmen" of their class, were a wild set last century, and among them the Jacobite Earl of Perth found refuge after Culloden. The banks of the stream, crowded with busy and grimy colliery rows and coal staithes, the lines of rail and tramway that run up and athwart the inclines, and the fleets of coal-barges ascending and descending, help to announce the close neighbourhood of Sunderland. Before we reach the seaport of the Wear, however, Hylton Ferry is passed. In spite of the increasing sounds and sights of shipping industry and manufacture, a little bit of superstition and romance continues to linger about dilapidated Hylton Castle, for a fabulous number of centuries the home of the fighting race of Hyltons, now extinct as county landlords: the countryside has not quite forgotten the family goblin or brownie—the "Cauld Lad"—the eccentric ghost of a stable-boy who was killed in a fit of anger by a former lord of Hylton; though it remembers and points out with more pride Ford Hall, where the Havelocks, a martial race of later date and purer fame, were born and bred.

It is not easy in these days to associate the three townships comprehended within the municipal and parliamentary bounds of Sunderland with cloistral seclusion or warlike events, or with romance or mystery in any form—more especially when the place is approached by road, rail, or river from the colliery districts that hem it in on the land side. Yet busy, smoky, and in some spots ugly and squalid as it is, Sunderland hardly deserves the censure that has been heaped upon it as a town where "earth and water are alike black and filthy," through whose murky atmosphere the blue sky seldom shows itself, and whose architectural features are utterly contemptible. Sunderland has a number of fine buildings and handsome thoroughfares, and a large part of the town is lifted clear of the dingy streets by the wharves and river-bank. The animation on water and shore, the passing stream of coasting and river craft, and the other signs of shipping, ship-building, and manufacturing trade, spanned by the huge arch of the Cast Iron Bridge; the larger vessels—evidences of an ocean-going commerce—in and around the docks on either hand; even the smoke and shadows, and the dirt itself in the streets and lanes, might have been reckoned fine pictorial elements of interest in a foreign sea-port.

Coal, lime, and iron; timber, glass, and chemicals; ship stores, ship fittings, and fishing, are the businesses to which modern Sunderland, Bishop Wearmouth, and Monkwearmouth, chiefly give mind and time. It was very different when they first began to be mentioned in history. The little harbourage at the mouth of the Wear was a shelter for ships, but it was also a place of refuge for studious and pious men. We hear of it first in the seventh century, when, soon after Aidan became Bishop of Lindisfarne, St. Hilda, or Bega, obtained a grant of land on the north side of the river and founded the convent of St. Bee's. Biscopius, a Saxon knight in the service of King Oswyn of Northumberland, resolved to renounce war and the world, and having prepared himself by making a pilgrimage to Rome, whence he brought back many precious books and relics, he obtained from the pious King Egfrith a grant of land near the nunnery—the modern Monkwearmouth—and set to work in 674 to build the monastery of St. Peter's; and a few years later he founded St. Paul's, at Jarrow. It has to be noted that Biscopius, who took the name of Benedict, brought over from France masons and glaziers to instruct the natives in these arts, and that glass-making has ever since flourished on the Wear and Tyne. All this we know from the Venerable Bede, who, when quite a young boy, resided in St. Peter's, under the Abbot Ceolfrid, before he took up his abode for life in the sister monastery at Jarrow. It is thought by archæologists that part of the original building is to be seen to this day in the west porch and west wall of the old church of Monkwearmouth. Sunderland already existed at that date; and the name was probably confined to the peninsula between the natural harbour on the south side of the Wear and the sea. Of

Bishop Wearmouth, or "the delightful vill of South Wearmouth," as it was called, we do not hear until Alfred's time, when large additional grants were made to Benedict's monastery, partly in exchange for a "Book of Cosmogony," which had been brought from Rome. The Danes, the pest, and the Scots troubled much the place, and reduced the number of the inmates of the house. Sometimes these were as many as six hundred; sometimes they were like to have perished altogether, and for two centuries the place lay "waste and desolate." Malcolm was here on a plundering excursion when St. Margaret and her brother, the Atheling, happened to be in the Wear, waiting for a fair wind to carry them to Scotland —a meeting that probably changed the rude monarch's life and the national history. In 1083 the brethren of both Wearmouth and Jarrow were removed to Durham, and, as we have seen, both houses were reduced to cells dependent on the monastery of St. Cuthbert.

The mouth of the Wear had compensation in the growth of other and more secular interests. Seven centuries ago Bishop Pudsey granted a charter to Sunderland; and the liberties and privileges of the borough were extended by subsequent holders of the See, in consideration of its increasing trade and consequence. In the sixteenth century, as we learn, the coal trade was already of some importance, and Sunderland was "enriched every day thereby;" grindstones also became a far-famed article of export from the Wear. Its industrial development was temporarily checked during the Civil War, when Sunderland became a centre of fighting between Cavaliers and Roundheads. The Scots army, under Leslie, Earl of Leven, encamped on what is now part of the long High Street of Bishop Wearmouth, and not far from the Building Hill, which local tradition points out as a Druidical place of worship. The King's forces from Newcastle drew out to face the "blue bonnets," first on Bolden Hill and afterwards at Hylton; and skirmishing took place, which was not attended with decisive results. The commercial development of Sunderland has since been steady and often rapid. Including Bishop Wearmouth and Monkwearmouth, it now contains some 130,000 inhabitants, and it ranks high among British ports in ship-building tonnage and coal output. It has other claims to distinction: Paley was rector of Bishop Wearmouth last century, and wrote his "Evidences" there; and further proofs could be given that learning and piety did not come to an end at Wearmouth in Biscopius's and Bede's time, any more than did the worldly enterprise of the "canny" inhabitants.

Outside, the North Sea beats against the long piers and lighthouses, and rocks the fleets of steamers and sailing craft lying at anchor, or plying between the Wear and the Tyne; and on either hand, at Roker and Whitburn, Ryhope and Seaham, are the bold cliffs and bathing sands, the caves and cloven "gills" and wooded "denes," to which the dwellers by the Wear resort to fill their lungs with fresh air.

JOHN GEDDIE.

CROSS FELL.

THE TEES.

Among the Fells—The Weel—Caldron Snout—High Force—Gibson's Cave—Bow Leys—Middleton-in-Teesdale—The Lune and the Balder—Scandinavian Names—Cotherstone Cheese—History in Teesdale—Scott's Description of the Tees—Egliston Abbey—Greta Bridge—Dickens and Mr. Squeers—Brignal Banks and Rokeby—The Village of Ovington—Gainford—Pierce Bridge—High and Low Coniscliffe—Croft—Yarm—The Industries of the Tees—Stockton—Middlesbrough—The Sea.

YOU can stand in fower keaunties at yance at Caldron Snout," said the companionable whip whom I had engaged to drive me, for such distance as the roads went, towards the first joyous springing up of the Tees at Cross Fell. The statement was a palpable exaggeration; no mere biped can stand in four counties at once; the most that is practicable is to straddle from one county to another. But from Caldron Snout the nearest point of Cumberland is distant at least five miles; so that only the counties of Durham, Yorkshire, and Westmorland touch each other where this marvellous waterfall pours through its rocky and precipitous gorge. However, the information was passably accurate. From the natives of Upper Teesdale no exact knowledge is to be extracted, by hook or by crook. They are chiefly remarkable for what they don't know. From Middleton, Cross Fell was five miles away—six miles, ten miles, fifteen miles, and so on, through an ever-lengthening road. A landlord, who was really not stupid-looking, and who was certainly not indifferent to matters of business, was unable to name the beck which flows within a few yards of his own door. "You will have h'ard o' th' High Force?" queried a Middletonian. "It's a famous place, is th' High Force. Well, no; I've never seen it myself; but I've lived five miles from it all my life, an' it's a fine, famous place is th' High Force." A fair sample of what the inhabitant of Upper Teesdale knows, or cares to know. This singular incuriousness is almost general. The facts of Nature are accepted as matters of course, and without inquiry. The report of the adventurous traveller is enough. In the first fifty miles of wandering by Tees-side I encountered only one man who was proud of his information, and this related exclusively to the places of public entertainment in the village of Yarm. Mr. Samuel Weller's knowledge of London was not more extensive and peculiar. In a slow, cautious, and yet eager style of speaking, he gave a detailed and exhaustive account of every public-house in the village, with sidelong glances at the characters of the various landlords, and an evidently cultivated criticism of the quality of the refreshment supplied by each.

The long ridge of Cross Fell was grey and cloudlike, as seen in the morning sunshine, from where our pair of horses finished their journey at the Green Hurth Mines. The intervening space of undulating moor was as parched and brown as if some sudden flame had swept across it; and where the clouds moved slowly across the grey-blue of the sky, long bands of dark shadow fell, so intense as to lend the brightness of contrast to what otherwise might itself have seemed to be a mass of shade. Not a single tree was in sight, but only whin-bushes and their yellow bloom. A white gleam of water in occasional hollows of the hills indicated the sluggish beck which divides Durham from Cumberland; and to the left, in a winding course well marked by the depression of the moorlands, the Tees wandered towards Caldron Snout, flanked by the steep side of Dufton Fell. It is here but a thin and narrow stream on dry summer days, but in times of rain it broadens and swells with an amazing suddenness, rushing downwards with a great roar and tumult of waters, so unexpected, sometimes, and with a character so much resembling the opposite phenomenon of the bore on the Severn, that holiday visitors, inapprehensive of calamity, have before now been carried headlong over the terrible cataract of High Force.

The guide-book accounts of Upper Teesdale are mainly remarkable for their singular inattention to facts, and their following of each other. "Murray" confidently places High Force at a distance of five miles below the source of the river at Cross Fell. As a plain matter of fact, it is five miles from High Force to Caldron Snout, a much more amazing waterfall, and there are more than seven miles as the crow flies between Caldron Snout and Tees Head. It is a country bare of inhabitants and abounding in game. There is no village beyond Langdon Beck, where we begin the ascent of the moors. The Tees is joined by numerous little streams before it leaves Cumberland, and flows through the four or five miles of stern valley where Westmorland and Durham face each other. Just before reaching the wild extremity of Yorkshire it thrusts out a broad arm through a deep, long recess of the hills, and "as with molten glass inlays the vale." The Weel is the odd and unaccountable name which has been given to this winding lake. It lies, white and weird and still, where scarcely even the winds can reach it; and so deserted is it

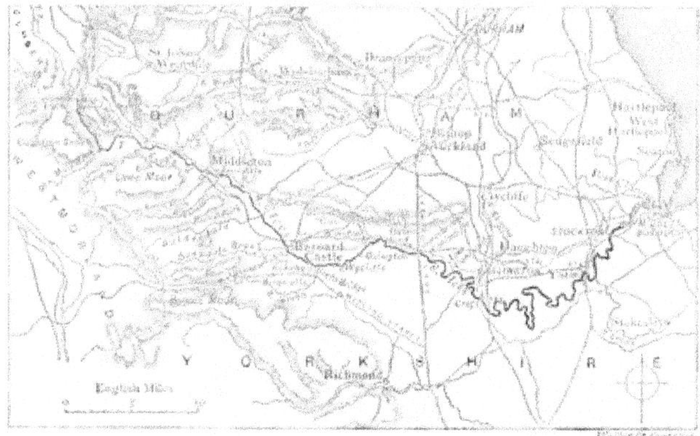

THE COURSE OF THE TEES.

that not so much as a single wild fowl breaks the surface of its ghastly calm. There is henceforth no more rest to the Tees water during the whole of its curiously devious journeying to the sea. Below the Weel it tumbles with desperate tumult over Caldron Snout, foaming down into a pool two hundred feet beneath. Had Southey beheld this waterfall when it was in flood he would scarcely have had the heart to write of the Falls of Lodore. Here there are no mossy rocks or sheltering trees to dapple the scene with their brightness and shadow. The river dashes in a succession of leaps over the bare basalt, swirling and boiling after such manner as easily explains the name given to this most lonely and most splendid of English cataracts, where the creamy waters—

> "With many a shock
> Given and received in mutual jeopardy,
> Dance, like a Bacchanal, from rock to rock,
> Tossing her frantic thyrsus wide and high!"

Here the Tees, in a succession of violent cascades, makes a descent, as we have seen, of two hundred feet. At High Force it falls by only seventy-five feet; but, whereas the lonelier cataract is a long and broken slope, the water at High Force falls with plummet-like directness, in a vast broad sheet when the river is in flood, in two straight white columns when the floods are subsiding, and in a single glittering fall when the river is at its normal height. Here the contrast between the Yorkshire and the Durham side of the Tees first makes itself decisively felt. The steep but still gradual declivity of the Durham side is veiled

HIGH FORCE.

FROM YORK SIDE.

in woods of birch and beech and fir; on the Yorkshire side the basalt descends sheer to the river's bed, and beyond and above it there is a bare expanse of unprofitable fields, darkened here and there by patches of whin-bush and long streaks of broom. This barren character is maintained, with a gradual decrease of sternness, until the little town of Middleton-in-Teesdale comes in sight.

Middleton is a long, straggling town, starting away from a stone bridge over the Tees, and climbing far away up the sides of the hills. It is built entirely of stone, even to the roofs and the chimneys. This is a peculiarity of all the houses in Upper Teesdale. Slates, in small quantities, have penetrated thus far into the wilds; but of baked clay, otherwise than in the form of pottery, there is no suggestion until the village of Cotherstone is reached, whence emanates the famous Cotherstone cheese. Below the bridge at Middleton the Tees leaves behind it the stern Yorkshire moorlands and scaurs, the hills on either bank withdrawing themselves that it may glitter in the sunbeams over a pebbly bed. Henceforth, until it approaches the large towns, and when it encounters the sea-tides, it flows, broad and open, past richly-wooded banks. In all England there is no more pleasant valley than that which the Tees waters between Middleton and Pierce Bridge. There is an almost equal beauty in the valleys of its numerous tributaries. "All the little rills concealed among the forked hills" have their individual features of loveliness, and hide sweet secrets of their own. About a mile below Middleton the river Lune ripples sunnily down into the Tees. Rising in Westmorland, it flows across that portion of Yorkshire which interposes itself between Westmorland and Durham, wearing one of the deepest of channels for itself, and giving token of frequent floods in the large stones by which its bed is thickly strewn. The river Lune is a favourite stream for trout, but it is still more renowned as a spawning ground for salmon; for as that kingly fish cannot ascend the Tees beyond the seventy-foot precipice at High Force, and as some of the higher tributaries are polluted with water from the lead mines, the Lune and the Balder, a smaller stream which flows into the Tees at Cotherstone, are almost the only accessible breeding beds.

BARNARD CASTLE.

"Fish! I should think so!" says a man who has fishings to let. "Why, there are times in the year when you could take salmon out by the armful." To the remark that this is not the time when salmon ought to be taken, he replies that there are good trout at any time of the year; and a very cursory observation of the Tees proves this to be true. The keen observation of Sir Walter Scott led him to remark on the blackness of this river. Coming down from the moorlands, it is thickly stained by the peat; but the peaty colour does not in fact obscure the clearness of the water, and looking down from above, one may everywhere see the fish shooting athwart the stream in little shoals. The river is exceedingly well preserved; indeed, on one side it is in the hands of the Duke of Cleveland, on the other it is well tended by Mr. Morritt of Rokeby, the Earl of Strathmore, and Sir Talbot Constable. Nevertheless, fishing is to be had on easy terms—from Henry Ludgate, of Winston, for example, who was formerly gamekeeper to the Earl of Brownlow, and who now keeps a public-house and writes verses. His political ideas take that turn, he observes, and the visitor to Henry's hostelry may hear some of the verses repeated if he should be so minded as to listen to them.

There are no towns on the Tees until one of the most horrible in all England is reached—Stockton, to wit; but there are innumerable villages. Some of these are quite remarkable for their cleanliness and beauty. Romaldkirk, the second village from Middleton, on the Yorkshire side, is an incomparable village, far scattered, but bound together by a plenitude of trees. Romaldkirk—anciently "Rum auld kirk," a serious-minded old villager observed, with a trenchant faith in his etymology—is noticeable not only for its combination of all the charms that an English village can possess, but also on account of its parish church and its parish stocks. The stocks are unique, indeed. Shackles of this ancient description are usually of wood; but the stocks at Romaldkirk are bars of iron, fastened in stone posts, and ingeniously bent so that one of the bars, locked down on the other, will imprison two pairs of feet. In winter the parish stocks of Romaldkirk must have been the most uncomfortable parish stocks in all England. The villagers preserve them now with genuine and reasonable pride, and the oldest inhabitant sits upon them and relates sad stories of the last persons who were imprisoned therein. The church has been so little restored that it remains one of the finest examples of early ecclesiastical architecture. It is unusually large for so small a village, a fact which is explained by its erection by the Barons Fitzhugh, who were buried here whenever they chanced to die in their beds. The building dates from the twelfth century, and is in the Early English style. One of the Lords Fitzhugh is kept in remembrance by a statue in chain-armour, still contemplated by the villagers with a mixture of awe and delight.

The Fitzhughs are again in evidence at the village of Cotherstone, two miles farther down the Tees. They had a castle there, of which a small portion still remains, bearing the same proportion to a complete feudal castle that an odd brick will bear to a modern house. Cotherstone is a smart, businesslike village, for these parts. Some of its stone roofs have a coping of red tiles, the first to be seen in Upper Teesdale. It has recently built itself a very pretty little church. Above all, it is renowned for its cheese. This cheese of Cotherstone is in shape similar to Stilton; but, however long Stilton cheese may be kept, it can never approach that of Cotherstone in aroma. A Cotherstone cheese, truly, requires a large room all to itself; it is not the kind of cheese that one can live with, even for the short space of lunch; it is a militant sort of cheese—fit to defeat armies. Those who produce it were formerly thought to be rather pronounced rustics by the inhabitants of Teesdale. They were called "Cotherstone calves," and uncomplimentary references were made to the strength of their heads; but the School Boards have changed all that, and a young Cotherstone calf now speaks with a certain air of refinement, and is not above feeling pleasure in giving information to the intruding stranger.

The Tees is not a river of traditions and memories. It must have a marvellous history, indeed, but it is, for the most part, unknown. Up among the fells, where it rises, one is constantly in danger of falling into pits in which the Romans or the Britons worked for lead; there is scarcely a space of fifty yards by the present roadside which does not bear traces of former mining; from which one surmises that the very road over which one travels has existed from the time when Rome conquered Britain for the sake of the metals which it was supposed to contain. The Watling Street approached the Tees at Greta Bridge; the Leeming Lane went through the river at Pierce Bridge, to cross the Watling Street near Middleton Tyas, in Yorkshire. There are almost innumerable remains of Roman camps and British defences; but, nevertheless, there is no history to speak of. When Sir Walter Scott sought a story with which to connect the scenery of the Tees he went back no further than to the conflict between the Cavaliers and Roundheads. The records of this wide district have, in fact, perished; between the present population and that of the earlier centuries of the Christian era there is no relationship of blood and no inheritance of tradition. The solitary fragment of the Castle of the Fitzhughs is more like a satirical commentary on the past than its memorial.

The Balder joins the Tees at Cotherstone; it is a shady little river flowing through a deep ravine. The Tees itself is at this point exceedingly lovely, streaming in a fine curve from beneath overhanging woods, and winding past a quaint old mill, which nestles by the waterside under high banks that are crowned by a tall fringe of trees. There is, probably, no English river which journeys for so many miles through such beautiful and unbroken woods. From the slope which is occupied by the village of Cotherstone one may see the domes of the Bowes Museum at Barnard Castle, rising out of what appears to be a vast forest, interspersed here and there with patches of cultivated ground. No sparkle of water is anywhere visible in the whole wide landscape, but the course of the Tees may be traced by a wavy and depressed line in the woodland verdure; and one guesses how, over many a mile, the bright river is making a sunshine in the shady place.

"Romantic Deepdale" joins the Tees a little above Barnard Castle. It is such a tributary as Wordsworth speaks of, a

> ——"torrent white,
> The fairest, softest, loveliest of them all!
> And seldom ear hath listened to a tune
> More lulling than the busy hum of noon,
> Swollen by that voice whose murmur musical
> Announces to the thirsty fields a boon
> Dewy and fresh, till showers again shall fall"

Deepdale Burn winds away across Yorkshire, over Bowes Moor, and to the borders of Westmorland, through one of the most lovely valleys in the whole of the north country.

"Barnard Castle standeth stately upon Tees," says Leland. Stately it is to this day, though it is no more than a group of ruined towers and crumbling walls, and though where the Tees must have flowed deep and wide from below the castle rock there is now at ordinary seasons only a thin stream, threading its way through what might very well be mistaken for a stone-yard. Before the castle is reached we have, in fact, come to the first salmon weir, which, besides its other purpose, is employed to divert the river to the service of industry.

From Barnard Castle these weirs become very frequent, and are, in all cases but this, an addition to the attractions of the stream. It was the weir just below Barnard Castle that supplied Creswick with a subject for one of his most famous and successful pictures. The artist visited the town very frequently, and stayed there for weeks on end; wherefore he is still well remembered by some of the older inhabitants, not always with that kindliness which one would have been glad to associate with his name.

Barnard Castle is one of the oddest and most interesting towns in the North. There is a wholly individual character in its buildings, as if its architects had devised a style of their own. Few of the houses are older than the period of Elizabeth, but they are almost all of them of respectable age. The building material is stone in all cases, and the houses are unusually high and substantial, often of four and sometimes of five stories. On either bank below the castle they are built down into the bed of the river, and as, in Scott's words, the Tees here "flows in a deep trench of solid rock," the houses by the riverside descend as much below the level of the street as they rise above it. Yet despite the stoutness and the elaboration of these buildings, the riverside streets present that appearance of misery and squalor which seems inevitable in every manufacturing town, however limited may be the field of its industry. Dwellings which were clearly built for persons of wealth and position are let as tenements, and, there is, consequently, an odd contrast between their stateliness and the dress and appearance of those who lounge about their doors. However, the wide central street of Barnard Castle, sloping down from the Market Place to the river, still preserves an air of old-time respectability,

BARNARD CASTLE: THE TOWN.

and has the sleepy aspect of a country town, as if it had dozed away a century or two without activity or change. There is in this street a remarkable old Elizabethan house, in which Oliver Cromwell is said to have lodged himself for a while.

The Castle, which enclosed a circuit of six acres or more, was built by Bernard Baliol, a son of that Guy Baliol whom I have had occasion to mention in connection with Bywell-on-Tyne. A descendant of Bernard climbed to the Scottish Throne, doing homage for the Crown at Newcastle to the first Edward. Edward Baliol did like homage to Edward III. for the crown and kingdom of Scotland. It was a short and unfortunate dynasty which the Baliols founded, brought to an end by the battle of Bannockburn. John Baliol presumed too much on his independence as a king, wherefore his patron, Edward I., seized upon his castle and his English estates, and the stately building on the banks of the Tees was given to the Beauchamps of Warwick. Thence it passed by marriage into the hands of the Nevilles, and was part of the dower of Anne Neville, the daughter of the King-maker, when she married the scheming politician who was to become Richard III. Gloucester not only dwelt here for some time, but left decided marks of his tenancy, the latest portions of the building being held by antiquarians to have been erected under his superintendence. Since 1592 Barnard Castle has been a ruin, the survey of that year exhibiting it as tenantless, mouldering, and weather-worn, "the doors without locks, the windows without glass."

Below Barnard Castle there is an open space of greensward extending over a few acres, and then the river, after falling over Creswick's salmon pass, plunges once more into the woods. Between this point and the village of Wycliffe lies the most lovely scenery of the Tees. At about a mile from Barnard Castle, on the Yorkshire side, Thor's Gill flows into the river through a deep ravine, and out of the neighbouring trees rise the impressive ruins of Egliston Abbey. Tired indeed of the world must have been those who came to this wild and lonely place for service and prayer. With Thor's Gill beside them, and the Tees far down below, in the front of their dwelling, they would look in all other directions over miles of barren moor, now subdued and cultivated by the plough. In time of flood the noise of waters must have drowned the intoning of their psalms, for at this section of its course the river is confined between rocky precipices, and ploughs its way over an amazing bed of that marble for which Barnard Castle formerly had a sort of fame.

There is a fine stone bridge below the Abbey, of one enormous span, with the river flowing a hundred feet beneath,

"Through paths and alleys roofed with sombre green."

The Abbey of Egliston was founded about the beginning of the thirteenth century, and was dedicated to St. Mary and St. John the Baptist. Its inhabitants were the Premonstratensian or White Canons, whose alleged object was to ensure a pure and contemplative life, and who, in coming here, certainly removed themselves from the reach of worldly temptations, and secured plenteous leisure for meditative calm. They must have seemed like ghosts amid these woodlands, their

ON THE GRETA AT ROKEBY.

dress being a long white cassock, a rochet, a white cloak, and a white cap. They are supposed to have been the schoolmasters of John Wycliffe, who was born some four or five miles away, and who would find only one other place of education within his reach. In Scott's time some portions of the religious house attached to the Abbey were still habitable, and until quite recently a hermit dwelt in one of the chambers; but the progress of decay has, during the last five or six years, been exceedingly rapid, and before long, probably, this interesting ruin will be no more than a heap of grey stones. At my own recent visit parts of the walls were being removed lest they should fall in, and the materials were being employed in some farm buildings near. There were signs of impending collapse elsewhere, and only such restorations as would be a disfigurement could now save what remains of the Abbey for future generations.

About two miles from Egliston, still on the Yorkshire side, is the fine domain of Rokeby Park, along one side of which the Greta flows to the Tees. Greta Bridge is known to all lovers of literature through the mention of it which is made by Dickens. It was there that Nicholas Nickleby descended from the coach which had brought him thus far on his way towards Dotheboys Hall. "About six o'clock that night he and Mr. Squeers and the little boys and their united luggage, were all put down together at the George and New Inn, Greta Bridge." Dickens insists that whilst he was not exaggerating the cruelties practised on boys at schools resembling Dotheboys Hall, Mr. Squeers was the representative of a class and not of an individual. This is a view of the facts that the people around Greta Bridge cannot be induced to accept, and there is no doubt that the novelist really did—without intending it, probably—very serious injury to one who is held by those who knew him to have been a very estimable man.

JUNCTION OF THE GRETA AND THE TEES.

There is now no one living to whom a relation of the facts can give pain, and so they shall be stated briefly here. The school which has been generally accepted as the subject of the great novelist's savage exposure was situated at Bowes, four miles from Greta Bridge. Bowes is no more than one straggling street, stretching away towards the desolation of Stanmore, and the school which was identified with Dotheboys Hall is the last house in the village, which lies along the Roman road of the Watling Street. The place was kept by a Mr. Shaw, who is said to have died of a broken heart. He had "only one eye," as Dickens remarked of his grim tyrant; he had also a wife and a daughter who assisted him in the management of the school. So far he "realises the poster," as an actor would say. There is no doubt, either, that his school was visited, and that he was seen by Dickens and by Hablot Browne. The one eye was in itself, unfortunately, a sufficient means of identification, there being no other one-eyed schoolmaster within any known distance of Greta Bridge. Dickens may have meant no more than to make use of this personal characteristic, combined with characteristics derived from other sources, as in the almost equally unlucky Miss Moucher case; but he had so associated a one-eyed schoolmaster with a place not far from Greta Bridge that no amount of explanation could remove the impression that Mr. Squeers was intended for Mr. Shaw, or could repair what was unquestionably an injury to one who stood high in the good opinion of his neighbours. All the members of the Squeers group of characters, indeed, were identified with persons then living in or around Bowes. John Browdie, for instance, is said to have been a farmer named Brown, and of the Browns there are still several families among the substantial farmers of the district. Of the good-feeling of which Mr. Shaw was the subject there are evidences still remaining in the resentment which is felt by the older inhabitants of Bowes when any inquiry is made as to Dotheboys Hall. "You'd better gan and inquire somewheere else," one of these remarked when

WYCLIFFE.

questioned on the subject. "Yow folks come here asking all manner of questions, and then you gan and write bowks about us." The name of Dickens is absolutely detested by some of those who know the circumstances. As to the lady who was identified with Fanny Squeers, and who died but recently, she is declared to have been distinguished by great kindness of heart, "the sort of woman a dog or a child leaps to instinctively." In fact, however true it may have been that "Mr. Squeers and his school are faint and feeble pictures of an existing reality," it seems to be placed beyond question by common testimony that this reality did not exist at the village of Bowes, though nothing whatever can now remove the impression that Dickens intended to represent the school of Mr. Shaw.

Besides the "George," mentioned by the novelist, there is at Greta Bridge another well-known place of entertainment, the "Morritt Arms." The village is scarcely of consequence, except as the site of a Roman station, of which the remaining indications are now "a grassy trench, a broken stone." The Greta is between here and the Tees so beautiful a river that Scott exhausted upon it all his powers of description, both in verse and prose. Having skirted Rokeby Park, it sweeps over a shelf of rock under a moss-covered bridge half-hidden in trees, and there meets with the obstacle of gigantic rocks, which seem as if they had been carried down in some tremendous flood and piled together in the central bed of the stream. Round these the Greta swirls to the Tees in two long rushing curves when the river is high, but in quiet, dry seasons it has one channel only, down which it rushes impetuously out of the leafy shade into the open sunlight.

Two miles above Rokeby are those Brignal banks of which the poet sings—

"O, Brignal banks are wild and fair,
And Greta woods are green,
And you may gather garlands there
Would grace a summer queen."

The present mansion of Rokeby is modern, and occupies the site of a manor house which was burned down by the Scots after the battle of Bannockburn. The Rokebys were a powerful family in these parts up to the occurrence of the civil wars. It was a Rokeby who, according to Holinshed, defeated the insurrection of the Earl of Northumberland, in the time of Henry IV., and slew the earl. Scott gives the whole of the family pedigree in the notes to his poem, showing how the Rokebys were High Sheriffs of Yorkshire through many generations, as well as justiciaries, Secretaries of State, and members of Council. They were destroyed by their loyalty and the bad faith of the Stuarts, as was the case with so many other ancient families, and their estates, after passing through the hands of the Robinsons, have been in the possession of the Morritts through several generations.

There is a remarkable peel tower, with singularly light and graceful battlements, broken into varying heights, on the ridge of a hill just beyond the junction of the Greta with the Tees. It is now surrounded by farm buildings, but is much visited on account of the spectre called the Dobie of Mortham, a murdered lady whose blood the eye of strong faith may still see on the steps of the tower.

High above the Tees on the Durham side, when Mortham has been passed, may be seen the pretty village of Whorlton, the first red-tiled village that we have so far encountered on Tees-side. It is approached by an iron suspension bridge, which crosses the river at a point where its broad bed of solid rock is curiously broken into long uneven steps, giving it the appearance of having been quarried at some remote time, and making a series of falls that, instead of crossing the river, as ordinarily occurs, shelve along one side of it, and continue for long distances, turning the current in an almost indescribable way

GAINFORD.

These singular breaks in the river bed mark the course of the Tees until the Yorkshire village of Wycliffe is reached, something over a mile from Mortham Tower. Except for the fact that the great Reformer was born here, the place is as unimportant as a newly-planted city in the American wilds; it consists, indeed, of no more than four or five scattered cottages, a parsonage, a church, and Wycliffe Hall. The parsonage is very large, and the church is very diminutive, seeming to be only an ornament of the parsonage grounds. But around this little church many of the Wycliffes lie buried, and among the monumental brasses there is one recording the death and the burial of the last of the name. Even yet, however, the Wycliffe blood is not extinct, for it flows in the veins of Sir Talbot Clifford Constable, the owner and tenant of Wycliffe Hall. If the "Morning Star of the Reformation" did not receive his first teaching at Egliston Abbey, as Dr. Vaughan has surmised, he must have ascended the hill from Wycliffe to where now stands the pretty village of Ovington, for here was formerly a priory of Gilbertine canons, though no traces of it now remain. Ovington stands higher than any other village on Tees-side, and from the level of its green the woods through which the river surges are far down below, so that even their highest tops do not reach to the crown of the ridge. Ovington is a right sweet and pleasant and prosperous village, much beloved of anglers, there being abundant fish. Nowhere is the Tees more shaded and beautiful, with its stream broken up into many currents by a series of wooded islands, on which the easy-going.inadventurous fisher may lie under the leafy branches through torrid summer days.

Ovington is a village with a maypole in the middle of its green — a maypole with tattered garlands still clinging to its iron crown. The neat cottages all have their little gardens in front, and are roofed with rich brown tiles. There is a hostelry with the curious sign of "The Four Alls," where one may find such entertainment as few villages in England can provide, and sit in rooms over the decoration of which an obviously æsthetic taste has presided. The sign of "The Four Alls" is weather-stained unduly, but one may still discern pictures of a crowned king, with the motto, "I govern all;" of a soldier, with the motto, "I fight for all;" of a bishop, with the motto, "I pray for all;" and of a husbandman,

CROFT.

BLACKWELL BRIDGE.

with his motto of "I pay for all." This is possibly a product of the native Yorkshire wit, of the same variety as that which has designed the Yorkshire coat of arms, "A flea, a fly, a flitch of bacon, and a magpie."

The Tees has much loveliness but little variety between Ovington and Yarm;

YARM.

it has lost most of its wilder features, and—through many a winding curve, for it is an erratic river, bending and turning with a strange wilfulness—its deep woods

"in seeming silence make
A soft eye-music of slow waving boughs,
Powerful almost as vocal harmony."

At Gainford, which clusters round a large village green, there is an air of rustic fashion and luxury, for here reside many prosperous persons who have places of business in Darlington, which is seven miles away. Gainford boasts of a medicinal spring, or spa. It is a pretty strong fountain of water, situated about half a mile from the village, and close to the banks of the Tees, which at this place has a pathway through the woods. It is affirmed of the Gainford spa that whilst the water has the usual "smell of rotten eggs" it is innocent of unpleasant taste, an asseveration which, having tested it, I cannot conscientiously confirm. The church of Gainford, it is stated in all the guide-books, is of great antiquity, having been built by Egred, Bishop of Lindisfarne, between the years 998 and 1018; but as a matter of fact scarcely anything of this old church remains, except a few sculptured stones and fragments of crosses which have been built, in an exceedingly *olla podrida* manner, into the porch of the present building, where I found displayed a carefully detailed statement of the week's revenue, amounting to the sum of fifteen shillings and eightpence-halfpenny. On the Yorkshire bank, opposite to Gainford, there is the end of an ancient earthwork, which runs across country from the Swale to the Tees, and which is surmised to be older than the Roman conquest of Britain. At Gainford, Samuel Garth, the poet of the "Dispensary," was born.

Two miles from this village, and by so much nearer to the wealthy "Quaker town" of Darlington, a noble stone bridge crosses the Tees, connecting the Yorkshire bank with the site of the ancient Roman station of Magis. Pierce Bridge carries the old Roman road—the Leeming Lane—from Durham to Yorkshire. Careless antiquaries call it the Watling Street, which, however, we left behind us at Greta Bridge. For twenty miles or so, or for an equal space on either side of the Tees, the Leeming Lane, which has various local designations, is probably the straightest road in all England. One may see it rising and falling for miles in front, always keeping the direct course, whatever may be the depressions in the land. At Pierce Bridge, which is famous for its fishing, and where the trout may be seen lightly disporting themselves, the forces under the Earl of Newcastle had a skirmish with those of Lord Fairfax in 1642, at the hottest period of the civil war. A mile further down the river is High Coniscliffe, which is quaintly situated above a sudden cliff, so that it seems as if the first buildings erected here must have been intended for defence. It is but a very little cluster of buildings, this High Coniscliffe, taking its name, perhaps, from the fact that the river banks hereabouts are much frequented by rabbits, as, indeed, is the case with the banks of the Tees from Rokeby downwards. The one prominent building is the church, which has the peculiarity of being seven times as long as it is broad. The other singularity is that the pillars supporting the arches of the nave are no more than six feet in height. Low Coniscliffe, two miles away, is a more humble place, with no appearance of a cliff to account for its designation, and with an aspect of old-world poverty such as is presented by no other place with which we have, so far, met. At this point the interest of the river is, for the present, exhausted, and its beauty is gone, for just beyond Low Coniscliffe there is a quarter of a mile or so of waterworks, stretching on either side of the main road to Darlington, the three towns of Stockton, Darlington, and Middlesbrough, here pumping their water from the Tees. Darlington itself we leave to our left, but pass the mansions of some of its wealthy men—the Peases, the Backhouses, the Frys—who, however much they may retain of the old Quaker simplicity, certainly make no striking exhibition of it in the character of their dwellings.

Three miles from "the Quaker town," and a much greater distance from High Coniscliffe, as the river winds, is the ancient village of Croft, occupying both banks of the Tees. On the Yorkshire side is the famous spa, to which invalids resort to drink the waters and to take the baths, and where marvellous cures are said to have been effected in times past. There are four sulphureous springs, of a much more decided character than the one already visited at Gainford, and owing, it may be, some part of their attractiveness to the sweetness of their situation. Croft is very commonplace on the Durham and very lovely on the Yorkshire side. The stone bridge which connects the two portions of the village, built in 1676, is the finest which crosses the Tees at any part of its course. It is on the site of an older structure, which was deemed greatly important by Henry VIII., as "the most directe and sure way and passage for the king our Sovereign Lord's army," when it was necessary to march against the Scots. The present bridge has a series of seven ribbed arches of fair width, and is so substantial that it is likely to endure until it can boast a more than respectable antiquity.

Croft Church is a half-brown, half-grey old building of mixed materials and of most evident age. It has an appearance more worn and dilapidated even than its years warrant, though it was built at least as early as the fifteenth century, seeing that it contains a tomb of one Richard Clervaux, who died in 1492. The interior of the church has great architectural interest, and the exterior is, in its quaint way, one of those "things of beauty" which deserve to remain "joys for ever." In this church Bishop Burnet may have listened to his first sermon, for it was at Croft that he was born

The Lord of the Manor of Croft, by the way, formerly held his lands on the peculiar condition that he should meet every newly-appointed Bishop of Durham on Croft Bridge, and, presenting him with a rusty old sword, declare—"My lord, this is the sword which slew the worm-dragon, which spared neither man nor woman nor child." Traditions of these worm-dragons are plentiful in the north of England. There was, for example, "the Lambton worm," slain by an ancestor of the present Earl of Durham, which used to devour a maiden at a meal; and there was "the loathly worm of Spindleston Haugh," with a similarly voracious appetite. The lands of Croft had evidently been given to some supposed dragon-slayer, and were continued to his descendants by the yielding up and the immediate return of the famous sword.

We are now more than ever reminded that the Tees is the dividing line of two counties. Though the river has constantly increased in width, all the towns from Croft downwards are situated more or less on each side of the stream. The first of these is the quiet and sleepy town of Yarm, with a single broad street on one side of the river, and a few scattered houses and windmills on the other. Up to Yarm the tide reaches, and here also the net-fishing for salmon begins, small cobles, with salmon-nets on board, being plentiful in the neighbourhood of Yarm Bridge. What else the people of Yarm do for a living in these days is not readily discernible. In former times they were shipbuilders on a limited scale, though they must have been exceedingly small vessels which could be launched in such a situation. Yet there must have been some period of great prosperity in the previous history of the place, as will be guessed from the fact that the houses are almost all of great width and height, and—as is evident from a peculiarity of style not seen elsewhere—were built with some thought of show. The one street of the place is of the width of three or four streets in the more crowded quarters of the larger towns lower down the Tees, and has in its centre an odd sort of Town Hall, like a large sentry-box

STOCKTON.

on arches. At Yarm we set our faces towards the great, growing Tees-side towns, passing the pretty bridge at Blackwell, where Sir Henry Havelock-Allan has a beautiful seat. Already the smoke of great industries is darkening the atmosphere, and when the wind is still and the clouds are low, a black, unpleasant haze creeps over the face of the country and spreads itself far inland.

By the time it reaches Stockton Bridge the Tees has been transformed from one of the most wild and lovely to one of the most tame and repellent of existing rivers. Its soiled waters henceforth flow between banks of blast-furnace slag; unpleasant odours float about its shores; it is ploughed by great steamships; all around there is the smoke of furnaces, the noise of hammers, the ugliness of trade. Stockton is a town of ancient foundation, which, after sleeping beside the Tees for ages, suddenly woke up to find itself in the nineteenth century, and, full of the nineteenth century desire to "get on," shook off its old apathy, measured itself against the age, deepened its river, built ships, smelted ironstone, cast and forged and manufactured, until it found itself accepted as one of the most spirited and enterprising of English towns. In the process of growth everything that may have been beautiful in its surroundings has been destroyed, and now, glorying in its ugliness, it flaunts its frightful aspect as one of its claims to consideration.

Stockton Manor was granted to the see of Durham after the Conquest. A fortress was built, as was so necessary in those days, and the place was visited in

HIGH STREET, STOCKTON.

1214 by King John. In the sixteenth century Stockton was a town to which a Bishop of Durham might retreat from the Plague. The castle was taken by the Parliamentarians in 1644, and destroyed, the only stone houses in Stockton a few years ago being such as were built from the castle walls. There is one fine street and a Borough Hall, but every other part of Stockton bears witness to the fact that a town which is engaged in growing and prospering has neither time nor inclination to attend to its looks. As to the growth of the last half century, there is only one town—the neighbouring Middlesbrough—by which it has been excelled.

At the beginning of the century Stockton had already a shipping trade, but one that could seem important only in the eyes of its 11,000 inhabitants. At that time the river kept a tortuous, shallow course until it arrived at the wide, sandy flats which stretched far eastward to the sea. The first improvement was a straightening of its course, which dates back to the year 1810. The effect was a heightening of the tide from eight to ten feet at Stockton Quay, and little short of a doubling of the shipping trade. The construction of the first public railway came just in time to encourage the town in its efforts at development. A Tees Conservancy was formed, with the consequence that the river was so dredged, banked up, and reformed generally, that Stockton is now not only a considerable port and an important manufacturing town, but a centre of shipbuilding, the vessels built here being as large as many of those which are constructed on the Tyne. Wealth and population have increased enormously, and there seems no necessary limit to further industrial development.

Any accurate description of Stockton is in many respects applicable to Middlesbrough, a still more wonderful town, which has, within living memory, sprung up close to the estuary of the Tees. Fifty years ago there was only a single farmstead where the great town of Middlesbrough now stands. The United States have few examples of such marvellous growth. At the census of 1831 there were 154 persons in Middlesbrough, and at the census of 1881 the population was 55,281. It was in 1830 that the present town was founded, on 500 acres of marshy land. It has been assisted both by enterprise and good fortune. Originally it was intended as a port for the shipping of coals; but iron was discovered in the Cleveland hills, and blast furnaces were built where it was supposed that only coal-staiths would be seen. The first ton of Cleveland ironstone was mined in 1850, and in sixteen years the output was no less than two and three quarter millions of tons. When the iron trade was declining, a decade since, Middlesbrough men set themselves to devise new methods of manufacturing steel, with the result that Middlesbrough steel is now in demand all over the world. Talent, enterprise, the bounty of Nature, have all combined to make of Middlesbrough one of our large centres of population and industry, and to bring about a growth so rapid as has not previously been witnessed in the history of our country.

The brief voyage down the Tees from Stockton to below Middlesbrough should be made in the night time, when clouds of smoke are shot through by columns of flame; when the furnace fires are blazing out into the darkness; when seething bars of iron, crushing and straining through the rolling-mills, make the forges look like some huge Vulcan's smithy; when the steel converters are sending out a fiery rain; and when the Tees is reflecting all manner of strange lights and weird coruscations—an appalling sight to one not accustomed to such spectacles, but grand and deeply impressive and wonderfully characteristic of the age in which we live.

Middlesbrough has its fine docks, crowded with shipping. Where, a few years ago, the Tees spread itself over a broad estuary, the channel of the river has been divided from the wide stretch of mud and sand and creeping waves by a curving groin of slag; lines of light stretch downward as far as the eye can follow, guiding ships to the desired haven. Henceforth the Tees—

"Not hurled precipitous from steep to steep;
Lingering no more 'mid flower-enamelled lands
And blooming thickets; nor by rocky bands
Held; but in radiant progress towards the deep."—

flows broadly onward to the Northern Sea.

During the last quarter of a century the river below Stockton has been constantly undergoing a process of enlargement and improvement, necessarily accompanied by a destruction of its former picturesque beauty. The work done is in the highest sense creditable to northern enterprise. The foundation stones of two great breakwaters were laid in 1863, these defences against the incoming waves being appropriately built of slag from the furnaces of Middlesbrough and Stockton. The large quantity of 443,000 tons of this material was deposited in a single year, and by 1874, when close upon £100,000 had been spent, it was possible to report that a shifting bed of sand had been replaced by a solid and immovable wall. The breakwaters have cost close upon a quarter of a million sterling at the present date, a sum well expended, for a fine harbour has now been constructed only less important than that of the Tyne. On good authority it has been declared that the recent improvements on the Tees are to be ranked amongst the most successful engineering works of the century.

FERRYBOAT LANDING, MIDDLESBROUGH.

Messrs. Besant and Rice have made the marvellous development of Middlesbrough the leading motive of one of their most striking novels. The mere history of the place is in itself a romance. So recently as in 1831 the place had only 154 inhabitants, and it has now, it is believed, considerably more than 60,000. Until iron was discovered in the Cleveland Hills the smelting works of the North of England were situated almost solely on the Tyne and the Wear. The finding of Cleveland iron made a vast change in the *locale* of a great industry, and covered the low-lying and desolate lands near the estuary of the Tees with mighty forges, and blast furnaces, and iron shipbuilding yards and crowded streets. Where, sixty years ago, a shallow stream wound down to the sea, with only an occasional house discernible along its banks, there is now one of the finest outlets of our commerce and manufactures, and a deep river flowing through thickly populated towns. And as regards development the end is not yet. It has seemed more than once that Middlesbrough would collapse almost as rapidly as it has grown up, but it has risen stronger from every depression, and some new invention or discovery has at each crisis brought its assurance of continued life and growth.

However, it is an unlovely Tees that the eye alights upon since the smoke of the blast furnaces came in sight. It would scarcely be possible for a river so beautiful in its upper reaches to undergo a more surprising and spirit-depressing change. Yet standing on the lofty quays at Middlesbrough and looking seaward, one is conscious of a throb of exhilaration, such as the hero of "Locksley Hall" must have felt when, imagining the future, he—.

> "Saw the heavens fill with commerce, argosies of magic sails,
> Pilots of the purple twilight, dropping down with costly bales."

In the perpetual coming and going of great steamers, bringing in cargoes of "wheat and wine and oil," and carrying out to all lands the produce of English industry and skill, there is a spectacle which very well atones for the destruction of some little picturesqueness here and there. What was bright and pleasant only is often enough in these cases replaced by what, when properly considered, is sublime.

AARON WATSON.

BLAST FURNACES, FROM THE RIVER, MIDDLESBROUGH.

IN THE POTTERIES.

THE HUMBER AND ITS TRIBUTARIES.

CHAPTER I.

THE TRENT, FROM THE SOURCE TO NEWTON SOLNEY.

The Course of the Trent—A Lowland Stream—Etymological—A Fish-Stream—The Source—The Potteries—Burslem, Etruria, and Josiah Wedgwood—Stoke-upon-Trent—Trentham Hall—Stone—Sandon—Chartley Castle—Ingestre and its Owners—The Sow—Tixall—Essex Bridge—Shugborough—Cannock Chase—Rugeley—Beaudesert—Armitage—The Blyth—Alrewas—The Tame—Burton-upon-Trent—Newton Solney.

SOME of our chief English rivers seek out paths for their waters, the motive of which is by no means easy to explain. Father Thames, indeed, goes about this work in a fairly business-like way. Born on the eastern slopes of the Cotswolds he makes his way to the sea by a tolerably direct course. Not so Trent. Rising on the western slopes of the backbone of England, one would have expected that, like the Weaver on the one side of it, and the Dane on the other, it would have made its way towards the estuaries of the Dee or the Mersey; but it flows first of all nearly south, parallel with the trend of the great hill district of Derbyshire and North Staffordshire, and then after this has sunk down to the lowlands of the latter county, Trent bends towards the east, until the hills are left behind, when it sweeps round to the north, and so makes its way towards the Ouse and the Humber. Thus its course, like that of Dee, still more of Severn, may be roughly likened to a fish-hook. But, unlike these rivers, and like Thames, Trent, throughout its whole course, is a lowland rather than an upland stream. The hill region already mentioned is, indeed, drained by some of its tributaries, and its western slopes give birth to the little stream which first bears the name of Trent, and for a time traverses the North Staffordshire coal-field, but the river soon enters the district composed of sandstones, gravels, and marls (referred by geologists to the Trias), and as these are but rarely either hard or durable, the scenery is neither bold nor conspicuously varied. Such change as it exhibits is due rather to difference of productiveness than to diversity of physical features. In regard to the latter the extremes are only from level plain to undulating hills of moderate elevation, but the former affords every variety between barren moorland and densely wooded or richly cultivated ground.

Michael Drayton thus explains the etymology of Trent, and assigns to it a mystic significance when he tells the tale of

> . . . A long-told prophecy, which ran
> Of Moreland, that she might live prosperously to see
> A river born of her, who well might reckoned be
> The third of this large isle: which saw did first arise
> From Arden, in those days delivering prophecies.
> * * * * *
> To satisfy her will, the wizard answers, Trent.
> For, as a skilful seer, the aged forest wist,
> A more than usual power did in that name consist,
> Which thirty doth import; by which she thus divined,
> There should be found in her of fishes thirty kind;
> And thirty abbeys great, in places fat and rank,
> Should in succeeding time have builded on her bank:
> And thirty several streams from many a sundry way
> Unto her greatness should their watery tribute pay.

On the same side may be quoted Camden and Spenser and Milton, yet philology is too strong for poetry, and modern scholars declare that the name Trent has nothing to do with the Latin word for thirty or any of its modifications in the Romance languages, but is of Celtic origin, is only a contracted form of Derwent, and means river-water. The first of the two words which compose the dissyllable Derwent, and enter into the monosyllabic Trent, is that which appears in the Doire, Dora, Douro, Durance, and other European rivers; the second is indicated by the Latin Venta, a name borne by more than one river-side town in Roman Britain.

The Trent and its tributaries were noted of old as fish-streams, and even now, after years of neglect and poaching, it would not be difficult to make up the "thirty kinds of fish" which were once said to people its waters. Isaak Walton has made the upper reaches of the Dove classic ground; and there, as in the Blyth, and in gravelly parts of the main river, one may yet see "here and there a lusty trout and here and there a grayling." Eels were and still are numerous in the more muddy parts of its bed; pike are also common, though the giants of olden days are vanished like the Rephaim; for in the last century, a county historian tells us, fish weighing more than twenty pounds were not seldom caught, and one monster of thirty-six pounds is said to have been found dead. The barbel also is a Trent fish, and the stream may claim the salmon. One was caught many years ago so far away from the sea as Rugeley, but it was white and out of season. Swans in several districts add to the beauty of its waters, and build their nests by its side among the willow-beds and reeds.

The river is navigable only as far as Burton, for above that town it is interrupted by weirs and by shallows; but canals follow the valley, and in the year 1819 the railroad uniting Rugby with Stafford passed along it for a few miles, and directed through a district, hitherto secluded, the traffic between London and Holyhead or the great towns of western Lancashire. This railway quitted the Trent near its junction with the Sow, but a few years later the towns higher up the river, forming the important district of the Staffordshire Potteries, were reached by a line which branches off from the main system of the London and North-Western Company at Colwich.

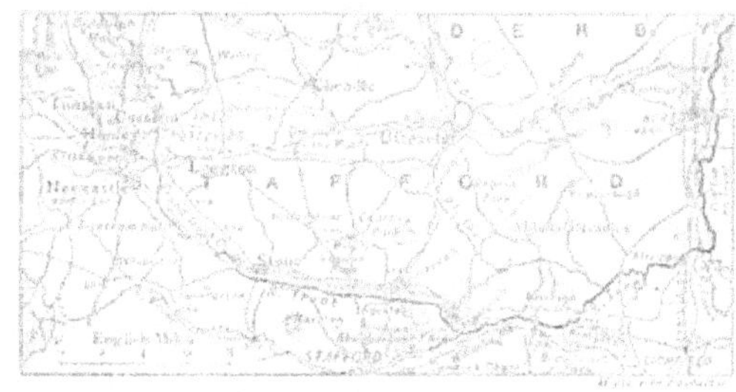

THE TRENT, FROM THE SOURCE TO NEWTON SOLNEY.

The birthplace of Trent, like that of many persons afterwards famous, is inconspicuous. The river, according to Erdeswick, "hath its first spring in the moorlands between Bidulph and Norton, and divideth the shire almost into two equal parts, north and south." There is little to note in its earlier course. One or two of the adjacent villages possess some link with our older history, notably "Stanleghe," of which the author just quoted says, "of this small village do all the great houses of Stanley take their name." But before long a district is entered, unpleasing indeed to the artist, but welcome to the man of commerce—a land of chimneys and smoke, of kilns and furnaces, not only for earth but also for metal. This is the district popularly called the Potteries, a group of towns often so nearly confluent as to defy distinction by all but residents. Tunstall and Burslem, Newcastle-under-Lyme, Hanley and Stoke-upon-Trent: these, with such suburbs as Etruria, occupy a strip of country some ten miles long, drained by the youthful Trent and its tributaries, a composite or confluent hive of human bees. We will venture but on one positive statement, that Stoke-upon-Trent is the last of these towns, and below it the river emerges into more attractive scenery. In this district the smelting furnaces and iron-works are industries comparatively modern, but for centuries it has been noted for its earthenware. Burslem, one of the towns more distant from the Trent, appears to be the oldest, for under the name of Bulwardsleme it is mentioned in Domesday Book, and its "butter-pots" were noted in the days of the Stuarts. When Dr. Plot wrote his History of Staffordshire—that is, during the short reign of James II.—it was the chief place for the potter's industry, and he tells us that "for making several sorts of pots they have as many different sorts of clay, which they dig round about the town, all within half a mile's distance, the

ETRURIA.

JOSIAH WEDGWOOD.

best being found near the coal." This earthenware was all coloured, for the white clay from Cornwall had not yet been imported into the district. The most marked advance was due to one man—Josiah Wedgwood, who was born to the trade in 1730. The effect of an illness in youth led him to turn his thoughts to the more delicate work, and he soon exhibited great skill in manufacturing ornamental pottery. When nearly thirty years old he established himself in business at Burslem, and produced such results as the white-stone ware, green glazed earthenware, cream-coloured Queen's ware, and the unglazed black porcelain. The works, however, at Burslem soon proved too small for his needs, and in 1766 he purchased an estate, built a large establishment on the bank of the Grand Trunk Canal, between Hanley and Newcastle, calling it Etruria, in remembrance of the so-called "Etruscan vases," which were among his favourite models. Aided in business by his partner, Bentley, in art by the talent of Flaxman, Wedgwood prospered, and Etruria under his management surpassed the fame of Worcester, and rivalled that of Sèvres or Dresden. Wedgwood, in fact, by the graceful form and harmonious decoration of his wares, did not a little to educate the national taste and raise it from the easy contentment with opulent ugliness which is the general characteristic of the "Hanoverian period" of British Art. Since his days the village has become a town; the iron-works of Shelton have helped in blackening the precincts of Etruria Hall, which Wedgwood built, and in the cellars of which he made his experiments; Spode and Minton and Copeland have added to the fame of the Potteries; villages and towns have grown beyond recognition, and houses have hid what once were fields; but though these and other makers have produced, or still produce, many admirable and characteristic works, "old Wedgwood ware" maintains a unique position among the masterpieces of ceramic art.

We must not linger over the Grand Trunk Canal, nor the fame of Brindley, the engineer, a native of this part of Staffordshire, nor shall we be much tempted to tarry in Stoke-upon-Trent—at any rate, for æsthetic reasons—unless we confine ourselves to the interior of its show rooms, though there is many a worse place to live in. It is mightily changed since the days when Erdeswick wrote of it, "Of Stoke I can report no more but that the parson of the parish is the best man in the town, being lord thereof, and it being one of the best parsonages in the county." The parson now is a bishop and a baronet, but the town is yet more important.

It contains many buildings which larger towns could not despise: a handsome modern church, a fine town-hall, and a school of science and art, which is a memorial to the late Mr. Minton. Statues, or monuments of some kind, to several

TRENTHAM.

members of the great potter families—Wedgwood, Spode, Minton, and others—will be found here, and the town itself is regarded as the centre and show place of the district.

Below Stoke, and almost within sight of its chimneys by the side of Trent, stands one of the "stately homes" of England—Trentham Hall, a seat of the Duke of Sutherland. The mansion lies low on the flat bed of the valley; the park mounts the slopes on the right hand, thus affording great variety of scenery, from richly-wooded meadows to rather open moorland. There is nothing to suggest a settlement of great antiquity, yet a monastery was founded here in the days of Alfred. Enlarged by Ranulf Earl of Chester, it passed, after the Dissolution, into the hands of the Levesons, ancestors of the present duke. One of them built on its site a fine Jacobean house, of which Plot gives a plate together with the following quaint note: "The stone-rail upon the wall built about the green-court before Trentham House is a pretty piece of work, it being supported with Roman capital letters instead of ballisters, containing an inscription not only setting forth the name of the ancient Proprietor and builder of this Seat, but the time when it was done, the Numeral Letters put together making up the year of our Lord, when it was finish't, viz., 1633."

This house was pulled down early in the last century, when the nucleus of the present mansion was erected, which, however, was greatly enlarged and altered by Sir Charles Barry in the time of the late duke. The church, which adjoins the house, contains remnants of very early work and some interesting monuments. There is a large sheet of water in the gardens, which are famed for many a mile round for their beauty, and surpass any that will be found elsewhere near the margin of the Trent.

After passing Trentham the river gradually loses the traces of the grime of the potteries and coal-fields, and glides along through pleasant pastoral scenery till it reaches Stone. This, for long a sleepy little country town, has been awakened by the railway and other causes, and seems now to be a fairly busy and thriving place, devoted chiefly to malting, brewing, and shoemaking. There is little to indicate antiquity, except a few fragments of an old nunnery, for the church dates from the last century, when that which had once served the religious house tumbled down.

Stone, nevertheless, begins its history more than twelve centuries ago. There lived then a certain Wulfere, king of Mercia, who had a residence somewhere near Stone: tradition asserts at Bury Bank, rather higher up the Trent, where an earthwork still exists. Wulfere was a heathen and a persecutor, but a holy hermit, named Ceadda, better known as St. Chad, who died bishop of Lichfield, was dwelling hidden in the neighbouring forest. The king's two sons were hunting one day, and were led by the chase to the saint's abode. The young men felt the charm of his words, repeated their visit, and became converts. Of course this was soon made known to their father; the parent was forgotten in the persecutor, and the young men were put to death. But time brought its revenges, though in this case merciful. Before many years were over Wulfere himself became a Christian, and then, as a monument of sorrow and penitence, he founded a monastery at Stone, where also a nunnery was established by his queen.

The last statement, as to the date of the foundation, is probably true, but all the rest of the story, like many another concerning Chad, is only legend. Since then Stone, as is the case with many other country towns, has shared in the beatitude of having no history. The suppression of its convents, the ruin of its church, and a connection with the Rebellion of 1745—the latter events happening in the same decade—appear to have been the chief incidents that have ruffled its even existence. The last-named incident might have given it a place in national history, had things taken another course. The young Pretender Charles Edward, after his triumph in Scotland, had crossed the Solway, and begun his invasion of England. He was expected to advance upon London along the line of the main road from Manchester, so the Duke of Cumberland encamped in the neighbourhood of Stone to dispute his passage. Charles, however, as is well known, struck eastward, and on arriving at Derby, was a long day's march nearer London than the duke's army. The inherent weakness of his forces averted the danger, and the Hanoverian troops had only to pursue the retreating enemy till he made his last hopeless stand on the moor of Culloden.

Below Stone the river passes Sandon, an old village. There are not many prettier places in all the valley of the Trent than the park of the Harrowbys with its slopes of grove and sward, the higher parts of which command views of unusual extent, not only over the rich river valley of the Trent, but also as far as the Wrekin and Caradoc hills. On elevated ground, at the edge of the park, is the parish church, containing several interesting remains of olden time, the most conspicuous, though by no means the most ancient, being the monument to Sampson Erdeswick, the historian of Staffordshire, and former owner of the estate, who died in the year 1603. The property ultimately passed into the hands of the Duke of Hamilton, and a lawsuit in regard to it is reported to have occasioned the quarrel between the duke and Lord Mohun which, as is well known, had so tragic an ending. Erdeswick's house, of which the site is still marked, was a fine old brick and timber edifice, surrounded by a moat; but in the last century a new and uninteresting mansion was erected by Lord Archibald Hamilton, which was burned down in 1848, and replaced by a more handsome building in the Tudor style. From him the property was purchased by an ancestor of the present owner, the Earl of Harrowby.

Rather below Sandon, near the little village of Shirleywich, brine is obtained. Fortunately, however, for the beauty of the scenery, there has been no temptation to establish extensive salt works. The quiet little villages on the lowlands, near the river, offer nothing to delay the traveller; but the grey ruins, high on the left bank, mark a place of some note. Those two broken towers, those fragments of curtain-wall, are remnants of Chartley Castle; the moorland, which extends back from the park, is one of the few spots in England where the descendants of *bos primigenius* still linger on in a semi-wild condition. The castle, though it carries back its history to early in the thirteenth century, makes little figure in

INGESTRE HALL.

history. The present house is on lower ground, and parts of it are older than the reign of Elizabeth, who not only visited it herself, but made it one of the prisons of Mary Queen of Scots. The estate formerly was included among those of the great Earls of Chester, but has for long been part of the family property of the present owner, Earl Ferrers. There is a tragic tale about a former earl, who was a man of ungovernable temper—probably insane, and shot his own steward. Feudal times were then too far away, and his coronet could not save him from the halter.

The wild cattle, of which it is not generally easy, and, at certain seasons, not always safe, to obtain a near view are, according to Shaw, the historian of Staffordshire, "in colour invariably white, muzzles and ears black, and horns white, fine-tipped with black." If a black calf be born it is promptly destroyed, not only because it might alter the constancy of the breed, but also because it is deemed an evil omen, for its birth, so folk believe, is followed by the death of a member of the family.

Some distance away, on the opposite bank of the Trent, just where the ground begins to rise from the level of the valley, stands one of the most picturesque, and formerly one of the most interesting, mansions along the whole course of the river. This is Ingestre, the home of the Chetwynd-Talbots, now Earls of Shrewsbury.

WOLSELEY BRIDGE.

Formerly it was a perfect specimen of an Elizabethan mansion, but in the year 1882 it was reduced by fire to a mere shell of masonry, and many family relics of interest were destroyed. It has, however, been rebuilt, and as in many places the old walls had remained uninjured, the external appearance is little changed. The plate in Plot's "Staffordshire" represents a formal garden and courtyard in front, with the church close at hand, near the eastern end

SHUGBOROUGH.

of the house, to which some additions have been subsequently made. The other features, though they can still be traced in part, have been modified in compliance with the less formal taste of later ages; but the church is unaltered—a grey stone structure of little architectural beauty, erected in the latter part of the seventeenth century by the owner of the estates in place of one which occupied a less convenient situation, and was in a dilapidated condition. This is the history of its consecration, as it is given by Plot, who tells us that milled shillings, halfpence, and farthings "coyn'd that year (1673) were put into hollow places cut for that purpose in the larger corner-stone of the steeple." Afterwards he continues, "The church being thus finisht at the sole charge of the said Walter Chetwynd, in August An. 1677 it was solemnly consecrated by the right Reverend Father in God Thomas Lord Bishop of Coventry and Lichfield; the Dean of Lichfield preaching the Sermon, and some others of the most eminent Clergy reading prayers; baptizing a Child; Churching a woman; joyning a couple in Matrimony and burying another; all which offices were also there performed the same day. The pious and generous Founder and Patron offering upon the Altar the tithes of Hopton a village hard by, to the value of fifty pounds *per Annum*, as an addition to the Rectory for ever: presenting the Bishop and Dean at the same time, each with a piece of plate double guilt, as a gratefull acknowledgment of their service: and entertaining the Nobility, Clergy, and Gentry, both Men and Women, of the whole County in a manner, which came that day to see the solemnity performed, with a most splendid dinner at his house near adjoyning."

The owners of Ingestre were descendants of the great Talbot family which fills so large a space in English history during the middle ages. The titles of Earl Talbot and Viscount Ingestre were conferred in the eighteenth century, and in the year 1856, in the lifetime of the third earl, the great law-suit was begun to establish his right to the earldom of Shrewsbury, and the large estates covered by the entail. For at least a century and a half the Earls of Shrewsbury had been Roman Catholics, and during all that time the title had not gone by direct descent, so it had become a saying in the county that so long as a Romanist held the title, no heir would be born to him. Thus, on the death of Earl Bertram, while still a young man and unmarried, great doubt existed as to the succession. The suit "involved two separate questions, namely, who was really the next-of-kin, and whether the estates were separable from the earldom. These had been entailed by an Act of Parliament obtained by the Duke of Shrewsbury, in the beginning of the eighteenth century, but it was doubtful whether the entail did not expire in the person of the young Earl Bertram. He was of opinion that it did, and being an ardent Roman Catholic, left the estates and all the art treasures contained in Alton Towers (the principal seat of his ancestors) to the Duke of Norfolk, so that they might still be owned by an obedient son of the Pope of Rome. It was, however, contended that the entail was yet valid and the estates were inseparable from the title. For the latter two claimants appeared, the one Earl Talbot of

Ingestre in Staffordshire, the other Major Talbot of Castle Talbot, county Wexford. The former claimed as descendant of a son of the second wife of a certain Sir John Talbot of Albrighton, grandson of the second Earl of Shrewsbury; the latter as a descendant of a son of the first wife of the same person. If Major Talbot could have proved his pedigree, obviously he would have succeeded. This, however, he failed to do to the satisfaction of the House of Lords, who decided that Henry John Chetwynd, the Earl of Talbot, had made out his claim. He accordingly took the oath and his seat as eighteenth earl, June 10th, 1858. The important suit about the estates was not decided till 1860, when the Court of Exchequer pronounced the will of the late Earl Bertram, as far as concerned the entailed property, to be invalid." *

Neither the winner, nor his son and successor, lived long to enjoy their victory, and the title devolved upon the present earl when he was still a boy. However, the charm seems broken, and the popular belief has been confirmed, for the earldom has already twice descended in the direct line.

Beautiful as is Ingestre Hall, its situation is hardly less attractive. The ground swells up from the old-fashioned garden into low hills, carpeted with grass, and shaded by fine old trees and clustering copses, which at last sink down into the rich meadows, through which the Trent winds slowly on. Rather below Ingestre it receives its first important affluent, which bears the prosaic name of the Sow. It is a stream of hardly less magnitude, but of less beauty and interest, which comes down a broad and well-marked valley from Stafford; this, though the chief town of the county, possesses little to interest the traveller; it is, however, an important railway junction, and is, besides, busied in shoemaking. The Sow also, before reaching the Trent, receives an affluent which is hardly less than itself. This is the Penk, which rises on the edge of the industrial district of South Staffordshire, and follows a northerly course through pleasant scenery on the western border of Cannock Chase until it meets the Sow.

Between the latter river and the Trent lies the estate of Tixall, once the property of the Astons and then of the Cliffords, but purchased some forty years since by the Talbots. The house, which stands nearer to the Sow, is a comparatively modern stone structure, plain and heavy in style, very inferior to the picturesque old dwelling which is represented by Plot, and of which he remarks that "the windows, though very numerous, are scarce two alike;" but the grey and ivy-clad old gateway "a curious piece of stone-work," built in 1580, though dismantled, still remains much as it was when his plate was engraved. It stands just at the foot of the slope, where the low hills die away to the river plain, which here is perhaps half a mile in width; fine old trees cluster thickly in the neighbourhood of the house and around the little village, almost masking its cottages and its tiny church. Down the valley we see the woods of Shugborough closing the view and clothing the opposite slope beyond the union of

* "Our Own Country" (Alton Towers), Vol. IV., p. 221.

the two rivers, and above them rises a triumphal arch, a memorial of a former owner of the hall, who was a man of note in his day and generation.

The Trent, after it has taken large tribute from the Sow, flows through the park of the Earls of Lichfield, which is certainly not the least beautiful of

RUGELEY, FROM THE STONE QUARRY.

those on its banks. The house, indeed, is not well situated, for it is built on the valley plain near the river, and is an uninteresting structure in the plainest Hanoverian style, but the scenery of the park is no less varied than beautiful. Here are broad and level meadows, shaded by groups of aged trees, and extending to the margin of the river; the plain gradually breaking into picturesque undulations as it approaches either border of the valley. On the left bank this is quickly reached. Here the slopes descend steeply to the river; on the opposite side, at a greater distance, the park begins to climb the outlying moorlands of Cannock Chase, on which, at intervals, cultivation wholly ceases.

The ancestors of the present earl have resided on this estate since the reign of James I., but the first to reach the peerage was Admiral George Anson, who, in 1740, began a protracted voyage, during which he circumnavigated the globe, and inflicted great injuries on the Spanish settlements in the New World. Afterwards he defeated the French in a naval engagement. As a reward for these and other services he was created Baron Anson, but the title expired with him. A nephew, however, who succeeded to his estate, was ultimately created Viscount Anson, and the earldom of Lichfield dates from 1831.

Shortly below its junction with the Sow the Trent is crossed by a curious old bridge, which, if only for its view of the valley, is worth a visit. Just above it the stream is divided by a wooded island and the western branch tumbles over a tiny weir: then the united waters, after passing beneath the bridge, contract as they flow between banks overhung by trees; these are backed on the left by the steep slopes already mentioned, but on the right stretch away till the wooded plain mounts to the uplands of Cannock Chase. The Essex Bridge, as it is called, from some connection with the family of Devereux, once owners of Chartley, even now consists of fourteen arches, but, according to the old county histories, was formerly of greater length. It is, however, difficult to see on which side the bridge has been cut short; but possibly the road across the valley may have been continued by a causeway, which was included with the bridge. This is a singularly picturesque old structure of grey sandstone, only about four feet in width, with an angle of refuge for foot passengers at every one of the piers—a convenience which will be appreciated by the traveller even if he encounter only a tricycle in crossing.

In the park of Shugborough, and for a short distance below this, Trent approaches nearest to the edge of Cannock Chase. Indeed, for rather more than a mile above Wolseley Bridge, opposite the villages of Great Heywood and Colwich, a walk of a furlong, through a mere belt of cultivated land, leads on to an open moor which in some directions extends without a break for miles. The Chase is an undulating upland rising some three or four hundred feet above the valley of the Trent, and often not far from six hundred feet above sea level, a plateau consisting of rolling hills and narrow valleys with steeply shelving sides, composed almost wholly of the "pebble beds"—thick masses of a rather hard and sandy gravel containing pebbles which often are three or four inches in diameter. There is practically no surface soil, and thus the moors offers little temptation to the "land-grabbers." Of late years indeed its area has been diminished, and its beauties not augmented, by considerable enclosures in the neighbourhood of

CANNOCK CHASE, FROM THE TRENT.

Rugeley and Hednesford, and by the opening of collieries near the latter place. But the new fields do not seem likely to do much more than pay interest on the first expenditure, and the collieries have not been so uniformly successful as to cause apprehensions that, at any rate in the present generation, the moorland will become a "Black Country." Another danger has lately threatened its solitudes, for a tract of Cannock Chase was one of the sites proposed for the meeting of the National Rifle Association in succession to Wimbledon Common. Bisley has been preferred, but there is still a possibility that this tract may be used as a practice ground for the Volunteers of the Midland and Northern counties, in which case the charm of another large segment of the Chase will quickly vanish.

At present, notwithstanding the occasional prospect of distant collieries, there are few districts in the Midlands which offer more attractions than Cannock Chase. The contour of the ground, it is true, does not exhibit much variety. It is, as has been said, an undulating plateau from which fairly well-marked valleys, gradually deepening, descend towards the lowlands, but there is much diversity in the minor details. Here sturdy oaks are scattered or graceful birches cluster close on slope or valley. Here only some weather-beaten sentinel of either tree, or a wind-worn thorn breaks the barrenness of the hill, or a few Scotch firs crown its crest. Almost everywhere the bracken flourishes, and heath or ling grows thick on the stony soil. So, in the late summer, the Chase for miles glows with the crimson bloom of the heath, or is flushed with the tender pink of the ling, while as autumn draws on the fern turns to gold on the slopes, and on the barer brows the bilberry leaf changes to scarlet, and the moor, soon to don the russet hue of its winter garb, seems to reflect the rich tints of the sunset sky. But this is not all. Among its many charms is the contrast of scenery: one moment you may be quite shut in by the undulations of the moorland—sweeps of fern and heath and ling bounding the view on every side—seemingly as far from the haunts of man as among the Sutherland Hills; but the next, on gaining the crest of some rounded ridge, many a mile of fertile lowland spreads out before your eyes—many a league of the rich vales of the Trent and the Sow, one vast and varied tapestry of woodland and corn-field and pasture, while beyond and above, rise, in this direction, the Wrekin dome and the Caradoc peaks, in that the great rounded uplands of Derbyshire, and in that the more broken outlines of the Charnwood Forest Hills. Deer once were common, black-game and grouse abundant, the snipe and even the woodcock made their nests in the valleys, and other rare birds were to be seen. But now the deer are few and the game is scanty. Cannock Chase, like the rest of Great Britain, suffers from the congestion of humanity.

But we must return to the Trent, from which we have wandered away into the moors. For a few miles, after leaving Shugborough Park, though it affords much pretty scenery, there is no place of special beauty or of historical interest near its banks. It passes under a new bridge, close to one of the approaches to the Chase; it leaves on the left the village of Colwich and its neat church, on the right Oakedge Park, from which the residence has now disappeared. This, more than a century since, was the scene of a local scandal—a fascinating widow, a midnight marriage, and a verification of the old proverb about haste and leisure in regard to that bond. Then the river glides beneath the three arches of Wolseley Bridge—deservedly held in repute for its graceful though simple design—and passes at the back of Wolseley Hall. The estate has been owned by Wolseleys from before the Norman Conquest—but the house is comparatively modern, is of little interest, and is placed too near the water. Of this family Viscount Wolseley is a member, tracing back his descent to a younger son of a former baronet, and is thus a distant cousin of Sir Charles Wolseley, the present owner of the estate.

About half a mile from the Trent, and almost at the foot of the uplands of Cannock Chase, lies Rugeley, a small market town, the chief industry of which is a tannery. This place some thirty years ago acquired an unenviable notoriety as the scene of a case of poisoning, which attracted much attention and presented points of legal interest. The chief railway station is near the river, and so at some distance from the town, of which little is seen. The slender spire which rises above its houses is that of the Roman Catholic Church; the Anglican Church is at the nearer entrance of the town. It was built early in the century, and if ugliness were a merit might claim the first rank, but on the opposite side of the road are the tower and some portions of the old church, which are not without a certain picturesqueness. The tall chimneys on the hill slopes, a mile or more beyond the town, indicate the northern boundary of the South Staffordshire coal-field. Here the escarpment of the moorlands is not very far away from a fault by which the coal measures are thrown down for so many hundred feet that no attempt has yet been made to sink shafts in the valley of the Trent.

Also on the uplands, and rather further away from Rugeley, is another of the great houses which are the chief interest of this part of the Trent. This is Beaudesert. Once a country seat of the Bishops of Lichfield, it passed into the hands of the Pagets in the reign of Henry VIII. A peerage has been long in the family, but the first Marquis of Anglesey was a dashing officer, who highly distinguished himself in the great war with France, and lost his leg at the battle of Waterloo, where he commanded the cavalry. The house, which stands in a commanding position high up on the slope of the uplands, is built of brick, and not a little of it dates from the reign of Elizabeth, though it is not a striking example of the architecture of that era. Several small villages are dotted over the low-lands near Trent side, each offering some little bit of antiquity or fragment of history, such as Armitage, with its church looking down on canal and river, or Mavesyn Ridware, with some tombs of interest in its highly restored Trinity aisle, and its story of a feud between Mavesyn de Ridware and Sir William of Handsacre; though over these we must not linger, but follow the Trent as it pursues its course through grassy meadows in a widening valley, leaving the old cathedral town of Lichfield some four miles away amidst the undulating ground on its southern bank. It glides by various small villages, and receives the tributary stream of the Blyth, which

FROM THE MEADOWS NEAR ALREWAS.

ARMITAGE.

traverses one of the prettiest districts of Staffordshire, coming down by the park of the Bagots, and the remnant of the ancient forest of Needwood, where many a grand oak still flourishes. By the water side are many fair pictures — pleasant groupings of trees, and reeds, with wide straths of grass and glimpses of scattered farmhouses, or grey towers of village churches—each with its little cluster of memories, sometimes of more than local interest. Of these perhaps the most noteworthy is Alrewas, once famed for its eels. Excerpts from its registers are quoted by Shaw, and make interesting reading. Here they tell of a murder, there of a suicide, now of a death by drowning in Trent or Tame, now of heat, or drought, or frost. Fires and storms also figure in the record, even an earthquake, but the strangest tale of all is the following: "This 21st day of December, anno 1581, was the water of Trent dryed up and sodenly fallen so ebb that I, John Falkner, vicar, went over into the hall meddow, in a low peare of showes, about 4 of the clocke in the afternoone: and so it was never in the remembrance of any man then living in the droughtest yeare that any man had knowuen, and the same water in the morning before was banke full, which was very strange."

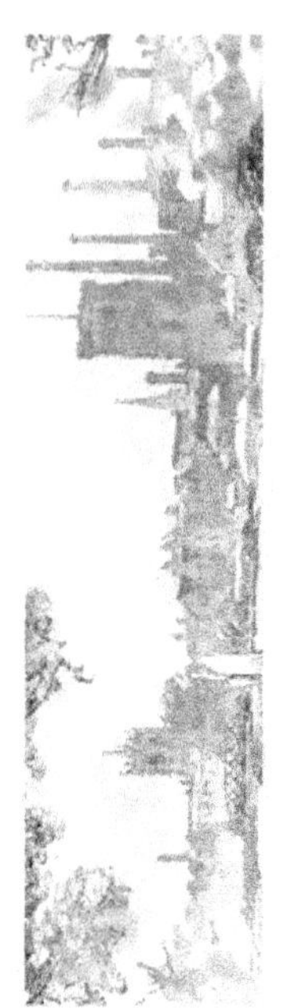

The Tame, which joins the Trent near Alrewas, coming down by "Tamworth tower and town," nearly doubles the volume of the latter, which afterwards flows towards the north, that is in prolongation of the course of the former river. The valley widens yet more between the low hills of Leicestershire and the upland which formed part of Needwood Forest—that region "richly placed," as Drayton says, "'twixt Trent and battening Dove," which, though curtailed of its ancient extent by enclosure, still exhibits more than one grand old oak, and many a choice nook of forest scenery, while the views from the hilly district between the Blyth and the Dove are often of singular variety and beauty.

But now chimneys begin to bristle from the river-plain, and smoke to dim the brightness of the air. Is it fancy, or does a pleasant odour of brewing mingle with the scent of meadow-sweet and riverside herbs? It may well be, for we are approaching Burton-upon-Trent, the metropolis of beer. The description written of it for other pages may be given here:—"If the visitor to Burton care neither to drink of beer nor think of beer, he will not find much to detain him there. Though an old place, it possesses little of antiquity; nor is there any picturesqueness either in its houses or in its streets. It gives one the idea of a typical Staffordshire town—that is to say, a very uninteresting one—which during the last half century has developed into an important mercantile centre. There is thus a certain air of incompleteness about it. Homely buildings of the times of our grandfathers are mixed with handsome modern structures; a fine church, school, or institute rises among dwellings of the most ordinary type; one shop is appropriate to the quiet country town of the last generation, another to the bustling country town of the present. But there is one dominant characteristic—Burton is wholly given over to beer. The great breweries occupy whole districts of the town, and are intersected by the streets; these are traversed again and again by rails; and locomotives, dragging laden wagons—trains of beer—pass and repass in a way unprecedented in any other English town. Great piles of barrels—the Pyramids of the Valley of the Trent—greet the traveller's eye as he halts at the station, and the air is redolent with the fumes of brewing." *

The development of this industry is comparatively of late date, though the ale of Burton has long enjoyed a local reputation. Even the monks of its abbey were noted for the excellence of their beer; but Leland and Camden speak only of its alabaster works. "But in the earlier part of the seventeenth century, beer from the district—which, probably, was in part brewed at Burton—was introduced into London. This, however, bore the name of Derby ale, and by that name is favourably spoken of by Camden. He, however, states that there were diversities of opinion, for a Norman poet had termed it 'a strange drink, so like the Stygian lake.'" The original Burton ale was, however, very different from that for which it is generally celebrated, for it was a strong drink, the India pale ale dating only from the present century. "In the year 1822, one Hodgson, a London brewer who had

* "Our own Country," Vol. VI., p. 155.

settled at Burton, brewed something like the present bitter ale, which he accomplished in a teapot in his counting-house, and called it 'Bombay beer.' A retired East India captain named Chapman improved on this, and Burton ale soon attained the celebrity that has made the names of Bass and Allsopp household words all over the world." The heads of each of these firms (now converted into limited companies) have mounted on steps of barrels to the peerage; but there are other firms of slightly younger standing though of hardly less importance.

One noteworthy fact in the later history of Burton is the liberality of these its leading citizens. Not a few of the principal public buildings—churches, schools, baths, and other institutions—are gifts from members of this or that firm; the latest is a suspension bridge for foot passengers over the Trent, at the southern end of the town, which is the gift of Lord Burton. Previous to this the river was only bridged in one place. At this spot a bridge has existed for several centuries; but the present structure is quite modern. It is far more commodious, but to the artist less attractive, than its predecessor. That was narrow, built on a curve, consisting of thirty-six arches, hardly any two of which were alike; this is wide, uniform, and strikes straight across the broad valley from bank to bank. Like most old bridges, the former had above its piers the usual nooks for the retreat of passengers, and few who remember it will not feel some regret at the change. But this was inevitable; the old bridge was totally inadequate for the needs of the new Burton, which had become a very different place from the little town pictured by Shaw at the end of the last century, and sentiment was obliged to yield to utility. As might be supposed, the old bridge, in early days, was the scene of more than one conflict.

But the history of Burton Town goes back earlier than that of Burton Bridge, even if this, as some have asserted, dated from the reign of William the Norman. Full a thousand years ago there dwelt at Bareton, or Buryton, a noted lady of Irish birth, Modwena by name, who, for curing Alfred, son of Ethelwolfe, of some disease, received a grant of land. Her home for some years was the island between the two branches of the Trent, and the well from which she had been wont to drink sympathetically retained healing virtues, being in repute, as Plot tells us, with those who suffered from the "king's evil." A monastery was afterwards founded by Ulfric Spot, Earl of Mercia, to which her body was translated, and which endured till the suppression of such institutions. The church which was attached to it has been rebuilt, and only some fragments of the conventual buildings remain about the house, which still bears the name of Burton Abbey.

The arms of the Trent unite below Burton, and the right bank of the river affords some varied and pleasant scenery, the ground sloping rapidly down to the level water-meadows, with scattered houses, hamlets, and groves of trees. A castellated mansion of pretentious aspect stands on the hill above fine old trees; beyond, on lower ground, embosomed in yet larger and not less ancient groves, is Newton Hall, near the village, called for distinction Newton Solney, which stands nearly opposite to the junction of the Dove with the Trent.

T. G. Bonney.

DOVE HEAD.

THE HUMBER AND ITS TRIBUTARIES.

CHAPTER II.

THE DOVE.

What's in the Name—Axe Edge and Dove Head—The Monogram—Glutton Mill—Hartington—Beresford Dale—Pike Pool—Izaak Walton and Charles Cotton—Beresford Hall—Dove Dale—Its Associations—Dam—The Manifold—Ashbourne—Doveridge—Uttoxeter—Sudbury—Tutbury—The Confluence.

HERE are two rivers bearing the beautiful name of the Dove—a name derived from "the shimmering gleam of water, corresponding to the lustre of the dove's white wing." There are also two Dove Dales. In Longfellow's "Poems of Places," Wordsworth's tender verses beginning—

> "She dwelt among the untrodden ways
> Beside the springs of Dove,"

are often ascribed to the Derbyshire river, which is more than worthy of such a dedication. But the Dove which the venerable recluse of Rydal Mount referred to is the wayward mountain streamlet of his own beloved Lakeland; and the Dove Dale of that district, in its romantic beauty and historic associations, is but a wayside dell in comparison with the enchanting glen where Izaak Walton discoursed upon philanthropy and fishing, and the gallant Charles Cotton alternately entertained the ancient angler, and hid himself in caves to escape the polite attentions of unpleasant creditors. The phrase, however—

> "A violet by a mossy stone
> Half hidden from the eye,"

aptly, if unconsciously, describes Dove Head, where the Derbyshire Dove escapes from the morose moorlands of Axe Edge, the mountain cradle of four other rivers—the Wye, the Dane, the Goyt, and the Manifold.

Axe Edge is a wild heathery table-land, in which the counties of Derby, Stafford, and Cheshire meet in a savage solitude. The loneliness of this region is impressive, although fashionable Buxton, the spa of the Peak, is only three miles away. There are whisperings of water everywhere on these breezy highlands, now purple under a passing cloud, now a vivid green in the slanting sunlight, as shadow and shine succeed each other over the rugged slopes. They are mere liquid lispings. Their articulations are not so loud as the crow of the blackcock, the clamour of the peewit, or the call of the grouse. But the imperceptible tinkling, the mere tracery of moisture among the rank grass and ebony peat, grow until the rill has become a rivulet; and now we are at Dove Head. There is an isolated farmstead, the whitewashed buildings of which stand out in strong relief from the sombre moorland background. Over the doorway of this solitary old farmhouse are carved the words "Dove Head." Exactly opposite to this house is a moss-grown trough with bubbling water, clear and cold, not topaz-coloured like most streams that have their origin in mountain mosses. On the slab the initials of Izaak Walton and Charles Cotton are entwined in cypher, after the manner of the monogram in the fishing-house in Beresford Dale. This spot indicates the county boundary. Staffordshire claims one side of the Dove, but Derby has greater pretensions to the ownership of the river, for both its head and its foot are in the latter county.

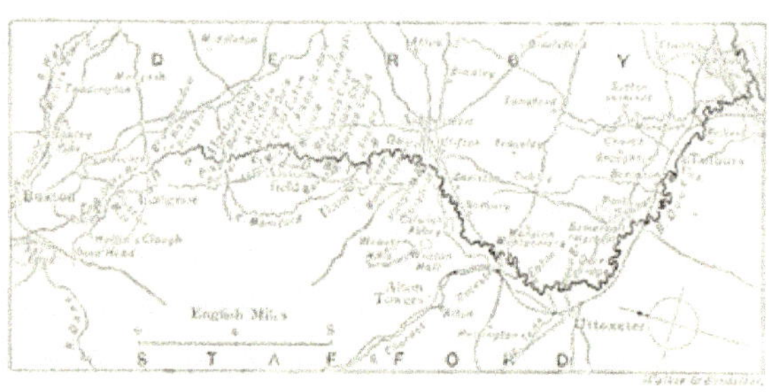

MAP OF THE DOVE.

Dove Head is one of the view points of the "Peake Countrie." The panoramic prospect over bleak height and verdant dale is one to transport the landscape painter. Yet it is too near Buxton, with Manchester only forty minutes' railway ride away, to tempt the English artist. There exist, in a relative sense and with due respect to proportion, few wilder or more picturesque "bits" of scenery than are comprised in the ramble from Dove Head to Glutton Mill. For three or four miles the river, a mere brook, passes through a gritstone gorge, with rocky escarpments above, boulders below, and a paradise of ferns around. At Glutton Mill the character of the scenery changes with the geological nature of the country. The limestone now crops up, and there are peculiar volcanic upheavals, such as Chrome Hill and Parker Hill. The rocky glen has widened suddenly into a green and spacious valley, and the harsh and hungry stone walls give place to park-like pastures and hawthorn hedgerows. Chrome Hill and Parker Hill rise steep between the "Princess Dove" in her infancy and her maidenhood; while green High Wheeldon and austere Hollins Clough are the sentinels of two jealous counties. Glutton Mill, with its red-tiled roof, idyllic surroundings, and sleepy atmosphere, might have inspired the Laureate when he confessed—

"I loved the brimming wave that swam
  Through quiet meadows round the mill,
The sleepy pool above the dam,
  The pool beneath it never still,
The meal-sacks on the whiten'd floor,
  The dark round of the dripping wheel,
The very air about the door
  Made misty with the floating meal."

Glutton Dale, a rocky gorge, gives access to the odd, old-world village of Sterndale, with a tavern the sign of which is "The Silent Woman." It is a pictorial sign in the most pronounced Van Daub style; but the designer must have been a satirical humourist, for the lady depicted is without a head!

The Dove for the next few miles loses its wild features. There are no deep gorges or rocky chasms. The walk now is through lush meadows, and the progress of the stream, so swift and tumultuous in its upper reaches, is in comparison almost sluggish. It ripples with soothing murmur over pebbly shallows, or reflects patches of blue sky in deep and glassy pools. Here and there a water-thread from either the Staffordshire or the Derbyshire side, is welcomed, and trout and grayling invite the angler. Past Beggar's Bridge, Crowdecote Bridge, Pilsbury, Broad Meadow Hall, and a fertile country dotted with dairy farms, and we are at the patrician village of Hartington, with its Elizabethan hall on the hill, and its venerable church with pinnacled tower, dating back to the first part of the thirteenth century, *temp.* Henry III. Hartington, which gives the Marquises their title, is eleven miles from Dove Head, and the length of the river from its source to its junction with the Trent is exactly fifty-six picturesque unpolluted miles, without an uninteresting point along the entire course. A river-side path brings us to Beresford Dale, perhaps the most secluded portion of the valley, for the Dove Dale tourist and the "cheap tripper" rarely penetrate so far up the zig-zag windings of the river. Here the stream resumes its romantic features. Limestone tors embroidered with foliage shut it out from the world. There is a strip of white cloud above, and a gleam of liquid light below. Pellucid pools reflect wooded height and gleaming crag. All around is the sense of solitude and the rapture of repose, broken only by the soliloquy of the stream and the song of the wild birds.

At Pike Pool (there are no pike), alluded to in the "Compleat Angler," rises from the centre of the Dove a pinnacle of weather-beaten limestone forty feet high. Izaak Walton and Charles Cotton indulge in a characteristic colloquy concerning this isolated needle, "one of the oldest sights." The intimacy of the reckless young squire who penned the indecencies of "Virgil Travestie," and the rigid moralist who wrote the Lives of Hooker and George Herbert, is one of the curiosities of famous friendships. It can only be accounted for by the conclusion that true love is like the law of magnetism—the attraction of opposites. Here, however, "Piscator" and "Viator" cease to be abstractions, for, behold! this is the classic Fishing House, wherein "my dear son Charles" entertained his "most affectionate father and friend." Externally it is the same as when Izaak and Charles smoked their morning pipe, which was "commonly their breakfast," and discoursed of the joys and contentment of country life. The little temple is built on a green peninsula at a pretty bend of the river, with the swing of trees above and the song of the stream below. "It is"—says the author of "Pictures of the Peak"—"a one-storied building, toned with the touch of time. In shape it is a perfect cube of eighteen feet, with a pyramidal stone roof, from which springs a stone pillar and hip knob. There are lattice windows and shutters on all sides. The doorway, with its three moss-grown steps, faces the dale, and over it is a square panel with the inscription—

THE MONOGRAM AT DOVE HEAD.

Piscatoribus
Sacrum
1674.

A monogram, similar to the one at Dove Head, declares the affinity between the two old-world fishermen!" Formerly the oak wainscoting was covered with paintings of river-side scenes, and the portraits of the "father" and his "adopted son" decorated the panels of the buffet. The old fireplace, the marble table, and the carved oak chairs, however, remain intact.

Not far from this fishing house stood Beresford Hall, the ancestral home of Charles Cotton. It was pulled down some years ago, when it was condemned as being structurally unsafe. But the owner (the late Mr. Beresford Hope) had all the stones carefully numbered and marked with a view to their re-erection somewhat after the old style. They now lie in an adjacent meadow. Beresford Hall in Charles Cotton's days was a noble building. It stood in plantations among the rocks with woodland vistas opening out to the windings of the water. The hall was wainscoted in oak. It was rich in old carved furniture, ebony coffers, and trophies of the chase. The most prized possession, surrounded with arms and armour, hunting horns and falcons' hoods and bells, antlers and fowling-pieces, was the fishing rod presented to Charles Cotton by old Izaak, whose bed-chamber, "with sheets laid up in lavender," was one of the choicest apartments of the house. There were figured patterns over the chimney-piece, and angels' heads stamped in relief on the ceiling. On the rocks above the site of the hall are to be seen vestiges of the

THE BANKS OF THE DOVE.

Prospect Tower, the basement of which was Cotton's study, and the summit a beacon where flambeaux were lit by his wife to guide her husband home in the darkness, even as Hero's watch-fires brought her beloved Leander to her bosom. Cotton himself called this observatory "Hero's Tower," and in a poetic epistle, describing his journey from London to Basford Hall, he thus alludes to the building:—

"Tuesday at noon at Lichfield town we baited,
But there some friends, who long that hour had waited,
So long detain'd me, that my charioteer
Could drive that night but to Uttoxeter.
And there, the Wednesday being market-day,
I was constrain'd with some kind lads to stay,
Tippling till afternoon, which made it night,
When from my Hero's Tower I saw the light
Of her flambeaux, and fancied, as we drave,
Each rising hillock was a swelling wave,
And that I swimming was, in Neptune's spight,
To my long long'd-for harbour of delight."

Dissipated Charles! devoted wife!

Leaving Beresford Dale, we come to many enticing passages on the Dove, troutful and leafy, where rock and water and woodland make combinations that are the despair of artists. Wolfscote Ravine, Narrow Dale, Cold Eaton, Alstonfield, Load Mill, and Mill Dale are but topographical expressions, but to those who know the Dove they cease to be words, and become scenes of enchantment. And now we are in the Dove Dale of the tourists and the trippers, the painters and the picnic parties, the fly-fishermen and the amateur photographers.

The guide-books have done Dove Dale grievous injustice by "heaping Ossa upon Pelion" with such misleading epithets as "grand," "majestic," "stupendous," "terrific," "awful," etc., *ad nauseam*. Dove Dale is only imposing by its surpassing loveliness, its perfect beauty. A romantic glen three miles long, narrow and winding, it is a dream of pretty scenery. Limestone cliffs close in the clear and voiceful water. Their precipitous sides are draped to the sky-line with a wealth and wonder of foliage, the white tors shining through the green gloom. The wooded slopes, rich with wild flowers, ferns, and mosses, just admit of a pathway by the water, which is now white and wavy with cascades, and now a dreamy calm in reflective pools. Each turn in this romantic valley has its surprise in scenery. A revelation awaits each step.

Some of the impending crags have such an individual character that they are known by particular names, such as Sharplow Point, the Twelve Apostles, Tissington Spires, the Lion's Head, the Watch Box, the Straits, the Sugar Loaf, the Church Rock, etc.; whilst perforations in the rock forming natural arches and caverns are entitled Dove Holes, Dove Dale Church, Grey Mare's Stable, Reynard's

ILAM HALL.

Cave, Reynard's Kitchen, the Crescent, the Arched Gateway, the Amphitheatre, the Abbey, and so on. These limestone tors, standing out from their green setting, assume castellated shapes. Here they suggest a bastion, there a spire; now an assemblage of towers, anon a convent church.

Dove Dale possesses many literary associations apart from those attached to Izaak Walton and his "adopted son" Charles. Surly Samuel Johnson frequently visited his friend Dr. Taylor, the Ashbourne divine who made his will in favour of the Fleet Street philosopher, but who lived to preach his funeral sermon in Westminster Abbey. In Dove Dale Dr. Johnson discovered the Happy Valley of "Rasselas." Morbid Jean Jacques Rousseau found a hospitable asylum at David Hume's house at Wootton Hall. It was another sort of "asylum" to which he should have been admitted, for he quarrelled with his benefactor. In Dove Dale he wandered scattering the seeds of rare plants that still flourish, and pondering over his "Confessions," the most introspective of autobiographies. Thomas Moore lived by the banks of the Dove, and his letters to Lord Byron abound with references to the "beauty spots" of the neighbourhood. He rented a little cottage at Mayfield, where he passed the early years of his married life, buried his first-born, wrote most of "Lalla Rookh," and in "Those Evening Bells" swung into undying music the metallic chimes of Ashbourne Church. Congreve wrote several of his comedies at Ilam. Canning was one of Dove Dale's devotees, and the reader will remember his political squib beginning—

> "So down thy slope, romantic Ashbourne, glides
> The Derby Dilly, carrying six insides."

The law of association links the Dove with other illustrious names: with Alfred Butler, the novelist, author of "Elphinstone," "The Herberts," and other works of fiction famous in their day; with Michael Thomas Sadler, author of the "Law of Population;" with Ward, the author of "Tremaine;" with Richard Graves, who wrote the "Spiritual Quixote," and whose portrait Wilkie painted; with Hobbes, the philosopher of Malmesbury; with Wright of Derby; and Edwards, the author of the "Tour of the Dove."

Dove Dale proper is at its extremity guarded by two imposing hills—Thorpe Cloud, a cone-shaped eminence of 900 feet, and burly Bunster, less conspicuous, but considerably higher. Passing these portals we come to the Izaak Walton Hotel, with the Walton and Cotton monogram of 1660 over its lichened gateway. The house is even older, and it serves to introduce us to the delightful village of Ilam, with its trim Gothic cottages, its magnificent Hall, its elegant Cross and Fountain, and its pretty church. In the church is Sir Francis Chantrey's masterpiece. It represents David Pike Watts on his death-bed taking leave for ever of his wife and children. The scene is an affecting one, and the composition one of pathetic beauty. It is a sermon in stone, and insensible to all feeling must be the man who can gaze upon this touching group without emotion. In the grounds of

Ham Hall the Manifold joins the Dove. Both rivers had their birthplace on Axe Edge, and throughout their course have never been far apart, although not within actual sight of each other. They have kept a "respectful distance," and not been on "speaking terms." The two rivers might have cherished a mutual aversion, if you can imagine such a repugnance. Before the Manifold emerges into the larger stream it has pursued a subterranean course for several miles. It bursts into daylight from a cave in the limestone rock, and at once plunges into the pure and placid waters of the Dove.

After leaving Ham, the Dove again assumes a pastoral character. It flows with graceful curves through a rich and reposeful landscape, where green woods cover gentle slopes. Passing Okeover and Mappleton, it just avoids Ashbourne, that only needed its silvery, shimmering waters to complete the charm of its dreamy old-world streets, as drowsy and quaint now as they were in the days of the '45, when Prince Charlie raised his standard in the market-place, and the ancient gables framed a Highland picture of targets and claymores and dirks, of unkempt, wild-haired clansmen in bonnet and kilt, ready to face any foe or endure any danger in the cause of the young Chevalier, whom they proclaimed King of England. A local tradition states that the Ashbourne men caught a Highlander, killed him, and found his skin so tough that it was tanned, and made most excellent leather! The church is the pride and glory of Ashbourne, and it is, indeed, a possession worthy of its fascinating surroundings and historic associations. It was dedicated in 1241; its tower and spire attain a height of 212 feet. The long series of Cockayne monuments, dating from the middle of the twelfth century to the end of the sixteenth, are worthy of a volume to themselves. In the chancel is Banks' pathetic monument to the memory of Penelope Boothby. The portrait of this sweet child was painted by Sir Joshua Reynolds. One of the illustrated papers has reproduced the picture, and made the innocent little face familiar in every home. Sympathetic inscriptions in English, French, Latin, and Italian on pedestal and slab vainly express Sir Brooke Boothby's poignant grief over his great loss. One of these inscriptions reads:—"She was in form and intellect most exquisite. The unfortunate parents ventured their all on this frail bark, and the wreck was total." One of the legends of art is that Chantrey stole into the church to study this poem in marble, and that it gave him the idea for his "Sleeping Children" in Lichfield Cathedral, which he designed in an Ashbourne hostelry while the inspiration was fresh upon him.

After leaving Ashbourne, the Dove, alder-fringed and willowed over, broadening through sweet-smelling pastures and passing prosperous farmsteads, makes its first acquaintance with a railway. The North Staffordshire line and the river play at hide-and-seek all the way down to the Trent, and the traveller has many gratifying glimpses—carriage-window pictures—of the glancing stream. The Dove is now not quite half-way on its journey to the strong and stately Trent. The scenery is very much like that of the Upper Thames, and should tempt some of our bright open-air school of painters. In succession follow Hanging Bridge and Mayfield, associated with the genius of Tom Moore; Church Mayfield, Clifton, Colwich Abbey, and Norbury, with its grand old church glorious in old stained glass, perfect of its

ASHBOURNE CHURCH.

kind, and its manor-house rebuilt in 1267. Then comes Rocester, inviting alike the artist, the angler, and the archæologist. The Dove here receives the rippling waters of the Churnet that flows past Alton Towers, and at Marston Montgomery it is joined by the Tean Brook, a tributary of considerable volume.

Passing Eaton with its rich verdure and hanging woods, once part of Needwood Forest, we come to Doveridge, the Hall—the seat of Lord Hindlip—rising above the wooded ridge. If the house itself, because of its debased style of architecture, is not an attractive addition to the landscape, its situation, on the green heights above the valley of the Dove, with the rolling Staffordshire moorlands and the obtuse peaks of the Weaver Hills in the distance, is enchanting. The Dove winds in the rich pastoral "strath" below in the most capricious curvatures, and the eye follows the course of the wilful stream by meadow and upland, by deep dell and dusky slope, for many miles. Presently comes Uttoxeter, the spire of the church being a conspicuous feature in a landscape filled with sylvan beauty. The pronunciation of the word puzzles the visitor, and even the natives grow gently disputations on the subject. A local bard, however, comes to the rescue of the stranger. In a fine patriotic outburst he declares:

"In all the country round there's nothing neater
Than the pretty little town of Uttoxeter."

Uttoxeter is a characteristic specimen of an old English market town, which neither the railway nor what Carlyle contemptuously calls "the age of gin and steam-hammers" has left unspoiled. It has many interesting literary and historical associations. Here Mary Howitt was born; and Dr. Johnson's father, bookseller at Lichfield, kept a stall in the market-place. On one occasion he asked his son to attend the market in his place, but the future lexicographer's stubborn pride led to insubordination. Fifty years afterwards, haunted by this disobedience of the paternal wish, Dr. Johnson made a pilgrimage to Uttoxeter market-place, and in inclement weather stood bare-headed for a considerable time on the spot where his father's stall used to stand, exposed to a pelting rain and the flippant sneers of the bystanders. "In contrition," he confesses, "I stood, and I hope the penance was expiatory." The incident says much for Johnson's character, and the scene may be commended to a painter in search of an historical theme.

At Uttoxeter the Dove is thirty-eight miles from its mountain home. It now winds past Sudbury, where it is crossed by a strikingly handsome bridge giving access to Lord Vernon's domain, with its deer park of 600 acres and model dairy farm. The Hall is a red-brick mansion in the Elizabethan style, and was erected in the early part of the seventeenth century. This delightful retreat was the residence of the Dowager Queen Adelaide from 1840 to 1843. The church, which is within the park, is a large and venerable structure, grey with age, and green with glossy ivy.

THE STRAITS, DOVEDALE.

Presently comes Tutbury, where the Dove is fifty miles from Axe Edge. It flows under the commanding castle hill, where the ruins of a building that existed before the Norman Conquest look down grim and gloomy upon the glad Dove, glancing up at its dismantled walls with their chequered history from the green plain to which she lends such grace. The three towers associated with John of Gaunt make a diversified sky-line. Tutbury Castle has all the credentials necessary to make the reputation of a respectable ruin. For fifteen years it was the prison-house of Mary Queen of Scots, and it suffered from the cannon of Cromwell. The west doorway of the Priory Church, with its "chevron" tracery, is a glorious specimen of Norman architecture. The village was notorious for its bull-baiting, and everybody has heard of "the fasting woman of Tutbury," one Ann Moore, who professed to live without food. She added an assumption of piety to her imposture, and by this means collected £240. She was subsequently sent to prison for fraud. An interesting feature in connection with the history of the place should receive notice. In 1831 an extraordinary find of coins was made in the bed of the river, over 100,000 in number. People flocked from all parts to dig up the auriferous and argentiferous river-bed, until at last the Crown despatched a troop of soldiers to protect the rights of the Duchy of Lancaster. Still stands the notice-board on the bridge threatening prosecution to all trespassers. It is supposed that the coins formed part of the treasury of the Earl of Lancaster when he had taken up arms against Edward II., and that in the panic of retreat across the Dove the money chests were lost in the swollen river, at that time scarcely fordable.

The Dove valley downward from Tutbury past Marston, Rolleston, and Egginton, is full of quiet and stately beauty. At Newton Solney the stream, as crystal as it was in the limestone dales, is greeted by the Trent, its clear waters soon losing their shining transparency in the darker tinged tide of the larger river.

Edward Bradbury.

JOHN OF GAUNT'S GATEWAY, TUTBURY CASTLE.

JUNCTION OF THE TRENT AND THE DOVE.

THE HUMBER AND ITS TRIBUTARIES.

CHAPTER III.

THE TRENT, FROM NEWTON SOLNEY TO THE DERWENT.

Newton Solney—Repton: The School and the Church—Swarkestone: Its Bridge and its Church—Chellaston—Donington Park and Castle Donington—Cavendish Bridge.

RULY a pretty spot is the little village of Newton Solney, rising up the slope from a low scarp which overlooks the Trent, with its scattered houses, its small church spire, and the fine old trees around the hall. This indeed is a modern structure, and certainly not picturesque, but there has been a mansion on this site for many a year, for the De Sulneys had the estate full six centuries ago, and there is a fine monument to one of them in the interesting church. Trent sweeps on through the broad and level meadows, now become a strong full stream, which near Willington Station—where it is bridged—is about eighty yards wide. Here, in the valley indeed, but nearly a mile away from the actual margin of the river, is a little town of great antiquity and unusual interest. Repton, distinguished from afar by the slender and lofty spire of its church, is the Hreopandum of the Anglo-Saxon chronicle. Some suppose it to be the Roman Repandunum; certainly it was a place of importance more than twelve centuries since, for it was selected by Diuma, the first Bishop of Mercia, as the centre of his huge diocese, and here, about the year 658, he died and was buried. Soon after this a nunnery was founded, and before St. Chad removed the "bishop's-stool" to Lichfield, St. Guthlac had started from Repton to float down the Trent, and to wander

REPTON.

through the fenland of East Anglia till he settled down on the swampy island of Crowland. So many of the Princes of Mercia were buried here that the abbey is described by a Norman chronicler as "that most holy mausoleum of all the Kings of Mercia." Hither, for instance, in the year 775, the body of Ethelbald was brought for burial from the fatal field of Secandun. No trace of his tomb, or indeed of that of any other Mercian King, now remains. Since those days changes have been so many that monuments have had little chance of escaping; but probably these and the monastery were alike destroyed when a horde of Danish plunderers swept through the Midlands of England, and Buthred of Mercia, in the year 874, had to fly before them. These unwelcome intruders spent the winter at Repington. At their hands Mercian monuments and monastic buildings would fare ill. Prior to this calamity the body of St. Wystan, a devout Prince, heir to the throne of Mercia, was laid here by the side of his mother Alfleda. On Whitsun-eve, 849, he was assassinated by a cousin, and before long miracles in plenty were wrought at his tomb. His relics, on the approach of the Danes, were transferred for safety to Evesham, and when the church was rebuilt, in the tenth century, the new structure was dedicated to his memory. Repton, at the time of Domesday Book, was a part of the Royal demesne; then we find it included in the estates of the Earls of Chester. The nunnery in some way or other had come to an end, for a widowed countess of this line founded on the site a priory of Black Canons in the year 1172, of which considerable remnants may still be seen.

The little old-fashioned town occupies some gently rising ground. This is separated from the broad and level water-meadows by a step or craglet a few feet in height, the scarp of an old river terrace; nearest to this are the church and priory buildings, which occupy a considerable tract of land, and look down upon the remnants of the monks' fishponds. The old trees that have here and there fixed their roots in the broken bank-side, the graceful steeple of the church, rising to an elevation of more than sixty yards, the great group of the school buildings—

THE "CROW TREES," BARROW-ON-TRENT.

which occupy the site of the old priory, and in which new and old are mingled together in a picturesque confusion—offer, as we approach Repton from the railway station, along the flat and otherwise uninteresting valley, a series of pictures of no little beauty. The school owes its foundation to Sir John Porte, who in the year 1556 endowed it with lands, and assigned to it the buildings of the old priory. These had originally been granted to one Thomas Thacker, but, as is often the case with ill-gotten gains, had brought him little good. Fuller, the Church historian, tells a tale which shows him to have been a man not easily thwarted. At Repton St. Guthlac had a shrine, where was a wonder-working bell, a grand specific for the headache. Public gratitude had found expression in a fine church or chapel, and this was included in Thacker's share of monastic plunder. He had heard that Queen Mary had set up the abbeys again, so he lost no time, but "upon a Sunday (belike the better day the better deed) called together the carpenters and masons of that county and pulled down in one day (church work is a cripple in going up but rides post in coming down) a most beautiful church belonging thereto, saying he would destroy the nest lest the birds should build again."

The gateway of the priory, a fine pointed arch, still serves as the entrance to the school premises, and several parts of the buildings evidently carry us back to the days of the Black Canons, while others probably indicate the hands of Elizabethan workmen, when the ruined monastic buildings were converted into a school. Mingled with these are structures of later date, among which those of the present reign are conspicuous, owing to the growth of the school and the development of education in recent days. Thus the whole group, in which new and old are mingled, almost entangled, is always interesting and not seldom picturesque. The school chapel, which is modern, and has been further enlarged of late years in commemoration of the tercentenary of the foundation, stands at some little distance from the other buildings, and on the opposite side of the churchyard. The estate bestowed upon the foundation by Sir John Porte, by whom also a hospital was established and maintained at Etwall, a village some four miles away, has proved valuable, so that the endowment is considerable. The school from a very early period enjoyed a considerable local reputation, which has gradually extended, till at the present day it claims a place in the second group of the great schools of England, for some three hundred lads have replaced the Black Canons, a change which means a good deal for the little town. Among its scholars in olden time were Lightfoot the Hebraist and Stebbing Shaw the historian of Staffordshire, whom we have more than once quoted. The constitution of the school was materially altered by the results of the Endowed Schools Act, for it was originally founded simply as a Free Grammar School for Repton and Etwall.

The ample churchyard allows of a good view of the church and its slender spire. At the first glance it would be put down as a rather simple but pleasing structure, most of which would be assigned to some part of the fourteenth century. On entering the interior a diversity of dates would become more obvious; but the general impression made is of a large and well-proportioned rather than of a richly adorned or of a specially interesting church. Monuments also are fairly numerous, but these are in no way remarkable, except for some connection with local history. Repton Church, however, has one treasure, but this is almost hidden underground. Underneath the chancel, approached by a narrow staircase, is a crypt. It is small, for it is only some seventeen feet broad and long, but one would have to travel not a few miles in order to find another remnant of ancient days equally interesting. The roof is rudely vaulted, supported by four columns, which have a spiral ornament of peculiar character, and rather plain flat capitals; the corresponding piers are relieved by a shallow grooving. The work indicates the influence of Classic patterns, with much rudeness of execution. To assign its date is difficult; its style is certainly anterior to the Norman Conquest, and probably the actual date is the same. A recent authority (Dr. Cox) considers this crypt to have been part of the first church dedicated to St. Wystan, erected after the destruction of the older edifice by the Danes, probably in the reign of Edgar the Peaceable (958–975). This is most likely correct, for the work appears a little too highly finished for a date anterior to the tenth century. Dr. Cox, however, remarks that portions of the outer walls of the crypt have been proved to be of earlier date than the pillar-supported roof, and may thus be a remnant of the church in which the Mercian Kings were entombed.

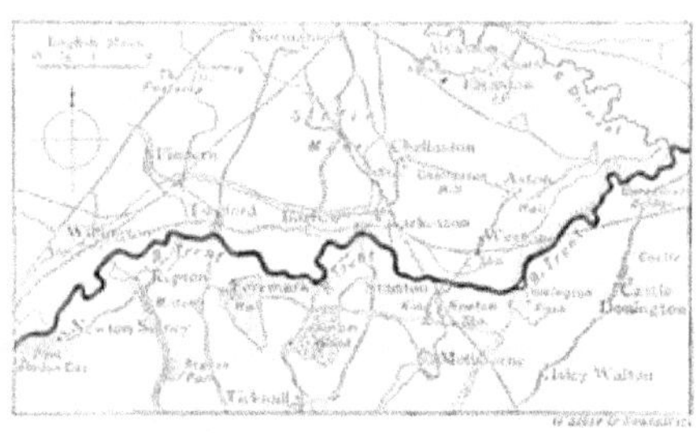

THE TRENT, FROM NEWTON SOLNEY TO THE DERWENT.

There is in the crypt an alabaster tomb of a knight in armour, dating from the fifteenth century; and in front of the old gateway is another relic of ancient days. This is the base of a cross, which, to judge from the number of steps, must have been of considerable size, and probably indicated the original market-place; for its proximity to the church and the priory would enable the country folk to attend to the affairs of this world, while at the same time they did not entirely neglect the concerns of the other. One trace both of ancient name and ancient importance is still retained by Repton, for all Derbyshire south of the Trent is called the "Hundred of Repington." This part of the river-course is about twenty-four miles in length. Previous to this it separates for a space Derbyshire from Staffordshire, and it leaves the former county at the junction of the Erewash, a stream from Sherwood Forest, which, for the greater part of its course, forms a parting from Nottinghamshire. Below Repton for several miles there is no place of special interest in the valley of the Trent, though some of the villages in or near it are of considerable antiquity. The sketch of the "Crow Trees," now fewer than formerly, at Barrow, gives a good idea of the quiet but pleasant river-side scenery. At Swarkestone the river is crossed by a curious old bridge, the raised approaches across the water-meadows being about a mile in length. The bridge is assigned by the guide-books to the twelfth century, and is traditionally reported to have been the work of two maiden sisters, who spent upon it all their living. It was the cause of a smart struggle in the civil war of 1643, and was occupied by the advanced guard of the Jacobites in 1745. Chellaston, a short distance from the opposite bank, is a name familiar to geologists. There are extensive workings here for gypsum, and the occurrence of a number of minute fossils (*foraminifera*) in a deposit usually destitute of the remains of organic life has attracted especial attention to the locality. It is, however, now doubted whether these organisms have not been obtained from a deposit of later age. After Stanton-by-Dale and Weston-on-Trent comes Donington Park, with its ample lawns and shady groves extending around the mansion, which was the home of the Hastings family, of one of whom more than enough was heard some few years since. Behind the park the village of Castle Donington straggles down and along the high road leading from Ashby-de-la-Zouch towards the Trent. Here some remnants of a castle are to be seen, said to have been founded by John of Gaunt, and from which the village obtains its distinctive name. Beyond this are Ashton-on-Trent and Cavendish Bridge, which crosses the river a short distance above the confluence of the Derwent. This bridge obtains its name from the family of Cavendish, by members of which it was erected about the middle of the last century.

T. G. Bonney.

TRENT LOCKS.

JUNCTION OF THE DERWENT AND THE TRENT.

THE HUMBER AND ITS TRIBUTARIES.

CHAPTER IV.

THE DERWENT.

The Derwent in its Infancy—Derwent Chapel and Hall—Hathersage—Eyam—Grindleford Bridge—Chatsworth—The "Peacock" at Rowsley—Haddon Hall—The Wye and the Lathkill—Darley Dale and its Yew-tree—The Sycamores of Oker Hill—The Matlocks and High Tor—Cromford and Willersley Castle—Ambergate—Belper—Derby—Elvaston.

IT might be interesting to ask how many Englishmen have made the tour of the Derwent—a river so rich in pictorial beauty and historic interest. If the country were polled upon the subject, the result would probably not be gratifying to local patriotism. And yet no more romantic revelations of river scenery exist than those traversed by the Derwent from its source among the dusky moorland heights of the Peak to its junction with the Trent, sixty-three miles from its mountain home, after collecting the waters of 300,000 acres of country. Other streams there are, of course, of greater magnitude, with mountain surroundings more stupendous; but beauty is not to be measured by bulk, or rivers by their breadth and volume, nor is the artistic charm of hills ascertainable by an aneroid.

There are several English rivers of the name of Derwent, which is derived from the British *dwr-gwent*, the water of "Gwent," or of the high lands, and the word is often locally pronounced "Darent." There is Wordsworth's Derwent in Lakeland; a Derwent which falls into the sea near Scarborough; and again a Derwent that is a tributary of the Yorkshire Ouse. But it is the Derbyshire Derwent that we now propose to trace down from its source. In the north-east corner of the Peak district, on the stern and austere Yorkshire borderlands, where the Langsett moors are most lonely and impressive, the stream spends its earliest infancy, and you hear its baby prattle in a rocky region, wild and desolate, where the Titans might have been hurling in space gigantic boulders to bring about chaos. The place where the river actually rises is called Barrow Stones. The traveller on the line from Sheffield to Manchester, when he is at Woodhead, with its dismal tunnel and long-linked reservoirs, passes as near as civilisation touches the spot. For some distance the river bubbles and babbles down a boulder-strewn valley, and is the line of demarcation between the counties of York and Derby. It is here a swift tawny streamlet, with effervescent cascades, and deep pools in which you can discern the pebbles at the bottom of the topaz-coloured water. Weather-worn masses of rock are strewn over this heathery wilderness—silvered with rare lichens, and cushioned with delicate mosses. Here and there picturesque little rills pour out their trickling tributaries from numerous mountain springs and musical ferny hollows. The only sound beside that of running water is the cry of the grouse, the blackcock, or the peewit. The Derwent cleaves its rocky way down the valley into Derwent Dale, past Slippery Stones, Rocking Stones, and Bull Clough and Cranberry Clough, with the Bradfield moors rolling away in petrified billowy waves to the horizon line. Before reaching Derwent Chapel it has received the Westend, a considerable stream, and the Abbey Brook, another important contributor, foaming down a deep rugged ravine, with gritstone ridges. In Derwent Dale alder-trees add a shade to the waterside, and the landscape, although still wild in its mountain beauty, is diversified by their green grace.

And now we are at the lonely little village of Derwent Chapel, with its grey scattered houses. The hamlet in the pre-Reformation times had four chapels belonging to the ancient Abbey of Welbeck. At Derwent Hall, charmingly placed by the river bridge, are preserved several relics of the monkish days. But the most interesting possessions are the old carved oak pieces of furniture. They form a unique collection, and are of historic value. Some of the cabinets and bedsteads are four hundred years old. The Hall, which formerly belonged to the Balguys, bears over the doorway the arms of that family and the date 1672. The Duke of Norfolk is the present proprietor, and has added a new wing at the expense of £30,000. The pack-horse bridge makes a pleasing picture, and the surrounding prospect is as fair as any that ever inspired poet's pen or painter's pencil. By leafy labyrinthian ways, in fascinating aquatic vagaries, our river, brown with peat-moss, ripples over the shallows or becomes demonstrative when obstructed by boulders on its way to Lady Bower and Ashopton, sentinelled by the bold peaks of Win Hill and Lose, so called from a sanguinary battle having been fought here between two Saxon kings. The victorious army occupied Win Hill, and the vanquished the opposite height. There are other magnificently grouped hills all around. Ashopton is haunted by painters and anglers. Pleasant it is to lounge lazily over the time-stained bridge that spans the Derwent near its confluence with the Ashop, which has found its way down the "Woodlands" from Kinderscout—famous as the highest point in the Peak, 2,088 feet; while from the opposite side the Lady Bower brook adds its trouty current. Here

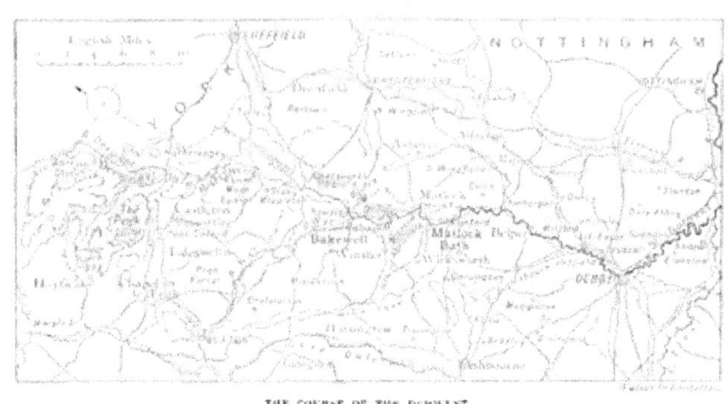

THE COURSE OF THE DERWENT.

we are tempted to make a *détour* to visit Castleton with its caverns, almost as wonderful as the famed Congo cavern in South Africa, the Elephanta cave in India, or the Mammoth cave of Kentucky; to climb up the crag to Peveril's ruined castle; to explore the beautiful green basin suggestively called the Vale of Hope; and to penetrate the Edale pass until the frowning Kinderscout morosely blocks the way. But we must keep to Derwentside.

The river is now a large stream, and—passing Bamford—at Mytham Bridge it receives the greeting of the Noe. Here we strike the Dore and Chinley Railway, a branch line of the Midland system, at present in process of construction. It follows the course of the Derwent valley for some miles, and is not likely to add to the beauty of the scenery. The noisy puff of the locomotive in this Paradise seems a profanation. The line, however, will open out a new holiday ground, and will give the traveller an alternative route between Sheffield and Manchester, London and Liverpool. This railway extension is twenty miles in length. There are five miles of tunnelling under the mountainous moorland, and the cost will not be covered by an expenditure of less than one million sterling. One of the tunnels is three miles in length, and next to the Severn tunnel the longest in the United Kingdom. At Hathersage, moss-grown and still, and one of the prettiest of Peak villages, a station will be erected, and much of its old-world charm will then have gone for ever. In the churchyard on the hillside may be seen the grave of Robin Hood's stalwart lieutenant, Little John. The resting-place of this romantic outlaw is marked by two stones which by their distance from each other would indicate that he was ten feet high.

The famous Forester was born at Hathersage, and fought in the ranks of Simon de Montfort's rebellious barons at Evesham in 1265. After the many vicissitudes of his adventurous life, he returned to his native village to die. Until recent years his cottage was pointed out to visitors, and at the beginning of the present

AT ASHOPTON, DERWENTDALE.

century Little John's bow and green cap were suspended in the church. They were carried away to Cannon Hall, near Barnsley.

Hathersage is surrounded with places of interest, and the Derwent is here thirteen miles from its source. Mention should be made of Padley Wood and the ruins of the Roman Catholic Chapel; Burbage Brook, another of the Derwent's many feeders, that brawls through a defile as sweetly wooded as the Fairy Glen at Bettws-y-Coed; Longshaw Lodge, the shooting-box of the Duke of Rutland, with its pretty grounds and rockeries; Fox House, a famous moorland hostelry; Hu Gaer, a hoary rocky platform which is marked on the Ordnance map as a Druidical relic; Caelswark, an old British fort; the Toad's Mouth, a huge and hoary block of gritstone bearing a curious resemblance to that unattractive reptile; Stoney Middleton, whose houses seem to hang dangerously from the bordering cliffs; and Eyam, the scene of the great plague of 1666, when out of a population of 350 no less than 260 were swept away by the pestilence. The infection was brought to the village in a box of clothes from London. The place is hallowed by the devotion of the saintly rector, the Rev. Wm. Mompesson. He never deserted his parishioners (although his wife was one of the first victims); and it was by his exertions that the plague was prevented from spreading far and wide.

CHATSWORTH.

But we are now at grey Grindleford Bridge. What a view there is down the richly wooded reaches of the river by Froggatt Edge, Stoke Hall, Curbar, Calver, and Bubnall to Baslow—the threshold of Chatsworth! The Derwent has here accomplished a distance of exactly twenty miles, and received numberless and nameless tributary outpourings from the moors on both the eastern and western sides. It is now a fine river, and lends additional beauty to the Duke of Devonshire's magnificent park, surely the most glorious domain in the wide world. The river sweeps in front of the Palace of the

Peak, with ancient trees reflecting soothing shadows in the shining water. So much has been written about Chatsworth — its great hall, its superb state apartments, its miracles of wood-carving, its unique sketch-gallery, its noble

libraries, its priceless picture-gallery, its grand drawing-rooms, bed-rooms, and banqueting-rooms, its superb sculpture gallery, its gardens, terraces, conservatories, woods, and fountains — that little fresh can be said upon a subject so well worn. A well-known writer, when he was at Niagara, and was supposed to write a description of the scene, simply remarked, "There are some waterfalls hereabouts, which are said to be pretty." In a similar manner the grandeur of Chatsworth may be summarily dismissed, we being content with the accounts of a thousand and one admirable authors. Enough to say that this treasure-house of art is apt to give the visitor a sense of general splendour on the brain. The house and park are open every week-day to the public, and many thousands of people each year avail themselves of the privileges so freely granted by the generous owner. Sightseers pour into the ducal palace, with its gilded casements and princely saloons, just as if the place belonged to them instead of to the Duke of Devonshire. It is open for them to enjoy, and all their pleasures are prepared for them. They can inspect the carvings by Grinling Gibbons, the masterpieces of Landseer, and Sir Joshua Reynolds' picture of the beautiful Duchess; admire the work of Verrio and Laguerre, and the chisellings of Canova and Thorwaldsen; dwell upon rare tapestry and the choicest products of Sèvres and Dresden; pause at tables of malachite and porphyry, be delighted with the plants and orchids of tropical climes, including the *Victoria Regia*, and stand and watch the Emperor Fountain and all the *grandes eaux* playing. All this

THE TERRACE, HADDON HALL.

gratification belongs to the public without the slightest cost of maintenance or responsibility of possession, for the head of the illustrious house of Cavendish keeps these precious treasures for his fellow-men rather than for his own private enjoyment.

There is a pleasant field-path through park and pasture, past Beeley, to Rowsley, three miles away. Just below the grey arches of the bridge at the sign of the Peacock—a quaint ivied Elizabethan building with many gables and battlements, an abundance of heavy-mullioned windows, and green lawns gently sloping down to the water—the Wye has its confluence with the Derwent. It is a pleasant Mesopotamia, the smaller stream issuing from the limestone dales transparent as glass, and so swift in motion as to at first push back the Derwent—flowing slow and strong and stately, the colour of cairngorm through its association with the moors. But the deeper river soon asserts its superior weight and strength, and the two streams—happy in their union—amalgamate in one undivided current, recalling—in, of course, a minor degree—the junction of the Thames and Medway, the alliance of the Rhone and Arve, the coalition of the Moselle and the Rhine. We are now in contact with the Midland Railway, which

HADDON HALL, FROM THE WYE.

crosses and recrosses the Derwent by bridge or viaduct fifteen times during the remainder of its course. A short walk from the russet Peacock—half-way between Rowsley and the bonnie town of Bakewell—stands, on a wooded eminence, Haddon Hall. The Wye winds in many a graceful curve, overhung by gnarled trees, at the foot of the grey old pile. The antique appearance of the hostelry has assisted to subdue the contrast that must strike every observer between the comparative newness of Chatsworth (although it is 200 years old) and the venerable aspect of Haddon—a revelation of a bygone age, a memorial of ancient chivalry which is almost unique, for some portions of this perfect baronial castle date back to the twelfth century. Haddon, the property of the Duke of Rutland, is uninhabited, although it is not a ruin, and promises to remain intact for centuries to come. It has never suffered from the violence of war, stronghold as it is, but has always been the home of hospitality.

"Lightly falls the foot of Time,
That only treads on flowers."

"The kitchens and larders all look as if the domestics had only retired for a short time. We come to the dining, drawing, and ball-room, all clean and dry as when abandoned as a human habitation; and as we pace along this latter room with its polished floor, the hollow sounds of our footsteps lead us to the contemplation of the time when the gay Elizabeth, surrounded by her Court, honoured the Vernons with her presence, and made the rooms echo with shouts of merry laughter. A long day may be spent in wandering about the terraces, gardens, and shady walks; the door is pointed out to us through which eloped Dorothy Vernon with her faithful lover (Sir John Manners). Which route they took is left to the visitor's imagination; perchance they crossed the remarkable stone foot-bridge. Suffice it to say the escape was perfected, and adds additional interest to the romance of Haddon Hall."

The Wye is the most important feeder of the Derwent, and runs through scenery that is romantically beautiful. Its length from Axe Edge to its junction with the Derwent at Rowsley is twenty-two miles, although the distance as the crow flies is considerably less. But the little river winds about in capricious curvatures, and its serpentine wanderings add much to its peculiar charm. There are two distinct Wyes, uniting in the Buxton Gardens, to which pleasaunce they add attraction. The larger stream issues from the gritstone formation; the other comes from the limestone. The one is coloured by the peat of the mosses; the other is of pellucid purity. The limestone water has its birthplace in the gloomy recesses of Poole's Cavern, and you may hear it fretting in the chill darkness, as

DERWENT TERRACE, MATLOCK.

if it were impatient to greet the glad sunlight. In Ashwood Dale, just below the Lovers' Leap, and a mile from the fashionable watering-place, the character of the scenery with which the Wye is for the most part associated begins. Limestone tors, of great height and beautifully wooded, rise above a contracted valley along which the stream pursues its lively course. The river leaves Topley Pike abruptly to the right, and enters Chee Dale. Nature here is in the imperative mood. Chee Tor soars to a height of 300 feet sheer above the water—a solemn limestone headland, its gaping fissures here and there clothed with a pendent tree. It is convex in shape, and is faced by a corresponding bastion, concave in form. In the narrow channel between these bold walls of rock the Wye forces its way through the pent-up space, making a tumult over the obstructing boulders. A scanty footpath is carried over the abyss, making a passage of unequivocal sublimity, for the defile has no superior and few equals in all Derbyshire. Miller's Dale afterwards opens out its picturesque features, although its idyllic charm is marred by the screaming railway junction and by the quarrying operations that are toppling bastions of rock—ancient landmarks—into limekilns. Two miles from Miller's Dale is Tideswell, with its grand old church—"the Cathedral of the Peak"—its secluded valleys and immemorial hills. Litton Dale and Cressbrook Dale follow—both wild glens that will repay lovers of rocks, ferns, and flowers. At Monsal Dale the scenery is no longer savage as it was at Chee Tor, but is of winsome loveliness. The Wye winds in green meadows below wooded heights, with here and there a rocky pinnacle jutting out like a spire; "lepping" stones cross the stream, and rustic cottages, with blue filmy smoke curling from their chimneys, stand just where an artist would have placed them. Well might Eliza Cook sing—

> "And Monsal, thou mine of Arcadian treasure,
> Need we seek for Greek islands and spice-laden gales,
> While a Temple like thee, of enchantment and pleasure,
> May be found in our native Derbyshire Dales?"

Close by is Taddington, an abode of miners, which contests with Chelmerton the claim of being the highest village in England. There is a quaint church, and in the churchyard an ancient cross which archæological authorities argue is the work of the monks of Lindisfarne, who introduced Christianity into Derbyshire. The Peakrels, in their caustic humour, gravely furnish the visitor to Taddington with the information that "only blind, deaf, and dumb persons, and those who do not live in the parish, are buried in the churchyard."

Past Demon's Dale, and we are at the pleasant village of Ashford-in-the-Water, celebrated for its inlaid marble manufactures. In the old church are hung five paper garlands. They are the relics of the obsolete custom of carrying garlands before the corpses of maidens in the funeral procession, and subsequently suspending them in the church. The custom is alluded to by Shakespeare. These garlands are Ophelia's "virgin crants" in *Hamlet*. The Priest tells Laertes that but for "just command" Ophelia would have been buried—as a suicide—

in "ground unsanctified," and "shards, flints, and pebbles" only would have been "thrown on her"—

> "Yet here she is allowed her virgin crants,
> Her maiden strewments, and the bringing home
> Of bell and burial."

The innocent observance lingered longer in Derbyshire than anywhere else, and was not abandoned at Ashford-in-the-Water until 1820. The Wye at this point spreads out its waters, turning weedy wheels, and wandering through lush meadow-lands, finely timbered. At Bakewell the stream is of considerable width, and is spanned by a handsome old bridge evidently the work of an architect of imagination. The town itself is of considerable antiquity, and the church, one of the oldest and finest in the county, stands on a commanding hill, and is a picturesque feature in a glorious landscape. Time has made furrow and wrinkle on the grey old fabric, but

> "Still points the tower and pleads the bell,
> The solemn arches breathe in stone;
> Window and walls have lips to tell
> The mighty faith of days unknown."

Bakewell is the Paradise of anglers, and wonderful stories are told of the trophies captured when the May-fly is on the water. The river now narrows, and winds in many a tortuous curve through the Haddon pastures. Below Haddon Hall, at Fillyford Bridge, it receives the limpid Lathkill, a stream to-day as clear as when Charles Cotton described it to "Viator" in "The Compleat Angler" as "by many degrees the purest and most transparent stream that I ever yet saw, either at home or abroad, and breeding the reddest and best trouts in England."

After it has welcomed the meandering Wye, the Derwent spreads through an open verdant country of contemplative beauty, with rounded wooded hills in the distance. This spacious golden-green strath is Darley Dale. Lord John Manners (now the Duke of Rutland), viewing this scene from Stanton Woodhouse, a wooded knoll close by, with weather-beaten tors, lofty hunting tower, and Druidical remains, was inspired to crystallise in verse the deep impression

THE HIGH TOR, MATLOCK.

that the pastoral scene and its mountain surroundings had made upon his mind:—

"Up Darley Dale the wanton wind
In careless measure sweeps,
And stirs the twinkling Derwent's tides,
Its shallows and its deeps.

"From many an ancient upland grange,
Wherein old English feeling
Still lives and thrives, in faint blue wreaths
The smoke is skywards stealing.

"The simple cheer that erst sustained
The Patriarch Seers of old,
Still in these pastoral valleys feeds
A race of ancient mould.

"And should fell faction rear again
Her front on English ground,
Here will the latest resting-place
Of loyalty be found."

In the churchyard at Darley Dale is the most venerable yew-tree in the world. Many authorities claim for it a fabulous age, making it as much as 3,000 years old. It is thirty-three feet in girth, but its trunk has suffered not a little from the modern Goths and Vandals who have carved their names in the bark, and employed other methods of mutilation. The tree is now fenced round to save it from further insult; and "whatever may be its precise age," says the Rev. Dr. John Charles Cox, "there can be little doubt that this grand old tree has given shelter to the early Britons when planning the construction of the dwellings that they erected not many yards to the west of its trunk; to the Romans who built up the funeral pyre for their slain comrades just clear of its branches; to the Saxons, converted, perchance, to the true faith by the preaching of Bishop Diuma beneath its pleasant shade; to the Norman masons chiselling their quaint sculptures to form the first stone house of prayer erected in its vicinity; and to the host of Christian worshippers who, from that day to this, have been borne under its hoary limbs in women's arms to the baptismal font, and then on men's shoulders to their last sleeping-place in the soil that gave it birth."

On the left bank of the Derwent, amid rocks and plantations, is the royal residence of the late Sir Joseph Whitworth; and on the opposite side rises, sharply defined, Oker Hill—a green isolated eminence that was once an important Roman station. Growing on the summit of this lofty peak are two sycamores. A legend is attached to the planting of these trees, which Wordsworth has recited in his tender sonnet:—

"'Tis said that to the brow of yon fair hill
Two brothers clomb; and turning face from face
Nor one look more exchanging, grief to still
Or feed, each planted on that lofty place

MATLOCK BATH.

> A chosen tree. Then eager to fulfil
> Their courses, like two new-born rivers they
> In opposite directions urged their way
> Down from the far-seen mount. No blast might kill
> Or blight the fond memorial. The trees grew,
> And now entwine their arms; but ne'er again
> Embraced those brothers upon earth's wide plain,
> Nor aught of mutual joy or sorrow knew,
> Until their spirits mingled in the sea
> That to itself takes all—Eternity."

The trout and grayling fishing in the Derwent here is of excellent quality, the water being stocked and preserved by zealous local angling societies, supported by the Trent Conservancy Board.

After leaving Darley the wooded banks contract, and the hills press forward, and at Matlock, nine-and-twenty miles from Barrow Stones, the stream runs through a deep gorge, where limestone precipices, festooned with foliage, rise sheer from the water's edge. This romantic ravine, overtopped by higher hills, extends for about three miles. Matlock is a misleading title. The little town is only a small watering-place, but it is split up into several principalities, governed by two Local Boards, and known as Matlock Bath, Matlock Bridge, Matlock Bank, Matlock Town, Matlock Cliff, and Matlock Green. There are two railway stations, the Bridge and the Bath, a mile apart; but passengers wishful to get to the one place find themselves alighting at the other, and the divisions and sub-divisions are most confusing. Matlock Bank (for which the Bridge is the station, distant a quarter of a mile) is given up to hydropathic establishments, of which there is a colony. Here John Smedley introduced the cold-water treatment many years ago, and the building devoted to his system of cure has developed into one of colossal proportions. Between Matlock Bridge and Matlock Bath the High Tor intervenes, occupying nearly the whole distance. It is a most impressive example of rock scenery, rising in one perpendicular face of grim grey limestone, 400 feet above the Derwent, which brawls angrily over the rocky bed at its stupendous base. The Midland main line perforates this mighty mass, and the dull roar of the trains may be heard reverberating in the gloomy tunnel with strange echoing resonance. There are natural fissures in the rock abounding in dog-tooth crystals, fluor-spar, lead-ore, and other minerals, and at the summit of the giddy cliff are pleasure-grounds. More than one disastrous accident has occurred through people venturing too near the edge and falling into the abyss beneath. Matlock Bath is a continuation of the poetic gorge, the Derwent being almost enclosed on the right by the towering Heights of Masson (commonly called the "Heights of Abraham"), and on the left by the Lovers' Walks. For about a mile the stream is deep and stately, and lends itself admirably to boating. Matlock Bath is a favourite resort of cheap trippers, who find innocent enjoyment in climbing the hills, exploring the caverns, investing their coppers at the petrifying wells, and driving to the Via Gellia, a charming valley within easy distance. The Pavilion is a large modern building standing on a terrace under the Dungeon Tors, and commanding panoramic views of great extent and variety. The Bath is also a much-frequented resort, and contains hotels that favourably compare with the caravansaries of other fashionable watering-places. The New Bath Hotel stands on the site of the old hotel, where Lord Byron met Mary Chaworth, and the lime-tree under which the poet sat with the proud beauty still flourishes. This tree has weathered the storms of more than three hundred winters, and is a marvel of arboreal growth, its wide-spreading branches covering an area of 350 square feet. Byron was a frequent visitor to Matlock, and in one of his letters to Thomas Moore he declares "there are prospects in Derbyshire as noble as in Greece or Switzerland." Mr. Ruskin visits the New Bath Hotel, and the author of "Modern Painters" writes in a characteristic manner:—"Speaking still wholly for myself, as an Epicurean Anchorite and Monastic Misanthrope, I pray leave to submit, as a deeply oppressed and afflicted Brother of that Order, that I can't find anything like Derbyshire anywhere else. '*J'ai beau*,' as our polite neighbours untranslateably express it, to scale the precipices of the Wengern Alp with Manfred, to penetrate with Faust the defiles of the Brocken—the painlessly accessible turrets of Matlock High Tor, the guiltlessly traceable Lovers' Walks by the Derwent, have for me still more attractive peril and a dearer witchery. Looking back to my past life I find, though not without surprise, that it owes more to the Via Gellia than the Via Mala, to the dripping wells of Matlock than the dust-rain of Lauterbrunnen."

Leaving Matlock Bath, the Derwent is utilised for commercial purposes by the Arkwrights, in connection with their mill machinery, and a very dangerous weir is the *bête noir* of the oarsman. Cromford, the cradle of the cotton manufacture, follows. Here are the immense but cleanly factories founded by Sir Richard Arkwright, the Preston barber's apprentice; and here is Willersley Castle, the seat of the family whose fortunes he made, looking down from a natural rocky plateau, embowered in trees, upon the windings of the river. Cromford bridge is a curious old structure. The arches on one side are pointed Gothic in style, and on the other side they are of a semicircular character. The same incongruity in architecture is to be observed in the bridges at Matlock Town and Darley. This is to be accounted for by the fact that they were once pack-saddle structures, and have been widened with no regard to the preservation of uniformity.

The river now passes down a contracted valley, deeply wooded, to Whatstandwell. A prominent feature on the steep crags to the left is Lea Hurst, the Derbyshire home of Miss Florence Nightingale, and on the other the forest of Alderwasley, a surpassing example of sylvan scenery. Ambergate is the next point of interest, where the Derwent receives the Amber, which has watered the delightful Ashover Valley, and wound under the steep hill dominated by the ruined towers and gables of Wingfield Manor. Then our river flows under hanging woods to Belper, where all its energies are required to turn the ponderous wheels at Messrs. Strutt's

MARKEATON BRIDGE.

cotton mills. Nowhere in all its course is it more picturesque than at Belper bridge. Above the weirs it is lake-like in its wide expanse, reflecting the green verdure at its side, the undulating uplands beyond, and the hill-side cemetery that by its delectable situation seems to render Death beautiful. The weirs make the water a live thing. One of these is a merry sluice, with several gates liberating the flood above, which comes down like Southey's torrent at Lodore. The large weir is of great width, and of crescent shape, with a wooded island at its foot. But the best view of this tumult of sunlit foam is obtained when we have for a moment turned to the river-path on the right; then, as we look up the stream, the graceful stone arches frame a picture of dancing water. Above, in the woodland park, is Bridge Hill, the residence of Mr. G. H. Strutt. The ivy-embroidered windows flash back the sunlight, as they look out over the valley of the Derwent. At Belper the river is forty-three miles from its birthplace. Milford comes next, with more of Strutt's mills and more turbulent weirs; and at Duffield, a mile or two farther south, the river Ecclesbourne pours its cheerful waters into the Derwent. It has come from the Wirksworth country, where George Eliot found character and scenery for "Adam Bede." Past pleasant pastoral scenes, farmsteads, and country houses, past Little Eaton and Breadsall, and Allestree Hall, with its

ALLESTREE.

ancestral woodlands, the seat of Sir William Thomas Evans; past Darley Abbey, where Evans's cotton mills break up the river into miniature Niagaras, the Derwent pursues its course, until presently we are at Derby, fifty-one miles from where we first made the acquaintance of the stream. An accession of considerable importance, the Markeaton Brook, falls into the river at this point; but we must get into the meadows at the west end of the town to see it, for it follows a subterranean course through the principal streets, being arched over in the year 1845. The upper windings of the Brook afford the painter many pretty "bits," and are held in high favour by lovers of Nature and other lovers.

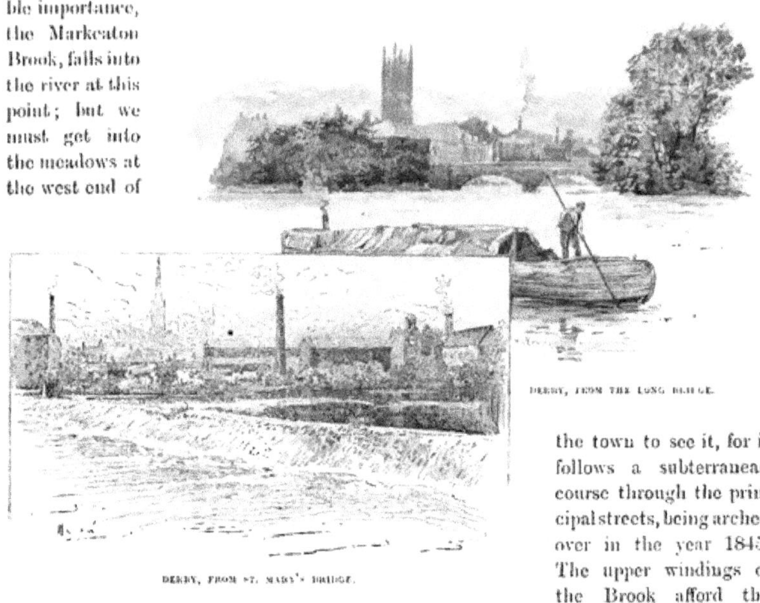

DERBY, FROM THE LONG BRIDGE.

DERBY, FROM ST. MARY'S BRIDGE.

About the ancient borough of Derby there is much that is historically interesting; and although the leading thoroughfares abound in pretentious examples of modern architecture, there still remain some of the old-world buildings that were in existence long before Prince Charlie in the winter of '45 began his disastrous retreat from Derby market-place, the most southerly point to which his army penetrated. A pilot guard advanced, it is true, six miles farther, to Swarkestone Bridge, but the Rubicon, that is the Trent, was not crossed.

The Derwent was formerly navigable up to Derby, but the right of communication was sold to the proprietors of two canal companies, who, before the introduction of railways, monopolised the traffic. In this place one peculiarity of the Derwent should not escape notice. The late Dr. Spencer T. Hall observed a distinguishing characteristic of the river, and described it in the following happy manner:—"Of all the rivers of England there is perhaps not one so noted for the sudden rise and lapse of its waters, on the melting of the snows, or the occurrence of summer storms. Even no higher up the stream than Chatsworth, there is an annual average of thirteen inches more rain than at Derby, and farther up the country a higher average still. For this, and for all the ordinary supply, such rapid descent is afforded by the steep cloughs and gullies and mountain roads, that, whenever a sudden thaw or unusual downpour occurs, the normal channel of the river is very soon overfilled, and on rushes the swelling and boiling torrent till it becomes majestic—almost terrific—as it breaks at last from the confines of the mountain gorges into the plain. It is sometimes easy to tell as low down as Derby, by the colour of the water, over which of the tributaries an up-country storm has broken. If out on the heather-side, about the Yorkshire border or the Longshaw and Chatsworth moors, down comes the deluge somewhat the colour of good coffee; if from the limestone districts, almost the colour of cream to it; and in the proportion in which both colours happen to be blended you may calculate pretty nearly how far the storm has been partial or general. Some fine morning you may walk as far as Derwent Bank or Darley Abbey, and see the river winding quietly along with its wonted grace and its usual flow. At noon you look again, and on it comes with the force of a little Niagara through the open flood-gates and over the great weir of Darley Mills, and thence spreads out until the meadows, as far as the Trent, form a series of lakes, which, if that river be also full, soon extends as far or farther down than Nottingham."

The Derwent at Derby is spanned by several handsome bridges. The oldest and most picturesque of these structures is St. Mary's. At the foot of the bridge is an ancient chapel where "the busy burgesses or men-at-arms turned aside for a brief silent prayer before crossing the Derwent and plunging into the forests that stretched out before them on the other side of the river." This mediæval bridge-chapel of Our Lady is now used as a mission-room in connection with the church of St. Alkmund. Just below the bridge, on an island, stands the first silk-mill ever erected in England. It is a vast pile of time-toned brick, pierced with as many windows as there are days in the year, and surmounted by a curious bell-tower. The history of the silk trade in Derby dates back to the opening days of the last century. At that period the Italians held secret the art of silk-throwing, and monopolised the market. John Lombe, an ambitious young fellow, full of spirit, an excellent draughtsman, and a capable mechanic, determined to acquire the secret. He visited Italy, and brought to Derby from Piedmont models of the coveted machinery, together with two native craftsmen who had favoured his enterprise and secured his safety. The Derby Corporation leased to Lombe the island swamp in the Derwent, where he erected in 1718 the present immense mill on a foundation of oaken piles. It cost him £30,000, but his manufactures were a superlative success, and the Italian monopoly was driven out of the market. But Lombe did not live more than two years to reap the rich result of his labours.

Treachery was at work, and he was poisoned at the hands of an Italian woman who was employed by the Piedmontese, and who contrived to escape the punishment due to her crime. Lombe, who was only twenty-nine when he thus tragically perished, was buried at All Saints', a church whose tower is one of the glories of the midland counties. Here, too, rest several members of the Cavendish family, their virtues commemorated in monumental marble; and there is a magnificent monument to the famous Countess of Shrewsbury, the friend of Queen Elizabeth, but better known as "Building Bess of Hardwick."

For many years Derby has been associated with the production of artistic porcelain. The making of china in the town has really never been discontinued since Duesbury commenced his labours here in the middle of the last century, amalgamating the historic works of Bow and Chelsea with his famous factory at Derby. There are now three china-works in the thriving town, which boasts of more than 100,000 inhabitants within the borough boundaries. The factory of the Derby Crown China Company, Limited, is a Palace of Porcelain where poems in pottery are produced. It is one of the sights of the neighbourhood, and is much visited by Americans and foreigners. Established in 1877, the works have been greatly developed, the business connections increased, and an advanced and higher tone given to most of the productions. All the usual services, such as dinner, tea, breakfast, trinket, and *déjeûner*, are made both in porcelain and in semi-vitrified "crown" ware, as are also figures and perforated vases in Parian. The specialities of the Company are vases of every conceivable design and style of decoration, from the most sumptuous Oriental schemes, wrought in raised gold of various hues upon full and lusciously coloured grounds, to the dainty and refined shapes and ornaments of the classic and of the best periods of the Renaissance. Other productions of the Company are the egg-shell specimens of fictile ware, which demand the most artistic skill of the potter. They are of extraordinary thinness; and the beauty of the colouring and the dainty jewelling and enamelling of the ornamentation equal anything achieved at the old works visited by Dr. Johnson in 1777, when he observed:—"The china was beautiful, but it was too dear; for that he could have vessels of silver of the same size as cheap as what were made here of porcelain." Derby, however, is largely dependent for its industrial prosperity upon the Midland Railway Company, who have their chief offices, locomotive, carriage and waggon, telegraph and signal works in the town. They employ in Derby alone a staff of 12,000 officials and workmen, and their estate covers 500 acres. It extends for some distance along the Derwent, which at this point receives the entire sewage of the town. This pollution of the beautiful river calls for legislative interference. What should be a source of delight becomes an object of disgust, and what was lovely is degraded with all that is loathsome. The South Sea Islanders pelt with filth the people they specially wish to honour: Derby treats the Derwent to a similar distinction.

But a truce to sanitation and economics. Let us follow the Derwent, unfragrant as it has become, past Spondon and the pretty mills at Borrowash, to Elvaston, the noble domain of the Earl of Harrington. The stream supplies with water a spacious ornamental lake, with four islands, concerning which the first Duke of Wellington, walking round it in company with Charles, the fourth Earl, stopped suddenly, and looking round, exclaimed, "Harrington, this is the only natural piece of artificial water I ever saw in my life." The gardens and grounds themselves are a triumph of arboriculture and landscape gardening; and who is there that has not heard of their avenues of quaintly clipped trees? The church tower and castle rise above a forest of patrician trees, while umbrageous aisles of green give vistas of scenes "where Boccaccio might have wooed and Watteau painted." These poetic perspectives look upon rockery and statuary, lawn and fountain, borders and beds of flowers. There is an avenue of elms a mile in length, framing at the extremity a view of the Gotham hills. The "golden" gates at the entrance-lodge belonged to the first Napoleon, and once occupied a position near the royal palace at Paris; they were erected here in 1819. The castle and church adjoin each other. The former is a Gothic mansion, which in 1643 was plundered by the Cromwellian troops. A costly monument in memory of Sir John Stanhope was demolished, and outrages were committed in the family vault. The church is a picturesque edifice, with a lofty perpendicular tower; in it are effigies of Sir John Stanhope and his wife, dated 1610, and other interesting family memorials.

Below Elvaston the Derwent flows through a flat country, and at its estuary at Wilne, near Shardlow, has greatly contracted its banks, so that it presents a striking contrast to the broad and powerful Trent. The Derbyshire river, indeed, is not worth following for its own sake below the county town.

Edward Bradbury.

IN THE SOUTH GARDENS, ELVASTON.

TRENT BRIDGE, NOTTINGHAM.

THE HUMBER AND ITS TRIBUTARIES.

CHAPTER V.

THE TRENT, FROM THE DERWENT TO THE HUMBER.

The Soar—Trent Junction—The Erewash—Gotham and its Wise Men—Clifton Hall and Grove—Nottingham and its History—Colwich Hall and Mary Chaworth—Sherwood Forest—Newark—Gainsborough—Axholme—The Confluence with the Humber.

SHORTLY after it has received the Derwent and passed by the locks communicating with the Erewash canal, the Trent is joined by another affluent, on its opposite bank. This is the Soar, which, for the latter part of its course, bounds on the west a portion of the county of Nottingham. Rising in the Leicestershire uplands, some miles to the south of the county town, it passes—traversing a rather wide and open valley—by Leicester itself, skirting the precincts of the Abbey—now marked by but scanty ruins—where Cardinal Wolsey died in the "winter of his discontent," disgraced by the king whom he had too well served. Then it flows northward by the lime-kilns of Barrow, and near the granite quarries of Mount Sorrel, wandering through water meadows, flat and at times flooded, but for several miles bounded on its western side by the rugged hills of Charnwood Forest, that insular outcrop of old-world rock which so strangely interrupts the monotonous opulence of the "red marl" scenery, and makes a little Wales in England. To the Soar come tributary streams from the pasture lands of Leicester, dear to the fox-hunter, which tributaries, like the river itself, glide past many a quiet village, of which the churches are often of no little interest, and the houses not seldom afford to us excellent specimens of the domestic architecture of our country from the sixteenth to the eighteenth century. The junction of the Soar is not far from another junction, which has given both an origin and a name to what is rapidly becoming a town. Here the main line of the Midland Railway receives one or two important tributaries, and as the result, Trent Junction has sprung up. As we approach, tall factories are seen to rise above lines of red-brick houses, and the College—a young but important school, which has helped to make the name of the place familiar—is conspicuous just on the outskirts of the town. The valley here is wide and level, and the scenery naturally becomes a little monotonous, but its right bank, near to which the river, for a time, is flowing, is sometimes rather steeply scarped. One of the prettiest spots is near to the place where the railway crosses the Trent, shortly after emerging from the cutting which conducts it from the valley of the Soar to that of the main river. The side of the valley is steep and broken, a pleasant combination of rough grassy slope and clustering trees. The uniform flow of the water is interrupted by a weir, and its surface is flecked with white bubbles, roughened and broken for a time with ripples, while above and below the bridge our eyes range up and down the level meadows broken but slightly with lines of green hedges and dots of trees.

Shortly below this place the Trent receives another tributary, the Erewash, a river which traverses the Nottinghamshire coal-field, and is now blackened in many places with collieries and ironworks. Attenborough Church, with its monuments, is of some note, and in the village was born Henry Ireton, son-in-law to Cromwell. Some two miles south of the river is a village known throughout the length and breadth of England, for its inhabitants in olden time have made it a household word. This is Gotham, where wisdom was once to be found; for are not its wise men proverbial? Thoroton, the county historian, thus relates the origin of the saying:—"King John, passing through the place towards Nottingham, and intending to go through the meadows, was prevented by the villagers, who apprehended that the ground over which a king had passed would for ever become a public road. The king, incensed at their proceedings, sent some of his servants to inquire of them the reason of their incivility, that he might punish them by way of fine, or any other way he thought proper. The villagers, hearing of the approach of the king's servants, thought of an expedient to turn away His Majesty's displeasure. When the messengers arrived, they found some of the inhabitants engaged in endeavouring to drown an eel; some were employed in dragging carts on to a barn to shade the wood from the sun; others were tumbling their cheeses down the hill to find their way to Nottingham; and some were engaged in hedging in a cuckoo which had perched upon a bush; in short, they were all employed in some foolish way or other, whence arose the old adage." Obviously, when we remember the monarch with whom they had to deal, they were not quite such fools as they seemed.

The Trent now begins to draw near to Nottingham, and the villages show signs of the approach to a great centre of manufacture. On a cliff above the river is Clifton Hall. According to the county historian, the house stands on a rock of alabaster, "curiously inlaid in many places with beautiful spars." It is approached by "an avenue of trees, a mile in length, upon gentle swells of the earth, which happily destroy the formal line which would have been shown upon a level surface. Below, the silvery Trent meanders." Tradition links a grim story of a murder to the pleasant groves of Clifton, for here, as we are told, "the Clifton Beauty, who was debauched and murdered by her sweetheart, was hurled down the precipice into her watery grave. The place is shown you, and it has been long held in veneration by lovers. Agreeable must be the shady walks above or below on the water's brink. Here the blackbird and the thrush whistle through the day, and the little redbreast in the evening sings the creation to calm repose in plaintive song. Here commerce is wafted from shore to shore, and industry flows for the reciprocal benefit of the human race." Since these words were written, industry has gone on flowing to an extent which would have astonished the historian, and would perhaps have rather deranged the measured progress of his periods. But, even now, the barges not seldom form groups—as they did when Turner sketched—tempting to the artist, and the natural beauty of the approach to Nottingham has not been wholly destroyed by tall mills and lofty chimneys. The Cliftons, from whom the Hall and Grove take their name, are an old and important Nottinghamshire family. Thoroton duly

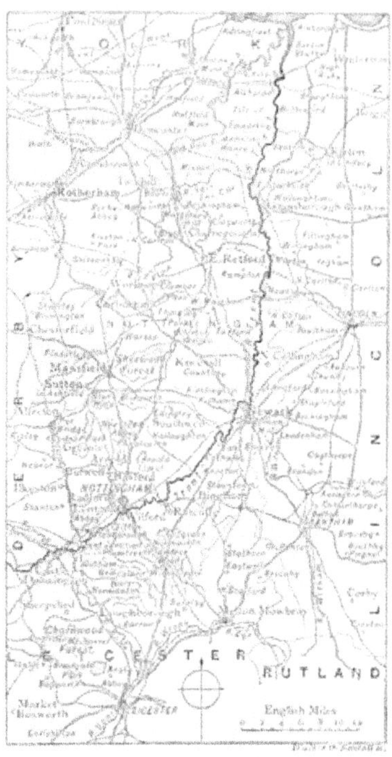

THE TRENT, FROM THE DERWENT TO THE HUMBER.

records the items of a feast given at the marriage of one of its members in the year 1530, which are so curious as to be worth repeating as an indication of the state of England some three and a half centuries since. For the more solid comestibles were provided two oxen, six calves, six wethers, seven lambs, and ten pigs. Among the lighter were "sixty couple conys," four dozen chickens, twelve swans, eight cranes, sixteen "hearonsews" (herons), and ten bitterns. To quench the thirst of the guests, there were three hogsheads of wine, "one white, one red, and one claret." The prices were very different from those of Nottingham market at the present time. A pig cost fivepence, a wether two shillings and fourpence, and a calf fourpence more. A chicken could be purchased for a penny, and a couple of rabbits for fivepence. A swan was priced at sixpence, and a crane at fivepence; for the sixteen herons and the ten bitterns the same sum was paid, viz., fourteenpence. One might visit Nottingham market now for a long time before getting a chance of buying any one of these four birds, and would then have to pay a fancy price for it. Cygnet, as everyone knows who has tasted it, is an excellent dish, but we should have thought that the other wild birds would have needed a hunter's appetite.

Clifton Grove is also inseparable from the memory of Henry Kirke White, the young poet who died at Cambridge, from overwork, in his twenty-first year. The following quotation from his poem on the place may serve as a specimen of his verses, which we think, in the present day, would not have greatly pleased "reviewers, men, or bookstalls," and may give an idea of the Grove at the beginning of the present century:—

"And oh, how sweet this walk o'erhung with wood
That winds the margin of the solemn flood!
What rural objects steal upon the sight!
What rising views prolong the calm delight!

"The brooklet branching from the silver Trent,
The whispering birch by every zephyr bent,
The woody islands and the naked mead,
The lowly hut half hid in groves of reed,
The rural wicket and the rural stile,
And frequent interspersed the woodman's pile.

"Above, below, where'er I turn my eyes,
Rocks, waters, woods in grand succession rise.
High up the cliff the varied groves ascend,
And mournful larches o'er the wave impend."

Not many towns in the Midland counties of England have a finer natural situation than Nottingham. The upland district on the western bank of the Trent terminates in an abrupt craggy scarp above the wide and level valley. The river, just opposite to the town, has swung away into the plain to a distance of more than half a mile from its ancient course, and a tributary stream called the Leen, which has cut deep into the plateau, intervenes between it and the ancient town. This, no doubt, was once limited to the scarped headland which rises between the two valleys, though probably it straggled down into the plain, and gradually extended along the road leading to the old bridge over the Trent. But during the present century Nottingham has gained enormously in size, and lost correspondingly in beauty. It has become less picturesque, though probably more healthy, and certainly more convenient; but now it is not wholly guiltless of smoke; it bristles in parts with chimneys, the utilitarian substitute for spires,

NOTTINGHAM, FROM THE CASTLE.

and it would require very subjective treatment at the hands of an artist who was desirous of depicting the beautiful. Still, there are some views of the town, from the side of the Leen, which are not even now without a certain beauty. Scarped cliffs of grey sandstone support the gardens and terraces of the castle, in the rear of which the town rises from the valley in alternating lines of trees and houses, broken here and there by the steeple or tower of a church. But in olden times, when the valley plain was free from railways, factories, and chimneys, Nottingham must have been a singularly picturesque town. Then the view from the valley of the Trent, especially from near the influx of the Leen, must have been a worthy subject for an artist. The southern wall of the town crowned the grey cliff; above it rose the noble tower of the principal church, and near the extremity of the headland, above the steepest crags, stood the keep and bastions of the castle. The church remains, but of the rest, as a glance shows, little is left to recall the Nottingham of the days of the Plantagenets.

A better site for a town could not readily have been found in the days when the "good old rule" in regard to taking and keeping prevailed. Thus there was a settlement on the headland at an early epoch, though the exact date of the foundation of Nottingham and its more ancient history are equally obscure. As this is not the place for an antiquarian discussion of the value of legends, we will pass over them in silence. As the Trent appears to have been bridged opposite to the town so long since as the tenth century, it is probable that even then a settlement of some importance was already in existence. Its subsequent history was for a time not altogether peaceful or prosperous. It was sorely harried by the Danes; it was taken and spoiled by the troops of Robert Earl of Gloucester in the days of King Stephen, when numbers of the townspeople were slain and no small part of the town was burnt; it was again besieged and captured by Duke Henry, afterwards the second king of that name. Since this time, though more than once the noise of war has been heard in its gates, the town has been, on the whole, much more fortunate. On two occasions only it occupies a prominent place in the history of England. At Nottingham Castle the young King Edward III. was residing with his mother Isabella and her notorious favourite, Roger Mortimer, when what would now be called a *coup d'état* was planned and successfully carried out. The insolence of this man had stirred the anger of the English nobles, and they rallied to the aid of the young king. He was lodged outside the castle; within its walls his so-called guardians appeared to be in safety. But one night Edward and his friends were admitted through a long underground passage, which is still shown under the name of "Mortimer's Hole," into the very interior of the castle; the Queen and Mortimer were arrested in their chambers, and the latter was hurried off to London, where the Parliament pronounced his doom, and he was instantly put to an ignominious death, meeting with a fate worse than that of Haman. This great act of justice done, the king, as Froissart says, "took new counsellors, the wisest and best beloved by his people."

The other episode occurred after a lapse of more than three centuries. At Nottingham was enacted the first scene of the long drama of the civil war termed by Royalist historians "the Great Rebellion." From York Charles I. had issued a proclamation requiring "all men who could bear arms to repair to him at Nottingham by the 25th of August following, on which day he would set up his royal standard there." On the morning of the day named he reached Nottingham, and took up his lodging at a house in the town, as the buildings of the castle had even then fallen into a dilapidated condition. The day was wild and stormy; but about six o'clock in the evening "the king himself, with a small train, rode to the top of the castle hill, Varney, the Knight Marshal, who was standard-bearer, carrying the standard, which was then erected in that place, with little other ceremony than the sound of drums and trumpets. The standard was blown down the same night it had been set up, by a very strong and unruly wind, and could not be fixed in a day or two, till the tempest was allayed." It was an evil omen, as many observed—not the first in that ill-fated career—and seemed a fitting beginning to the long series of calamities which was closed on the scaffold before the windows of the banqueting house of Whitehall.

But in days previous to those of the Stuarts, Nottingham Castle was a not unfrequent residence of the Kings of England. It was sometimes a prison for men of high estate, for here Owen Glendower and David II. of Scotland were immured, the latter for twelve years, after the battle of Neville's Cross. King Charles, after he had set up his standard, was not long able to retain possession of the town, and it fell into the hands of his opponents, who repaired the fortifications, and placed Colonel Hutchinson in command. Several attempts were made by the Royalists to regain possession of so important a centre; but though a metal more valuable than lead was also tried, all were unsuccessful, and the King was never again able to set foot within the walls. The castle was "slighted" at the conclusion of the war, and became ultimately the property of the Duke of Newcastle. He cleared away the ruins, and upon the site built a mansion, the design of which some ascribe to Sir Christopher Wren. If so, it is far from being among the happiest efforts of that great man. How ugly it is those who do not know it may see from Turner's early sketch of Nottingham, which gives an excellent notion of the leading features of the town before its later development. What an offence it had become to the feelings of his maturity may be seen in Turner's latest sketch of the town, engraved on the next plate of "Modern Painters" (vol. IV.), where the castle is almost thrust aside out of the picture, and is treated rather freely, in order to alleviate slightly the hardness of its rectangular walls and windows.

It was not, however, for long a favourite residence, and by the earlier part of the present century the ducal owner seldom passed any time under its roof. At last, on the rejection of the Reform Bill by the House of Lords in 1831, the Nottingham "lambs," as the town roughs are called—seemingly because that is about the last animal to which they present any resemblance—"determined to make the castle a burnt-offering to the shade of the outcast Bill." With the usual British negligence, no precautions had been taken against a riot, so they had for a season full opportunity to disport themselves. After a little preliminary diversion in the country they swarmed up the castle hill, forced the gates, piled up combustibles in the rooms, kindled them, and in a short time the whole building was in flames. Thus the duke got rid of a useless house, and as he recovered damages from the Hundred, he probably did not bear much malice against the rabble of Nottingham. For some forty years it stood a mere roofless, floorless, windowless shell, an unpicturesque ruin. The walls, however, were still in good condition, and were ultimately acquired by the municipal authorities, at whose expense the structure was thoroughly restored for use as a museum; this was opened in 1878, the adjoining grounds being laid out as an ornamental garden. The terrace commands a fine view over the valley of the Trent. "Striking at all times, it is never so remarkable as when that river is in flood. Formerly this was a common event,

NEWARK CASTLE.

but the inundations were mitigated by the removal, in the year 1871, of the old Trent Bridge, with its narrow arches, and the erection in its stead of the present handsome structure, which gives a more ready passage to the swollen waters. Still, it is not a rare occurrence to see the whole valley, as far as the eye can reach, converted into one huge lake. The roads in many places are submerged; the railway embankments barely overtop the waters; hedges almost disappear, and the trees rise forlornly from the flood; whole groups of houses are converted into a bad imitation of Venice, and the water disports itself on the ground-floors of warehouses, and among the chattels of store-yards, greatly to the detriment of their owners."

The stately tower of St. Mary's Church is still conspicuous in the views of the town from the neighbourhood of the Trent, and the whole structure is well worth a visit, for there are few finer churches in the county. It is a noble specimen of Perpendicular architecture, especially remarkable for the number and size of its windows —which, as Leland says, are so many "that no artificer can imagine to set more." The market-place also—a triangular area some four and a half acres in extent—is an interesting spectacle on Saturdays, when it is covered with booths for the sale not only of fish, flesh, and fowl, but of all sorts of wares; for Nottingham market still maintains its ancient repute in the town; and there, on its stony pastures, the Nottingham lambs were formerly wont to disport themselves at election times, and probably will do it again, whenever political feeling is running high. Of this spectacle one might say that distance would certainly lend enchantment to the view.

CARLTON.

On University College—a fine new structure, and a lasting monument to the public spirit of the municipality—on the modern churches and public buildings, the arboretum and the town gardens, want of space forbids us to dwell. But the sandstone cliffs so prominent in every view from the river call for the mention of one peculiarity, which is exhibited not only by Nottingham but also by some of the neighbouring villages. In these may be seen dwellings hewn in the rocks, for which some persons claim a remote antiquity, and see in them indeed a survival, if not an actual remnant, of the days when, as the Greek tragedian relates—

> Houses of wood or brick they could not frame,
> But underneath the ground, like swarming ants,
> In sunless caves they found a hidden home.

Be this as it may, houses partly excavated in the rock are still not very uncommon, and there are some singular caves in the cemetery which are now being utilised for vaults, so that "at the present day in the town of Nottingham, we find a return not only to primitive dwellings as at Petra, but to primitive sepulchres as at Jerusalem."

The secret of the rapid development of Nottingham during the present century, the cause, direct or indirect, of the great blocks of buildings that rise high above the level of the houses on the hill, and have spread so widely over the meadows of the Trent and Leen, is the manufacture of hosiery and lace. In early days Nottingham was noted for making malt and tanning leather, but the latter trade, happily for the noses of the inhabitants, is not now among the leading industries of the town. It became distinguished for hand-knit stockings not very long after this method of making them was adopted, and one of the first attempts at a weaving machine was set up in a Nottinghamshire village. It is needless to say that the inventor experienced the common fate of those wiser than their generation, and that others reaped the fruits of what he had sown in poverty and sorrow. The machine, after the death of the inventor, was adapted for use in London, and was brought back again into Nottinghamshire, where during the seventeenth century it became firmly established. Great improvements in the methods of weaving were made in the following century, and these during the present one have been carried to a high pitch of perfection. The machinery in the factories produces almost everything that can be woven, from the most ordinary articles of hosiery to the most delicate lacework.

From Nottingham to Newark the Trent continues to flow and to wind along a wide open valley, bounded here and there, as at the former town, by sandstone crags, which with their pleasant combinations of rock, wood, and water occasionally relieve the general monotony of the scenery. On the left bank runs the railway. Colwich Hall, which is in the valley not far from Nottingham, is noted for its memories of Mary Chaworth, who first awakened the youthful susceptibilities of Byron, and is commemorated in more than one of his earlier poems. She married the owner of Colwich Hall, and her fate was a sad one. At the time of the riots already mentioned, the house was attacked and plundered by the Nottingham mob; she escaped from the tender mercies of the playful "lambs" into a neighbouring plantation, but the fright and the exposure to the rain caused an illness which proved fatal.

West of the Trent lies Sherwood Forest, with its memories of Robin Hood, who more than once played his pranks in the town of Nottingham, and made its officials his victims. On this side also lies the group of ample estates and lordly mansions called the "Dukery"; but on the river itself there is no place of any note—though some of the village churches are of interest—till we reach the old ferry at Fiskerton, near to which is East Stoke, where the misguided followers of Lambert Simnel were crushed and scattered by the troops of Henry VII. Before the Trent reaches Newark it divides into two streams, the larger keeping to the western side of the valley, while the smaller flows nearer to the undulating plateau by which it is bounded on the east. Between the base of this plateau and the water is a broad strip of level land, on which the town is built. It was, in former days, a military post of some importance, for it guarded the line of the Great North Road, which is now carried across the island plain on a raised causeway, constructed by Smeaton. According to tradition, the first fortress by the river-side was erected by Egbert, but this was rebuilt by Leofric, the great Earl of Mercia, when it was called the New Work, and thus gave a name to the town. But of this fortress not a fragment is now visible, the oldest part of the present castle dating from about the year 1123, when it was rebuilt from the ground by one of the Bishops of Lincoln. He had a liking for castle-building, but as he doubted how far such work was episcopal, in order to keep his conscience easy, he always founded a monastery when he built a new fortress. Since this date also very much has been changed, and the ruin as it stands is for the most part distinctly less ancient. Within the walls of Newark Castle, King John, of evil fame, ended his unquiet life; and not long after it was occupied by the nobles who were in arms against him, and was defended for a few days against the Earl of Pembroke, guardian of the young king, his successor.

But the most stirring episodes in the history of Newark Castle occurred during the Civil War. After the troubles began, the town, which was exceptionally loyal, was held by a strong Royalist garrison, which for a time formed a serious obstacle to the progress of the other party. So it was beleaguered by three separate bands of the Parliamentary troops. This division of forces proved to be a disastrous policy. The band which had occupied Beacon Hill, to the north-east of the town, was attacked suddenly on one side by Prince Rupert, on the other by a sally of the besieged, and was crushed and captured, whereupon the others retreated hurriedly. Newark was again besieged after Marston Moor, and again relieved by Prince Rupert. But at last, after the fatal field of Naseby, the town was blockaded by the Scotch army. Yet even then it held out till the king had surrendered at Southwell, when, in accordance with his orders, it capitulated. Among the "siege pieces" which remain as memorials of the great struggle, those of Newark are familiar to the collector. The castle, of course, was duly "slighted," and for two centuries the ruins were abandoned to the ravages of the weather and of the local vandals. Now, however, they are carefully preserved. The river front, which consists of a lofty curtain-wall with three towers, is still fairly perfect, but the latter do not project sufficiently to produce an effective outline or a picturesque view.

Newark, though now a busy place, for it is the centre of an important agricultural district, and has a noted corn market, besides gypsum and farming implement works and malthouses, still retains several remnants of bygone times, particularly in its ample market-place, where one or two interesting old houses may yet be seen, as well as a curious though much-restored cross, called the Beaumont Cross, at the junction of two of its streets. In former days, as a halting-place on the Great North Road, it was noted for its inns, and two of those which now remain claim to have existed from very early times. The "Saracen's Head" (where Jeanie Deans is lodged by the author of the "Heart of Midlothian")

ON THE TRENT AT GAINSBOROUGH.

traces back its history to the reign of Edward III., and the "White Hart" to that of Henry IV. But its chief attraction to the antiquarian is the church, the lofty spire of which rises conspicuously above the houses in every view of the town. It yields to few parish churches in England either in size or beauty; and, now that Southwell is a cathedral, may claim to be, on the whole, the finest in the county of Nottingham. It incorporates a few remnants of a Norman building, but the lower part of the tower is Early English—the building as a whole, together with the spire, being Perpendicular. The steeple is at the western end, and the plan is cruciform, but the transepts do not project beyond the outer wall of the aisles. The stalls and woodwork of the choir and the roof are very fine, and some of the brasses are interesting. There is also some good modern stained glass, and an excellent organ. The large churchyard allows the church to be well seen from near at hand, and for many a mile along the broad and level valley of the Trent its steeple rises like a landmark, which in olden times served to guide the traveller to the shelter of the walls of the "New work."

The general course of the Trent is now almost due north to beyond Gainsborough, though the river sweeps through the broad valley in great sinuous curves.

The scenery loses its interest, for the slopes which rise from the plain are, as a rule, rather low, and comparatively distant from the water-side. Level meadows have, no doubt, a certain beauty of their own, particularly in the early summer, when the grass is dappled with flowers and the scythe has not yet laid low their beauty. There is a charm in the beds of rustling reeds, in the grey willows overhanging the water, in the clusters of meadow-sweet, willow-herb, and loosestrife, fringing the bank and brightening the ditches; in the swan that "floats double" on the still stream, and the kingfisher that glances over it like a flying emerald; but these after a time become a little monotonous; and neither the river itself, nor the villages near its bank, afford much opportunity for illustration or for description.

West of Lincoln, roughly speaking, the Trent ceases to traverse Nottinghamshire, and becomes the boundary between it and the adjoining shire of Lincoln. The only place of importance on the latter portion is Gainsborough, a town of considerable antiquity, for here the fleet of Sweyn was moored, and here he himself, on returning from his foray, "was stabbed by an unknown hand"; but it retains little of interest and is less picturesque than is the wont of riverside towns. The influence of the tide extends some miles above the town, and bare banks of slimy mud are exposed at low water on either side of the stream. The Trent is said to exhibit at spring tides the phenomenon called the "bore" or "eagre," when, at the first rise after low, the tidal wave, forcing its way up the contracted channel of the river from the broad expanse of the estuary, advances as a rolling mass of water, causing no little disturbance to the smaller craft which it meets in its course. A handsome stone bridge of three arches, with a balustraded parapet, spans the river at Gainsborough, and affords a good view both of it and of the town. The latter occupies a strip of level land between the water-brink and the well-defined slope which forms the eastern boundary of the valley. Mills old and new are its most conspicuous features. Not a few have their bases washed by the tide; but at intervals gardens, defended as usual by retaining-walls, come down to the Trent. Chimneys are more prominent than spires, and the principal church—at some distance from the bridge—has a tower inconspicuous either for height or for beauty. On the left bank houses are not numerous; flat meadows and hedgerow trees generally border the stream, and extend for a mile or more, till the ground gradually rises to the opposite slope of the valley. It must be confessed that neither the scenery nor the town itself is

AT AXHOLME.

particularly attractive; but the former is improved by regarding it from the higher ground on the east, from which also views are obtained across another expanse of comparatively level ground to a line of low hills forming the northern prolongation of the plateau on which stands the Cathedral of Lincoln. The parish church of Gainsborough is said to have been built early in the thirteenth century; but the greater part of the tower must be considerably later in its date, and the body of the church is a heavy stone structure in what its architects would probably have called the Italian style. It has, however, a churchyard, pleasantly—it might be said, thickly—planted with trees; and, to judge by its size, one would infer that Gainsborough at any rate was deemed a good place to die in, whatever it might be for the purpose of living. The town, however, possesses easy communication, by way of the Trent, with the Humber, and is thus an inland port of some rank.

MEADOW LAND AT AXHOLME.

The old chapel mentioned by Leland, the traditional burial-place of sundry Danish invaders, is gone; but the visitor who has traversed the rather long and, near the water-side, unlovely streets which intervene between the railway station and the central part of the town, will find, when he has reached the latter, something between it and the river to reward him for his pains. This is a remarkable specimen, in very fair preservation, of the older English domestic architecture. It is called the Old Hall, or Manor House, and John of Gaunt is popularly indicated as its builder; but it may perhaps be doubted whether the greater part, at least, does not belong to a rather later date. The house, which is of considerable size, stands at the end of a kind of open courtyard surrounded by cottages. Its general plan is that of a long central block from which two wings project at right angles. The former is chiefly —at any rate, in the upper portion—of timber-work; the latter are mainly built of brick. The mansion has suffered considerably from the effects of time and neglect, but it has been to some extent restored of late years, and portions of it are still either inhabited or in use. About a century and a half since it was the residence of one Sir Neville Hickman, but since his death it has served various purposes, one part for a time having been converted into a theatre.

The tidal river below Gainsborough passes on through scenery less and less interesting. After a time it ceases to divide the county of Nottingham from Lincoln, and is bordered on both banks by the latter. The district to the west is called the Island of Axholme. This, "though now containing some of the richest land perhaps in the kingdom, was formerly one continued fen, occasioned by the silt thrown up the Trent with the tides of the Humber. This, obstructing the free passage of the Dun and the Idle, forced back their waters over the circumjacent lands, so that the higher central parts formed an island, which appellation they still retain. From this circumstance it became a place so deplorable that Roger, Lord Mowbray, an eminent baron in the time of King Henry II., adhering to the interests of the younger Henry, who took up arms against his father, repaired with his retainers to this spot, fortified an old castle, and for some time set at defiance the king's forces who were sent to reduce him to obedience."*

The authority just quoted tells us that an attempt to regulate the drainage of Axholme was made so long since as the reign of Henry V. by one of the Abbots of Selby, who constructed "a long sluice of wood" upon the Trent "at the head of a certain sewer called the Maredyke," and this he did "of his free goodwill and charity for the care of the country." This was destroyed of malicious purpose in the days of his successor, who rebuilt the same of stone. But the chief reclamation of land, not only in the marshes of Axholme, but also in the adjacent fens called Dikes Mersh and Hatfield Chase, in the county of York, was undertaken in the earlier part of the reign of Charles I., when a contract bearing date May 24, 1646, was made with Cornelius Vermuden, which was successfully carried out during the next five years, so that many thousand acres of land were made available for agricultural purposes—"the waters which usually overflowed the whole level being conveyed into the river Trent, through Snow sewer and Althorpe river by a sluice, which opened out the drained water at every ebb, and kept back the tides upon all comings-in thereof."

The confluence of the Trent with the Humber takes place near Alkborough, "where Dr. Stukeley places the *Aquis* of Ravennas, having discovered a Roman *castrum* and a vicinal road. The Roman castle is square, 300 feet each side, the entrance north, the west side is objected to the steep cliff hanging over the Trent, which here falls into the Humber; for this castle is very conveniently placed in the north-west angle of Lincolnshire, as a watch-tower over all Nottingham and Yorkshire, which it surveys. I am told the camp is now called *Countess Close*, and they say a Countess of Warwick lived there, perhaps owned the estate; but there are no marks of building, nor, I believe, ever were. The vallum and ditch were very perfect. Before the north entrance is a square plot, called the Green, where I suppose the Roman soldiers lay *pro castris*. In it is a round walk, formed into a labyrinth, which they call 'Julian's Bower.'"

So, where Trent and Ouse unite to form the broad and "storming Humber," that "keeps the Scythian's name," our survey ends; the rivers have now become an estuary, and that, as another writer will presently show, soon begins to open out towards the sea, along which the vessels come and go to "merchandising Hull" and other ports which during this century have risen into notice.

T. G. Bonney.

* "Beauties of England and Wales," Vol. IX., p. 566.

BOLTON BRIDGE.

THE HUMBER AND ITS TRIBUTARIES.

CHAPTER VI.

THE WHARFE.

General Characteristics—The Skirfare—Langstrothdale—Kettlewell—Dowkabottom Cave—Coniston and its Neighbourhood—Rylstone and the Nortons—Burnsall—Appletreewick: an Eccentric Parson—Simon's Seat—Barden Tower and the Cliffords—The "Strid"—Bolton Abbey and Bolton Hall—The Bridge—Ilkley—Denton and the Fairfaxes—Farnley Hall and Turner—Otley—Harewood—Towton Field—Kirkby Wharfe—Bolton Percy.

THE Wharfe is typical of the broad shire. From beginning to end it is a Yorkshire stream. Having its origin on the slopes of the Cam mountain, in the north-west of the county, it traverses, in the sixty or seventy miles of its course to the Ouse, almost every description of the scenery for which this great division of England is famous. Over moorland and meadowland, rushing madly down precipitous rocks and flowing placidly along fertile plains, shut up in some parts within deep gorges and at other points spreading out to river-like dimensions, it has an ever-varying charm to all who trace its progress. And its physical characteristics are but a reflex of the incidents of the story to be gleaned along its banks. To make its acquaintance away up on the fells is to find it blending into many a choice bit of folklore and into old-world customs and superstitions. Here, in a favoured bend, it murmurs in sweet harmony with an idyll of country life; there it dashes wildly on its way, in keeping with the tragic tale of which at this particular spot it is the scene. Yonder it skirts, in a roofless monastery, a memorial of its treachery; here it has turned for generations the water-wheel of a mill that has never failed to find grist from a peaceful farming community. If in one place it sweeps round one of the great battle-fields of our country, in another it flows in undisturbed seclusion between wooded slopes where the over-hanging trees hide the sunlight from its waters, and dark rock-sheltered pools provide a safe retreat for the otter. Not anywhere, in fact, is the Wharfe devoid of interest or beauty. It retains throughout its freshness and its charm, and it is cheering to know that very watchful are the people who live on its banks to guard it from anything calculated to lessen its attractiveness.

A classic English river, tributes have been paid to the Wharfe from the days of the Romans. In our own time Wordsworth got from it the inspiration for some of his finest verse, and Turner found it yield subjects to him in generous abundance for his matchless drawings. Camden must have lingered by the Wharfe. He knew it better than any other early writer. There is evidence, in what he says about it, that he penetrated into those regions where its interest to the modern tourist too often ends, but where to the naturalist, the antiquary, and the artist, some of its choicest features begin to reveal themselves. In his quaint way, in his "Britannia," he tells us that "if a man should think the name of the stream to be wrested from the word Guerf, which in British signifieth swift or violent, verily the nature of the river conspireth with that opinion." Camden's description of the Wharfe is proof that he saw it chiefly in its mountainous aspect. He speaks of it as "a swift and speedy streame, making a great noise as it goeth, as if it were froward, stubborn, and angry." And he further speaks of it as being "verily a troublesome river, and dangerous even in summer time also," which he himself had some experience of, "for it hath such slippery stones in it that our horse had no sure footing on them, or else the violence of the water carried them away from under his feet."

The Wharfe is joined, at a point about fifteen miles from its source, by the Skirfare. Both rivers run on a parallel course from the direction of the Cam fells, and are close enough to each other to have a common interest. The Skirfare passes through what Wordsworth, in the "White Doe of Rylstone," using the ancient name, calls "the deep fork of Amerdale." "Amerdale" has for a long period, however, given place to "Littondale," Litton being the name of a village on the banks of the stream. Running north of the Skirfare, and starting from a point a few miles further west, the Wharfe passes down Langstrothdale in the fell country, and then through Kettlewelldale to the point of junction with the Skirfare. The name Langstrothdale has a Celtic ring, and has not inappropriately been translated to mean the long valley. From here are supposed to have come the two scholars of Soleres Hall at Cambridge, mentioned in Chaucer's "Reve's Tale"—

> "Of oo towne were they borne that highte Strother,
> Fer in the North, I cannot tellen where."

The spot is, however, pretty clearly identified otherwise by Chaucer himself, the dialect he uses in this tale in connection with the scholars bearing a close resemblance to the Langstrothdale folk-speech. It is a speech deserving the attention of the philologist, agreeing as it does in many of its peculiarities with early English forms.

The head waters of the Wharfe lie far out of the beaten track, in a district so broken up into hilly grandeur, and commanding from its heights so many fine glimpses into the dales "where deep and low the hamlets lie," as to form a fitting introduction to the river that in its course yields so much beauty and romance. At Beckermonds, "the mouths of the becks," two small streams unite, and from here the Wharfe passes downwards into Kettlewelldale. Hubberholme, the first village on the river of any note, is supposed to be of Danish origin, and is one of the oldest cluster of houses in this part of the country, possessing a church, dedicated to St. Michael, the history of which is popularly supposed to go back to the time of Paulinus. A short distance below Hubberholme lies Buckden, in a delightful setting of scenery. Then comes Starbotton, a village taking its name from a stream that runs through it, and below is Kettlewell, the best starting point for Upper Wharfedale, and the town from which this section of the river's course takes its name. Kettlewell figures in Domesday as Chetelwell, and is said by some authorities to be derived from "the weiler or dwelling of Chetel." A Norman church of an exceedingly simple pattern remained here until the beginning of the present century, when the existing edifice took its place, only the old font remaining as a memorial of the ancient structure. The town stands at the foot of Great Whernside (2,310 feet) and close to it also is Buckden Pike (2,304 feet). Magnificent views may be obtained from both heights. But one need go no further than the centre of the bridge at Kettlewell to find delightful glimpses of the course of the Wharfe, both east and west. The river at this point comes down with a great rush, the descent from its source, a little over ten miles, exceeding six hundred feet. Two miles or so south of Kettlewell is the well-known, although not easily found, Dowkabottom Cave, perhaps the most interesting of the many openings into the limestone formation in North-West Yorkshire. The entrance to the cave is on a level terrace on the mountain slope, at a point 1,250 feet above the sea. Five chambers and several passage-ways make up the cave, in which are many curious natural formations caused by the percolation of the water through the limestone. The scene inside is singularly weird and fascinating. But the Dowkabottom Cave is more than a curiosity. It was one of the homes of primitive man, and it seems to have been a place of shelter also in the Brito-Roman period. Bones and skulls of animals were found on the surface when the cave was discovered, and since then there have been scientific examinations of the interior, with the result that human skeletons have been unearthed, together with the bones of the wolf, the wild boar, the horse, the red deer, sheep, and other animals. Amongst the articles of domestic use found were bone pins and ornaments belonging to the primeval occupation, and bronze weapons, armlets, rings, coins, etc., of the Brito-Roman days. The theory as to the last-mentioned articles is that the inhabitants of the district found shelter here for a time after the departure of the Romans, when the Northern tribes, held no longer in check, came down into the Craven country. To account for the loose bones, it has been surmised that the wolf may have found a safe den in this cave long after it was driven out of other parts of England.

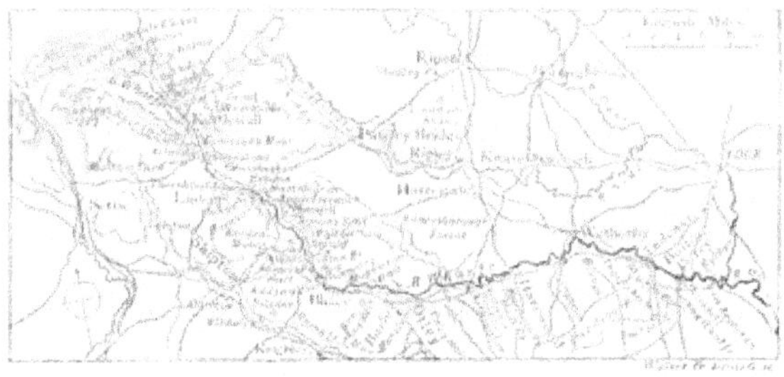
THE COURSE OF THE WHARFE.

Returning to the Wharfe, and following the river on its way from Kettlewell, Coniston is reached—a picturesque village, with a maypole, trim garden ground in front of most of the houses, and a church which, according to Whitaker, is the most ancient building in Craven. Since Whitaker's time the church has been much improved, but it retains many of its ancient features. From Coniston it is a short walk across country to Kilnsey, where is a grand stretch of overhanging limestone, "a promontory," says Phillips, "of the primeval sea loch, which is now the green valley of the Wharfe." The crag is nearly half a mile in extent, and rises at its highest part, whence there is a fine view, to 165 feet. A beautifully wooded walk of three miles leads from Coniston to Grassington, where at one time a good deal of lead was obtained and smelted. Here is what is said to be the oldest bridge on the river. What became of some earlier bridges on the same stream is told in an entry in the church books of Otley, under date 1673. On the 11th of September in that year there was "a wonderful inundation of waters in the northern parts," and on that occasion "this river of Wharfe, never known to be so big within the memory of man, overturned Kettlewell Bridge, Burnsey Bridge, Barden Bridge, Bolton Bridge, Ilkley Bridge, and Otley Bridge." It also swept away certain fulling mills of wood, and "carried them down whole, like to a ship." And when the flood had passed, "it left neither corn nor cattle on the coast thereof."

Close to Grassington is Threshfield, where there are several old buildings, and the Grammar School in which Dr. Whitaker, the historian of Craven, received his early education. Then comes Linton, where in the old time every woman in the place "could spin flax from the distaff, or rock as it was called, and could card or spin wool from the piece." Linton, in those days, was a veritable Arcadia in the

SKIPTON CASTLE, FROM ONE OF THE TOWERS.

hills, for here there was neither poor's rate nor public-house, and almost every housekeeper had his "three acres and a cow," or what was tantamount thereto. There has been a change in these conditions, but Linton has not lost its look of prosperity and comfort. Close to the village are what have been called the Falls of the Wharfe—a rocky break in the river, forming a fine study for the artist. Below Linton lies Hebden, a village whose character and position are well expressed in its name—heb, high; and dene, a valley; and across the river at this point lies Thorpe. At Thorpe we are on the road leading to Rylstone, the seat of the Nortons, who risked and lost so much in the "Rising of the North," 1569—

> "Thee, Norton, wi' thine eight good sonnes,
> They doomed to die; alas! for ruth.
> Thy revered lockes thee could not save,
> Nor them their fair and blooming youth."

The ballad is an exaggeration, two only of the sons having suffered on the scaffold.

The property, however, was cut off, and the "sequestered hall" mentioned in the "White Doe" fell into ruins. The name of the family clings to the district, and is perpetuated in what remains of the Norton Tower.

"It fronts all quarters, and looks round,
O'er path and road, and plain and dell,
Dark moor, and gleaming pool and stream,
Upon a prospect without bound."

The "White Doe" was the pet of "the exalted Emily, maid of the blasted family." It was presented to her by her brother, Francis Norton, of Rylstone.

ILKLEY BRIDGE.

Francis was one of those who perished in the rising of the North. He was buried in Bolton Abbey, and, according to the legend, the sister was a frequent visitor to his grave—

"But most to Bolton's sacred pile,
On favouring nights she longed to go;
There ranged through cloister, court, and aisle,
Attended by the soft-paced doe.
Nor did she fear in the soft moonshine
To look upon St. Mary's shrine,
Nor on the lonely turf that showed
Where Francis slept in his last abode."

Lying below Thorpe and Hebden is Burnsall, and here the scenery, especially along the banks of the river, is rich in picturesque beauty. Burnsall is Brinshale in Domesday. It is a place where well-worship must have prevailed from a remote time, as is evidenced in its "Thorsill" or Thor's well, and in its other wells dedicated to St. Margaret and St. Helena. Owing to a peculiarity in the division of the manor, the parish at one time rejoiced in two rectors and two rectories, with two pulpits and two stalls in the church. Originally Norman, the church has undergone repair at different times. The latest restoration was in 1859. An inscription on a tablet inside the tower speaks of an earlier work in the same direction, describing how in 1612 the fabric was repaired and beautified at the "onlie coste and charges of Sir William Craven, Knight and Alderman of the Citie of London, and late Lord Mayor of the same." Sir William was a native of Appletreewick close by. His career recalls that of Whittington. He went up to London under the care of a carrier, got employment in the family of a mercer, and eventually excelled his master in business. He was Lord Mayor in 1611. His eldest son distinguished himself in the service of Gustavus Adolphus and the Prince of Orange, and married the Queen of Bohemia. "Thus," says Whitaker, with a touch of pride, "the son of the Wharfedale peasant matched with the sister of Charles I."

Sir William Craven also erected and endowed the Grammar School of the village. At this school Eugene Aram is said to have been an usher. A more interesting character than Aram was the Rev. John Alcock, master of the school in Aram's time, and rector of a moiety of the parish. It is said of him that on one occasion, when preaching on behalf of some benevolent object, he noticed his congregation becoming restless. "Oh yes," he said, "I see how it is. You want your dinners; so do I. Very well, there's sermon enough left for another spell, and so we'll postpone the remainder till next anniversary." On another occasion he had no sermon to deliver at all; he had either mislaid or lost his MS. "It's no matter," he said to the clerk, loud enough for all to hear; "hand me up that Bible, and I'll read a chapter in Job worth two of it." Nor is this the only instance showing how coolly this eccentric clergyman could meet an emergency. There is a story to the effect that the pages of a sermon he had were stitched together in such a way as to confuse the argument. He did not discover this until about to announce the text, when he quietly explained what had happened, adding "I've no time to put the leaves right. I shall read them as I find them. You can put everything straight yourselves when you get home." "That's an awkward word," he said to a lady when she came to the "obey" in the marriage service; "you can skip on to the next!"

Leaving Burnsall, the Wharfe skirts Hartlington, and flows past Appletreewick. Both of these places trace their history back to Saxon times. There is much to see here, amongst other things caverns worth exploring, and a great collection of boulders known as "the Apronful of Stones." The legend of the stones is that the devil was carrying them, for some purpose best known to himself, when he stumbled over a knoll, causing the apron to give way with the weight that was in it, and the stones to assume their present position. On the river to the south lies Howgill, and we are now close to Simon's Seat (1,593 feet), from whose summit fine views of Upper and Lower Wharfedale and neighbouring valleys are obtained. The name Simon in this connection has been traced to the northern hero Sigmund; but the legend among the dalesmen is that a shepherd once found a male child on the top of the mountain, and adopted the infant, whom he named Simon. As the boy grew up the burden of keeping him was shared by different shepherds. The little fellow was cared for, in fact, "amang 'em;" and "Amanghem" became his surname—a name, whatever is to be said for the story, that is borne by some families in this part of the country.

Simon's Seat rises gradually from the Wharfe, and it is an easy descent from its slopes to Barden Tower, whose grey ruins look grandly over a wild and beautiful scene. Barden Tower was the home of Henry Clifford, "the Shepherd Lord," and may be taken as a landmark dividing Upper from Lower Wharfedale. The story of the Shepherd Lord, although some four centuries old, is known by oral transmission all over the countryside here. Unlike a good many of the other tales common among the dalesmen, it has the merit of truth. Its hero was the eldest son of John, "the Black Clifford," who was struck down on the eve of the battle of Towton, and whose estates were forfeited by the issue of that day. The Clifford heir, then a boy of five years, was sent for protection, after the battle, into Cumberland, where he was brought up as a shepherd. He pursued this life for about twenty-five years, and when, on the accession of Henry VII., he secured the inheritance of his ancestors, his desire for a quiet and simple life was shown in the selection he made of Barden Tower for his residence. He found the tower a small keep or lodge, and enlarged it sufficiently to provide accommodation for a few of his friends. Here he spent his time studying astronomy and alchemy, and enjoying the company of such of the monks of Bolton as had similar tastes. The Shepherd Lord could fight valiantly when the need arose, and the dalesmen rallied around his standard when, in his sixtieth year, he went onwards to Flodden:—

"From Penigent to Pendle Hill,
From Linton to Long Addingham,
And all that Craven coasts did till,
They with the lusty Clifford came."

The Shepherd Lord survived Flodden about ten years. After his death, Barden Tower was only occasionally used by the Cliffords, and was allowed to fall into decay. An inscription over the gateway states that it was repaired by Lady Anne Clifford, Countess of Pembroke, Dorset, and Montgomery, "and High Sheriffesse by inheritance of the county of Westmorland." This was in the years 1658-9, "after it had layne ruinous ever since about 1589, when her mother then lay in it, and was greate with childe with her, till now that it was repayred by the sayd lady." "The said lady" did a great deal for the houses of her family; hence a citation at the close of the Barden inscription (Isaiah lviii. 12)—"Thou shalt build up the

THE BRIDGE, OTLEY.

foundations of many generations, and thou shalt be called the repairer of the breach, the restorer of paths to dwell in." A small chapel adjoins the ruin, and a part of the tower adjoining the chapel is used as a farmhouse. The property, like the Bolton estate below, now belongs to the Duke of Devonshire.

From Barden Tower the Wharfe falls rapidly over a rocky course, densely wooded on both sides, towards the famous "Strid," a narrow gorge in the rocky bed, through which the water rushes at a furious speed. The name "Strid" has two derivations given to it. One, in common acceptance, is that it is so called because it is possible at this point to stride over the chasm. The more likely derivation is the Anglo-Saxon "stryth," or turmoil. The common meaning, however, suggests the tradition that gives romantic interest to the spot. It was here over seven centuries ago, as the story goes, that "the Boy of Egremond," the heir to the Romillys, perished in the flood while out hunting.

"He sprang in glee, for what cared he
That the river was strong and the rocks were steep!
But the greyhound in the leash hung back,
And checked him in his leap.
The Boy is in the arms of Wharfe,
And strangled by a merciless force;
For never more was young Romilly seen
Till he rose a lifeless corse."

Connected with this legend is the founding of Bolton Abbey, situated in the meadow land close to the river some distance below. It is said that the falconer hastened back to the Lady Alice, the mother of the boy, and broke the sad news with the significant question, "What is good for a bootless bene?" Wordsworth scarcely varies from the story as it is still told in the locality:—

"'What is good for a bootless bene?'
The Falconer to the Lady said;
And she made answer, 'Endless sorrow!'
For she knew that her son was dead;
She knew it by the Falconer's words,
And from the look of the Falconer's eye,
And from the love that was in her soul
For her youthful Romilly."

The story goes that when the Lady Alice fully realised what had happened she vowed, now all hope was gone from her, that many a poor man's son should be her heir. According to the legend, she selected a site for a priory, as near to the scene of the accident as she could find one, and when "the pious structure fair to see" rose up, she transferred it to the Monks of Embsay, in the bleak hilly region beyond. The charter and the romance do not, however, agree. The conveyance of the ground at Bolton to the monks appears to have been made before the accident at the Strid, as the son is named in the document as a party to the transaction, and the reading indicates that the land had been given over in a prosaic fashion by way of exchange. It has been surmised by believers in the story that

FARNLEY HALL.

after the drowning the monks came to the bereaved lady and induced her to build a priory on what was now their property on the Wharfe, as a memorial to her son. Her mother, Cecily, the wife of William de Meschines, and heiress of William de Romilly, had joined with her husband in 1120 in founding the Embsay Priory for Augustinian Canons, the site being two miles east of Skipton. The Embsay endowment, handsome enough to begin with, was increased by the gift of the village and mill at Kildwick and lands at Stratton, the deed setting forth that this was done by the heiress of the Romillys "for the health of her soul and that of her parents." It is stated in the charter that the conveyance in this instance was made by the Lady Cecily, mother of Alice, and William, her son-in-law, placing a knife on the altar of the conventual church. This William, a nephew of David, King of Scotland, was married to Alice, who in her turn became heiress of the estates, and adopted her mother's name. She bore her husband two sons and three daughters. The younger son, "the Boy of Egremond"—so named after one of the baronies of the family—survived his brother until, according to the legend, the sad incident at the Strid put an end to the bright promise of his life, and left his mother in "endless sorrow."

Situated on a bend of the Wharfe, with a mountainous background, and an open sylvan expanse of country in front, through which the river moves in a clear, uninterrupted course, the Abbey rises in a scene of great sweetness and beauty. The building, like most other works of its kind, shows traces of the workmanship of different periods; but, unlike similar structures in the same county, it is not wholly a ruin. The nave, roofed over, and partly restored, forms the parish church of Bolton. It is entered through the gateway of what was intended for a western tower, and retains fortunately the original west front, finely detailed, with much arcading, in the Early English style. The entrance, forming the first stage of the contemplated tower, shows excellent Perpendicular work. On the spandrels of the recessed doorway are the arms of the Priory and the Cliffords, and above is a lofty five-light window. The tower was begun by the last of the priors, Richard Moone, as set forth on an inscription (the name symbolised) on the cornice below the window, "In the yer of owr Lord MDCXX, R. ☾ begaun thes foundachon on qwho sowl God haue marce. Amen." The Dissolution put a stop to Prior Moone's work, but it is said that long after this the crane that was used to raise the stones remained fixed, and there was a belief among the dalespeople that the canons would return and complete the building. The nave, which is without a south aisle, is Early English on that side, and Decorated on the north. At the end of the aisle on the north is a chantry founded by the Mauleverers of Beamsley, and beneath is the vault in which members of the family are said to have been buried upright—

"Pass, pass who will, yon chantry door,
And through the chink in the fractured floor,
Look down, and see a grisly sight—
A vault where the bodies are buried upright!"

The ruined portions of the structure include the piers of a central tower, north and south transepts, and a long but aisleless choir, with the remains of chapels on the south side. With the exception of the lower walls, the work here is of the Decorated period, and shows many interesting features. There are monumental fragments, and in the south transept may be seen a tomb-slab with an incised figure representing Christopher Wood, the eighteenth prior, who resigned in 1483. Scant remains of the conventual buildings may be traced to the south of the Priory ruins. To the north is the churchyard. The Priory barn remains in good condition. It is still in use, and has some fine timber work.

A short distance west is Bolton Hall, a seat of the Duke of Devonshire. This mansion makes a framework to the gatehouse of the old Priory, the entrance-chamber being formed out of the ancient gateway. The chamber is represented in Landseer's picture of "Bolton Priory in the Olden Time," now at Chatsworth. There are other matters that recall the past conditions of the place even more vividly, as in the case of a Commission sent hither so early as 1274, in which certain irregularities are set forth in these blunt words:—"The whole convent conspired against the predecessors of the present Prior, William de Danfield. Nicholas de Broe, the present sub-prior, is old and useless. Silence is not observed, and there is much chattering and noise. John de Pontefract, the present cellarer, and the sub-cellarer, are often absent from service and refections, and have their meals by themselves, when the canons have left the refectory. The house is in debt," etc. But Dr. Robert Collyer of New York, a Wharfedale worthy, who has gone into the records, tells also how "the merry old rogues" had a certain rough humour, which came out in the names they gave their humbler brethren. "One poor fellow," he says, "has stood on their books these six hundred years as Adam Blunder, a sort of primitive Handy Andy, I suppose. Another, with 'a fair round belly,' no doubt, they dub Simon Paunch. A third is Drunken Dick. A fourth, the cooper, as I guess, and a great hand to spoil his work, is Botch Bucket. The carter is laughingly baptized The Whirl, perhaps because his wheels never do whirl by any accident. One is Rado the Sad; and the blackest sheep of the flock is Tom Nowt—'nowt' in the Dales as applied to a man being still a term of the utmost contempt."

The Priory was surrendered in 1540, and the estate was given, two years afterwards, by Henry VIII. to Henry Clifford, first Earl of Cumberland. The property next passed to the Earl of Cork, and thence by descent to the Cavendish family.

The grounds over the wide stretch from Barden Tower to Bolton Bridge are open daily (except Sundays) to visitors. Their natural attractions, with their relics and associations, make them one of the most interesting of the show places of Yorkshire. There are two memorials on the estate to Lord Frederick Cavendish, Chief Secretary for Ireland, assassinated in the Phœnix Park, Dublin, May 6, 1882. One, in the churchyard, in the form of an interlaced cross, rising seventeen feet, was erected by the tenantry. The other—a hexagonal fountain, rising into pinnacles with a small lantern crown—is in the Park, and was erected by the electors of the West Riding, of which division of Yorkshire Lord Frederick was for many years a representative.

It is a pleasant walk from the Priory to the bridge, across the field on which Prince Rupert encamped on the way to Marston Moor. At Bolton Bridge we get to what is now the nearest railway-station for Upper Wharfedale, a connecting line

RUINS OF HAREWOOD CASTLE.

between Ilkley and Skipton having been opened in 1888. From the bridge the river flows past Beamsley, behind which is Beamsley Beacon (1,314 feet). In the village is a hospital founded in the time of Elizabeth, and endowed for thirteen poor widows. Beamsley Hall, near by, retains some old features, including armorial bearings of the Claphams and Morleys, its early possessors. The road here follows the Wharfe through diversified scenery, and leads to Addingham, where is a church which was originally served from Bolton. Here also on the bank of the Wharfe is Farfield Hall, a fine mansion, from whose site commanding views are obtained.

Ilkley, three miles further down the stream, is a town of great interest and attractiveness in the modern sense, with a far reaching history. As seen to-day it is almost wholly new; half a century ago it was made up of a few old cottages and its ancient church. Its value as a health resort, and its delightful situation, have since then been fully recognised, and it is now a fashionable inland watering-place with well laid-out streets, and some fine buildings. The records of the town go back to the time of the Romans, and its existing name is supposed to be a corruption of the designation given to it by the Western conquerors. The Romans had here a strong fortress, the foundations of which may be traced. Some interesting Roman relics are preserved in the neighbourhood. On the grounds at Middleton Hall, on the opposite side of the river, is an altar dedicated to the Wharfe, the river figuring in the inscription as "Verbeia." In the churchyard at Ilkley are the shafts of crosses, very rudely sculptured, and undoubtedly very ancient. The church, dedicated to All Saints, is an old foundation, and has some curious features. Its earliest monument is a cross-legged effigy of Sir Adam de Middleton, who died in 1315. The ground rises steeply to the south behind Ilkley, and at a height of 1,300 feet spreads out into a magnificent heathery expanse known as Rombald's Moor. "Rombald" is said to be a corruption of "Romilly," the first Norman lord of the manor; but there is a tradition which speaks of the moor as a promenade of a certain giant Rombald, a mighty figure that is said to have made a stride one day across the valley from Almescliffe Crag far beyond in the north-east, and to have come down with such force as to leave the impression of his foot on the larger of the two rocks above Ilkley, known as the Cow and Calf. The impression is there, of course. The story may have had its origin in the manner in which the valley at this point was absorbed in the interest of the Romillys. From the high land at the Cow and Calf, and from many other points east and west, fine views are obtained of the valley, now opening out to a grand pastoral sweep. On the slopes are several hydropathic establishments of a public and private character. Nearly all are noted for picturesque architectural treatment. This is especially the case with Ilkley Wells, where there is an observation tower, and the still earlier house in the Scotch baronial style, a mile and a half east, at Ben Rhydding, opened in 1844.

Across the river from Ben Rhydding lies Denton, the home of the Fairfaxes; and from this point onwards to the Ouse incidents and houses connected with this great family present themselves. In Denton Church many of the name lie buried. The present Denton Hall occupies the site of the old mansion in which Sir Thomas Fairfax, the Parliamentary General, was born. At Burley, on the south bank of the Wharfe, a short distance from Ben Rhydding, is the Yorkshire house of the late W. E. Forster. Here, too, at the river side, are the worsted mills of which Mr. Forster was a part owner, and in the cemetery beyond is his grave, with an inscribed slab to his memory. On the other side of the river is Weston Hall, the property of the Vavasours through a long succession. Family papers at Weston date back to Henry III., and amongst other treasures is an original portrait of Cromwell. Farther east on the same side is Farnley Hall, where are relics of the Commonwealth, including the hat worn by Cromwell at Marston Moor, and the watch and sword of the Protector. Farnley Hall used to be notable also for a unique collection of about fifty drawings by Turner, which were sold in 1890. Turner was a frequent visitor at Farnley Hall, Mr. Walter Fawkes, uncle of the present owner, being one of his earliest patrons and friends. A curious gateway on the property was brought from Menston Hall, a Fairfax seat on the south bank of the river.

It is a pleasant descent from Farnley Hall to the Wharfe, on whose south bank at this point is Otley, one of the first towns in Yorkshire to engage in the manufacture of cloth. Otley was long the site of a palace of the Archbishops of York, who were lords of the manor, and is now the headquarters of the Parliamentary division bearing its name. Several of the Fairfaxes are buried in the church. Sloping from the town to the south is the hill familiarly known as "The Chevin" (probably from the Saxon "chevn," a back or ridge). The hill rises to a height of 921 feet, and commands fine views. Near the town is Caley Hall, famous at one time for a park in which many varieties of deer, wild hogs, zebras, and other animals were kept. At Pool, just below Otley, the river expands, and flows pleasantly through the open valley to Arthington (where was once a house for Cluniac or Benedictine nuns), and onwards to the Harewood estates. Here we are still on part of the wide domain held by the ancient Romillys, who are credited with the building of the first Harewood Castle. From the Romillys the Harewood lands passed to the Fitzgeralds, the Lisles, and others, and then to the Gascoignes, from whom they went to the Lascelles (Earls of Harewood), the present possessors. The ruins of a castle built in the fourteenth century rise boldly on a pre-Norman mound near the river. The church at Harewood has some interesting details, and a number of historic monuments—one to Sir William Gascoigne (the Chief Justice who is said to have committed the heir of Henry IV. to prison) and his wife. Harewood House, built in 1760, is seen to advantage from the church. It is a porticoed building, and was erected by the first Lord Harewood, to replace Gawthorpe Hall, the seat of the Gascoignes, and the birthplace of the Chief Justice. To Gawthorpe Hall came at times the great Lord Strafford in search of repose. "With what quietness," he wrote, "could I live here in comparison with the noise and labour I meet with elsewhere; and, I protest, put up more crownes in my purse at the year's end too." In the same parish is the village of Weeton, above which, on the summit of a hill, is a peculiarly shaped rock, known as "the Great Almescliffe." From the rock a fine view is obtained of Wharfedale on the one side, and of Harrogate and the district leading into Nidderdale on the other.

From Harewood the Wharfe sweeps placidly onwards to Netherby, and to Collingham and Linton, where there is fine farming country. Then Wetherby is reached on a bend of the river, hence the old Saxon name, Wederbi, "the turn." There is a bridge here of six arches, affording a good view of the stream. Boston Spa—a secluded inland watering place—is the next village. Then comes Newton Kyme, with a fine old church, and the remains of a castle that was held by the Barons de Kyme, the last of whom died as far back as 1358. We are now again on ground over which Roman legions passed, and from which relics of the Roman occupation have been unearthed. The church, dedicated to St. Andrew, is old and interesting, with an ivy-covered embattled western tower. Close to the church is Newton Hall, an old Fairfax seat, with portraits of members of that family.

A mile and a half further down is Tadcaster, the Calcaria of the Romans, and the "Langborough" of later times. The Roman name is supposed to have been given on account of the abundance of calx or limestone in the district. Tadcaster was an important outpost of York. Through it ran the road of Agricola —still known as the Roman ridge—from London to Edinburgh, and it was also on the ancient road between York and Manchester. Near the town, at a place called St. Helen's Ford, are traces of a Roman encampment. Of more interest, however, than what Tadcaster reveals of that remote period of its history are the associations that cluster round it in connection with the civil wars. Three miles distant, near to the village of Saxton, is the site of the battle of Towton, "the bloodiest and most fatal engagement fought on English soil since Hastings." Sore fought Towton was, "for hope of life was set on every part," and each side had its awful orders neither to give nor seek quarter. A force of 100,000 men in all mustered for the struggle—40,000 Yorkists with Edward IV. and the Earl of Warwick at their head on the one side; on the other, 60,000 Lancastrians, with whom were Queen Margaret and the Duke of Somerset. About a third of this force perished on the field, the greater number being Lancastrians. The date of the battle is memorable. All the villagers round about tell to this day how it was fought on a Palm Sunday in the long ago. The conflict really began on the Saturday (March 29th, 1461), was suspended during the night, and renewed with vigour in the morning. The issue was decided about noon on the Sunday, the Duke of Norfolk, with reinforcements for Edward, giving the Yorkists an advantage at the critical moment which was at once followed up. Twenty-eight thousand Lancastrians were left dead upon the field, and vast numbers perished in the rout that took place. A field near Towton Dale Quarry, half a mile south of Towton village, and known as "the Bloody Meadow," is pointed out as the scene of the thickest of the fight; but the conflict extended over a wide area, and Towton battle-field may be said to cover the whole ground between Saxton and Towton villages. The Cock, a tributary of the Wharfe, winds round the site. In the swollen waters of this stream many of the Lancastrians perished when they broke rank and fled. On the outskirts of Grimston Park (the seat of Lord Londesborough) near by, is a field called Battle Acre, where the Lancastrians are said to have made their last stand; and here there is annually a prolific growth of white roses—

> There is a patch of wild white roses, that bloom on a battlefield,
> Where the rival rose of Lancaster blushed redder still to yield;
> Four hundred years have o'er them shed their sunshine and their snow,
> But in spite of plough and harrow, every summer there they blow.
> Though ready to uproot them with hand profane you toil,
> The faithful flowers still fondly cluster round the sacred soil;
> Though tenderly transplanted to the nearest garden gay,
> Nor rest nor care can tempt them there to live a single day.

Opposite Towton is Hazlewood Hall, the seat of an ancient Yorkshire family, the Vavasours. The hall commands an extensive view, and it is said that from it on a clear day the towers of Lincoln on the one side, and York on the other, sixty miles apart, may be seen.

From two to three miles south-east of Tadcaster is Kirkby Wharfe, where there is a church with some fine Norman remains—notably the pillars of the nave, the porch doorway, and the font. There is also a Saxon cross. The church, which is dedicated to St. John the Baptist, was restored in 1861, in memory of Albert, first Baron Londesborough. The school is at Ulleskelf, one mile to the south-east, where there is a railway station, and a Jubilee memorial in the form of a chapel-of-ease. It is a short walk from here to Bolton Percy, where also there is a station. Bolton Percy was one of the manors granted by the Conqueror to William de Percy, founder of the great house of that name. From a wood in the neighbourhood, the Percys are said to have granted timber for the building of York Minster. The existing church dates from the early part of the fifteenth century, and nearly the whole of it is of that period. It is a noble Perpendicular building, with an exceptionally fine chancel. The east window, rising full twenty-three feet, with a depth of fourteen, presents five unbroken lights. Figured on it are full-length life-size portraits of Archbishops Scrope, Bowet, Kempe, Booth, and Neville, with the armorial bearings of these worthies. Above are representations of Scriptural characters. The living, which exceeds £1,200, is

AT TADCASTER.

in the gift of the Archbishop of York, and is the richest at his disposal. At Bolton Percy the Fairfaxes were a power in their time. Ferdinando, Lord Fairfax, has an elaborate monument in Bolton Percy Church. To make room for it, one of the chancel piers had to be cut away. The son of Ferdinando—"Black Tom,"

KIRKBY WHARFE.

the General-in-Chief of the Parliamentary forces—died at Nun Appleton Hall, on the south bank of the Wharfe, below Bolton Percy, and is buried at Bilbrough, in the same neighbourhood. Nun Appleton passed by purchase, on the death of the daughter of Thomas Lord Fairfax, to Alderman Milner, of Leeds, whose descendant (Sir Frederick Milner, Bart.) is the present owner. From Nun Appleton the Wharfe passes onward to Ryther (where is a church that was founded in 1100), and just below Ryther it falls into the Ouse.

W. S. Cameron.

THE OUSE AT YORK.

THE HUMBER AND ITS TRIBUTARIES.

CHAPTER VII.

THE OUSE.

The Ure and the Swale—Myton and the "White Battle"—Nun Monkton, Overton, and Skelton—The Nidd—York—Bishopsthorpe—Selby—The Derwent—The Aire—Howden—Goole—The Don.

THE Yorkshire Ouse (from the Celtic "uisg" or water) has one decided peculiarity among important British rivers: it has no natural beginning, and it loses its identity before its waters touch the sea. It is remarkable, further, for the number of other rivers that drain into it. Within the immense water-shed of Yorkshire, it absorbs in its course the Ure, the Swale, the Nidd, the Foss, the Wharfe, the Derwent, the Aire, and the Don. Looked at in connection with these streams and their tributaries, this chief Yorkshire river receives its supplies from over a considerable part of the North of England. Although covering a distance of about fifty miles, it keeps well within its own county, is almost wholly confined, in fact, to the great plain of York. Its value as a waterway was recognised from the dawn of our history. Up its waters rich argosies and primitive war craft have come, and its ramifications east, west, and north proved a convenient channel along which to carry weal or woe into the ancient Northumbria. It traverses beautiful and fertile land, and all its tributaries come to it over picturesque and classic ground. It springs into existence with a full flow of water in the neighbourhood of Aldborough, at the confluence of two of the prettiest rivers in the country, the Ure and the Swale. From this point in the plain of York the Ouse passes smoothly through rich agricultural lands, alongside quaint villages, and through the heart of the capital of the North, and so onwards until it in turn is absorbed in a greater waterway.

The Ure (from the Celtic "ur" or "brisk") rises on the mountainous boundary line of Yorkshire and Westmorland, and runs over a course of about fifty miles, passing through Wensleydale, and skirting Ripon on its way into the plain of York. In Wensleydale the progress of the Ure is broken by several fine waterfalls, notably the cataracts at Aysgarth. Close to Aysgarth the river passes Bolton Castle, a magnificent keep, well preserved as regards the external walls. This castle, the stronghold of the ancient Scropes, dates from the fourteenth century. It was one of the prisons of Mary Stuart on her way south to Fotheringay. A short distance further down the valley are the ruins of Middleham Castle, where Warwick the King-maker kept house and hall, and where Richard III., his son-in-law, spent the happiest part of his life. Near to Middleham the Ure receives the Cover, a stream on whose banks are the remains of Coverham Abbey, a house of White Canons. Coverdale is noted also as being the birthplace of the divine of that name to whom we owe an early translation of the Bible. Exceedingly pretty, if scant, monastic ruins are passed by the Ure at Jervaulx, just before Wensleydale comes to an end. The river then flows on through tolerably open ground towards Masham and Tanfield into the Marmion country, and onwards to Ripon, whose Minster dates from the twelfth century, and is the outcome of a much earlier foundation. Near by, on the Skell, a tributary of the Ure, is Fountains Abbey, a majestic and picturesque ruin, whose grounds form part of Studley Royal, the estate of the Marquis of Ripon. As the Ure nears its point of junction with the Swale it passes two towns of great historic and antiquarian interest, lying within touch of each other, namely, Boroughbridge and Aldborough. Boroughbridge is the site of the battle fought in 1322, at which was killed the Earl of Hereford, who, with the Earl of Lancaster, had risen against Edward II. Lancaster was taken prisoner, and conveyed to his own castle at Pontefract, where he was beheaded. Three rude blocks of granite, known as the "Devil's Arrows," form one of the sights of Boroughbridge. They vary in height from sixteen and a half to twenty-two and a half feet above the ground. There were four blocks in Leland's time. One theory is that these monoliths marked the limits of a Roman stadium or racecourse; but they may have had an earlier significance. Aldborough, the ancient Isurium, was, apart from York, the most important Roman station in the county. Here two Roman roads met—one from York and Tadcaster to Catterick, and the other, the famous Watling Street, running north from Ilkley. There was a strongly walled camp at Aldborough, and it is said that the present church occupies a position in the centre of the ancient possession, and is partly built of material from the Roman town.

The Swale (probably from "swale," the Teutonic "gentle") rises amidst bleak surroundings on the hills beyond Kirkby Stephen, but soon reaches the picturesque valley to which it gives its name. It takes in Richmondshire in its course, the wide district from which the Saxon Edwin was expelled to make room for the Norman Alan. The Earl Alan built the oldest part of the castle at Richmond. The massive keep was erected later on (about 1146) by Earl Conan. A mile below Richmond are the ruins of Easby Abbey, the ancient granary of which is still used. The river, on passing out of Swaledale, goes onward to Catterick (where the Romans had a walled camp), Topcliffe, and Brefferton. The church at Brefferton is on the brink of the river and is said to mark the spot where Paulinus baptised his converts in the Swale. There is an opinion also that the rite was administered at Catterick; but Bretherick, to judge by ancient place names derived from Paulinus, seems the likelier spot. A little below Bretherton the Swale unites with the Ure, the distance traversed from its source to this point being about sixty miles.

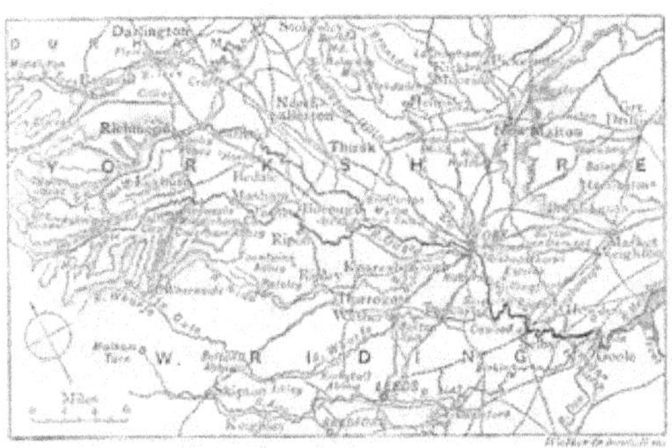

THE COURSE OF THE OUSE.

Close to where the Ouse takes form at the junction of these two rivers is Myton, the scene of a conflict sometimes spoken of as the Battle of Myton, but better known in Yorkshire as the "White Battle," and the "Chapter of Myton." The battle was fought on October 12, 1319. In the autumn of that year Edward II. had equipped an army and gone northward to lay siege to Berwick. While the King was thus engaged a strong detachment of Scots under Randolph and Douglas came into England by the west, and marched close up to the walls of York. They destroyed the suburbs, but failed to effect an entrance into the city. The inhabitants of York were not in a position to do more than protect themselves behind their barriers, all their fighting men being with the King. The Scots had, however, done and said things at the walls that were hard to bear, and on this account an aggressive movement was made from the city. Soon after the troops of Randolph and Douglas had started on their return journey they were surprised to find a motley army of some 10,000 on their rear, made up of clergy, apprentices, and old men, prepared to give battle. Though a valiant venture, it was a wild one. This strange force from York possessed but few weapons, and was without adequate leadership, while the Scots were largely men trained to warfare, well equipped, and skilfully led. The battle was soon over. The Scots turned upon their pursuers and effectually routed them. Great numbers of the English were killed, including the Mayor of York. Many others were drowned in the Swale. The

BISHOPTHORPE.

name "White Battle" is accounted for by the large number of priests and clerks who took part in the engagement.

From the junction of the two rivers out of which the Ouse is formed onwards to York is a distance of about fifteen miles. About midway over this stretch the stream passes three villages lying near together—Nun Monkton, Overton, and Skelton—each of which has an interesting church. The Skelton Church is Early English throughout, and is dedicated to All Saints, but is popularly known as St. Peter's, from a tradition that it has a claim to be considered part of the Metropolitan Church, it being a common belief that it was built from stones left over after the completion of the south transept of York Minster. The church at Overton shows Transition Norman features, and is close to the site of a Roman settlement, and in the neighbourhood also of a Priory of Gilbertine Canons founded in the reign of John. Nun Monkton has mention in Domesday, and is supposed to be the site of a Saxon monastery. Here, too, in the reign of Stephen, there was a Priory (Benedictine); and the church, Early English, was the chapel of the nuns. At Nun Monkton, the Nidd, after a rapid course from Great Whernside, joins the Ouse. The upper section of Nidderdale is wild and secluded. From Pateley Bridge the tributary water passes Dacre Banks, above which are the curiously shaped boulders known as Brimham Rocks. Further down, Knaresborough, with its castle dating back to Henry I., and its memories of Eugene Aram and Mother Shipton, rises grandly over the river.

Both the Ouse and the Nidd skirt the grounds of Beningborough, where the Abbot of St. Mary's, York, had a choice park. At Red Hall on the Ouse, a mile and a half below Nun Monkton, Charles I. slept on his way from Scotland in 1633. The building was a seat of the Slingsbys, who were active Royalists. Sir Henry Slingsby, the entertainer of the King, suffered on Tower Hill in 1658.

The minster towers of York are seen to advantage from the plain as the Ouse approaches the ancient city. It is said of York that it was founded a thousand years before Christ, by one Evrog, son of Membyr—hence the ancient British name of the place, Caer Evrog, or Evrog's City. This belongs to Celtic mythology, but it is pretty certain that the Roman Eboracum is a variation of the name possessed by York when the Western conquerors settled here. York in the Roman era was "the seat of the Prefect, with the official staff and the ministers of his luxury, when London was still a mere resort of traders." Here Severus died, and his memory remains perpetuated in Severus Hill. Here Constantine Chlorus also died, and although it is doubtful whether his son, Constantine the Great, was "a born Englishman," and a native of York, as some have asserted, he was certainly proclaimed Emperor in this famous city. Here, too, Paulinus preached, and Edwin of Northumbria was baptised. Our own early Sovereigns held their Courts and Parliaments at York, and for many centuries it was a place of great military, ecclesiastical, and political importance. The Minster—one of the most impressive of all our cathedrals, with a superb west front, which is but one of many glorious features—has in its foundations traces of the Early Saxon Cathedral and Norman work. The superstructure is Early English and Perpendicular. From the platform on the top of the central tower (216 feet) magnificent views are obtained on every side. The ruins of St. Mary's Abbey, near to the river, are very fine, and are carefully preserved. This was a mitred Benedictine house, and was one of the earliest monastic establishments founded in the North after the Conquest. The castle ruins, also seen from the river, occupy the site of a structure raised by the Conqueror. The walls of York, with the ancient gateways or bars, remain one of the features of the city. On the inner side of the embattlements is a promenade, much used. The circumvallation is practically complete. It does not now, of course, embrace the whole city, but it has within its limits the historic York. So well do these old walls become the city, that to this day it is with a shock the fact is recalled that just before the Queen came to the throne the civic authorities actually petitioned Parliament for powers to demolish the ancient environment with its barbicans and posterns. The successors of the men who advocated such an act of vandalism have, however, atoned for the shameless proposal. They have put the walls into thorough repair, and in June, 1889, the Mayor and Corporation took part in the completion of the restoration by throwing open the remaining stretch of the walls running from Monk Bar to Bootham Bar.

The Foss enters York on the south, and passes into the Ouse on the east bank. It has a run of about sixteen miles from the Howardian Hills, and flows near Sheriff Hutton Castle, a seat of the Nevilles, originally built in 1140, by Bertram de Bulmer, Sheriff of Yorkshire. At Fulford, just below York, the Ouse skirts the scene of the defeat of the Earls Edwin and Morcar, by Hardrada (1066). A little farther down, on the west side, is Bishopthorpe, where the Archbishops have their palace. A palace was built here in the thirteenth century by Archbishop de Gray, and presented to the see. Of the original building there are but few remains. It was at Bishopthorpe that Archbishop Scrope and the Earl Marshal were condemned in the presence of the King (Henry IV.) for treason. The sentence was carried out in a field on the way to York. Old boatmen tell that it was common at one time to fire a salute of three guns from the river on passing the Archbishop's palace, and to be rewarded with a supply of the palace ale. At Naburn, on the east bank, a mile and a half below, is a lock (opened in 1888 by the late Prince Albert Victor) constructed for vessels of 400 tons. Three miles further down is Stillingfleet, and here the river is in the neighbourhood of Escrick Park, the seat of Lord Wenlock. Escrick Hall is Elizabethan, with fine pictures and statuary. Skipwith Common, with its tumuli and ancient turf dwellings, is also in this neighbourhood. East of Skipwith, and near the river, is Riccall. At this point on the Ouse was moored the fleet of Harold Hardrada while his troops advanced to York. A short distance above Riccall, on the west bank, the Wharfe enters the Ouse, and on the same side, half a mile below the point of junction is Cawood, where the Archbishops of York were established in residence from before the Conquest. Wolsey thought much of Cawood, and it was from his palace here that he was taken a prisoner, when he had perforce to bid farewell to all his greatness. There are some remains of the ancient buildings. The gatehouse stands, and in a room over the entrance the Court-leet of the Archbishops is still held.

Selby, further down the stream on the same side, is a thriving market town. It has the advantage not only of the navigable waters of the Ouse, but of canal communication with the Aire. Its Abbey church has many noteworthy features, not the least of which is its length (296 feet). The building has a double dedication—to SS. Mary and Germanus. The foundation is traced to Benedict, a French monk. That monk, while in the Convent at Auxerre, was, according to the legend, commissioned in a vision by Germanus to go to England, and find there a similar spot to one revealed in the vision, and there he was to halt, set up the Cross and preach. Benedict is said to have been so impressed by the mandate that he started at once, and continued his travels until, sailing up the Ouse, he found on the curve of the river at Selby a district corresponding exactly

CAWOOD.

to what had been revealed to him in the vision. Here he set up a Cross, and constructed a hut for himself by the riverside. The year 1068 has been assigned as the date of this undertaking. There was then, says the old chronicle, "not a single monk to be found throughout all Yorkshire, owing to the devastations of the Northmen by the Conqueror." Benedict found favour in the eyes of the Norman Sheriff, and acting on the suggestion of this functionary, he waited on the King, and succeeded in obtaining a grant of that portion of the manor on which he had settled. A monastery of wood was then erected, and Benedict became first abbot. He held the position for twenty-seven years, when he died. The second abbot was a member of the De Lacy family, and was wealthy enough to begin a permanent building of stone, portions of which may be traced in the existing fabric, which from the time of James I. (1618) has been the parochial church of Selby. Pope Alexander II. made Selby a mitred Abbey, the only other English establishment north of the Trent enjoying this distinction being St. Mary's at York.

SELBY

Selby was a place of strategic importance in the wars of the Commonwealth. It changed hands two or three times, but was eventually secured for the Parliament by the Fairfaxes, after a battle in which Lord Bellasis, the Governor of York, and 1,600 men were made prisoners, with much baggage and a useful supply of guns and horses. The victory at Selby, to quote Markham, was "the immediate cause of the battle of Marston Moor, and the destruction of the Royalist power in the North; and the two Houses marked their sense of its importance by ordering a public thanksgiving for the same." There is a tradition that Selby was the birthplace of Henry I., the youngest son of the Conqueror, and Freeman suggests that "William may have brought his wife into Northumbria, as Edward brought his wife into Wales, in order that the expected Atheling might be not only an Englishman born, but a native of that part of England which had cost his father most pains to win."

Some three miles below Selby is Hemingborough, where there is a fine church with a lofty spire (180 ft.), and between here and Barmby-on-the-Marsh, the Derwent, after a long, winding course from the high moorland south of Whitby, unites with the Ouse. The Derwent passes Malton, the Roman Derventio, the site of which is still traceable. Here there is an interesting Gilbertine Priory. The river also passes Kirkham, where there are remains, notably an exquisite Early English gateway, of an Augustinian Priory; and on its northern bank at this point is Castle Howard, the Yorkshire seat of the Earl of Carlisle. Many smaller rivers are absorbed by the Derwent, particularly the Rye, on whose banks are the ruins of Rievaulx, the earliest of the Yorkshire Cistercian houses; the Costa, which runs past Pickering Castle, where Richard II. was held a prisoner just before his tragic death at Pontefract; and the Bran, which runs close to the celebrated Kirkdale Cave.

Two miles further down, on the west side, the Ouse receives another important feeder in the Aire. Turbid enough is the Aire at this point, after its contact with Leeds and other West Riding manufacturing towns; but no river has a more romantic beginning. Rising mysteriously from its underground source at the foot of Malham Cove, "by giants scooped from out the rocky ground," it flows onward through a scene of surpassing grandeur; and very beautiful still is its course through Airedale proper, from beyond Skipton on to Kirkstall Abbey. The Aire is joined at Leeds by the Liverpool Canal; at Castleford by the Calder; and at Birkin by the Selby Canal; and after a run of about seventy miles it passes into the Ouse at Arnim, opposite the village of Booth.

Howden lies a short distance to the north-east of Booth. It possesses a fine old church, dedicated to St. Peter, and is the site of a famous horse fair. Howden boasts also of several celebrities, beginning with Roger de Hoveden, the chronicler, and coming down to the stable boy who became Baron Ward, and was Minister to the Duke of Parma. The church at Howden was handed over by the Conqueror to the Prior and Convent of Durham, and was made collegiate in 1267. The choir and chapter-house are in a ruinous state, and of the former, which was erected in place of an earlier structure about 1300, only the aisle walls and the eastern front remain. The chapter-house, even in decay, is an exceptionally fine example of Early Perpendicular work, with elaborate tracing and arcading. An archæological authority (Hutchinson) writes enthusiastically of "its exquisite and exact proportions," and speaks of it as the most perfect example of its kind in the country. After the dissolution of the collegiate establishment the church at Howden began to be neglected. It suffered much more from natural wear and tear than from vandalism, and much of it was easily restored. The portions in use include the nave, the transept, with eastern chantries, and a central tower. Over a graceful west front rises a central gable, finely crocketed, and flanked with hexagonal turrets. A head carved over the south porch, supposed to be that of Edward II., but also claimed for Henry III., gives some indication of the date of the erection of this part of the building. The tower, lighted by tall and handsome windows, rises 130 feet, and from its summit a commanding view is obtained. Its chambers are of unusual size, and are said to have been constructed to serve as a place of refuge to the inhabitants of the neighbourhood in the event of inundation, the country here having been originally marsh land and subject to floods. The Bishops of Durham took a lively interest in their collegiate church at Howden. Here they had a palace, and here several of them died.

From the point where it receives the Aire, the Ouse flows eastwards and southwards, and at the end of the bend thus formed touches Goole—a place which was a quiet village some seventy years ago, but is now a busy commercial centre, and, moreover, a town which, although well inland, lays claim to the position of a seaport. Goole has the advantage of the Don as well as of the Ouse. The former stream comes into it along a straight, artificial channel, known locally as the Dutch river, after its constructor, Vermuyden the engineer. The Don rises in Cheshire, and has branches running out of Derbyshire. It passes Doncaster, Sheffield, Rotherham, and other towns, on its way to the Ouse, and is the last of the streams to fall into the great Yorkshire waterway; the Ouse, after a short run eastward from Goole, uniting with the Trent to form the Humber.

W. S. Cameron.

BARTON-UPON-HUMBER.

THE HUMBER AND ITS TRIBUTARIES.

CHAPTER VIII.

THE ESTUARY.

Drainage and Navigation—Dimensions of the Humber—The Ferribys—Barton-upon-Humber—Hull—Paull—Sunk Island—Spurn Point—Great Grimsby—Places of Call.

GLANCE at that part of the map where Yorkshire is separated from Lincolnshire reveals the full extent of the Humber, but while it shows a wide estuary, it conveys a poor idea of the national importance of this arm of the sea. Nor is the value of the estuary in this respect much increased by the mere statement that the Humber is formed by the confluence of the Trent and the Ouse. These two rivers have to be considered in connection with their tributary streams before a fair idea is formed, not only of what the Humber is as a channel of trade, but of the wide extent of the water-shed of which it is the basin. The Ouse brings to the Humber nearly all the running water of Yorkshire, the collection having been made over an area exceeding 4,000 square miles; while the supplies from the Trent, though less in quantity because of the lower altitudes of their origin, drain about 4,500 square miles. This makes the Humber the largest river-basin in England, the Severn coming next with a total drainage of 8,580 square miles, as compared with 9,770 in the case of the Humber, made up as follows: Ouse, 4,100; Trent, 4,500; Humber proper, 1,170.

So far as navigation is concerned, the Humber is an open way, by means of river and connecting artificial links, with the Mersey, the Thames, and the Severn, and practically, therefore, its waters are in touch with the whole country. The Humber figures also in all our histories. From the earliest period the invader found passage along it to Mercia, on the one hand, and to Northumbria on the other; and along the valleys through which its tributaries run it is not a difficult task to trace, in place-names and surnames, the settlements that took place in this part of England in the long ago as a result of the encroachments of Angle, Dane, and Norse. From the date of the withdrawal of the Romans it was always to the Humber that the Vikings steered their course, and hither they kept coming until the Norman conquest was complete, and England out of many elements became compact and strong.

THE COURSE OF THE HUMBER.

At the confluence of the Ouse and Trent the Humber has a width of about a mile. From here to Paull, on the north bank—a point south-east of Hull—the width varies from a mile-and-a-quarter to two miles. From Paull south-east to Grimsby the width gradually increases to about four miles, and where the bank on the Yorkshire side curves inward like a sickle the width exceeds seven miles. Spurn Head, forming the point of the sickle, lies almost direct east from Grimsby, and here, at the mouth of the Humber, the width is about five miles. From the head of the estuary to Paull—a tolerably straight line east—the distance is 18½ miles. From Paull to Spurn the stretch is about a mile less than this, thus giving 36 miles as the full length of the Humber.

The towns on each side have from a remote period had ferry communication with each other. It is said that the Romans crossed from the Lincolnshire coast in the neighbourhood of Whitton to Brough on the north bank, and the latter town is spoken of as the Petuaria of Ptolemy. Just below Whitton, on the Lincolnshire side, is Winteringham, close to a Roman station on the route from Lincoln to York. It was to Winteringham Ethelreda came in that flight across the Humber from Egfrid, king of Northumbria. West Halton—anciently Alfham—where she obtained succour, is close by, and the church of this village still bears her name. The next place of interest on the Lincolnshire side of the Humber is South Ferriby, where there is a curious old church—at one time a much larger structure—

dedicated to St. Nicholas, of whom there is an effigy over the porch. Immediately opposite, on the Yorkshire side of the Humber, is North Ferriby. Hessle, which lies some three miles further east on the north bank, is noted for its flint deposits; hence its name (from the German *kiesel*). Barton, the Lincolnshire town opposite Hessle, is a place of great antiquity. This is obvious from the tower of the old church, St. Peter's. Usually the Norman evidences in an ecclesiastical building are in the basement, but in the case of this tower they form the superstructure. The lower part is Saxon. It is short and massive, rising seventy feet, and is in three stages. There are some curious features in the church, and amongst the monumental work are effigies of the time of Edward II. St. Mary's Church, close by, is also interesting. It was originally a chapel-of-ease to St. Peter's, and is Norman and Early English. Barton figures in Domesday as Brereton. It was held by the De Gants through Gilbert, son of Baldwin de Gant, a nephew of the Conqueror, who took part in the Norman invasion, and had the land here made over to him. The town carries on a brisk trade, and is noteworthy historically for the fact that it furnished eight vessels fully manned to assist Edward III. in the invasion of Brittany.

Hull boasts not only of being the chief port on the Humber, but claims to be the third port in the kingdom, giving precedence only to London and Liverpool. There was a time when it was a mere hamlet; but it has not only outgrown the towns near it that once did a greater business—such as Hedon and Beverley—but has seen what was a much larger commercial centre than either of these places literally pass from the map. What anciently was the chief port on the Humber lay, snugly enough to all seeming, just within the bend at Spurn Head. It was known as Ravenser. It had much shipping, and in the time of Edward I. sent members to Parliament. Henry IV. landed here in 1399. Unfortunately Ravenser, with neighbouring towns, was built on unstable ground. A process of denudation is continually going on at this the extreme point of Yorkshire, and from this cause the sea had left only a fragment of Ravenser in Bolingbroke's day. In no long time after this the town was wholly absorbed by the encroaching waters. Hull began to flourish as Ravenser began to decay. Another circumstance that led to the development of this great Humber port was the difficulty the Beverley merchants had in getting their supplies by river. Hull was originally one of many wykes (the Norse name for a small creek or bay). It got the name of the river (the Hull) on which it stands in the time of Richard I., and by this name it is known everywhere, its corporate title of Kingston-upon-Hull seldom being given to it in print, and still more seldom being applied to it in speech. The royal title was conferred by Edward I., who is said to have noticed the value of the site for commercial purposes while hunting here in 1256.

The parish church (Holy Trinity) is a magnificent Decorated and Perpendicular structure, cruciform in plan, with a tower rising to a height of 150 feet. It is one of the largest parish churches in England, its length from east to west being

272 feet, and its width 96 feet; and it is claimed for it that in its chancel and transepts it possesses the earliest examples of brick masonry since the Roman epoch. Holy Trinity was founded in 1285. St. Mary, in Lowgate, also a cruciform structure, with central tower, dates from the early part of the fourteenth century. The Dock Office is a fine structure of the Venetian type; the Trinity House is Tuscan; the Town Hall is Italian; and the High Street shows a picturesque blending of Domestic styles, dating from the thirteenth or fourteenth century onwards to work of the present time. In the Market Place is a statue to William III., "our great deliverer," as he was called here. The statue has the peculiarity of being gilt, probably as a further tribute from the Hull burgesses to the worth of the Prince of Orange. In the Town Hall are statues of Edward I., the founder of the town; of Sir Michael de la Pole, the first Mayor of the borough (1376); of Andrew Marvell, poet, wit, and statesman, a native of the place. A statue of another noted statesman, also a native of Hull, William Wilberforce, the anti-slavery advocate, surmounts a Doric pillar (72 feet) close to the old Docks. The river Hull, which rises in the wolds, and has a course of about thirty miles, flows through the older parts of the town. It is the passage way to several of the Docks, and is itself thronged with shipping on each side, and bordered by warehouses.

Paull, or Paghill (anciently Pagula), is about five miles south-east from Hull, and is noteworthy as the spot near which Charles I. in 1642 reviewed his forces. The shore continues in a sharp south-east dip from here to what is known as Sunk Island—a double name, which is now a misnomer, the land being well exposed and no longer an island. It is the peculiarity of this Yorkshire peninsula that while it continually suffers from denudation, it is also being recompensed by the same agency. Sunk Island has been reclaimed from the Humber, and is an interesting example on a small scale of land nationalisation. The soil is exceedingly fertile, and is let out by the Crown, to whom the cottages and other buildings on the estate belong. About 7,000 acres are at present under cultivation, and there is every prospect that the area will go on increasing. From the end of Sunk Island to Spurn Point the Humber takes a wide bay-like sweep inward and southward, the peninsula narrowing considerably as Spurn Point is reached. The Spurn Point of six centuries ago, with the lost town of Ravenspur, lay a little to the west of the present promontory, which has been almost wholly built up afresh by natural causes since that time. There are two lighthouse towers on the Point, the larger of the two being Smeaton's work.

It is almost a direct line west across the Humber mouth from Spurn to Grimsby—Great Grimsby as it is called, to distinguish it from the smaller Grimsby, near Louth, in the same county. Here on the Lincolnshire coast the country, viewed from the sea, is flat and Dutch-like, but close at hand it is decidedly English in its bustle and trade and signs of manufacturing progress. There is fine anchorage eastward, to which Spurn Point forms a natural breakwater.

Dock extension has done much for Grimsby as for Hull. Considerable trade is carried on here with the Continent, and immense quantities of fish are consigned direct from the North Sea through Grimsby to our leading markets. Some fine buildings surround the harbour. The principal street runs north and south, and is of great length, leading in a straight line to Cleethorpes, a neighbouring watering place. A Danish origin is assigned to Grimsby. Tradition speaks of it as Grim's town. Grim, we are told, was a fisherman who rescued a Danish infant from a boat adrift at sea. This infant was appropriately christened Havloch, or sea waif. He was adopted by Grim, grew up a fine boy, and was afterwards found to be a son of a Danish King. What followed may be readily surmised. Havloch was restored to his own country, and when he came to his own he did not forget his foster-father, on whom he bestowed riches, rights, and privileges, enabling him to become the founder of what is now called Grimsby. The tradition is perpetuated in the ancient common seal of the borough, which in Saxon lettering has the names Gryme and Habloc, and a design typifying the foundation of the town. British and Saxon remains in the neighbourhood show, however, that there were builders here before the somewhat mythical Grim.

While the vessels sailing from the Humber do business with every country, they have almost a monopoly of the North Sea trade. And as in the ancient era, so at the present time, this open channel into the heart of England continues to receive at its ports great numbers of Northern and Germanic peoples. The invasions of to-day are, however, chiefly of a temporary character. Hull and Grimsby are places of call for the emigrants from the Continent, who land here to find their way to Liverpool by rail, and from thence to the New World on the Atlantic Liners, or who re-ship into other vessels in the Humber and take the Channel route to New York.

W. S. CAMERON.

DISTANT VIEW OF GREAT GRIMSBY.

A BIT OF FEN.

THE RIVERS OF THE WASH.

THE WITHAM: Grantham—Lincoln—Boston. THE NEN: Naseby—Northampton—Earls Barton—Castle Ashby—Wellingborough—Higham Ferrers—Thrapston—Oundle—Castor—Peterborough. THE WELLAND: Market Harborough—Rockingham—Stamford. THE OUSE: Bedford—St. Neots—Huntingdon—St. Ives. THE CAM: Cambridge—"Five Miles from Anywhere"—Ely. FENS AND FENLAND TOWNS: Wisbeach—Spalding—King's Lynn—Crowland.

ON THE FENS IN WINTER.

IF ever a river could be reproached with not knowing its own mind it would be the WITHAM. Rising in the extreme south of Lincolnshire, it wanders northward along the western side of the county, and at one place seems almost minded to fall into the Trent, from which it is separated only by a belt of land slightly higher than the bed of either river. So slight, indeed, is the division between the present valleys of the Witham and the Trent that it has been urged by a very competent authority that the great gap traversed by the former river at Lincoln really represents the ancient channel of the Trent, which has only adopted the present course towards the Humber at a very late epoch in its geological history.* But the Witham at last, after submitting for a time to the influence of a limestone plateau, which rises to a considerable height on its eastern bank, suddenly alters its course, though low and level ground still continues along the same line, and cuts its way through the upland, which is severed by a fairly wide and rather deep-sided valley. Thus it gains access to the broad lowland tract between these hills and the wolds, which is here in immediate communication with the fenland, and along this it pursues a south-easterly course until it reaches the Wash.

* A. J. Jukes-Browne, "Quarterly Journal of the Geological Society." Vol. XXXIX., p. 606.

The streams which presently unite to form the Witham traverse more than ordinarily pretty pastoral scenery—a region now shelving, now almost hilly, of meadow and pasture, cornfield and copse, where is many a mansion pleasantly situated in its wooded park, and many a comely village clustered round a church, which is often both interesting and beautiful—till we arrive at Grantham, once a quiet market town, now rapidly developing into a very important manufacturing centre. The situation of the town on gently undulating ground sloping down to the Witham is rather pretty, though its rapid increase during the last quarter of a century has not made it more acceptable to the artist. The steeple of its church is beautiful, even for a county unusually rich in fine churches. Tower and spire are almost the same height, together giving to the capstone an elevation of 273 feet. The lower part is in the Early English style, the remainder and the body of the church, which is not unworthy of the steeple, belong to the Decorated and the Perpendicular styles, but a considerable part of the spire was rebuilt, without, however, any change being made in the design, in the year 1661. The Angel Hotel is "one of the three mediæval inns remaining in England," and within its walls Richard III. signed the death-warrant of the Duke of Buckingham. Grantham once had a castle, but this has disappeared, and so has a Queen Eleanor Cross, but some traces of its religious houses yet remain.

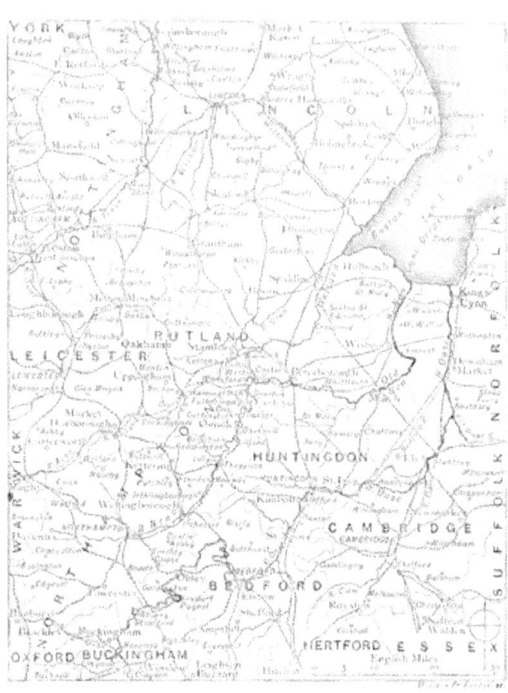

MAP OF THE RIVERS OF THE WASH.

Quietly and lazily, after leaving Grantham, the Witham works its way along a broader valley, cut down into the blue clays of the lias formation, and bounded on its eastern side by the low upland plateau formed by the harder limestone beds of the lower part of the oolite, which farther to the south are noted for their stone quarries. Little, however, calls for special notice till a triple group of towers looms up against the sky, and tells of our approach to the turning point in the river course, where for many a century the cathedral and the fortress of Lincoln have kept watch and ward over the gap in the hills, through which, as already stated, the Witham finds an outlet towards the fenland and the sea.

Durham Cathedral only, of all those in England, excels that of Lincoln in the beauty of its situation, for even Ely on its island hill, overlooking the wide Cambridgeshire fens, must be content to take a lower place. Like Durham, Lincoln occupies a site which seems to be indicated by Nature for a place of defence and offence in war, for a centre of commerce and industry in peace. Thus full eighteen centuries since it was crowned by a fortified camp, and eight centuries since it was chosen as the more fitting site of the bishop's stool, in a diocese which at that time was the largest in England. Told as briefly as possible and to the barest outline, this is the history of Lincoln. On the south-western angle of the limestone plateau, guarded on the one side by the steep slope which falls down to a level plain—that which prolongs in a northerly direction the valley of the Witham—on the other by the yet steeper slope which descends to the marshes fringing its actual course through the upland, the Romans established a great fortified camp. Of this, portions of the defences both in earth and masonry remain to the present day. It has been argued with probability that in the name, given by these invaders, *Lindum Colonia*, from which the present one has descended, there is evidence that the site was already in British occupation, the first word being compounded from *Llyn* a pool, and *dun* a hill fortress; thus signifying the hill by the pool in the marshy expanse of the Witham. Fragments of wall and a gate, the basements of pillars, probably belonging to a great basilica, a sewer, a tesselated pavement, and sundry other relics, remain to this day as memorials of the Roman occupation. From Lincoln also radiate the lines of five main roads, constructed, where they cross the marshes, on solid causeways. Of these the most important are the Fossway and the Ermine Street, which unite just south of Lincoln, then scale the steep slope below the ancient south gate, along the line of the present High Street, and pass out northward beneath the ancient archway, which still, such is the irony of time, retains its ancient name of Newport.

After the Romans departed, the history of Lincoln for a time is a blank. Doubtless the English invaders plundered, and burnt, and slaughtered, as was their wont, but we hear little more till after the missionaries of Augustine had begun to preach the Gospel to the heathen conquerors of the land. In Lincoln there is a little modern church, a short distance south of the Newport arch, and very near the remnants of the Roman basilica. This marks the site of the

LINCOLN, FROM CANWICK.

first Christian church in Lincoln, the first sign of its second and peaceful conquest by the followers of the Crucified. It was founded by Paulinus, Bishop of York, and his newly-made convert Blecca, the Governor of Lincoln. Within its walls, as Canon Venables tells us, Honorius, fourth Archbishop of Canterbury after Augustine, was consecrated by Paulinus. Doubtless the church of Paulinus—now St. Paul's—like that of St. Martin at Canterbury, was constructed of Roman materials—perhaps was a restoration of an earlier building, but of this unhappily no trace remains. The Danish invaders sorely harried Lincoln and all the region round. Indeed, in 876 the invaders parcelled out the county among themselves. "Lindsey became largely a Danish land, and Lincoln became pre-eminently a Danish city." Then for a time followed more peaceful days, till William the Norman became master of England. His eye was attracted by the natural advantages of Lincoln, so on the highest point of the plateau, at the south-western angle of the Roman *castrum*, he built a strong castle, remnants of which can still be discerned in the existing walls of that building. To secure space for its outworks he cleared away 166 houses, and in connection with this we have the first distinct notice of the lower town, which at the present day, commercially speaking, is the most important part of Lincoln. It is, however, probable that a suburb had already sprung up at the spot where the Roman road crossed the nearest channel of the Witham—obtaining from its situation the name of Wickerford or Wigford—to which the families dislodged from the upper town no doubt transferred themselves. For them—on land granted by the Conqueror—one Colswegen built some houses, and at the same time founded the churches of St. Mary-le-Wigford and St. Peter-at-Gowts. The towers, and in case of the latter some other portions, of both these churches still remain, and though built somewhere between the years 1068 and 1086 are so completely survivals of the rude style which prevailed in England before the Normans came that they are often quoted as examples of "Saxon" churches.

About the same time Remigius, a Norman monk, was consecrated to the See of Lincoln. At that time Dorchester, in Oxfordshire, was the site of the bishop's stool, but then, as now, it was a place of little importance, and inconveniently situated for the management of so vast a diocese; so he commenced the building of a cathedral at Lincoln, of which a part of the western front still remains incorporated into the grand façade of the present cathedral. The severe simplicity of this early Norman fabric was relieved by the more ornate work of a later bishop in the middle part of the twelfth century, which may still be seen in the entrance doors of the western façade and the lower parts of the two western towers. Then by degrees the remainder of the fabric was rebuilt. Most of the work from the eastern transept to the western façade dates from between the end of the twelfth and the middle of the thirteenth century, commencing with that of Bishop Hugh, afterwards St. Hugh, and ending with that of the illustrious Englishman Robert Grostête, who may be numbered with the "Reformers before the Reformation." To receive the relics of the former the famous Angel choir, or Presbytery, was built about the year 1280. The cloisters and upper part of the central tower were added some twenty years later, and certain alterations subsequently made, the most important being the upper stages of the western towers, which are assigned to the middle of the fifteenth century. Thus, while Lincoln Cathedral presents us

LINCOLN CATHEDRAL, FROM THE SOUTH-WEST.

with examples of English architecture from the very earliest Norman to the close of the so-called Gothic, and even, in its rebuilt northern cloister, of the classic Renaissance, it is in the main a specimen of the First Pointed or Early English style, from its beginning till it merged almost insensibly in the Middle Pointed or Decorated. Over its details and its history, its damage from earthquake and spoiler, the labours of St. Hugh of Avalon, and the tragedy of the little St. Hugh of Lincoln, its sieges and its narrow escape from destruction in the days of Cromwell, it is impossible to linger. Suffice it to say that the building is as beautiful as the site is commanding, and that the minster garth is girdled by ancient houses full of interest, although Lincoln was never, as the popular name would suggest, the centre of a great monastery.

We must endeavour to summarise the chief attractions of the town and the leading features of the scenery. Of the former it may be said that few towns in England are more full of relics of olden time or more fruitful in pleasant impressions. We never know what the next turn in the most unpromising street may disclose. The Roman relics have been already mentioned, but these and the cathedral do not nearly exhaust the list of its antiquities. Would you look at a wealthy burgess' residence in the earlier part of the twelfth century? You may find it in the Jews' House of the upper town, or "John of Gaunt's" stables in the lower. Would you seek for domestic architecture belonging to the later periods of Pointed work? The gate-houses of the close belong to the earlier part of the fourteenth century; "the chequer or exchequer gate with its shops in the side passage, and the Pottergate remain; several residentiary houses were erected at the same period, and are partly remaining, though much altered and disfigured." At every turn in the older parts of the town the eye falls upon some remnant of ancient days, doorway or gatehouse, window or corner of a wall; it may be merely a fragment, a little block, of mouldering masonry, or it may be an almost perfect example of mediæval architecture. But Lincoln is not only interesting in detail; the town, as a whole, when seen from the flat land by the Witham, is exceptionally attractive. True, it has lost much in recent days. It has become a manufacturing town of some importance; large foundries and other works have sprung up on the meadows by the Witham. The lowland begins to bristle up with tall chimneys, which discharge their clouds of dusky smoke. New and old are in sharp contrast. The tower of St. Mary-le-Wigford looks down on a railway, the quaint little conduit on its churchyard wall is close to a signal-box. Still, ugly as the foreground in many places has become, it cannot spoil the beauty of the town itself, as its houses and gardens climb the steep hillside to the summit of the plateau, where above all peer up the grey remnants of the ancient castle, and the vast mass of the cathedral with its lofty towers rises high above the picturesque buildings of the close and the green trees upon the slope beneath.

BOSTON CHURCH: THE TOWER.

From the walls of Lincoln the Witham can be watched as it passes onwards to enter the fenland, into which the level valley opens out as the plateau shelves down towards the east. This part of its course is naturally monotonous, so we shall not attempt to describe it in detail, and shall pause only at the old town which forms its port. Boston, anciently Botolph's Town, is a thriving market town, which, as every lover of architecture knows, possesses one of the finest churches in the county, or indeed in the whole country. It stands in an ample churchyard close to the left bank of the Witham; the magnificent tower, crowned by an octagonal lantern, which is supported by flying buttresses, is about 300 feet high, a beacon for many a league of fen and sea. The church itself is not unworthy of the tower, and is one of the largest in England, perhaps the largest of those built on a similar plan. The style is Late Decorated and Perpendicular, though doubtless there was an earlier structure on the same site. The tradition runs that "the first stone was laid in the year 1309 by Dame Margery Tilney, and that she put five pounds upon it, as did Sir John Twesdale the vicar, and Richard Stevenson, a like sum; and that these were the greatest sums at that time given."

NORTHAMPTON.

Progress, however, must at first have been slow, for most of the building is of rather later date. The interior, though rather plain, is very fine, producing an impression which may be summed up in the word "spaciousness." Lofty aisles are connected with the nave by corresponding arches; the clerestory is comparatively small. The chancel is large, and open to the body of the church, so that there is little interruption in any direction to the view. Formerly Boston Church was exceptionally rich in brasses, but most of these have perished; two, however, one of a merchant named Peascod, whose dress is appropriately ornamented with pea-pods, and another of a priest vested in a richly-ornamented cope, still remain at the east end. Among the many minor objects of interest to be found in this grand church, which was carefully restored about thirty years since, may be mentioned the stone roof of the tower, the lower storey of which is open to the church, the chancel-stalls, and the curious Elizabethan pulpit.

Above the church is a great sluice, below it a bridge, which may be reckoned as the head of the port of Boston. Here sea-going vessels may be seen afloat at high tide, or stranded on the mud bank at low water. The sea itself is about four miles away, and the dead level of the fens extends all around the town. Except the church there is little of interest in Boston, but probably its tower is surpassed by none in the kingdom, in either its fine design or its extensive prospects.

PETERBOROUGH CATHEDRAL.

From the table-land about Naseby, much of which lies at an elevation of some six hundred feet above the sea, flow two of the rivers which ultimately pass through the fenland into the Wash. These are a source of the Nen and the Welland. Near the springs of these rivers, on the undulating upland not far from Naseby, was the last great struggle in the field between Royalist and Roundhead; Charles and Rupert on one side, Cromwell and Fairfax on the other, "looked one another in the face." Both sides were brave enough; but on the one were rashness and incapacity, on the other discipline and skill; so that before four hours had passed the king's army was shattered before the "new model," and he became "like a hunted partridge flitting from one castle to another."

Thus the Nen has its sources quite on the western side of the county—thence each feeder flows through a pleasant rolling region, where pastures alternate with corn-fields, and both with copses, broadening its valley, as it proceeds, until they join and reach the chief town of the county, by which time the water meadows bordering its banks are of considerable extent. Northampton is a town which has increased rapidly in size, and in consequence diminished rapidly in attractiveness. While it possesses some very interesting remains of ancient days, its older buildings for the most part are those of a midland market town of the last century, and these have been seldom replaced with the more imposing structures erected at the present day; thus, if we except the new Town Hall, the chief additions to Northampton are blocks of factories, and rows of small houses, monotonous wildernesses of red bricks and purple slates. The place is very old, but the politics that prevail are very modern; for some years one of its parliamentary representatives was the late Mr. Bradlaugh.

ROCKINGHAM VILLAGE AND CASTLE.

GATEWAY OF THE CASTLE.

This slope above the Nen, where its course begins to bend towards the north, was a town full a thousand years ago, when it bore the shorter name of "Hamtune." For a considerable time it was in the hands of the Danes; it was burned by them in 1010, and harried by the forces of Morkere a year before the Norman Conquest. The successors of William often kept court here, for the Forest of Rockingham—which then spread over a large part of the county—was a favourite hunting ground, and many councils and parliaments were held in the castle. In its hall Becket confronted Henry II., and at a later date, the constitutions of Clarendon were ratified. Its annals have not always been peaceful. De Montford struggled for it with Prince Edward, and the Duke of York with Henry VI. Once Northampton seemed in the way to become a seat of learning, for owing to the state of feeling between "town and gown" in the year 1260 the students abandoned Oxford and settled there; their stay, however, was not long, the "town" found that a proud stomach would soon be an empty one, and made interest with the king to recall the "gown," so the Nen did not replace the Isis.

The ruins of the castle are inconspicuous, but Northampton possesses two churches of great interest, one, St. Peter's—a fine, and in some respects remarkable, example of a rather late Norman parish church—which, notwithstanding some alterations, retains in the main its original character, and is an unusually ornate example of that style—and St. Sepulchre's, one of the four churches in England which commemorate in their plan the ancient church of the Holy Sepulchre at

STAMFORD.

Jerusalem. This church has been much altered and added to, but the rotunda, or rather octagon, is still in fair preservation, and indicates a date rather later than that of its three companions. The Queen's Cross, on the higher ground about a a mile south of Northampton, is one of the three which remain to mark the resting-places of Queen Eleanor's body and the affection of her husband. Though somewhat injured, it is still in fair preservation.

The valley of the Nen below Northampton affords scenery which, if a little monotonous, is generally pretty. There are flat water meadows by the winding stream, forming a plain a mile or so wide, bounded by slopes, rising sometimes gently, sometimes more rapidly, to a low plateau on either side, and pleasantly diversified with copses and hedgerow timber. The district is an excellent example of the ordinary Midland scenery, quiet, peaceful, seemingly fairly opulent, notwithstanding agricultural depression, but offering few subjects, so far as the scenery is concerned, for pen or pencil, though occasionally an ancient bridge and frequently an old farmhouse of grey stone will attract the artist. As we pass along we note high on the left bank the church of Earls Barton, of which the solid and curiously ornamented tower was built before the Norman Conquest, and the body retains remnants of almost every succeeding period of architecture. Indeed, all this part of the valley of the Nen, which is followed for the most part by the railway to Peterborough, if comparatively uninteresting in its scenery, is exceptionally rich in its churches. In the words of the late Canon James: "The Saxon tower of Earls Barton; the complete Early English Church of Warmington, with its wooden vaulting and exquisite

BEDFORD BRIDGE.

capitals; the unique octagon of Stanwick; the lanterns of Lowick, Irthlingborough, and Fotheringay; the spires of Raunds, Rushden, and Irchester; Finedon, perfect in the best style; Strixton, the model of an earlier one; the fine steeple of Oundle—are but selections out of a line of churches, some but little inferior, terminating in the grand west front and more solemn interior of Peterborough Cathedral." Besides this, opposite to Earls Barton lies Castle Ashby, the home of the Marquis of Northampton, overlooking from its terrace a great extent of the valley of the Nen, and the wooded hills on its other bank. The house, which is built round a quadrangle, replaces a castle which had disappeared by Leland's time. Three sides were built in the reign of Elizabeth, the fourth was added by Inigo Jones. A lettered balustrade, a rather favourite device in Elizabethan and Jacobean work, is to be seen here. The house contains some interesting pictures and some memorials—according to the author of the account in Murray's Guide-book—of the famous spendthrift election, when my Lord Northampton, my Lord Halifax, and my Lord Spencer all ran candidates for the borough of Northampton, and the race cost the winner a hundred thousand pounds, and each of the losers a hundred and fifty thousand pounds! Yardley Chase, a fragment of one of the old Northamptonshire forests, adjoins the park.

The Nen winds on to Wellingborough, with its chalybeate spring, a town which began to prosper when the iron ore of Northamptonshire found favour in the market. The ore, which is the oxide of iron, popularly known as "rust," occurs in a group of sands of no great thickness at the base of the lower oolites, and overlying the stiff blue lias clay. According to Horace Walpole, quoted in the Guide-book, Wellingborough was not well provided with hotels in 1763. "We lay at Wellingborough—pray never lie there—the beastliest inn upon earth is there! We were carried into a vast bed-room, which I suppose is the club-room, for it stunk of tobacco like a justice of the peace! I desired some boiling water for tea; they brought me in a sugar-dish of hot water in a pewter plate." The church is a fine one, and interesting in more respects than space allows us to enumerate. For the same reason we must pass rapidly by Higham Ferrers, with its old bridge (the best of two or three over this section of the river), and the buildings founded by Archbishop Chichele as a mark of affection for his birthplace. The grand church dates from various periods, commencing with the Early English, and ending with the first half of the seventeenth century, when the steeple was rebuilt, but on the old pattern. The church was made collegiate by Chichele in 1415, to which date belongs the woodwork of the chancel. A brass indicates the burial-place of his parents, and there are several other monuments of great interest. The school-house on the north side of the churchyard, quite close to the steeple, and the bede-house on the south, are also Chichele's work, together with the college, which stood in the main street, but is now in ruins. Probably no townlet in England possesses such a remarkable group of ecclesiastical buildings. The shafts also of two crosses remain. The castle, however, which once belonged to the Earls Ferrers, has now disappeared.

Hence the Nen flows on by bridge or mill to the little town of Thrapston, noted for its grain market. "There is a very pretty view from the bridge which crosses the Nen between Thrapston and Islip. The river sweeps round between green meadows, overhung in the foreground by masses of fine trees. Loosestrife, arrow-head, the flowering rush, and many of the rarer water plants, abound, and the tall rushes which border the stream are used here for plaiting the outer portion of horse collars and mats, and for the seats of chairs." Then comes Thorpe with its fragment of a castle and the old bridge over a tributary of the Nen, which near here for a while parts into two channels. The scenery generally in this part of the valley is attractive, especially near Lilford, where the old mansion stands on rising ground surrounded by fine trees; and near to the river are the churches and the ruined Castle of Barnwell. Then, hurrying on, Oundle is reached, with its lofty steeple and fine church, its ancient bridge over the river, and its quaint old houses. Oundle has been inhabited since the days of the Romans, and is justly noted as "one of the pleasantest towns in Northamptonshire." Cotterstock with its memories of Dryden, Tansor with its curious church, come next, then Fotheringay with its "fair builded paroche church" and its ruined castle, in the hall of which stern justice was done to Mary Stuart, overlooks the valley of the Nen. At Wansford the river sweeps round to the east, and glides slowly through a less interesting district down to Peterborough, passing on its way Castor with its interesting church and relics of a Roman station. This, Durobrivæ by name, appears to have occupied both sides of the river, and was evidently a wealthy and important settlement. It was famed also for its pottery; "kilns and great works extended round Castor and its neighbourhood for about twenty miles up and down the Nen valley. Roman potters' kilns have been found nowhere else in England so perfect or in so great numbers."

Far above the lowland, far above the fens upon which the river is now entering, rises the huge mass of the Cathedral of Peterborough. The town, once a mere appendage to the great monastery, is now an important centre of railways and of works connected therewith. Within the last forty years the population has trebled; acres and acres of land have been covered with rather commonplace dwellings; but the nucleus of the town, the houses by the Nen bridge, the picturesque market-place, the old residences of the close, and above all the Cathedral, are little changed. A few years ago it was found necessary to rebuild completely the central tower of the Cathedral, for it was on the point of falling; much underpinning and other structural work has had to be done in the choir, during which some very remarkable remnants of the older fabric have been found; and it will probably be some years before the work of restoration is completed, for the expense is great, and neither the chapter nor the diocese is rich.

At Peterborough we stand on the brink of the lowland. It is not yet actual fen; the Cathedral, the town, stand on a thin bed of rock, which overlies clay and provides a foundation. Here, about the year 655, the place being then called Medeshamstede, a monastery was founded. For more than two centuries it flourished; then the Dane swooped down on the fenland abbey, and for nearly a hundred years it was desolate. It was rebuilt about 966, and in less than a century had become so wealthy that in the days of Abbot Leofric, a great benefactor, it was called the golden burgh of Peter. The splendour for a time was dimmed when the monastery was burnt, and the church sacked, by Hereward the Wake as an English welcome to the first Norman Abbot. All of this church that was above ground has long disappeared, but considerable portions of the foundation have been discovered during the recent alterations, and will not be again buried. The grand Norman structure which still remains—one of the most complete in the kingdom—was begun about 1118, and completed, except the west front, about 1190. That—a structure perfectly unique, a gigantic portico, in the form of three huge pointed arches—is assigned to the first quarter of the thirteenth century. For boldness of design and perfection of execution it is unsurpassed by anything of this period in

HUNTINGDON BRIDGE.

the kingdom. The small spires, the pinnacles, and the porch, unfortunately stuffed between the piers of the central arch, are of later date. The "new building" or lady chapel at the east end is a fine piece of Tudor work, but it has not improved the lower part of the Norman church. The Perpendicular architects have inserted poor tracery in many of the windows, and have made other alterations, seldom for the better, but less mischief has been done at Peterborough by these meddlesome blunderers than in most other Norman cathedrals.

The Welland rises, as has been said, on the high ground near Naseby, but runs parallel with the outcrop of the rocks, while the stream going to the Nen descends with their slope. Thus the valley of the former widens rapidly, and before reaching Market Harborough is already trench-like in outline. This, for long a sleepy little town, seems to have been stimulated into some life by the meeting of railways. Still it possesses one or two old houses, a chapel and a church of some interest; and from it Charles led his army to the fatal field of Naseby. Below Harborough the valley of the Welland continues to broaden and flatten its bed, the slopes often rising steeply on both northern and southern sides. Though sometimes pleasantly wooded around the site of some old family mansion, they are commonly rather bare, and the scenery is on the whole less attractive than is usual in this region of England. Such churches also as are near the river are not remarkable, and it is not till we come to Rockingham that we care to pause. Here, however, high on the right bank, backed by shady woods, are the terraces, gables, and the remaining bulwarks of Rockingham Castle. The road climbs through the picturesque village to the grey old gateway, which, with other portions, dates from the thirteenth century, but the part more conspicuous from the valley is mainly of the reign of

Elizabeth. "Anywhere the high site of Rockingham, backed with its avenues of limes and groups of forest trees, would be a fine one, but in Northamptonshire the wild and broken ground of the park, and the abrupt slopes and earthworks on which the castle stands, make it signally unique." The earlier kings of England not seldom used this for a hunting seat in the days when Rockingham Forest was a reality instead of a name.

The river winds on with little change in the general character of the scenery; the tower of Gretton looks down from the high scarp of the right bank, the little spire of Seaton rises among trees hardly less high on the left, the small village of Harringworth, with its grey stone houses, its interesting church, and its old cross still standing in the market-place, lies by the river side, near to which a branch of the Midland Railway crosses river and valley on a mighty viaduct of brick arches. Then Collyweston crowns the slope on the right. Here are the quarries of so-called slate, which in former days roofed all the churches and most of the mansions for miles round—a material in its slight irregularity of form and colour far more pleasing to the eye than the formal smoothness and dull tints of the slates of Wales or Westmorland, which now find favour with builders. Then near the river are more grey houses, always worth a passing glance, for they are often at least a couple of centuries old, and as stone was plentiful and good, men in those times forbore to do their work "on the cheap." But here is something more, for above them rises the steeple of Ketton church, perhaps the most graceful to be found in any village in England. High on the hills behind are the famous quarries, which for long took the place of those of Barnack, but are now in their turn becoming exhausted.

OLD BRIDGE, ST. IVES.

Then above the willow trees by the water, grey houses, towers, and spires, rise from the bed of the valley, climb the slope on the left, and that on the right also, till the suburb is arrested by densely massed woods. These hide from view the palatial mansion of Burghley; this is "Stamford town," once a noted halting-place on the great North Road. There is, perhaps, no town in England of the same size which is more picturesque or more interesting. Grey stone houses, often of excellent design, overhang the river, and border the streets; the steeple of St. Mary's is very similar, and hardly inferior, to that of Ketton; that of All Saints is also fine. In St. Martin's, near the gate, Burghley, the great Lord Treasurer, the founder of the houses of Exeter and Salisbury, lies buried; the Burghley Bede House, Browne's Hospital, and the ruined priory of St. Leonard's, are full of interest, and the town boasts that to it, as to Northampton, there was once a migration from Oxford.

At Stamford itself one would hardly suppose that the fens were near. The ground on either side is fairly high, the valley not notably broad, but the river, like the Witham at Lincoln, after cutting through the great limestone escarpment, passes out into the vast expanse of marsh-land that borders the Wash.

The Ouse rises in Buckinghamshire not far from Banbury, noted among children for its cross and cakes, and wanders leisurely on by the quiet county town of Buckingham, by Newport Pagnell, and Olney, known to admirers of Cowper, its scenery for the most part opulent, but rather monotonous, till it approaches Bedford —once a town wholly agricultural, now the site of important works of agricultural implements, and evidently prospering. Sleepily the Ouse glides along by its reedy banks through the wide lowland, silently it slides by the waterside houses, the pretty gardens, and the modern bridge which has replaced an earlier and more picturesque structure. Among the fields towards the south, the massive tower of Elstow church rises above the trees, indicating the birthplace of John Bunyan, who "lighted on a den" in Bedford gaol, and there "dreamed the dream" of the "Pilgrim's Progress." Bedford Castle has disappeared, the churches are of little interest, the houses commonplace. Except for a few memorials of Bunyan, Bedford does not offer much to detain the traveller, unless he would examine its excellent schools or search for the remains of palæolithic man in the neighbouring gravels.

Below Bedford the Ouse passes on through wide meadows, near the pine-clad hills of Sandy, and the market gardens, fertile from the happy mixture of the light sand of the slopes with the mud of the river; by the old town of St. Neots, with its fine church tower; by Huntingdon with its picturesque bridge and its memories of Cromwell, where the old mansion of the Earls of Sandwich looks from its terrace over the wide and often flooded river plain; and beneath the ancient bridge of St. Ives. The valley becomes less and less definite, the scenery flat, flatter, flattest, till somewhere or other in the fens the Ouse receives the Cam, and somewhere or other at last reaches the sea. This enigmatical sentence will be presently explained; let us now turn back to notice briefly the course of the last-named river.

The CAM is shorter than any which have been noticed, yet a stream which passes through Cambridge, and may claim to glide by Ely, may well demand a longer notice than any of them. This, however, the limitations of space forbid, so we shall pass over, as generally known, the history of Cambridge and of its University. We will merely glance at the site of the Roman camp on the low plateau and the old "Saxon" tower of St. Benet's on the plain across the Cam, indicating, as at Lincoln, an early separation of the military and the civil element. We will only mention the Round church, another memorial of the Holy Sepulchre. We will not discuss the rise and progress of the University, whether or no its founder was Sigibert, king of the East Angles, nor speak of the work of many a pious benefactor, royal, noble, and lowly born, or of its illustrious sons, its treasures of literature, its museums and colleges. We will merely trace the course of the Cam through the town, because there is no mile of river scenery in all England, or, so far as we know, in all Europe, which can be exactly compared with it.

The Cam at Cambridge results from the union of two or three streams which have stolen sluggishly down, from sources a few miles distant among the chalk hills or the yet lower undulations of the clay district, to form a river rather wider and deeper, but hardly more rapid than an ordinary canal. Meadows and osier beds end at a mill, up to which barges can come, and below the pool, at the first bridge leading into the town, the characteristic scenery may be said to begin. Close to this the buildings of Queen's College overhang the water, linked to the garden on the left bank by a picturesque wooden bridge. With tall trees to the left, with another garden on the right, we then glide beneath a single-arch bridge into the precincts of King's College. On the left bank are meadows bordered by tall trees; on the right, from smooth-shaven lawns, rise the master's lodge, the massive Fellows' Buildings, and the stately chapel, the pride of King's College. Overlooking the lawns, but parted by a garden from the river, is the single court of Clare College, an excellent example of seventeenth century domestic architecture, behind which is the group of buildings belonging to the University Library, the older part of which was erected for the students of King's College. A handsome three-arched bridge links Clare to its beautiful gardens on the opposite bank of the Cam, and almost closes the view along the stream, though beneath its arches glimpses are obtained of more gardens and yet more bridges. Rowing on, with some care for our oars, we pass beneath an arch, and glide by the gardens of Clare College and beneath the terraced wall which hides that of Trinity Hall, but not its stately chestnut trees. Then, through a single arch of iron, which carries one of the roads leading into the town, we enter the grounds of Trinity College, the largest, richest, and most aristocratic of the educational foundations of Cambridge. Before us is its bridge, interrupting the noble avenue of limes, which on the one side separates its tree-fringed meadows, on the other leads up to the gateway tower in the façade of the "New Court." There are now neither shrubs nor flowers by the river, but here and there a weeping willow overhangs the water. As we pass beneath one of the arches we obtain on the one side a clearer view of the Trinity meadows; on the other, of Wren's stately but rather ugly library adjoining the "New Court," and in front, across more meadows, and yet more aged trees, we see the grand mass of the "New Court" of St. John's College.

On approaching these the river bends to the right. Old elms border the

JUNCTION OF THE CAM AND THE OUSE.

meadows of St. John's, an ivy-clad wall bounds an old garden belonging to Trinity, and then, beyond another three-arched bridge, the Cam passes between the buildings of St. John's. They rise directly from the water, like the palaces of Venice; on the right, a picturesque group of red brick and old grey stone, dating from the seventeenth century, linked by a covered bridge of stone—a Gothicised Rialto—to the loftier mass of the New Court on the left. Bridge and buildings were erected rather more than half a century since; the material is a cream-coloured limestone; the style is late Perpendicular. Passing between these and by the gable of the college library, a view is obtained of the Master's lodge and of the west front of the chapel with its heavy inappropriate tower. Both are the work of Gilbert Scott, and the latter is by no means one of his successes. These left behind, some rather poor but not unpicturesque houses border the Cam, till it is crossed by an iron bridge, supporting the main street of the town. Then we glide past the buildings of Magdalene College, which of late years have been opened to the river. Soon after this we emerge from the town, to see, below a lock and weir, the boat-houses of the college rowing-clubs bordering the left bank of the Cam, and the grassy expanse of "Midsummer Common" on the opposite side. For the next three or four miles the margin of the Cam, uninteresting as its scenery may be, is often lively enough, for skiffs, pairs, four-oars, eight-oars, dart up and down, propelled by the strong arms of sturdy rowers. Dingeys or "tubs" progress more leisurely, while now and again a long string of

QUEEN'S BRIDGE, CAMBRIDGE.

barges is towed or punted onwards, and almost blocks the water-way. As a result of this, the representatives of learning and of commerce exchange compliments, when the language is vernacular rather than classic. Brightest of all is the scene on occasions of the college races. Carriages and spectators crowd the right bank, on the left runs a yelling crowd, which, as it follows the boats, resembles in its motley mixture of uniforms a huge party-coloured water-snake. Age and youth, don and undergraduate, mingle in one confused mass, like a pack of hounds in full cry. Oh, the music of that shout! Oh, the memories of those days when friends were many and cares were few—when many a face was bright which has now faded away into the shadow-land, many a heart was warm which is now mouldering in the dust!

Before long the Cam fairly enters the fen-land, and creeps along by willows and reeds, by wide tracts of black earth, once marshy and malarious, now rich plains of corn land. Here and there a cluster of trees, a tower or a spire, marks the spot where some insular bank afforded in olden times a site for a village among the wild waste of flooded fen. When the winter frost has gone, when the spring north-easter is still, when the summer sun is high, it is indeed a sleepy land. The spirit of the scenery may be not inappropriately summed up in the words written over the door of a water-side inn, half-way between Cambridge and Ely: "Five miles from anywhere; no hurry!" One object only breaks the monotony of the horizon; this is the vast mass of Ely Cathedral towering up from its island hill, and overlooking the fens of the Cam and of the Ouse.

This isle of Ely, a large but low plateau surrounded by meres and marshes, was of old a place of note. It was the dower of Etheldreda, daughter of Anna, king of the East Anglians, and she, soon after the year 673, founded a monastery near to the site of the present cathedral. Of this she became abbess, and here she died and was ultimately enshrined. To her memorial festival pilgrims crowded from all quarters, and the trifles sold at "St. Awdry's" fair have left their mark upon our language. The Danes came and the monastery was devastated, but it was founded anew about a century before the Norman Conquest. At that epoch it became a "Camp of Refuge" for the patriots who refused submission to the invaders. The deeds of Hereward the Wake are too well known to need recounting; suffice it to say that the resistance was long and stubborn, and that the Normans were more than once beaten off from the isle with heavy loss. The scene of their gravest defeat is still marked by an old causeway which crosses both the fens and a channel of the Ouse to a spot near Haddenham, about four miles distant from Ely.* Along this William advanced from Cambridge to the attack. By the river brink there was a desperate struggle, but at last the dry reeds above the causeway on the Norman side were fired by the English; the flame fanned by the evening breeze came roaring down on the invader's column; then was a wild rush for dear life, but between fire and morass many a Norman never got back again to his camp.

The monastery which sheltered Hereward's men, the church where they worshipped, have now disappeared. The foundations of the present cathedral were laid by Simeon, the first Norman abbot, who was appointed in 1082. Most of it belongs to a yet later date. The oldest work is found in the transepts; the upper parts of these, with the nave, are Late Norman, the west tower and remaining part of the façade not being completed till near the end of the twelfth century. The singularly beautiful choir is partly Early English, partly Decorated; the eastern bays dating from about 1240, the western nearly a century later. In the year 1322 the Norman central tower fell in with a mighty crash, and was replaced by the octagon and lantern, which form the unique glory of Ely. About the same time

* It is called Aldreth; there was here some twenty years since an old wooden bridge, of which the late Professor Freeman (with whom I first visited the place) wrote in his "Norman Conquest" (vol. iv., p. 465), "It looked very much as if it had been broken down by Hereward, and not mended since." A few years later I found it had almost disappeared.

the great Lady-chapel at the east angle of the northern transept was added. The beautiful western Galilee porch was built in advance of the western façade, perhaps a quarter of a century after the completion of the latter, which has lost, at what date it is uncertain, its northern wing or transept.

Of the additions and alterations made by the architects of the Perpendicular

ELY CATHEDRAL, FROM THE RIVER.

period—rarely improvements—it is needless to speak, and through want of space we must pass over the beautiful monuments, the stall work ancient and modern, the decoration of the roof, and the many enrichments which the cathedral has received during the latter part of the present century. Nor can we do more than mention the interesting remains of the annexed monastery—the ruins of the infirmary, the ancient gateway, the deanery and other old houses, or the Bishop's Palace, which stands a little apart from these to the south-west of the cathedral. In this respect its precincts are not less interesting than those of Lincoln and Peterborough.

We have not attempted to follow either Nen, Welland, or Ouse, to the sea, because their courses through the fen-lands are now to a considerable extent artificial, forming part of a connected system of drainage; and because the whole district is an almost unbroken plain. A description written for one part will apply to any other; a few trees, more or less, grouped a little differently by the dykes or on the low shoals which rise a few feet above the plain; a little more or less of marsh or peat still left among the enclosures: that is all; the only differences are in the sluices, pumping-stations, windmills, houses, churches—in short, in the artificial, not in the natural features of the scenery.

The history of the drainage of the fens and the rectification of its river courses is a long and complicated one.* Restricting ourselves to the vast plain west and south-west of the Wash, the silted-up estuary, rather than the river delta of the Welland, Nen, and Ouse, it may suffice to say that, while works were executed so far back as Roman times, the first great effort for the reclamation of the land dates from the seventeenth century. Formerly these rivers branched in the fen-land. The Welland divided at Crowland, one arm passing by Spalding, the other inosculating with an arm of the Nen, which was thrown off near Peterborough; of this river the other arm passed through Whittlesea Mere to Wisbeach, and so to the sea. The Ouse also divided at Erith, one arm passing northward to join part of the Nen, the other, that mentioned above, flowing south of the Isle of Ely and uniting with the Cam. The part of the fens which lay north of the Nen was partially reclaimed in the reign of James I. The drainage was completed by Rennie in the beginning of the present century, but some sixty years afterwards powerful pumps had to be added to his work to discharge the drainage into the sea. The reclamation of the district south of the Nen was undertaken by Vermuyden with the help of the Earl of Bedford. His scheme was elaborate and open to criticism, its history complicated and unsatisfactory. It may suffice to say that the work, begun under Charles, was completed under Cromwell; that the rivers were conducted along channels, mainly artificial, enclosed by banks, and that before long, owing to the drying of the peat, the consequent reduction of the slope of the ground, and the silting-up of the outfalls, it was found necessary to introduce windmills for pumping. Since then many improvements and alterations have been made. Whittlesea Mere, for example, a sheet of water from 1,000 to 1,600 acres in extent, has been drained, new sluices have been added, steam pumping engines erected, and the drainage of the fens may now be regarded as complete. The wild marsh-land, once a steaming swamp in summer, a vast sheet of water in winter, is now a plain of dry black earth, "green in springtime with the sprouting blade, golden in autumn with the dense ears of grain. It is a strange, solemn land, silent even yet, with houses few and far between, except where they have clustered for centuries on some bank of Jurassic clay, which rises like a shoal not many feet above the plain; with water yet dank and dark, but brightened in summer with arrowhead and flowering rush and the great white cups of water-lilies. Strange kinds of hawks yet circle in the air, the swallowtail butterfly yet dances above the sedges, though the great-copper no longer spreads its burnished wings to the sunshine. Few trees, except grey willows or rows of rustling poplars, break the dead level which stretches away to the horizon, like a sea.

* Much information not only on this, but also on many other questions relating to the fens, will be found in Messrs. Miller and Skertchly's book "The Fenland."

beneath a vast dome of sky kindled often at sunrise and at sunset into a rare glory of many colours." *

With the progress of cultivation the peculiar flora and fauna are gradually disappearing. The bittern, the spoonbill, the crane, and the wild swan, are becoming rare visitants, the ruffs and reeves, once so common, are now scarce; the decoys are falling into disuse, and the strange unearthly cry of the wild fowl less often breaks the frozen silence of the winter night; but if this is a loss to the naturalist and the sportsman, there is a gain to the labourer and the farmer. Ague and marsh fever have all but disappeared. Though the fen-land is less wild and strange than in days of yore, he who has gazed in the early autumn from one of the high church towers over the vast expanse has seen a sight which he will never forget, for all around the endless fields of grain

"Are like a golden ocean,
Becalmed upon the plain."

A word must be said of the fen-land towns. Wisbeach claims to be the metropolis. Built upon the Nen, which is navigable up to it for vessels of moderate tonnage, and a prosperous town, it has little of special interest besides its principal church, for its castle has practically disappeared. Spalding, also a bright and thriving place, among shady trees; and King's Lynn, at the mouth of the Ouse, with a fine church, an old Guildhall, and the curious pilgrimage chapel of the Red Mount—claim more than mention. Nor must we forget the once mighty Abbey of Crowland, that grey broken ruin which towers still so grandly over the fens, or its singular triangular bridge, or the memories of St. Guthlac and of Waltheof.

AMONG THE FENS.

T. G. Bonney.

* The Author, "Cambridgeshire Geology," p. 8.

A NORFOLK BROAD.

THE RIVERS OF EAST ANGLIA.

THE CROUCH: Foulness—Little Barsted and Langdon—Canewdon—Rayleigh—Hockley Spa. THE BLACKWATER: Saffron Walden—Radwinter—Codham Hall and Bather—Bocking—Braintree—Felix Hall—Braxted Lodge—Tiptree—Maldon. THE CHELMER: Thaxted—The Dunmows—Great Waltham—Springfield—Chelmsford—Mersea Island. THE COLNE: Great Yeldham—Castle Hedingham—Halstead—Colchester. THE STOUR: Kedington—Sudbury—Flatford and John Constable—Harwich. THE ORWELL: Stowmarket—Barham—Ipswich. THE DEBEN: Debenham—Woodbridge—Felixstowe. THE ALDE: Aldborough—Southwold—Halesworth. THE WAVENEY: Diss—Bungay—Mettingham—Beccles—Breydon Water—Horsey Mere. THE BURE: Hickling Broads—St. Benet's Abbey—Salhouse and Wroxham Broads—Hoveton Great Broad—Horning Ferry—Fishing in the Broads. THE YARE: Norwich—Yarmouth.

AFTER the Medway and the Thames have delivered their great contributions to the sea, the peculiar Essex coast country—flat, marshy, and often very uninteresting—is sufficiently served by a number of small streams of little note in literature, and generally as commonplace in appearance as in the duties they perform. There are exceptions, which will be duly indicated, but with regard to the majority of the streams of East Anglia, poet has not sung nor painter wrought his magic art. If not remote, unfriended, or melancholy, they are, it cannot be denied, slow. During the hot summer-time, when the level fields through which they meander are quivering with heat-haze, and the pastures and hedgerows are ablaze with the wild flowers which love fat pastures and flourish upon them, the upper waters are choked with luxuriant tangles of aquatic vegetation, and the current is barely sufficient, without the frequent application of scythe and water-rake to the thickets below water, to turn the rustic mills planted upon their banks. The dainty trout loves not the muddy beds and lazy flow of these rivers, which will be found to be much more numerous than is commonly supposed; but the waters are the natural home of the eel, pike, roach, bream, and other specimens of the so-called coarse fishes, or summer spawners, of Great Britain. A purely pastoral country is that watered by these narrow reed-margined rivers, famous for grain, roots, and grassy acres, with good soil where the solid earth lies so low that the hand of man must perforce sometimes exert itself to save it from the inroads of the salt sea. Let us follow the coast-line from the north shore of the Thames, abounding in marshes that have been so well described by Dickens in "Great Expectations," and by the author of "Mehalah" in his novels.

The first river is the CROUCH, whose estuary is still the groundwork of a remunerative oyster fishery. Anything more dreary than the shores of this long and gaping river-mouth can scarcely be imagined. The beacons out at sea tell the tale of danger, and point to the dread Maplin sands, and the treacherous shoals that culminate in the fatal Goodwins. True, upon Foulness the tenants of Lord Winchilsea most successfully reclaimed a space of forbidding foreshore from the sea, but as a rule these expanses yield little better than coarse marsh grass, wild fowl, and everlasting salt; and the island of Foulness, which is formed by the curvature of one of the smaller channels, half river and half creek, that abound in these parts, is the oasis of this marshy desert. Yet the church on the island, which was built less than forty years ago, occupies the site of one which was founded in the twelfth century, and the Danes, as every schoolboy is taught, built themselves forts hard-by, and made camps that have left their landmarks to this day. At high water the Crouch estuary is a pleasant enough arm of the sea, and as the river is navigable for brigs of respectable tonnage at Burnham, and for smaller craft to Fambridge Ferry, the ruddy and white-sailed boats impart a refreshing liveliness to the scene. Especially is this the case when the little fleet of oyster boats are on active service.

The Crouch rises from a couple of springs in Little Bursted and Langdon, the district lying between the high and picturesque uplands of these parts, Billericay (where the Romans had a station) and Langdon Hill. A small stream for a while, the Crouch passes several villages, the branches joining forces at Ramsden Crays; it becomes navigable for barges at Battle Bridge, and for sea-going brigs and schooners at Hull Bridge, near which place the scenery is pretty and undulating. From North Fambridge, however, the normal marsh-land of the estuary begins to assert itself, and Burnham is to all intents and purposes the seaport of this portion of the Hundreds—a local term applying to the aguish levels between the Crouch and the Colne, which latter stream will presently engage our attention. Before leaving the Crouch, however, the village of Canewdon should be mentioned, as being well situated above the flats, and as being in the neighbourhood of a battle-field upon which Canute defeated Edmund Ironside. The discovery of relics from time to time shows that the

CADHAM HALL: PORTRAIT OF SAMUEL BUTLER.

Romans as well as the Danes were located on the shores of the Crouch, and the ancient village of Rayleigh is claimed to have been the home of the Saxon. The mineral waters of Hockley Spa are credited with peculiar virtues, and the place is in consequence growing in importance.

The BLACKWATER, sometimes called the Pant, which is the next river as we proceed northwards, waters a pleasant, flourishing, and populous part of the county of Essex. It is the kind of landscape that delights the agriculturist, and that gives to rural England its distinctive charm, its combination of pasture and arable land, wood and water, village and town. The Blackwater rises near the borders of Cambridge, not far from Saffron Walden, the wooded slope of the Saxon, the strategic position upon which the Britons had formed an ancient encampment, and

Geoffrey de Mandeville built his castle in the early days of the Norman Conquest; the place where in more recent times the cultivation of the saffron suggested a suitable prefix to "Weald den." The tower and spire of Radwinter Church forms a conspicuous object from the surrounding country, but the church has been restored and enlarged in our own times. Here, towards the close of the sixteenth century, Robert Harrison, the author of the "Decay of the English Long Bow," and an historical description of the "Land of Britaine," was rector. Lower down the river, in the village church of Hempstead, a monument stands to the memory of William Harvey, the discoverer of the circulation of the blood, but the hall where Harvey's brother Eliab resided no longer exists. Butler is said to have written the greater part of "Hudibras" at Cadham Hall, below Shalford; and at Finchingfield, on a hilly site near a tributary of the main stream, Spains Hall, an Early Tudoresque mansion in a fine park, represents the free hand of the Conqueror, who gave the estate to one of his Normans.

Bocking Church, as we descend the river, now running almost due south, stands high, and is of some note as a building of the time of Edward III., in which ministered the Dr. Gauden who, in the opinion of some of the authorities, was the author of *Eikon Basilike*. Bocking is virtually an outlying suburb of the neat market town of Braintree, where a colony of Flemings, settling in the time of Elizabeth, founded the weaving establishments which, with ironworks, corn mills, and malting-houses, maintain the present population in general prosperity.

MALDON.

The vale and park of Stisted succeed, and by-and-bye the old-fashioned little town of Coggeshall, partly covering the rising ground of one of the river banks. Weaving is still carried on, though not to the extent of former days, when the town was a valuable centre of the woollen manufacture; and of the Cistercian Abbey founded by Stephen and Maud nothing remains but an antiquated barn appropriating portions of the ruins. John Owen, chaplain to Oliver Cromwell, was born at Coggeshall; and Bishop Bonner probably resided at Feering Bury Manor House, by the village of Feering, nearer Kelvedon, where the Blackwater is crossed by a strong, handsome bridge. Felix Hall is the show-place of the neighbourhood, and its noble park and the works of art contained in the mansion attract numerous visitors. Another beautiful specimen of "the stately homes of England" is Braxted Lodge, perched upon an eminence, with commanding views of one of the most richly cultivated prospects to be found in all Essex, and including, amongst the landscape features of the lovely demesne, a lake some twenty acres in extent. Tiptree, once a notable waste, boasting of nothing but heath, within the memory of living man became even more notable as Tiptree Hall Farm, which was created out of most unpromising materials into a model homestead by the late Mr. Alderman Mechi, a scientific agriculturist who expended large sums of money in machinery for the treatment of sewage and irrigation. The town of Witham, on the further side, stands on the tributary Brain.

MAP OF THE EAST ANGLIAN RIVERS.

The borough and seaport of Maldon, marking the junction of the Chelmer with the Blackwater, stands at the head of a long, uninteresting, marshy estuary of the same pattern as that of the Crouch, and extending a dozen miles before the open sea is reached. Camden infers that Camulodunum was on the site of Maldon, and another historical tradition is that Edward the Elder encamped here to oppose the invasion of the Danes. Local antiquarians point to remnants of the ancient encampment, and assert that though at first the Danes were beaten back, Unlaf in 993 sailed hither and successfully led his Vikings to the rout of the Saxons and capture of the station. Landseer, the painter, lived at Maldon in the early part of his artistic career, and many of his drawings have been preserved in the town and neighbourhood. The Royal Academician Herbert was a native of the town.

The river Chelmer has been referred to as a tributary of the Blackwater, but it is a navigable river on its own account, and brings the county town, by means of an improved canal system, into communication with Maldon and the sea. Though in the meadows above Chelmsford it, from a not excessive distance, looks but a silver thread trailed across the grass, it has a distinct value in the commerce of the county. Thaxted, near which it takes its rise, is a typical specimen of the decayed country town that, once of some importance, has been left to sleepiness by the march of progress, which somehow passed it by. Its fourteenth century church, with massive tower and lofty octagonal spire, is amongst the finest in a country where good churches are plentiful. Horham Hall was a residence of Queen Elizabeth before she came to the throne; and the pleasantly situated village of Tilty, in the valley of the Chelmer, environed by hills and graced by a wood along the banks, boasts the remains of a Cistercian Abbey dating from the middle of the twelfth century. Easton Park is in the valley; its fine old Elizabethan mansion is in good preservation, and the church contains many interesting memorials of the Maynards, who have long been in possession of the estate. Great Dunmow is the next place touched in our downward course, a comfortable town set upon a hill, with a charming suburb thrown out to the river bank. In the neighbourhood, but on the other side of the stream, is Little Dunmow, associated with the memories of the Fitzwalters, one of whom is credited with the famous bequest of a flitch of bacon to any married couple who could prove that for twelve months and a day they had lived in perfect harmony. The custom of awarding the flitch has been almost forgotten, though Ainsworth made a gallant attempt to revive it, and the prize was claimed as recently as 1876. It was first offered by Robert de Fitzwalter in 1244, the actual conditions being "That whatever married couple will go to the Priory, and kneeling on two sharp-pointed stones will swear that they have not quarrelled nor repented of their marriage within a year and a day after its celebration, shall receive a flitch of bacon." Whether the people of the generations past felt the conditions impossible, or treated the affair as a farce, no one may decide, but it is remarkable that the first prize was not claimed until two hundred years after it was established. Up to 1751 only five flitches had been won, and there have been two since. The parish church of Little Dunmow owes its fine columns, richly carved capitals, and windows, to what is left of the Priory Church of the Augustinian establishment founded in 1104.

Onwards through farms and parks, with many a hamlet and village rich in relics of the Middle Ages, the Chelmer flows, laving no land more fair in its disposition of deer parks, woods, lawns, and mansions, than that around the village of Great Waltham. An excellent view of the valley, the river, and a widespread scene which includes the town of Chelmsford, is obtained from Springfield Hall. The village of Springfield is one of many in England which are said to have given Goldsmith the theme of his

"Sweet Auburn! loveliest village of the plain,
Where health and plenty cheered the labouring swain,
Where smiling Spring its earliest visit paid,
And parting Summer's lingering blooms delayed."

Had the poet been standing on any of the eminences from which on every side the wayfarer seems to descend upon Chelmsford, he might have noted all the points which are so sweetly made in "The Deserted Village;" but the same remark would apply to many a spot in many an English county. Yet the following lines do chance to answer with happy accuracy to the Springfield outlook:—

"How often have I paused on every charm—
The sheltered cot, the cultivated farm,
The never-failing brook, the busy mill,
The decent church that topped the neighbouring hill,
The hawthorn bush with seats beneath the shade,
For talking age and whispering lovers made."

But Springfield is in these days a portion of Chelmsford, from which it is separated by the Chelmer and the smaller Cann, both crossed by bridges. Chelmsford is one of the characteristic county towns of the smaller type (its population is about 12,000), which thrive in a centre of agricultural activity. The attempts made to restore to the town the privileges of a borough were at last successful, as it was strange they were not before, for though it sent four members to the Council at Westminster in the time of Edward III., it was at last the only county town in England, except the little capital of Rutlandshire, that was not a borough. With its markets and fairs as important periodical events, the Corn Exchange may be regarded as in some respects the principal building, though a more imposing edifice is the older Shire Hall, in which the assizes are held, and in which, so recently as 1879, a precious discovery of ancient documents was made in one of the upper rooms. The papers related to matters of the sixteenth and seventeenth centuries, and comprised records of the persecutions of Episcopalians, Catholics, and Nonconformists, and of punishments, in which the community enjoyed some notoriety, for witchcraft. Chief Justice Tindal was one of the worthies of Chelmsford, and his name is inscribed upon the elegant conduit in the market-place. The Chelmer, as already stated, becomes an established navigation from the county town, and continues its course to the east. The most noticeable feature of the north side of the vale is Boreham House, with its park, avenues of trees, water, and tastefully laid-out gardens. In the parish is New

THE SHIRE HALL, CHELMSFORD.

Hall, an educational establishment, on the site of Henry VIII.'s palace of Beaulieu, and used subsequently as a residence by Monk, when Duke of Albemarle. The modern visitor is shown the sculptured initials, with love-knots, of bluff King Hal and Anne Boleyn. To the west of Ulting church, the Chelmer receives the Ter, fresh from the well-wooded park of Terbury Place. Considerably increased in volume by this addition, it hastens to Maldon and its confluence with the Blackwater.

In discharging its waters at the termination of its long estuary, the Blackwater, with the Chelmer in union, sweeps along the southern shore of a charming little island in the bay between St. Peter-on-the-Wall and Colne Point. This is Mersea Island, five miles long from east to west, and three miles at its widest portion. The oysters which have made Whitstable famous have good breeding ground in Pyefleet—the creek, passable at low water, which separates the mainland from this prettily wooded and verdant isle, with a bold front to the North Sea. In common with all the coast from Southend to Harwich, the foreshores at low water present a melancholy expanse of ooze, upon which the sea-birds may forage without fear of the approach of man. But while at its lower end Mersea Island faces the outflow of the rivers we have been considering, its upper shores are in a similar position with regard to the Colne, which will next engage our attention.

Of the four rivers of this name in England three are spelt with the final "e," and this stream in the north-eastern portion of the county is often described as the Essex Colne to distinguish it from its namesake, which is a tributary of the Thames. Rising near Moynes Park, the river pursues a south-easterly course to Great Yeldham, a village embowered in trees, amongst which must be reckoned, as of particular account, the gnarled oak, of which the inhabitants are not a little proud. A larger village is Castle Hedingham, standing upon its breezy acclivity, and favoured with a delightful prospect of highly cultivated valley. What remains of the Castle which gave name to the place is in grand condition, the great tower or keep, with its stupendously solid walls, standing almost externally entire upon its turfy mound. The Norman masonry is square and lofty, with walls twelve feet in thickness, and the keep, as a whole, is 100 feet high. So well preserved is the structure, that the grooves for the portcullis in the gateway facing the west might still be used for their original purpose.

Halstead, lower down the widening river, is doubtless what its name signifies, a healthy place, covering the gentle ascent from the stream. The market is one of the oldest in the country, and for many years the population has prosecuted the trade of straw-plaiting, and manufactures of silk and crape. A tributary feeds the Colne from the extensive lake of 100 acres in the park of Gosfield Hall, three miles below Halstead. Gosfield Hall was the seat of the Nugents, one of whom wrote the life of Hampden, and it afterwards came into the hands of the Marquis of Buckingham. Four villages, three on the left and one on the right, take a portion of their name from the stream:—Colne Engaine, so called from its ancient lords of the manor; Earls Colne, once the residence of the Earls of Oxford; White Colne, a modern rendering of Colne-le-Blanc; and Wakes Colne. This is the Colne village near which, at Chappell, the valley is crossed by the Stour Valley railway viaduct, 1,000 feet in length, and 80 feet above the level of the stream.

By the villages of Fordham, West Bergholt, and Lexden, the river at length, by devious ways, arrives at Colchester, the largest town in Essex, the ancient fortified post which historians nominate the capital of the Trinobantes; and Mr. J. H. Round, who has written a history of Colchester Castle, identifies the town with the British Camalodunum. A similar honour, as we have seen, has been claimed for Maldon on the Blackwater. This "hill-town at the head of the river" has figured often in history, and the relics exhibited in the Colchester Museum, and the writings of early historians, sufficiently warrant us in beginning with the Romans. The number of remains unearthed at Colchester has been enormous, and Romans, Saxons, and Danes, in succession, occupied this valuable position on the eastern coast. It became the point of contention in civil war, sent ships and men to Edward III., was visited by both Mary and Elizabeth, and was a staunch contributor of men and money to the Parliament against Charles I.

The river Colne, to which Colchester owes so much of its importance past and present, is navigable to Hythe, where the newest bridge, a construction of iron, replaced a brick bridge which was washed away by a winter flood in 1876. North Bridge is also an iron structure, and East Bridge, with its five arches, is of brick. The public buildings of Colchester are handsome and mostly modern, and the business of the place has been much increased since the extension of Colchester Camp as the headquarters of the Eastern Military District. The picturesque portion of the town must be looked for on the high ground where stand the remains of the Castle, supposed to have been built by the Romans. The monastic ruins in the town are also of more than common interest. The river Colne, widening as it goes, passes Wivenhoe Park, receiving a small tributary called the Roman river, and henceforth it is an estuary proper, with salt water, fishing-boats, oyster-beds, and marshes intersected by creeks dear to the wild-fowler. One of the best known landmarks for the incoming mariner is the tall tower of the church of the fishing village of Brightlingsea.

Dividing for some distance the counties of Essex and Suffolk, next in order comes the Stour, born upon the borders of the adjoining county of Cambridge, and running an almost parallel course with the Colne, but longer. Three brooks contend for the reputation of starting the Stour upon its journey, and the matter is not placed beyond dispute until the three become one. The river begins to act as a county boundary at Kedington, where Archbishop Tillotson was rector at the time of the Commonwealth. Birdbrook and Whitley, Baythorn Park and Stoke College, the village which gave a name to the Cavendishes, the old hall of Pentlow, the village of Long Melford, with Melford Hall and Kentwell Hall, and Liston Park opposite, bring us, with a curve of the river, to the borough town of Sudbury, the birthplace of the painter Gainsborough, and the point from whence the Stour becomes navigable. With smaller villages in close succession planted along its course, the Stour at Higham is joined by the Bret, and the district between Higham and the town of Manningtree is the veritable country which inspired in the heart of John Constable a love for rural scenes, and stored his mind with the knowledge which in after life served him so well. The artist was never tired of saying that these soft pastoral landscapes in the Stour valley made him a painter. He was born at East Bergholt, and numbers of his pictures were actually representations of scenes at Flatford. The flocks and herds, the swelling uplands at different periods of the year, the shade of the woods, the sunlight on the corn, the dripping water-wheel, the cottage, and the church—they are still the common objects of the country on either side of the river. At Manningtree the Stour is lost in the sea long ere it arrives at the thriving port of Harwich, where the channel is commanded by a port on either side, and vessels are directed by a couple of lighthouses, one of which is a lofty erection surmounted by a powerful lantern. A new town, the watering-place of Dovercourt, which in all probability has a future before it, is growing up a near neighbour to Harwich.

1. MILL ON THE COLNE. 2. HIGH STREET, COLCHESTER.

If the Stour has its Harwich, the river ORWELL, which farther north joins the same estuary, has its Ipswich; and while the name of Constable has been mentioned in connection with the former, that of Crabbe belongs to the latter. The river, rising near the village of Gipping, is generally known to the country people by that name in its freshwater course; and it is formed by three small tributaries which become united near Stowmarket, the ancient county town of Suffolk. This town, celebrated

ON THE ORWELL AT IPSWICH.

in these later days for the manufacture of the new explosives, fed the fire of genius in former times, for hither came Milton to visit his tutor Young, and until modern times a mulberry tree in the vicarage garden was called the Milton tree. George Crabbe received the rudiments of his education at Stowmarket. The river subsequently passes Needham Market, and a number of country seats and villages; Barham being the parish where Kirby, the entomologist, lived for more than half a century pursuing his patient and successful studies. The stream is navigable to Stowmarket, and in the channel between that town and Ipswich there is a total descent of ninety-three feet, with fifteen locks in a distance of about sixteen miles. It is not until the river approaches the tidal end that it is termed the Orwell.

Ipswich is well situated on rising ground with a southern aspect, and Gainsborough, who lived here, and Constable, who knew it well, thought highly of the district of which it is the capital. Constable said of it, "It is a most delightful county for a painter. I fancy I see Gainsborough in every hedge and hollow tree." Ipswich in many a quaint corner and irregular street gives evidences of its age. The merry dog Rochester, boon companion of a merry king, saw Ipswich once in the small hours of the morning, and described it as a town without people on the banks of a river without water. The tide was out at that time, and the banks of the Orwell are to this day a marvellous acreage of muddy foreshore at low water. But Ipswich has always been a prosperous town, and its leading inhabitants flourishing men of mark. In these days it is the headquarters of agricultural implement manufacture, sending labour-saving machinery to all parts of the world. The busy ironworks extend along both banks of the river. New docks are established where a new cut has been made to serve them. Ocean-going ships and fleets of "billy-boys" from Goole and elsewhere lie along the wharves. Public buildings, in a fine modern group, attest the progress of Ipswich with the advancing times. Even the Grammar School, one of Queen Elizabeth's foundations, has been reared in the newer town. The wealthy merchants, trading with the Continent, used to live in the midst of the people on the lower land; their villas now stud the heights overlooking the river. Yet here and there an antique chimney, an old-world doorway, indicate where the solid old houses once stood. In the Butter Market there is a marvellous piece of ancient architecture, a house front quaintly timbered and embellished with carvings chiselled centuries ago; and the inhabitants love to believe that this is one of the numerous houses in England in which Charles the Second hid from those who sought his life. Also is the visitor taken to see a gate through which it is affirmed entrance was obtained to Cardinal Wolsey's cottage. The Ipswich of to-day, however, with its water and steam mills, its export business in boots and shoes, its great ironworks, is, in East Anglia, the conspicuous type of go-aheadness, and when the Orwell is at high tide the outlook from the heights is of extreme beauty. The estuary then is a lovely stretch of scenery; gently rising hills laid out with grounds and country seats, diversified by woods and high cultivation, appear on either side, and the estuary from grassy shore to grassy shore is covered with water, dotted with white-sailed yachts and craft of more serious order.

The river Deben runs in a parallel direction with the Orwell, rising a short distance northward of Debenham, becoming navigable at Woodbridge (where Crabbe learnt surgery), and making estuary near Felixstowe, the favourite watering-place of southern Suffolk. Bernard Barton, the Quaker poet, thus grandiloquently described the section of the coast:—

> "On that shore where the waters of Orwell and Deben
> Join the dark heaving ocean, that spot may be found:
> A scene which recalls the lost beauties of Eden,
> And which Fancy might hail as her own fairy ground."

The poet Crabbe, to whom passing reference has been already made, was born at Aldborough, the quiet seaside town which receives its name from the little river Alde, and which was the subject of the poem "The Borough." The stream passes close to the town, but instead of making for the sea close by, turns abruptly south, and follows the line of the coast, within sound of the ocean, for several miles, past Orford, to Hollesley Bay. North of Aldborough is Southwold at the mouth of the river Blythe, another minor stream, navigable to Halesworth, a picturesquely situated town below Hevingham.

A district in many respects quite unique meets us at the estuary which is marked on the maps, though scarcely known by the country folk, as Lake Lothing, this being, in point of fact, an estuary harbour a little south of Lowestoft railway station. Following the coast northward, past Great Yarmouth, and up to a trifle beyond Cromer, we have that extremely interesting district known as the East Anglian Broads, which have now become one of the most popular summer resorts for boating and fishing men, and a well-frequented haunt of the wild-fowler who is not afraid to brave the bitter winds of winter, cruising over the great watery wastes in search of the game which can be found in such quantities in this part of the country. Till within a comparatively few years this extraordinary network of waterways connecting fresh-water lakes was comparatively little known, but the increase of railway communication, and the spread of knowledge consequent upon the multiplication of cheap literature and the new departure taken by the daily press, brought the rivers and broads of both Norfolk and Suffolk before the public. Now for months together wherries and yachts peculiar to the locality sail by day and anchor at night upon the Broads; and camping-out parties may be encountered at all the villages connected therewith. This may also be described as savouring of Dutch-land, the salient features of which are in some wise reproduced here in our own country. Although elsewhere changes are continually taking place in the habits and customs of the people, and often in the aspect of the country, the Broads so far remain unaltered.

The rivers are characterised by a slow rate of speed. Many of them for miles together resemble canals in the appearance of their banks, and in their tardy, discoloured currents. It is difficult sometimes to imagine that the sheets of water are connected with them at all, but, as the name Broad would indicate, the apparent lakes are nothing but openings-out of the waterways, which sooner or later send their contents to the sea. There are two or three exceptions, which will be pointed out, but the Broads are for the most part fed by such rivers as the Bure and the Yare. The southernmost river is the Waveney, which at first runs from west to east, until it approaches within a few miles of the estuary above named. Then, however, it takes an arbitrary turn northwards, gives the go-by to Lowestoft, and, joining the river Yare at Breydon Water, empties itself into the sea outside of Gorleston Pier.

The Waveney, one of the largest of the Norfolk rivers, waters both Norfolk and Suffolk. The talented Agnes Strickland, who wrote of the Queens of

England, calls this river the sweet stream of her childhood, and in its upper part it certainly does merit that somewhat poetical description. It rises from springs near Lopham Gate, and the little Ouse, which takes a contrary direction, is also

HARWICH: THE QUAY.

born in the same neighbourhood. The first town on the banks of this river is Diss, which is very prettily situated on high ground, with a considerable lake with steep banks on the eastern side. The little river called the Dove, which passes the borough of Eye, joins the Waveney. The town of Harleston is near the Waveney proper, and at Bungay, on the borders of Norfolk and Suffolk, where the river describes a curious loop towards the village of Ditchingham, the Broads district is held to have its south-western boundary. There are no Broads, however, near, but the tourists who hire their wherries and make water parties for periods of weeks and months frequently push on to this point. The ruins of Bungay Castle remind us of the old days when Barons held their sway, and there is a parish church which was once connected with a nunnery.

For the most part, the Broads district is a dead level that becomes monotonous until one gets accustomed to its quietude and freedom. But occasionally there is an exception to the rule, and we have an example at Mettingham, a portion of which parish spreads over a range of hills, upon which are the remains of a castle. Sir John Suckling, the poet, was lord of the manor in the parish of Barham, which has its Hall some distance from the river, and a stretch of marshes bordering it. The mother of Nelson, and Captain Suckling, his uncle, were both born in the Rectory House of Barham. Beccles, with its fen to the north, its race-course to the right, and the Gillingham marshes on the other side of the river, are important stations connected with the line from Lowestoft and Yarmouth. Beccles was a favourite resort of the poet Crabbe. This little town is finely situated on a promontory, giving a pleasant view of the broad valley, with villages and country houses dotted along its banks.

In its northward course the Waveney passes Somerleyton station, then St. Olaves, and finally, running parallel with the terminal course of the Yare, winds through reedy marshes and becomes lost in Breydon Water, a huge expanse of estuary, which visitors to Yarmouth will remember as presenting such a dreary waste of muddy flat at low water. The Yare and the Waveney are connected by an artificial channel, called the New Cut, making the course by water to the ancient City of Norwich complete from the south-eastern portion of the district. Away to the east of the river at St. Olaves is Fritton Decoy, one of the smaller, but at the same time typical, Broads of Norfolk.

The district of the Broads is computed to hold not less than 5,000 acres of lake, and 200 miles of river, or canal-like waterway that passes as such; but the Broads, as they are popularly known, mostly cluster along the banks of the BURE. Towards the coast in the north-east is delightful little Horsey Mere, the outlying lake in that direction connected with the combination of watery stretches, generally known as Hickling Broads, the largest of the entire series, and brought into the common watery highway by means of the Thurne, sometimes called the Hundred Stream. As a rule, the water of these East Anglian Broads is discoloured by sand in solution, and sometimes, as at Fritton, it assumes a greenish hue. But Hickling, which is a very beautiful sheet of water, though, by reason of its shallowness, not wholly beloved by yachtsmen, has the enviable peculiarity of being clear. Upon the hard gravelly bottom the loveliest of water plants grow; and sailing over them in a small boat, brushing them lightly even with your keel, and the breeze not being sufficiently strong to ruffle the surface, you look down upon a submerged panorama, upon a subaqueous fairyland of mossy meadows and weedy bowers, from and into which the zebra-barred perch and the silvery cyprinidæ glide.

From Hickling it is a long sail down to Thurne mouth, where we regain the main stream of the Bure, and the scenery is thoroughly characteristic of East Anglia. Truly there is nothing like it elsewhere in this country. League upon league we steal along the placid waterway, between rustling sedge, flag, reed, and coarse grasses, protecting all the aquatic flowers in their season. Sleek cattle graze upon the low, fat, boundless pastures; everywhere weather-worn windmills catch the breeze, and work devoted to the perpetual service of pumping out the intersecting dykes. Beyond the marshes, undulating country swells gently to picturesque and distant woods; square church-towers peep above the trees. There are corn-fields and patches of turnip surrounding the ruddy buildings of many a happy homestead. Hour after hour we silently move between margins gay with the bold purple loosestrife, the free-blossoming willow-herb, the fragrant meadow-sweet, and the dark glossy-leaved alder, which never thrives so well as when its feet are in the water, and which seems to be most strong in the sap when other trees are on the verge of decay.

The Broads connected with the upper part of the Bure are the most generally known, following each other in close succession, and having a number of villages in their neighbourhood. The trip from Yarmouth up this river is at first monotonous in the extreme, but the traveller soon gets accustomed to the Hollandish land and water. The smaller the boat for this excursion, the better the speed; the mast has to be lowered at the low, modest bridges, and to meet this requirement the so-called wherries and the una-rigged boats are provided with special appliances. Very soothing it is, when the breeze is merry, to loll upon the cushions aft, gaze up at the heavens, and list to the ripple at the bows. The shivering willows present an everlasting intermingling of moving grey and green as the slender leaves expose now the upper and now the under covering, after their kind. Water-fowl scuttle off to cover as you heave in sight. By-and-bye there will bear down upon you one of the famous East Anglian wherries, half-sister to the sailing-barges of the Medway and the Thames. Her large ruddy sails are hoisted by machinery, and as she sweeps round a bend, running free, she will seem to be dooming you to destruction. Yet she flies past, making splendid speed, and docile as a child under the management of the skipper at the helm.

One of the show-places on the Bure is St. Benet's Abbey, to which all strangers resort. The ruins that attract attention long before the landing-place is reached are the remains of an ecclesiastical establishment of the early part of the eleventh century. It was a strong post, and the monks offered a stubborn resistance to William the Conqueror. Eventually the abbey was annexed to the bishopric of Norwich; and, inheriting the old right of the Abbot to a seat in the House of Lords, the Bishops of Norwich, who are in legal parlance Abbots of St.

Benet's-at-Holme, as well as Bishops, have a double claim to a seat on the Episcopal Bench. The river Bure was, in those old fighting days, a line of defence to the abbey on the south, and the position of the moat, which completed the isolation, may still be traced. The gateway of the abbey, which was a cruciform building with a plain round tower in the centre, stands, but it is blocked by the rubbish of a large windmill which tumbled upon it in the last century. There are other relics, and the prettiness of the place, its historical associations, and the soft turf that contrasts so agreeably with the rougher herbage of the marshes, make it a resort of picnic parties.

Walsham, Ranworth, Hoveton, Woodbastwick, Salhouse, and Wroxham Broads are a close constellation. Wroxham is a typical specimen of the larger Broads upon which regattas are held, where a large yacht may cruise, and the shores of which present diversity of woodland, private grounds, farm lands, and village life. Equally typical of the smaller lakes is Salhouse Broad. I visited it last in the late summer, the boat slipping out of Wroxham Broad through an inviting opening in the reeds. To my mind there is nothing prettier in all Norfolk than this sheltered lakelet, a watery retreat which, like many of the Broads, is private property. The reeds around its margin on one shore, which presents a series of bays within bays, are of gigantic height. They stand out of the water in thickets, lofty walls of slender growth, coped with nodding plumes and restless tassels. On the opposite shore the scenery is park-like. At the time of my visit there were a number of small yachts moored at Salhouse, and upon the weedy shore there was, at points, a striking intermixture of ash trees, alders, and the guelder rose, vieing with one another as to which could thrive best nearest the water's edge. The guelder rose bushes were bright with their clumps of red berries, glittering and transparent like Venetian glass.

Out of this small enclosure you push through a narrow waterway into Hoveton Great Broad, a lake of quite another type, particularly Dutch-like in its surroundings. Productive arable land stretches right and left, and windmills mark the horizon all round; no point of the prospect is without its square-towered church or red-tiled houses. So shallow are many portions of Hoveton Broad, that as you sweep through the light beds of reeds, forcing the graceful growths out of your course, there are often not eighteen inches of water beneath your keel, and the Dutch flavour before mentioned is intensified by the appearance of large clumsy boats, laden high with cut reeds, to be used hereafter as fodder.

Horning Ferry, a well-known waterside resting-place, may be taken as a typical feature of village life in these parts. At a bend in the river Bure you arrive at a village with granaries, and the red-tiled cottages of a long street close to the water's edge. There are heaps of produce on the bank, a fleet of boats-of-all-work, wherries waiting for cargoes, and a huge windmill on the low ridge behind this quaint country settlement. You sail close to the walls of the village street, and it is expected that you offer a largesse of coppers to the sunbrowned children who run along, keeping pace with the boat, and singing a hymn, as the Horning children have done from time immemorial, in praise of John Barleycorn. All the yachtsmen coming and going halt at Horning Ferry, lounge upon the smooth-shaven lawn, and enjoy the comforts of a civilised inn;

THE BEACH, YARMOUTH.

for the first time, perchance, for days, in the case of men who have been roughing it in wherries or smaller boats. In the hotel parlour may be noticed a case of stuffed birds, containing excellent specimens of the beautiful summer teal, black tern, solitary fowl, and jack-snipes, and two or three rare visitants, all shot by the proprietor of the hotel. Guns, fishing-rods, hunting pictures, whips and spurs, adorning the walls, give an air of sport to the place both welcome and fitting.

The largest Broad in the north-eastern part of the district I have already nominated as Hickling, which also includes Whitely and Chapman's Broad. Horsey Mere is, however, still further east, and it is a lovely bit of wild water, with an abundance of tall poplars around the shores, and most picturesquely reeded. By proceeding up Palling Dyke, on the trip to which I have once or twice referred, I was able to stroll across to the beach, through the sand dunes, and inhale the real odour of brine from the ocean. On the way I passed the blackened ribs of a wrecked ship protruding from the silver sand which had been drifting year by year with the kindly object of burying them out of sight. The dunes here are high embankments of sand, covered with spear-like grass. Looking east was the blue sea and its ships and steamers; west was a sunshiny land, dotted with villages and farms. Barton Broad is a detached lake of considerable size; and in an opposite direction, south-east, is the long, narrow collection of Broads—Filby, Rollesby, and Ormesby—one expanse of water, independent of the rivers and cuts which abound in every other part of the district of the Broads. This peculiar piece of water straggles along a length of three miles, and throws out queerly shaped arms both east and west.

The attractions for visitors to the Broads are sailing, and sport with rod and gun. The country is so sparsely populated that the visitor has to provide rations for himself, and is, when once upon the Broads, far away from the noise of the world. The angler who has read glowing accounts of the sport to be obtained is likely to be disappointed at the large proportion of the water which is in private hands. The Broads and rivers abound with bream and roach; and there are pike, perch, and eels. In some of the Broads the rudd, which is first-cousin to the roach, occurs in incredible quantities, and affords capital fly-fishing on summer evenings off the fringes of the reedy thickets. A wholesale system of poaching, which has not been completely stopped by the special legislation provided by the Norfolk and Suffolk Freshwater Fisheries Act of 1877, has, however, of late years inflicted much injury. In his description of the marriage of Thames and Medway, Spenser selects the Yare as having—

"With him brought a present joyfully
Of his own fish unto their festival,
Which like none else could show; the which they ruffins call."

By "ruffins" Spenser means the pope or ruffe, the voracious little impostor that pretends to be a perch, and that is often a nuisance to the East Anglian fisherman. According to Cuvier, this fish was discovered by Dr. Caius, who was a native of Norwich, and who, taking a ruffe in the Yare, sent it to Gesner.

Though the Episcopal City of Norwich is its great inland headquarters, Yarmouth is considered to be the capital of the Broads district. In the literal sense of the term these are well-known towns. Norwich abounds with old streets and houses, as becomes a city said to be of more than fourteen centuries date. Kings of East Anglia dwelt in its castle, or were ejected from it, as Saxons and Danes in turn carried it by storm. The keep and outer vallum are well preserved, and in celebration of the Queen's Jubilee the building has been dedicated to the purposes of a County Museum. The cathedral, with its lofty steeple, and the Bishop's Palace, are fine monuments of an historical past, and one of the palace apartments is lined with a carved oak wainscot, brought from the St. Benet's Abbey mentioned on a preceding page.

Yarmouth, at the mouth of the Yare, is the Margate, if not the Brighton, of East Anglia. The narrow "rows" or connecting alleys between the main thoroughfares of the oldest portion of the town have a renown all their own.

They are the principal curiosities of this emporium of fish-curing, and may be taken as a foil to the magnificent market-place, covering nearly three acres of flagged area. The types of men and women who gather here at the Saturday market are of a most varied and interesting kind; and the booths, like the comfortable country folks who furnish them, are just what they have been during the lifetime of the oldest inhabitant. The far-stretching yellow sands are the abiding strength of Yarmouth as a watering-place, and they give the place a steady average of prosperity which seaside resorts without so noble a beach cannot reckon upon. Of the remains left of the ancient walls, North Gate, bearing the date of 1396, is the best, but there are many venerable buildings worthy of inspection, such as the Elizabethan house on South Quay, built in 1596. The Market Place, as before indicated, is one of the largest in the country; and the grand parish church of St. Nicholas at its foot enjoys the same distinction. In all but name it is a cathedral of which any diocese might be proud.

W. Senior.

OUTWARD BOUND.

INDEX.

Printed by Cassell & Company, Limited, La Belle Sauvage, London, E.C.

STACKS AT DUNCANSBY, CAITHNESS

(From Lazonde, *The British Isles*)

ST MICHAEL'S MOUNT

(From TAYLOR, *St Michael's Mount*)

www.ingramcontent.com/pod-product-compliance
Lightning Source LLC
Chambersburg PA
CBHW030900270326
41929CB00008B/514

* 9 7 8 3 3 3 7 2 4 0 7 3 8 *